WOMEN RIGHTS
Violation *vs.* Restoration

WOMEN RIGHTS
Violation *vs.* Restoration

Sukanta Sarkar
Manaswini Patra

KALPAZ

ISBN: 978-93-5128-155-9
Price: ₹ 1250/-

First Published 2015

Published by

Kalpaz Publications
C-30, Satyawati Nagar,
Delhi - 110052
E-mail: kalpaz@hotmail.com Ph.: 9212142040

Laser Typesetting : Rajender Vashist, Delhi
Printed at : G. Print Process, Delhi

Cataloging in Publication Data--DK

Courtesy: D.K. Agencies (P) Ltd. <docinfo@dkagencies.com>

Sarkar, Sukanta, author.
Women rights : violation vs. Restoration / Sukanta Sarkar, Manaswini Patra.
pages cm
Includes bibliographical references (pages).
ISBN

1. Women's rights--India. 2. Women--Crimes against--India. I. Patra, Manaswini, author. II. Title.

DDC 305.420954 23

Contents

Preface

A woman is a female human. The term woman is usually reserved for an adult, with the term girl being the usual term for a female child or adolescent. Womanhood is the period in a female's life after she has passed through childhood and adolescence, generally around the age 18. The role of women in society has been greatly overseen in the last few decades but now is coming to a more perspective to people. In the early days women were seen as wives who were intended to cook, cleanand take care of the kids. They faced discrimination like and other race that faced it. Women are faced with more responsibly than men but also are faced with a lot more problems than men because they are looked at like a woman a bearer of children. Women's rights are the rights and entitlements claimed for women and girls of many societies worldwide. Although males seem to have dominated in many ancient cultures, there are some exceptions.

We desire to express our heartiest thank to Prof B.K. Panda, Department of Economics, Berhampur University, Odisha who despite his busy schedule and hectic academic engagements, all the time encouraged and supported us. We have also beholden to Dr N.G. Pendse, Department of Economics, Rani Durgabati University, Jabalpur who's erudite and scholarly tidbits for preparing such a vast work are still fresh in our mind. We also thanks to Dr Pradeep Kumar Pandey, Centre of Judicial Studies, Dibrugarh University, Assam; Dr Suman Kalan Chaudhury, Department of Business Administration, Berhampur University,

Odisha; Dr Rakesh Joshi, Department of Economics, Saurashtra University, Gujarat; Dr D. Pulla Rao, Department of Economics, Andhra University; Dr Vibhuti Patel, Professor cum Director, Centre for Study of Social Exclusion and Inclusive Policy, SNDT Women's University, Mumbai; Dr WakarAmin, Department of Social Work, University of Kashmir, J and K.; Dr Shazia Manzoor, Assistant Professor Department of Social Work, University of Kashmir, J and K; Dr Pallab Kanti Ghoshal, Department of Commerce, Netaji Subhas College, Udaipur, for their valuable suggestions and moral support.

We are heartily grateful to Prof A.K. Tomar, D.S. College Aligarh and Prof S.K. Mishra, Varanasi, Prof A.K. Gaur, BHU Varanasi, Prof P.K. Pandey, M.G. Kashi Vidyapeeth, Varanasi, Prof A.D.N. Vajpayee, Vice-Chancellor, Shimla University, Shimla, who always encouraged us to carry on this constructive work. Further, we express our heartily thankfulness to each and every person who directly/indirectly helped us in preparing this work.

It is hoped that this book will be very useful society in general and students of women studies in particular. Comments and suggestions are most welcomed.

Dr Sukanta Sarkar
Dr Manaswini Patra

Acknowledgment

Women's rights are the rights and entitlements claimed for women and girls of many societies worldwide. Although males seem to have dominated in many ancient cultures, there are some exceptions. We desire to express our heartiest thank to Prof B.K. Panda, Department of Economics, Berhampur University, Odisha who despite his busy schedule and hectic academic engagements, all the time encouraged and supported us. We have also beholden to Dr N.G. Pendse, Department of Economics, Rani Durgabati University, Jabalpur who's erudite and scholarly tidbits for preparing such a vast work are still fresh in our mind. We also thanks to Dr Pradeep kumar Pandey, Centre of Judicial Studies, Dibrugarh University, Assam; Dr Suman Kalan Chaudhury, Department of Business Administration, Berhampur University, Odisha; Dr Rakesh Joshi, Department of Economics, Saurashtra University, Gujarat; Dr D. Pulla Rao, Department of Economics, Andhra University; Dr Vibhuti Patel, Professor cum Director, Centre for Study of Social Exclusion and Inclusive Policy, SNDT Women's University, Mumbai; Dr WakarAmin, Department of Social Work, University of Kashmir, J & K.; Dr Shazia Manzoor, Assistant professor Department of Social Work, University of Kashmir, J & K; Dr Pallab Kanti Ghoshal, Department of Commerce, BBMC, Agartalar, for their valuable suggestions and moral support.

We are heartily grateful to Prof A.K. Tomar, D.S College Aligarh and Prof S.K. Mishra Varanasi, Prof A.K. Gaur BHU Varanasi, Prof P.K Pandey, MG Kashi Vidyapeeth Varanasi, Prof ADN Vajpayee, Vice Chancelor, Shimla University, Shimla, who always encouraged us to carry on this constructive work. Further, we express our heartily thankfulness to each and every person who directly/indirectly helped us in preparing this work.

It is hoped that this book will be very useful society in general and students of women rights in particular. Comments and suggestions are most welcomed.

Dr Sukanta Sarkar
Dr Manaswini Patra

Introduction

Indian woman bearing the torch of cultured living through self-sacrifice, physical and mental endurance, and compassion is waxing eloquence for retrogressive drudgery. It lends rationale for under-nutrition of girls, unequal health care, inequitable access to resources, and denial of property rights all reserved for women born into a tradition that hails women's capacity for forbearance. Although Women may be victims of any of the general crimes such as murder, robbery, cheating etc., only the crimes which are directed specifically against women are characterized as Crimes against Women. The United Nations defined Violence against Women in 1993 in Declaration on the Elimination of Violence against Women

Women are facing various types of crimes, i.e. Force Marriage, Dowry, Women Trafficking, Marital Rape, Acid Attack, Domestic Violence, Sexual Harassment, Eve Teasing, Honour Killing, Molestation, Rape, Female Genital Multination, Child Marriage etc. Forced marriage is a marriage in which one or both of the parties are married without his or her consent or against his or her will. It is a form of child/domestic abuse and violence against women; it should form part of existing child and adult protection structures, policies and procedures. Dowry is the transfer of parental property to a daughter at her marriage rather than at the owner's death. A dowry establishes a type of conjugal fund, the nature of which may vary widely. This fund may provide an element of financial security in widowhood or against a negligent husband, and may eventually go to provide for her sons and daughters.

Human trafficking is the trade of humans, most commonly for the purpose of sexual slavery, forced labor or commercial sexual exploitation for the trafficker or others. It can occur within a country or trans-nationally. It is a crime against the person because of the violation of the victim's rights of movement through coercion and because of their commercial exploitation. Marital rape is non-consensual sex in which the perpetrator is the victim's spouse. It is a form of partner rape, of domestic violence and of sexual abuse. The issues of sexual and domestic violence within marriage and the family unit, and more generally, the issue of violence against women, have come to growing international attention from the second half of the 20th century onwards. Acid throwing is usually an act of revenge, motivated by jealousy or hatred, because of a personal relationship problem such as a broken love affair or marriage, unfaithfulness, or rejection. The perpetrator blames the victim for the problem, and wants to inflict as much physical and mental suffering as possible.

Domestic violence is control by one partner over another in a dating, marital or live-in relationship. The means of control include physical, sexual, emotional and economic abuse, threats and isolation. The term 'domestic violence' refers to interpersonal violence which takes place in domestic settings, family relationships, and intimate relationships, and is most commonly applied to violence by a man to his wife, female sexual partner or ex-partner. Generally, international instruments define sexual harassment broadly as a form of violence against women and as discriminatory treatment, while national laws focus more closely on the illegal conduct. Eve teasing is a ridiculous form of enjoyment for men and a physical as well as mental torment for women. This is one of the daily problems women in Indian society face. Of all the forms that violence against women can assume, eve teasing is the most ubiquitous and insidious because it is considered normal behaviour and not an assault to females.

Honour killing is a form of violence that is almost without exception directed towards women. It is a murder which is an intentional, often especially malicious act with few causes that is, however, judged by family and society as a legitimate killing of a girl or a woman by a family member, when she is suspect of breaking the family honour code. Molestation means forcing undesired sexual behaviour by one person upon another. When that force is immediate, of short duration, or infrequent, it is called sexual assault. The offender is referred to as a sexual abuser or molester. Rape is a type of sexual assault usually involving sexual intercourse or other forms of sexual penetration perpetrated against a person without that person's consent. Child marriage is a formal marriage or informal union entered into by an individual before reaching the age of 18.

Globally, violence within the home is universal across culture, religion, class, and ethnicity. In the last two decades, the Indian women's movement has contributed to a growing public awareness of violence against women. Recently, after a student was raped and murdered in Delhi, a committee headed by former Indian Supreme Court chief justice J.S. Verma made a number of recommendations for improving India's rape laws, including doing away with the marital rape exemption. According to the Verma Committee's report-Under the Indian Penal Code sexual intercourse without consent is prohibited. The widespread contemporary exploitation of men, women and children is unacceptable to people of conscience the world over. Traditional approaches to preventing trafficking in human beings, to protect and assist trafficked persons and bring criminals to justice have had some small impact on the global phenomenon, but not enough.

Abbreviations

ACRWC	: African Charter on the Rights and Welfare of the Child
CAT	: Committee against Torture
CEDAW	: Convention on the Elimination of All Forms of Discrimination against Women
CIA	: Crime Investigation Agency
CMA	: Christian Marriage Act
CMRA	: Child Marriage Restraint Act
CRC	: Convention on the Rights of the Child
CrPC	: Code of Criminal Procedure
CSA	: Childhood Sexual Abuse
CSW	: Commission on the Status of Women
DRDA	: District Rural Development Agency
DV	: Domestic Violence
DWCRA	: Development of Women and Children in Rural Areas
ESCR	: Economic, Social and Cultural Rights
FGM	: Female Genital Mutilation
FIWE	: Federation of Indian Women Entrepreneurs
GB	: Grameen Bank
GBV	: Gender-based Violence

GoI	: Government of India
IAY	: Indira Awaas Yojana
IBPs	: Individual Banking Programmes
ICC	: Internal Complaints Committee
ICESCR	: International Covenant on Economic, Social and Cultural Rights
ICPD	: International Conference on Population and Development in Cairo
ILO	: International Labour Organisation
IOM	: International Organisation for Migration
IPC	: Indian Penal Code
IPV	: Intimate Partner Violence
LAC	: Latin America and the Caribbean
MDGs	: Millennium Development Goals
MFDEF	: Micro-finance Development and Equity Fund
MFIs	: Microfinance Institutions
MGNREGA	: Mahatma Gandhi National Rural Employment Guarantee Act
MKSP	: Mahila Kisan Sashaktikaran Pariyojana
MoWA	: Ministry of Women's Affairs
MSME	: Micro, Small and Medium Enterprises
MTPA	: Medical Termination of Pregnancy Act
NABARD	: National Bank for Agriculture and Rural Development
NCRB	: National Crime Records Bureau
NCW	: National Commission for Women
NMEW	: National Mission for Empowerment of Women
NPA	: Non-Performing Assets
NRLM	: National Rural Livelihood Mission
OHCHR	: Office of the UN High Commissioner for Human Rights
OSCE	: Organisation for Security and Cooperation in Europe

PCMA	: Prohibition of Child Marriage Act
PIL	: Public Interest Litigation
PWDVA	: Protection of Women from Domestic Violence Act
RFA	: Revolving Fund Assistance
RMK	: Rashtriya Mahila Kosh
SEWA	: Self Employed Women's Association
SGSY	: Swarnjayanti Gram Swarozgar Yojana
SHG	: Self Help Group
SIDBI	: Small Industries Development Bank of India
SIDO	: Small Industries Development Organisation
UAE	: United Arab Emirates
UDHR	: Universal Declaration of Human Rights
UN.GIFT	: United Nations Global Initiative to Fight Human Trafficking
UN	: United Nations
UNICEF	: United Nations Children's Fund
VAW	: Violence against Women
WEAI	: Women's Empowerment in Agriculture Index

Part I
Preservation of Women Rights

1

Status of Indian Women

"LORD God said, "It is not good that the man should be alone; I will make him a helper fit for him." ... And the rib that the LORD God had taken from the man he made into a woman and brought her to the man. Then the man said, "This at last is bone of my bones and flesh of my flesh; she shall be called Woman, because she was taken out of Man." Therefore a man shall leave his father and his mother and hold fast to his wifeand they shall become one flesh."

—***Bible-Genesis* 2:18, 22-24**

Introduction

'Adam and Eve, according to the creation myths of the Abrahamic religions were the first man and woman. The story of Adam and Eve is central to the belief that God created human beings to live in a Paradise on earth. It provides the basis for the belief that humanity is in essence a single family, with everyone descended from a single pair of original ancestors. In Islam, Adam role is being the father of humanity, is looked upon by Muslims with reverence. Eve is the "mother of humanity." In the Bahá'í Faith, Adam is seen as a Manifestation of God. The Adam and Eve narratives are seen as symbolic, but are also seen as having mythical features. The story of Adam and Eve contradicts the scientific consensus that humans evolved from earlier species of hominids.'[1]

'A woman is a female human. The term *woman* is usually reserved for an adult, with the term girl being the usual term for a female child or adolescent. Womanhood is the period in a female's life after she has passed through childhood and adolescence, generally around the age 18.'[2] 'The role of women in society has been greatly overseen in the last few decades but now is coming to a more perspective to people. In the early days, women were seen as wives who were intended to cook, cleanand take care of the kids. They faced discrimination like any other race that faced it. Women are faced with more responsibly than men but also are faced with a lot more problems than men because they are looked at like a woman a bearer of children.'[3]

'In the ancient Indian writings the feminist principle is part of a cosmic whole and the woman is seen as a coequal being at the spiritual level; means she is honoured and dreaded as a goddess. Durga who is riding on a tiger can serve as an example as well as Kali, dancing and terrifying at the same time. Shakti, who is the elemental force of the universe, is omnipresent. The epics of the Mahabharata contain innumerable feminist role models. Looking at those wisdoms in India, it is difficult to understand the discrimination of girls and women or the assaults happening on them at present.'[4]

'Historically Indian women are equal to men. The concept of woman as Shakti, the primal energy force, finds expression in the famous epic Mahabharata. In this epic woman is glorified as a light of the house, mother of the universe and supporter of the earth and all its forests. Manu in his Manusmriti, who was the first to codify the laws in India, also writes about this, "Where women are verily honoured, there the gods rejoice. Where, however, they are not honoured, there all sacred rites prove useless." In another epic Ramayana, when Rama intended to perform the Ashwamedha Yajana in the absence of Sita, the religious norms advised Rama to keep a golden statue of his wife beside him during the ceremony.'[5]

Indian Women during British Period

'During the British rule several changes were made in the socioeconomic structure of our society. During this period some substantial progress was made in eliminating inequalities between men and women in matters of education, employment, social and political rights. Education which has been identified as the major instrument for raising the status of women was started during British period. After the Bhakti movement, the Christian Missionaries took interest in the education of girls. During British period there were two major movements which affected the position of women. These were the Social Reform Movement of the nineteenth century and the Nationalist Movement of the twentieth century. Another very powerful force which helped to change the attitude towards women was the Nationalist Movement, particularly during Gandhian phase.'[6]

'At the end of the nineteenth century women in India suffered from disabilities like, child-marriage, practice of polygamy, sale of girls for marriage purposes, severe restrictions on widows, non-access to education and restricting oneself to domestic and child-bearing functions. The Indian National Conference started in 1885 by Justice Ranade contained these disabilities. Raja Ram Mohan Roy, who played an important role in getting the Sati system abolished, raised voices against the child-marriage and fought for the right of inheritance for women. Ishwar Chandra Vidyasagar launched a movement for the right of widows to re-marry and also pleaded for educating women.'[7]

'The turn of the twentieth century saw a challenge to traditional social structures at both the level of ideology and practice. The rise of feminism in Europe and North America has over the past hundred years seen most of the male bastions fall and spread an increasing awareness of a woman's wants, aspirations and outlook to life, empowering her to evaluate her own 'self' and the society around her from her own perspective. Feminism asks for restoring the dignity of women and for granting her equal rights, power and opportunity with men.'[8]

Prostitution in Colonial India

'The practice of prostitution in colonial India was influenced by British rule dating back to the nineteenth century. Although the governments of many Indian princely states had regulated prostitution prior to the 1860s, such regulation in British India was first ushered in by the Cantonment Act of 1864. The Cantonment Act regulated and structured prostitution in the

British military bases. The structuring features of the Cantonment Act provided for about twelve to fifteen Indian women for each regiment of British soldiers. Each regiment contained about a thousand soldiers. They were licensed by military officials and were allowed to consort with soldiers only. In the early twentieth century, European prostitutes were visible in the major cities and seaports of British India. Although the British were proactive in state regulation and even importation of prostitution in the possessions they controlled, they had misconstrued ideas about Indian culture and local religions.'[9]

'The British drafted legislation as the Contagious Diseases Act of 1864. Under this Act and the Cantonment Rules, the British and other European soldiers in India were not only permitted but promoted to hold native young and good-looking girls as prostitutes for their carnal pleasure.'[10] 'From Farida Begum (2012) project "The Creation of Difference: Empire, Race and the Discourse on Prostitution in Colonial Bengal, 1880-1940", we know that in the beginning of the twentieth century, the international concern over trafficking of women raised philanthropic and political interest in saving the victims, specifically once it was acknowledged that there were 'white' women living as prostitutes in the colonies. This heightened the racial fears of the West. The international furor over 'white slavery' shifted the focus on how to differentiate Indian prostitutes from European prostitutes. In the 1920s and 1930s, a series of laws were passed to regulate brothels and trafficking, which mostly served to demarcate separate spaces for the prostitutes from respectable society. The Bengal Suppression of Immoral Traffic Act was passed in 1933 with pressure from the All Bengal Women's Union and followed the Bombay Immoral Traffic Act of 1923 and the Calcutta Immoral Traffic Suppression Act of 1923.

In sum, concern over the health of the British army in India led to regulation and medical examinations for prostitutes in the late nineteenth century. This led to the differentiation of prostitutes as the 'Other' to almost everyone in society. According to changes made in the structure of prostitution in Bengal under the British, certain medically policed groups were created to cater to the needs of the British soldiers and these were set apart from other prostitutes who were closed off to the

Europeans. The British created a market for prostitutes as they sought to provide for the sexual needs of their soldiers. In India, public attention to prostitution heightened in the twentieth century as international pressure focused on how to stop trafficking of women and girls, particularly with regard to European prostitutes. In the League of Nations reports from the 1920s and 1930s, the focus was on foreign prostitutes. In British India, after the Rebellion of 1857, colonial officers and politicians "stipulated new codes of conduct that emphasised respectability, domesticity and a more carefully segregated use of space," and these measures were concerned with European women.'[11]

Social Upgrading of Women during British Period

'Many important changes have taken place in the situation of women since the time the British ruled India. Samual Stanely and Santosh Kumari (2011) in their paper "Position of Women in Colonial Era" discuss about the condition of women in British period. According to them, in Colonial India, the social status of women seemed to be dependent on their men. The first and foremost social problem that attracted enlightened opinion was the need for a better deal for women in society. Though the East India Company broadly adhered to its declared policy of non-interference with the social custom of the people, yet early Governor General like Cornwallis, Minto and Lord Hasting had taken some steps to restrict the practice of Sati by discouraging compulsion forbidding administration of intoxicating drugs to the sorrow stricken widows, putting a ban of the Sati of pregnant women and widows below the age of 16 years and above-all making compulsory the presence of police official at the time of sacrifice who were to see that no compulsion proved inadequate and achieved limited success. Another horrible and cruel rite particularly common among the Bengalis and Rajput was killing their infant daughter at birth, taking female children to a great economic liability. When persuasion alone could not help, in Bengal regulation XXI of 1775 and III of 1804 declared infanticide illegal and equivalent to committing a murder as a precautionary measure, the Government of India passed an Act in 1870 (Pamphlet on the Right of Women, 1975). It is making compulsory for parents to register the birth of all babies and providing for verification of female child for some years after birth.

The central legislative of Indian enacted law in 1928 for the degenerated system of Devdasis. The Bombay legislature also passed a legal enactment to stop the immoral practice of prostitution. In 1872, the colonial government enacted the native Marriage Act II which was fixed the age of marriage for girls at 14 and for boys at 18. It also contained provision to ban Polygamy; the progressive section of Indian intelligentsia welcomed the provision of this Act. The Hindu Remarriage Act (Act XV of 1856) legalised marriage of widows and declared issues from such marriage as legitimate. Many widows became its beneficiaries.'[13]

Women Education during the British Period

'When the English began ruling India, they encouraged the growth of traditional *paathshaalas* and *madrasas*. In the paathshaalas, students studied the shastras, puranas and Sanskrit grammar, while in the *madrasas* the Quran and other religious texts were taught. The English knew that they could bring some people from England to India and make them government officers, but it would be too expensive to appoint English officers and servants for all the jobs, big and small. So, at least for the posts of clerks, workers and junior officers, they needed Indians with some English education. Like Ram Mohan Roy, thousands of other people in India put pressure on the British government to make immediate arrangements for English education in India. People were greatly affected by English thoughts and manners and by the advancements in science and technology.'[14]

'Although education in India started receiving some attention under British rule with the Charter Act of 1813 and obtained full recognition in the famous Macaulay's Minute of 1835, education of women in India still remained absent from the Indian society. It is only when the "Wood's Dispatch", containing Educational development programme was passed in 1854 by the East India Company that a special reference was made of education and employment of women and the Government assumed direct responsibility for making women literate. The two decades from 1902-22 witnessed a more active role of the Government in the field of women's education on the one hand and impact of Freedom Movement on women's education on the other. It is during this period that Lord Curzon supported the cause of Women's education and the similar policy was enunciated by a Government Resolution on Education Policy (1913). Women's University in 1916 in Bombay catering to the needs of higher education of nearly 10 thousand girls and women every year.'[15]

'A decade later in 1791 due to the sincere efforts of the British resident, Jonathan Duncan, a Sanskrit College was established to promote the study of Hindu laws and philosophy in Banaras. In 1829, after assuming the office of the Governor-General of India, Lord William Bentinck, emphasised on the medium of English language in Indian education. In 1854, Sir Charles Wood sent a comprehensive dispatch as a grand plan on education. The establishment of departments of public instructions in five provinces and introduction of the pattern of grants in aid to encourage private participation in the field of education were recommended.'[16]

'Arya Samaj in North India, Brahmo Samaj in Bengal, Christian Missionaries came into aid of Indian girls and women in all sphere of life. First school was opened by Mrs Meada in Nagaercoil in 1819. Mrs Norton opened a school for women at Allepey in 1920; Mrs Wilson opened a school for girls in Bombay in 1830, known as St. Columbia School where Parsees girls sent 16 girls to the school. In 1875, Calcutta, Madras universities did not permit admission of girls. In 1882, Girls were permitted to get admission for higher education.'[17]

Role of Women in Indian Freedom Movement

'The history of Indian Struggle would be incomplete without mentioning the contributions of women. The sacrifice made by the women of India will occupy the foremost place. They fought with true spirit and unafraid courage and faced various tortures, exploitations and hardships to earn us freedom.'[18] 'The entire history of the freedom movement are replete with the saga of bravery, sacrifice and political sagacity of hundreds and thousands of women of our country. Their participation in the struggle began as early as 1817 when Bhima Bai Holkar fought against the British Colonel Malcolm and defeated him in guerilla warfare. Another woman whom we remember in this context was Hazrat Mahal Begum. Kasturba, the wife of Mahatma Gandhi, was one of the foremost supporters of the Gandhi's programmes. One of the first women to be imprisoned in Transvaal, she took part in the Quit India Movement (1942) and was arrested. She died while imprisoned in Poona. Many women of Nehru family joined the freedom movement. Sarojini Naidu holds pride of place among women freedom fighters of India. She was responsible for awakening the women of India. She was first woman President of the Indian National Congress in 1925 at the Kanpur Session.

Rani Gaidineliu was a prominent Naga nationalist woman leader from Manipur who took over the movement of Naga nationalists against the British. Kalpana Dutta was another prominent woman revolutionary leader who was influenced by the revolutionary idea of Surya Sen. Sucheta Kriplani was an ardent nationalist with socialistic orientation. She was a close associate of Jai Prakash Narayan who actively participated. Annie Besant, Irish by birth, was a staunch supporter of India's struggle for freedom. She founded the Home Rule League in Madras in 1916. Meera Behn and Sarla Behn Mahatma Gandhi's two English daughters helped for the cause of freedom. Raj Kumari Amrit Kaur was a close follower of Gandhiji from 1919 onwards.'[19]

'The history of Indian Freedom Struggle would be incomplete without mentioning the contributions of women. The sacrifice made by the women of India will occupy the foremost place. Woman's participation in India's freedom struggle began as early as in 1817. Many women including Bhima Bai Holkar, Rani Channama of Kittur, Rani Begam Hazrat Mahal of Avadh fought against British East India company in the ninteenth century; 30 years before the "First War of Independence 1857". The role played by women in the War of Independence of 1857 was creditable and invited the admiration even leaders of the Revolt.'[20]

'Many women stood up to the colonial patriarchy, such as Pandita Ramabai, Anandi Gopal and Savithribai Phule. Gandhiji was also instrumental in bringing women into the fold of the national movement. He believed that marriages should take place only when there is a desire for progeny. One of the greatest contributions of Gandhiji to the emancipation of women is his insistence on their participation in politics. He felt that women should have as much a share in winning swaraj for India as men. They were active in participating in the Swadeshi movement, or the boycott of foreign goods, non-payment of taxes, picketing of liquor shops and so on.'[21]

Women Empowerment since Independence

'The empowerment of women is located within the discourse and agenda of gender equality and is increasingly being taken in the agendas of international development organisations, perhaps more as a means to achieve gender equality than as an end in itself. Constitution of India guarantees equality to women (Article 14). There are other articles too which ensure rights of women e.g. no discrimination by the state [Article15 (1)] equality of opportunity (Article 16) etc. Feminist activism picked up momentum in India during later 1970's. Later on many groups and NGO's have been working for the empowerment of women. The Constitution Framers were very much conscious of the problem of women empowerment hence they ensured that the Principle of Gender Equality is enshrined in the Indian Constitution in its Preamble, Fundamental duties and Directive Principle.'[22]

'Right to improve the status and position of women is necessary factor to have the removal of all the anomalies in the rights of men and women the Hindu Code Bill covered all the aspects regarding the rights of women.'[23] 'The cases of trafficking of young girls and women have been reported. These women are either forced into prostitution, domestic work or child labour to prevent this, the Immoral Traffic (Prevention) Act was passed in 1956. In 1961, the Government of India passed the Dowry Prohibition Act and the Dowry Prohibition (maintenance of lists of presents to the bride and bridegroom) rules were framed in 1985. In India, all the medical tests that can be used to decide the sex of the child have been banned. The Government of India passed the Muslim Women's (Protection of Rights upon Divorce) Act, on the base of Supreme Court Judgment in 1986. Women-oriented NGOs were formed with the help of grants from foreign donors in 1990s. Self Help Groups, Self Employed Women's Association (SEWA), etc. played a key role in protecting women's rights by which many women have emerged as leaders of local movements in India.'[24]

'The United Nations Development Programme constituted eight Millennium Development Goals (MDG) for ensuring equity and peace across the world. The third MDG is directly related to the empowerment of women in India. The MDGs are agreed-upon goals to reduce certain indicators of disparity across the world by the year 2015. The Ministry for Women and Child Development was established as a department of the Ministry of Human Resource Development in the year 1985 to drive the holistic development of women and children in the country. The National Commission for Women is a Department within the Ministry of Women and Child Development. It was set up exclusively to help women via the Constitution by reviewing Legal and Constitutional safeguards for women, recommending remedial legislative measures, by facilitating quick redressal of grievances and by advising the Government of India on all policy matters affecting women.'[25]

Women Rights in India

'Women in India face a lot of social inequalities ranging from gender specific abortions, mistreatment by their spouses, to eve teasing. Most women are not aware of women rights in India and other times their legal rights are not protected as they should be.'[26] 'The Constitution of India not only grants equality to women but also empowers the State to adopt measures of positive discrimination in favour of women for neutralising the cumulative socio-economic, education and political disadvantages faced by them. Fundamental Rights, among others, ensure equality before the law and equal protection of law; prohibits discrimination against any citizen on grounds of religion, race, caste, sex or place of birth and guarantee equality of opportunity to all citizens in matters relating to employment. Articles 14, 15, 15(3), 16, 39(a), 39(b), 39(c) and 42 of the Constitution are of specific importance in this regard.'[27]

'Women-Specific Legislations

- The Immoral Traffic (Prevention) Act, 1956
- The Dowry Prohibition Act, 1961 (28 of 1961) (Amended in 1986)
- The Indecent Representation of Women (Prohibition) Act, 1986
- The Commission of Sati (Prevention) Act, 1987 (3 of 1988)
- Protection of Women from Domestic Violence Act, 2005

- The Sexual Harassment of Women at Workplace (Prevention, Prohibition and Redressal) Act, 2013
- The Criminal Law (Amendment) Act, 2013

Women-Related Legislations

- The Indian Penal Code, 1860
- The Indian Evidence Act, 1872
- The Indian Christian Marriage Act, 1872 (15 of 1872)
- The Married Women's Property Act, 1874 (3 of 1874)
- The Guardians and Wards Act, 1890
- The Workmen's Compensation Act, 1923
- The Trade Unions Act 1926
- The Child Marriage Restraint Act, 1929 (19 of 1929)
- The Payments of Wages Act, 1936
- The Payments of Wages (Procedure) Act, 1937
- The Muslim Personal Law (Shariat) Application Act, 1937
- Employers Liabilities Act, 1938
- The Minimum Wages Act, 1948
- The Employees' State Insurance Act, 1948
- The Factories Act, 1948
- The Minimum Wages Act, 1950
- The Plantation Labour Act, 1951 (amended by Acts Nos. 42 of 1953, 34 of 1960, 53 of 1961, 58 of 1981 and 61 of 1986)
- The Cinematograph Act, 1952
- The Mines Act, 1952
- The Special Marriage Act, 1954
- The Protection of Civil Rights Act, 1955
- The Hindu Marriage Act, 1955 (28 of 1989)
- The Hindu Adoptions and Maintenance Act, 1956
- The Hindu Minority and Guardianship Act, 1956
- The Hindu Succession Act, 1956
- The Maternity Benefit Act, 1961 (53 of 1961)
- The Beedi and Cigar Workers (Conditions of Employment) Act, 1966

- The Foreign Marriage Act, 1969 (33 of 1969)
- The Indian Divorce Act, 1969 (4 of 1969)
- The Contract Labour (Regulation and Abolition) Act, 1970
- The Medical Termination of Pregnancy Act, 1971 (34 of 1971)
- Code of Criminal Procedure, 1973
- The Equal Remuneration Act, 1976
- The Bonded Labour System (Abolition) Act, 1979
- The Inter-State Migrant Workmen (Regulation of Employment and Conditions of Service) Act, 1979
- The Family Courts Act, 1984
- The Muslim Women (Protection of Rights on Divorce) Act, 1986
- Mental Health Act, 1987
- National Commission for Women Act, 1990 (20 of 1990)
- The Protection of Human Rights Act, 1993 [As amended by the Protection of Human Rights (Amendment) Act, 2006 - No. 43 of 2006]
- Juvenile Justice (Care and Protection of Children) Act, 2000
- The Child Labour (Prohibition and Regulation) Act
- The Pre-Conception and Pre-Natal Diagnostic Techniques (Prohibition of Sex Selection) Act, 1994
- The Prohibition of Child Marriage Act, 2006'[28]

Role of Women in Indian Politics

'The Constitution of India establishes a parliamentary system of government and guarantees its citizens the right to be elected, freedom of speech, freedom to assemble and form associations and vote. The Constitution of India attempts to remove gender inequalities by banning discrimination based on sex and class, prohibiting human trafficking and forced labour and reserving elected positions for women. India has a federal form of government, with devolved powers. The electorate votes to elect a national parliament as well as state assemblies. Discussion of women's reservations was again introduced in 1974 by the

United Nations Commission on the Status of Women in India, but India did not fully establish quotas in local government until 1994. Local governing bodies in India are called Panchayati Raj Institutions (PRI) and one-third of seats and leadership positions must be reserved for women. States such as Andhra Pradesh, Bihar, Chhattisgarh, Jharkhand, Kerala, Maharashtra, Odisha, Rajasthan, Tripura and Uttarakhand have increased reservations to 50 per cent. The national government has also proposed to raise the level of reservations in PRIs to 50 per cent.'[29]

'India falls in the lowest quartile with respect to the number of women in parliament (9.1 per cent, 14th Lok Sabha). Even Rawanda (56.7 per cent), South Africa (44.5 per cent), Mozambique (34.8 per cent) and many others have much more women representatives, according to the UN's 2008 survey of women in politics. Some states, like Karnataka, had inducted women into rural politics even before it was mandated by the constitution. Several states, including Madhya Pradesh, Himachal Pradesh, Bihar and most recently, Uttarkhand, have allotted not just the required 33 per cent of panchayat seats for women but increased it to 50 per cent.'[30] '15th Lok Sabha elections have delivered a record 59 women as members of Parliament, the highest since independence, raising their parliamentary participation to 10.9 per cent. Seventeen of these women are under 40. And representation of women leaders at he grassroots level in India is nearly 50 per cent, especially since the passing of the 73rd amendment in 1992, which allotted one-third of all seats to women.

It is heartening to note that Indian women were among the earliest to get their political rights (right to vote) without any political movement like United States and many Western countries. They were among the foremost to take active part in politics even in pre-independence times. Indian women have a distinction to become UNO Secretary (Vijay Laxmi Pandit), Prime Minister (Indira Gandhi), Chief Minister (Sucheta Kriplani, Jayalalitha, Uma Bharati, Mayawati, Mamta Banarjee and Vasundhara Raje) and even President (Pratibha Patil).'[31]

Conclusion

During the British rule several changes were made in the socioeconomic structure of our society. During this period some substantial progress was made in eliminating inequalities between men and women in matters of education, employment, social and political rights. The turn of the twentieth century saw a challenge to traditional social structures at both the level of ideology and practice. The entire history of the freedom movement is replete with the saga of bravery, sacrifice and political sagacity of hundreds and thousands of women of our country. Women in India face a lot of social inequalities ranging from gender specific abortions, mistreatment by their spouses, to eve teasing. Majority of women are not aware of women rights in India and other times their legal rights are not protected as they should be. The Constitution of India attempts to remove gender inequalities by banning discrimination based on sex and class, prohibiting human trafficking and forced labour and reserving elected positions for women. India has a federal form of government, with devolved powers.

References

1. Adam and Eve (2015), Retrieved from http://en.wikipedia.org/wiki/Adam_and_Eve
2. Woman (2015), Retrieved from http://en.wikipedia.org/wiki/Woman
3. Role of Women in Society (2014), Retrieved from http://www.megaessays.com/viewpaper/100876.html
4. India – Women in the society, Retrieved from http://www.hss.de/fileadmin/india/downloads/India_%E2%80%93_ Women_in_the_society_01.pdf
5. Status of Women in India (2014), Retrieved from http://natrss.gov.in/pdf/reading/women%20in%20india.pdf
6. Puja Mondal, Changes in the Status of Indian Women during British Rule, Retrieved from http://www.yourarticlelibrary.com/india-2/changes-in-the-status-of-indian-women-during-british-rule-essay/4400/
7. Status of Women in India during The British Period, Retrieved from http://www.indiastudychannel.com/resources/144242-Status-women-India-during-British-period.aspx
8. Sudhanshu Bhandari, Prostitution in Colonial India, Mainstream, Vol. XLVIII, No. 26, June 19, 2010, Retrieved from http://www.mainstreamweekly.net/article2142.html
9. Prostitution in Colonial India (2015), Retrieved from http://en.wikipedia.org/wiki/Prostitution_in_colonial_India

10. Sudhanshu Bhandari, Prostitution in colonial India, Mainstream, Vol. XLVIII, No. 26, June 19, 2010, Retrieved from http://www.mainstreamweekly.net/article2142.html
11. Farida Begum (2012), The Creation of Difference: Empire, Race and the Discourse on Prostitution in Colonial Bengal, 1880-1940, pp.1-33.
12. Samual Stanely and Santosh Kumari (2011), "Position of Women in Colonial Era", International Journal of Educational Research and Technology, Vol. 1 [2], pp. 109-110.
13. New ideas and attempts at social reforms in the British periods, Retrieved from http://www.eklavya.in/pdfs/Books/SSTP/social_studies_8/history/7%20New%20Ideas%2 0and%20Social%20Reform.pdf
14. Educational development of girls and women, Retrieved from http://www.teindia.nic.in/mhrd/50yrsedu/s/3N/EP/3NEP0401.htm
15. Educational and social reforms of the British India, Retrieved from http://holisticthought.com/educational-and-social-reforms/
16. Achla Sharma, Status of Women: A Socio-Historical analysis in different Ages of Indian Society, Research Journal of Language, Literature and Humanities, Vol. 1(1), 10-14, January (2014), p.13.
17. Satwinder Kaur, Role of Women in India's Struggle for Freedom, International Journal of Management and Social Sciences Research, Volume 2, No. 4, p.112.
18. Siddhartha Dash (2010), Role of Women in India's Struggle for Freedom, Odisha Review, pp.74-76.
19. Role of women in India's struggle for freedom, Retrieved from http://www.eduresourcecollection.com/projects_women.php
20. Puja Mondal, The Role of Women in Indian National Movement, Retrieved from http://www.yourarticlelibrary.com/essay/the-role-of-women-in-indian-national-movement/32977/
21. Women Empowerment : A Challenge of 21st Century, Retrieved from http://www.rmttc.com/images/new_pdf/concept_paper.pdf
22. Dr Mathew Rosamma (2013), Empowerment of women through ages an analysis, Innovare Journal of Social Sciences, Vol. 1, Issue 1, p. 2.
23. Dr Ravi N. Kadam, Empowerment of Women in India- An Attempt to Fill the Gender Gap, International Journal of Scientific and Research Publications, Volume 2, Issue 6, June 2012, pp. 2-3.

24. Women Empowerment in India – A Burning Issue, Retrieved from http://www.womenempowermentinindia.com/
25. Women Rights in India, Retrieved from http://www.womenempowermentinindia.com/women-rights-in-india/
26. Constitutional and legal provisions for women in India, Retrieved from http://nlrd.org/womens-rights-initiative/legislations-laws-related-to-women/constitutional-and-legal-provisions-for-women-in-india
27. From official website of National Commission for Women.
28. Women's political participation in India (2015), Retrieved from http://en.wikipedia.org/wiki/Women%27s_political_participation_in_India
29. Vipul Pandey, Women in Indian Politics, Retrieved from http://www.civilserviceindia.com/subject/Essay/women-in-indian-politics.html
30. What is the Role of Women in Indian Politics? Growing Stronger..., Retrieved from http://knowledge.wharton.upenn.edu/article/what-is-the-role-of-women-in-indian-politics-growing-stronger/
31. Puja Mondal, Essay on the Role of Women in Politics, Retrieved from http://www.yourarticlelibrary.com/essay/essay-on-the-role-of-women-in-politics/31315/

2

Constitution of India

"You have the right to work, but never to the fruit of work. You should never engage in action for the sake of reward, nor should you long for inaction. Perform work in this world, Arjuna, as a man established within himself - without selfish attachments and alike in success and defeat."

–*The Bhagavad Gita*

Introduction

'Constitution is a set of fundamental principles or established precedents according to which a state or other organisation is governed. Constitutions concern different levels of organisations, from sovereign states to companies and unincorporated associations. A treaty which establishes an international organisation is its constitution. The Constitution of India is the longest written constitution of any sovereign country in the world, containing 444 articles in 22 parts, 12 schedules and 118 amendments.'[1] 'The term *constitution* literally means *creation* or *foundation*, because in the constitution the people create and found a government, which has no legitimate power apart from the people's will expressed in the constitution. The Constitution says there are three spheres of government - national, provincial and local. Each sphere has legislative (law-making) power over certain things and executive power and responsibility for certain things. The spheres of government are different to the old system in which most decisions were made at national level and merely implemented at provincial and local government level. The spheres of government are distinctive (each one is clearly separate from the others), interdependent (they depend on each other) and interrelated (their functions are related to one another).'[2]

'The Constitution of USA was written during the Philadelphia Convention, which took place from May 25, 1787 to September 17, 1787. The Constitution was signed on September 17, 1787 in the Assembly Room of the Pennsylvania State House. It did not go into effect until June 21, 1788 when nine states ratified it. James Madison is often referred to as the Father of the Constitution because many of his philosophies are reflected in the document. Other prominent figures in the Constitution's drafting include Benjamin Franklin, George Washington and Alexander Hamilton.'[3] 'Constitution Day is an opportunity for students to broaden their knowledge of the Constitution, with its short elegant language and it's far reaching ramifications that have both shaped our history and our lives.'[4]

'The Indian constitution is based on the theory of Parliamentary sovereignty and not constitutional sovereignty, as is the case in the U.S.A. Consequently, the Parliament may easily tamper with Indian fundamental rights. The capacity of the judiciary to afford protection to the fundamental rights is very limited. The Supreme Court verdict that the fundamental rights are not amendable was subsequently reversed. In the Keshavanand Bharati case, Supreme Court held that the Parliament may amend the entire Constitution. It cannot only alter any basic feature of the Constitution.'[5]

Significance of Constitution

'The Constitution places the government's power in the hands of the citizens. It limits the power of the government and establishes a system of checks and balances. The Constitution is important because it protects individual freedom and its fundamental principles.'[6] 'The Constitution is important for a great number of reasons primarily because it was the document that founded our government. It gives a complete list of all the things that we can do and the rights that we have. The Constitution and its amendments protects us, it protects us from each other and it protects us from our own government, it protects us from wrongful prosecution, incriminating ourselves, our right to speech, our right to bear arms, our right to freedom of religion.'[7]

Preamble of Constitution

'The preamble to the Constitution of India is a brief introductory statement that sets out the guiding purpose and principles of the document. The hopes and aspiration of the people as well as the ideals before our nation are described in the preamble in clear cut words. It may be considered as the soul of Constitution. The preamble can be referred to as the preface which highlights the essence of the entire Constitution. It was adopted on 26 November 1949 by the Constituent Assembly. The Preamble reflects the philosophy as well as fundamental values of Indian Constitution. It clarifies four important aspects: It mentions that the Constitution derives its Authority from the people of India: (a) It declares India to be Sovereign, Socialist, Secular, Democratic and Republican country; (b) It clarifies the objectives of the Constitution are Justice, Liberty, Equality and Fraternity: and it states the date of Adoption i.e., 26 November 1949.

Fundamental Rights

It is a charter of rights contained in the Constitution of India. It guarantees civil liberties such that all Indians can lead their lives in peace and harmony as citizens of India. These include individual rights such as equality before law, freedom of speech and expression and peaceful assembly, freedom to practice religion and the right to constitutional remedies for the protection of civil rights by means of writs such as habeas corpus. Fundamental rights for Indians have been aimed at overturning the inequalities of pre-independence social practices. They have also been used to abolish untouchability and thus prohibit discrimination on the grounds of religion, race, caste, sex, or place of birth. The fundamental rights were included in the constitution because they were considered essential for the development of the personality of every individual and to preserve human dignity. The writers of the constitution regarded democracy of no avail if civil liberties, like freedom of speech and religion were not recognised and protected by the State.'[8]

' The Fundamental Rights, Directive Principles of State Policy and Fundamental Duties are sections of the Constitution of India that prescribe the fundamental obligations of the State to its citizens and the duties of the citizens to the State. The Fundamental Rights, embodied in Part III of the Constitution, guarantee civil rights to all Indians and prevent the State from encroaching on individual liberty while simultaneously placing upon it an obligation to protect the citizens' rights from encroachment by society. The purpose of the Fundamental Rights is to preserve individual liberty and democratic principles based on equality of all members of society. The Fundamental Rights are defined as the basic human rights of all citizens. These rights, defined in Part III of the Constitution, apply irrespective of race, place of birth, religion, caste, creed or sex. They are enforceable by the courts, subject to specific restrictions.'[9]

'The Constitution of India guarantees certain Fundamental Rights to the Citizens of India. The Indian constitution contains a chapter on fundamental rights. Part III (Art. 12-35) contains fundamental rights of Indian citizens. The fundamental rights are called fundamental because they are basic to the development of human personality.'[10] 'The seven fundamental rights recognised by the Indian constitution are:

1. *Right to equality:* It includes equality before law, prohibition of discrimination on grounds of religion, race, caste, gender or place of birth and equality of opportunity in matters of employment, abolition of untouchability and abolition of titles.
2. *Right to freedom:* It includes speech and expression, assembly, association or union or cooperatives, movement, residence and right to practice any profession or occupation (some of these rights are subject to security of the State, friendly relations with foreign countries, public order, decency or morality), right to life and liberty, right to education, protection in respect to conviction in offences and protection against arrest and detention in certain cases.
3. *Right against exploitation:* It prohibits all forms of forced labour, child labour and traffic of human beings.

4. *Right to freedom of religion:* It includes freedom of conscience and free profession, practice and propagation of religion, freedom to manage religious affairs, freedom from certain taxes and freedom from religious instructions in certain educational institutes.
5. *Cultural and educational rights:* Preserve the right of any section of citizens to conserve their culture, language or script and right of minorities to establish and administer educational institutions of their choice.
6. *Right to constitutional remedies:* It is present for enforcement of Fundamental Rights.
7. *Right to life:* It gives the right to live with human dignity. This includes rights such as right to education, health, shelter and basic amenities that the state shall provide.'[11]

Constitutional Protection

'The Constitution of India not only grants equality to women but also empowers the State to adopt measures of positive discrimination in favour of women for neutralising the cumulative socio-economic, education and political disadvantages faced by them. Fundamental Rights, among others, ensure equality before the law and equal protection of law; prohibits discrimination against any citizen on grounds of religion, race, caste, sex or place of birth and guarantee equality of opportunity to all citizens in matters relating to employment. Articles 14, 15, 15(3), 16, 39(a), 39(b), 39(c) and 42 of the Constitution are of specific importance in this regard. Constitutional Privileges are:

1. Equality before law for women (Article 14).
2. The State not to discriminate against any citizen on grounds only of religion, race, caste, sex, place of birth or any of them (Article 15 (i)).
3. The State to make any special provision in favour of women and children (Article 15 (3)).
4. Equality of opportunity for all citizens in matters relating to employment or appointment to any office under the State (Article 16).
5. The State to direct its policy towards securing for men and women equally the right to an adequate means of

livelihood (Article 39(a)); and equal pay for equal work for both men and women (Article 39(d)).

6. To promote justice, on a basis of equal opportunity and to provide free legal aid by suitable legislation or scheme or in any other way to ensure that opportunities for securing justice are not denied to any citizen by reason of economic or other disabilities (Article 39 A).
7. The State to make provision for securing just and humane conditions of work and for maternity relief (Article 42)
8. The State to promote with special care the educational and economic interests of the weaker sections of the people and to protect them from social injustice and all forms of exploitation (Article 46).
9. The State to raise the level of nutrition and the standard of living of its people (Article 47).
10. To promote harmony and the spirit of common brotherhood amongst all the people of India and to renounce practices derogatory to the dignity of women (Article 51(A)(e)).
11. Not less than one-third (including the number of seats reserved for women belonging to the Scheduled Castes and the Scheduled Tribes) of the total number of seats to be filled by direct election in every Panchayat to be reserved for women and such seats to be allotted by rotation to different constituencies in a Panchayat (Article 243 D(3)).
12. Not less than one-third of the total number of offices of Chairpersons in the Panchayats at each level to be reserved for women (Article 243 D(4)).
13. Not less than one-third (including the number of seats reserved for women belonging to the Scheduled Castes and the Scheduled Tribes) of the total number of seats to be filled by direct election in every Municipality to be reserved for women and such seats to be allotted by rotation to different constituencies in a Municipality (Article 243 T(3)).
14. Reservation of offices of Chairpersons in Municipalities for the Scheduled Castes, the Scheduled Tribes and women

in such manner as the legislature of a State may by law provide (Article 243 T(4)).'[12]

Protection of Human Rights

'The concept of human rights incorporates three basic tenets: individualism, which implies that the individual is the basic unit of society; rights, which implies that the basic organising principle of society is rights; and legalism, which means that the primary method of securing these rights is through recourse to formal law, where rights are claimed and adjudicated upon, mainly in an adversarial manner.'[13]

'Human rights refer to the basic rights and freedoms to which all humans are entitled. Examples of rights and freedoms which are often thought of as human rights include civil and political rights, such as the right to life and liberty, freedom of expression and equality before the law; and social, cultural and economic rights, including the right to participate in culture, the right to work and the right to education. The Constitution of India is the most right-based constitutions in the world. It was drafted around the same time when the Universal Declaration of Human Rights by the United Nations came into force (1948). Indian Constitution provides the spirit of human rights in its Preamble and the sections on Fundamental rights and Directive Principle of State Policy. The development of constitutionally guaranteed fundamental human rights in India was inspired by England's Bill of Rights (1689), the United States Bill of Rights (approved on September 17, 1787, final approval on December 15, 1791) and France's Declaration of the Rights of Man (created during the revolution of 1789 and ratified on August 26, 1789).

The Fundamental Rights are included in Part III of the Constitution (Articles 12-35), these rights were finalised by a committee of the Constituent Assembly headed by Sardar Vallabhbhai Patel. The Fundamental Rights are not absolute; they can be subject to certain restrictions. There are six fundamental rights enshrined in the Indian Constitution. Right to Equality is included in Articles 14, 15, 16, 17 and 18 of the Constitution. The constitution also guarantees the right to life and personal liberty under Articles 20 and 21. Articles 25, 26, 27 and 28 of the constitution cover the right to freedom of religion. Articles 23 and 24 provides the right against exploitation.

Article 29 and 30 provides special measures to protect the rights of the minorities. Article 32 of the constitution deals with the right to constitutional remedies.'[14]

'The Apex Court has elevated the status of working women in India and confirms that women shall not be denied a job merely because she is a woman. This was decided in a landmark case, Air India vs. Nargesh Meerza AIR 1981 SC 1829. In another milestone case, Miss C.B. Muthamma vs. Union of India AIR 1979 SC 1868, the Hon'ble Supreme Court laid down that seniority promotion shall not be denied on the ground of sex. There are more than a few cases in point where the Hon'ble Supreme Court has elevated the status of women in India in accord with the Constitution of India. There are several statutes made by the state in the past as well as in the recent times for upliftment and progress of the status of women in India.'[15]

Conclusion

The Constitution places the government's power in the hands of the citizens. It limits the power of the government and establishes a system of checks and balances. The Constitution is important because it protects individual freedom and its fundamental principles. The Preamble to the Constitution of India is a brief introductory statement that sets out the guiding purpose and principles of the document. The Fundamental Rights, Directive Principles of State Policy and Fundamental Duties are sections of the Constitution of India that prescribe the fundamental obligations of the State to its citizens and the duties of the citizens to the State. The Constitution of India guarantees certain Fundamental Rights to the Citizens of India.

References

1. Constitution (2015), Retrieved from http://en.wikipedia.org/wiki/Constitution
2. Why the Constitution is so important, Retrieved from http://www.parliament.gov.za/content/4Why%20the%20Constitution%20is%20so%20important.pdf
3. See http://www.ask.com/government-politics/constitution-important-68a25cb89de153d0
4. Kathryn Kolbert, The Importance of Constitution Day, Retrieved from http://www.nytimes.com/ref/college/collegespecial2/coll-constitutionday-intro1.html

5. Article on Fundamental Rights Guaranteed by the Indian Constitution, Retrieved from http://www.importantindia.com/1994/fundamental-rights-guaranteed-by-the-indian-constitution/
6. See http://www.ask.com/government-politics/constitution-important-68a25cb89de153d0#
7. See http://answers.yahoo.com/question/index?qid= 2008090 2193605AA0t3Hy
8. Fundamental Rights in India, Retrieved from http://en.wikipedia.org/wiki/Fundamental_rights_in_India
9. Fundamental Rights, Directive Principles of State Policy and Fundamental Duties of India, Retrieved from http://en.wikipedia.org/wiki/Fundamental_Rights,_ Directive_Principles_and_Fundamental_Duties_of_India
10. Article on Fundamental Rights Guaranteed by the Indian Constitution, Retrieved from http://www.importantindia.com/1994/fundamental-rights-guaranteed-by-the-indian-constitution/
11. Fundamental Rights in India, Retrieved from http://en.wikipedia.org/wiki/Fundamental_rights_in_India
12. Constitutional and legal provisions for women in India, Retrieved from http://nlrd.org/womens-rights-initiative/legislations-laws-related-to-women/constitutional-and-legal-provisions-for-women-in-india
13. Nidhi Gupta, Women's human rights and the practice of dowry in India, p. 87.
14. Anurag Pandey, Protection of Human Rights and the Constitution of India, Retrieved from http://elearning.sol.du.ac.in/mod/book/view.php?id=453andchapterid=311
15. Manisha Singh (2012), Protection of Women under the Constitution of India, Retrieved from http://www.proud2bindian.com/women/protection-of-women-under-the-constitution-of-india/

3

Women Rights

"The happiness which comes from long practice, which leads to the end of suffering, which at first is like poison, but at last like nectar - this kind of happiness arises from the serenity of one's own mind."

—*The Bhagavad Gita*

Introduction

'Woman can be said as the God's complete creation. She is the symbol of independence, love, caring, gentleness and intensity, both in love and in hate. Women are emotionally stronger than man. Undoubtedly women endure much more pain than men do. No men do go through even half the pain a woman goes through during labour. Women have not been treated nicely by men all throughout time. They have been denied their rights, their opportunities. It is very common happening on a daily basis in offices, sports, factories, schools and entertainment.'[1] 'Males seem to have dominated in many ancient cultures, there are some exceptions. In the Nigerian Aka culture women may hunt, even on own and often control distribution of resources. Freeborn women of ancient Rome were citizens who enjoyed legal privileges and protections that did not extend to non-citizens or slaves. Starting in the late eighteenth century and throughout the ninteenth century, rights, as a concept and claim, gained increasing political, social and philosophical importance in Europe. Movements emerged which demanded freedom of religion, the abolition of slavery, rights for women, rights for those who did not own property and universal suffrage.

In 1791, the French playwright and political activist Olympe de Gouges published the *Declaration of the Rights of Woman and the Female Citizen*, modelled on the Declaration of the Rights of Man and of the Citizen of 1789. The Declaration is ironic in formulation and exposes the failure of the French Revolution, which had been devoted to equality. It states that: *"This revolution will only take effect when all women become fully aware of their deplorable condition and of the rights they have lost in society"*. During the ninteenth century some women in the United States and Britain began to challenge laws that denied them the right to their property once they married. Under the common law doctrine of *covertures* husbands gained control of their wives' real estate and wages.'[2] 'Despite great strides made by the international women's rights movement over many years, women and girls around the world are still married as children or trafficked into forced labour and sex slavery. They are refused access to education and political participation and some are trapped in conflicts where rape is perpetrated as a weapon of war. Around the world, deaths related to pregnancy and childbirth is needlessly high and women are prevented from making deeply personal choices in their private lives.'[3]

What are Women's Rights?

'*Women's rights* are the rights and entitlements claimed for women and girls of many societies worldwide. These are an essential component of universal human rights. They reflect the fact that men and women have very different experiences and the fact that women and girls often face gender-based discrimination that puts them at increased risk of poverty, violence, ill health and poor education.'[4] Women's rights are the rights and entitlements claimed for women and girls of many societies worldwide. In some places, these rights are institutionalised or supported by law, local custom and behaviour, whereas in others they may be ignored or suppressed.

Women's Rights Movement

'The women's rights movement of the mid-nineteenth century unified women around a number of issues that were seen as fundamental rights for all citizens; they included: the right to own property, access to higher education, reproductive rights and suffrage. World War I and II encouraged women to do their patriotic duty by entering the workforce to support the war effort. Many women assumed they would leave the working world when men returned from service and many did. In the four decades since, the women's movement has tackled many issues that are considered discriminatory toward women including: sexism in advertising and the media, economic inequality issues that affect families and violence against women.

The women's rights movement rose during the nineteenth century in Europe and America in response to great inequalities between the legal statuses of women and men. First proposed as a federal amendment in 1868, women's suffrage floundered for many years before the passage of the Nineteenth Amendment gave women the right to vote in 1920. The women's rights movement reformed during the 1960s as the women's liberation movement. The period would mark the revitalisation of feminism.'[5]

Role of United Nations

'UN support for the rights of women began with the Organisation's founding Charter. Among the purposes of the UN declared in Article 1 of its Charter is *"To achieve international co-operation ... in promoting and encouraging respect for human rights and for fundamental freedoms for all without distinction as to race, sex, language, or religion."* The landmark Declaration, adopted by the General Assembly on 10 December 1948, reaffirms that *"All human beings are born free and equal in dignity and rights"* and that *"everyone is entitled to all the rights and freedoms set forth in this Declaration, without distinction of any kind, such as race, colour, sex, language, religion, birth or other status."* In 1979, the General Assembly adopted the Convention on the Elimination of All Forms of Discrimination against Women (CEDAW), which is often described as an International Bill of Rights for Women. In its 30 articles, the Convention explicitly defines discrimination against women and sets up an agenda for national action to end such discrimination. The Fourth World Conference on Women, held in Beijing in 1995, went a step farther than the Nairobi Conference. The Beijing Platform for Action asserted women's rights as human rights and committed to specific actions to ensure respect for those rights.

On 2 July 2010, the United Nations General Assembly unanimously voted to create a single UN body tasked with accelerating progress in achieving gender equality and women's empowerment. The UN system continues to give particular attention to the issue of violence against women. The 1993 General Assembly Declaration on the Elimination of Violence against Women contained *"a clear and comprehensive definition of violence against women [and] a clear statement of the rights to be applied to ensure the elimination of violence against women in all its forms"*. In 2007, the theme of the International Women's Day was Ending Impunity for Violence against Women and Girls.'[6]

'Numerous international and regional instruments have drawn attention to gender-related dimensions of human rights issues, the most important being the UN Convention on the Elimination of All Forms of Discrimination against Women (CEDAW), adopted in 1979. In 1993, 45 years after the Universal Declaration of Human Rights was adopted and eight years after CEDAW entered into force, the UN World Conference on Human Rights in Vienna confirmed that women's rights were human rights. In 1994, the International Conference on Population and Development in Cairo (ICPD) articulated and affirmed the relationship between advancement and fulfillment of rights and gender equality and equity. It also clarified the concepts of women's empowerment, gender equity and reproductive health and rights. In every region of the world, UNFPA is working to promote women's rights and end discrimination against them. The Fund is increasingly involved in protecting the rights of women affected by conflict and ensuring that women can have an active role in peace building and reconstruction efforts.'[7]

'Discrimination based on sex is prohibited under almost every human rights treaty including the International Covenant on Civil and Political Rights and the International Covenant on Economic, Social and Cultural Rights, which under their common Article 3 provide for the rights to equality between men and women in the enjoyment of all rights. Gender equality is at the very heart of human rights and United Nations values. A fundamental principle of the United Nations Charter adopted by world leaders in 1945 is "equal rights of men and women" and protecting and promoting women's human rights is the responsibility of all States.'[8]

United Nations Women

'In July 2010, the United Nations General Assembly created UN Women, the United Nations Entity for Gender Equality and the Empowerment of Women. In doing so, UN Member States took an historic step in accelerating the Organisation's goals on gender equality and the empowerment of women. The creation of UN Women came about as part of the UN reform agenda, bringing together resources and mandates for greater impact. Over many decades, the UN has made significant progress in advancing gender equality, including through landmark agreements such as the Beijing Declaration and Platform for Action and the Convention on the Elimination of All Forms of Discrimination against Women.

The main roles of UN Women are: (a) To support inter-governmental bodies, such as the Commission on the Status of Women, in their formulation of policies, global standards and norms; (b) To help Member States to implement these standards, standing ready to provide suitable technical and financial support to those countries that request it and to forge effective partnerships with civil society; and (c) To lead and coordinate the UN system's work on gender equality as well as promote accountability, including through regular monitoring of system-wide progress.'[9]

'UN Women became operational in January 2011. As with UNIFEM previously, UN Women is a member of the United Nations Development Group. The organisation is governed by a multi-tiered intergovernmental governance structure in charge of providing normative and operational policy guidance. The General Assembly, Economic and Social Council and the Commission on the Status of Women (CSW) constitute the governance structure that sets forth the normative policy guiding principles of the Entity. The intergovernmental governance structure in charge of providing operational policy guidance to UN Women includes the General Assembly, the Economic and

Social Council and the organisation's Executive Board. The mandate and functions of UN Women consist of the consolidated mandates and functions of the Office of the Special Adviser on Gender Issues and Advancement of Women, the Division for the Advancement of Women, the United Nations Development Fund for Women and the International Research and Training Institute for the Advancement of Women.'[10]

Women Rights in India

'Constitution of India does not differentiate between males and females. Women have equal rights as that of a man in every sphere. Hindu Women's Rights to the Property Act, 1937 dealt with the rights of Hindu widow, on the death of her husband who does not make any Will. The Hindu Succession Act, 1956 brought out revolutionary changes in property rights of women. Section 14 of the Hindu Succession Act, confers absolute right to the female in any property possessed by Hindu female. The rights are of full nature including unfettered rights of disposal of property.'[11] 'Rights (in any form of property) are defined here as claims that are legally and socially recognised and enforceable by an external legitimised authority, be it a village-level institution or some higher-level body of the State.'[12] 'In South Asia, inheritance is often the vehicle that grants women property rights. Women's inheritance rights are mostly governed by formal and customary laws and the primary formal laws are personal laws which tend to be heavily influenced by custom and religion.'[13]

'One of the legal reforms in India that most clearly followed upon the efforts of British reformers was "age of consent". Law governing the age at which adolescents can legally consent to sexual intercourse. Nineteenth century age of consent laws in England and India arose in the context of prostitution and child marriage, respectively, which were social issues directly linked to Victorian notions of domesticity and sexual restraint. An important factor in the issue of widow remarriage was the supposed belief that Hinduism required an ascetic widowhood. The forfeiture provisions of the 1856 Hindu Widows' Remarriage Act of 1856 clearly envisioned a world in which widows deserved support but were not entitled to control marital property. In the nineteenth century, induced abortion became illegal in India, unless medically indicated to save the life of a pregnant woman, as governed by the Indian Penal Code and the Code for Criminal Procedure.'[14]

'The constitution of India confers special rights upon women. The state is directed to provide for maternity relief to female workers under Article 42 of the Constitution, whereas Article 51-A declares it as a fundamental duty of every Indian citizen to renounce practices to respect the dignity of women. Indian Parliament has passed the Protection of Human Rights Act, 1993 for the proper implementation of Article 51-A. Indian Parliament over the years have taken significant steps for through legislations to achieve the goal of empowering the women in India. The significant among them are the Equal Remuneration Act, the Prevention of Immoral Traffic Act, the Sati (Widow Burning the rights of) Prevention Act and the Dowry Prohibition Act etc. The government in India has enacted a variety of laws like Dowry Prohibition Act, Sati Prevention Act etc to guarantee the rights of the women.'[15]

'The National Crime Records Bureau (NCRB) had predicted that growth rate of crime against women would be higher than the population growth by 2010, which was found to be true.'[16] 'The National Commission for Women have taken up the cudgels for women's right and have vociferously demanded a separate criminal code for women and enhanced punishment for offences against women. The proposal for creating a separate criminal code for women was designed to provide quick justice to the aggrieved women and speed up the conviction rate. In India, it was state which initiated the first reform measure when after lot of debate it reformed the Hindu Succession Act in 1956 in which women were given equal right to inheritance.'[17]

'Women's right to property has been substantially improved by the Hindu Succession Act 1956. The concept of women being entitled to a limited estate when they acquire property by inheritance is abolished and women are entitled to an absolute estate like men when they inherit any property. Again the daughter of a predeceased son and the daughter of a predeceased daughter are raised to a higher rank. Under Section 14 of The Hindu Succession Act, 1956, the limited interest of Hindu female is converted into absolute rights. If she gets property from her husband she can sell it and the purchaser gets absolute right in the property. The stringent restrictions under the Shastric law on female inheritance were finally taken away by the Parliament to make it conform to the Constitutional mandate of equality. The disability of women in inheriting the father's property was undone under Section 6 of the 1956 Act. The Supreme Court through its judgment in fact went beyond legislative language. The Court said that Section 14 is wide in its scope and ambit. It says that any property possessed by a female Hindu whether acquired before or after the commencement of the Act shall be held by her as full owner. The words 'any property' are large enough to include her *stridhanam* obtained immediately before the commencement of the Act.'[18]

'Women are frequently caught up in a vicious social, cultural, religious, political and legal circle and may be unable to break out of it alone. To do so, they need, inter alia, the support of independent and impartial legal professions that are familiar with international human rights law and its application to women and are capable of exercising their responsibilities diligently and fearlessly. Enhancement of awareness among judges, prosecutors and lawyers of acts and practices that violate the most fundamental rights of women and girls constitutes an important step towards providing half of humanity with an acutely needed remedy and a means of redress.'[19]

Challenges before Women

'Growing up as females has never been easy. Social mentality about boys and girls are not same. Females may face a lot of disturbances or discrimination from people around them and worse, from their parents sometimes, in the case of determining their own happiness and their futures.'[20] 'Today, there are still problems for women. One of the big problems is sexual harassment. Many women have jobs outside and they get sexual harassment by their bosses. It is a very common problem and it is the worst problem for women. There is unfair payment between men and women. Many women work with men, they work the same time as men and they have the same abilities as men. There salaries are different. Men get more than women sometimes. It is not fair.'[21]

'The recognition of gender as an issue powered the post-colonial women's movement, supported by feminist critiques and women's studies in academia. Women mobilised to protest violence, legal discrimination and rising prices and agitated for better living conditions through higher wages, the prohibition of liquor and the provision of drinking water. In 1986, the developing tensions were exposed and fueled by the Shah Bano case. Discrimination against women in personal law had been on the women's movement's agenda since the 1920s, but the Shah Bano case catapulted the issue into a crisis of national proportions.'[22]

'Women in India, as well as elsewhere, are affected by conflicts in various ways due to their role in society. Discrimination, that women often have to face in times of peace, gets reinforced in war as the community becomes militarised. Militarism and masculinist values, such as domination, aggression and assertiveness, are closely intertwined. In patriarchic societies, men are expected to be strong and powerful, whereas women are valued in terms of their chastity and obedience. They have little independent status, as they are viewed by the communities only in connection with their fathers or husbands.'[23]

'Violence against women is partly a result of gender relations that assumes men to be superior to women. Cultural and social factors are interlinked with the development and propagation of violent behaviour. The World Human Rights Conference in Vienna, first recognised gender-based violence as a human rights violation in 1993. Technologies like amniocentesis and ultrasound used in most parts of the world, largely for detecting foetal abnormalities, has been used in large parts of the Indian subcontinent for determining the sex of the foetus so that it can be aborted, if it happens to be a female. The information of the sex of the unborn was being extensively misused. Medical Termination of Pregnancy Act (MTPA) 1971 allows abortion if the doctor is of the opinion that the continuance of the pregnancy would endanger the life of the pregnant woman or involve grave injury to her physical or mental health; or there is substantial risk that the child would suffer from disabling physical or mental abnormalities.'[24]

Conclusion

Women's rights are the rights and entitlements claimed for women and girls of many societies worldwide. They are an essential component of universal human rights. They reflect the fact that men and women have very different experiences and the fact that women and girls often face gender-based discrimination that puts them at increased risk of poverty, violence, ill-health and a poor education. The women's rights movement of the mid-nineteenth century unified women number of issues that were seen as fundamental rights for all citizens. They included the right to own property, access to higher education, reproductive rights and suffrage. UN support for the rights of women began with the Organisation's founding Charter. Constitution of India does not differentiate between males and females. Women have equal rights as that of a man in every sphere. The constitution of India confers special rights upon women.

References

1. Sanjib Kumar, Short Essay on Women Rights, Retrieved from http://www.publishyourarticles.net/knowledge-hub/law/short-essay-on-women-rights.html
2. Women's rights (2014), Retrieved from http://en.wikipedia.org/wiki/Women%27s_rights
3. Women's rights, Retrieved from https://www.hrw.org/topic/womens-rights
4. Women's Rights are Human Rights (2014), Retrieved from http://www.amnestyusa.org/our-work/issues/women-s-rights
5. Women's Rights Movement (2014), Retrieved from http://www.enotes.com/research-starters/womens-rights-movement
6. Women: global issues, Retrieved from http://www.un.org/en/globalissues/women/
7. The Human Rights of Women (2014), Retrieved from http://www.unfpa.org/resources/human-rights-women
8. Women's Human Rights and Gender Equality (2015), Retrieved from http://www.ohchr.org/EN/Issues/Women/WRGS/Pages/WRGSIndex.aspx
9. About the UN Women, Retrieved from http://www.unwomen.org/en/about-us/about-un-women
10. UN Women (2014), Retrieved from http://en.wikipedia.org/wiki/UN_Women
11. Puja Mondal (2014), Essay on Property Rights of Women in India, Retrieved from http://www.yourarticlelibrary.com/essay/essay-on-property-rights-of-women-in-india-625-words/4658/http://

www.yourarticlelibrary.com/essay/essay-on-property-rights-of-women-in-india-625-words/4658/

12. Bina Agarwal, Are We Not Peasants Too? Land Rights and Women's Claims in India, p.2.
13. Women's Inheritance Rights to Land and Property in South Asia: A Study of Afghanistan, Bangladesh, India, Nepal, Pakistan and Sri Lanka (2009), Retrieved from http://www.landesa.org/wp-content/uploads/2011/01/RDI_Report_WJF_Womens_Inheritance_ Six_ South_Asian_Countries_December_2009.pdf
14. Varsha Chitnis (2007), The Legacy of Colonialism: Law and Women's Rights in India, Retrieved from http://scholarship.law.ufl.edu/cgi/viewcontent.cgi? article=1148 &context=faculty pub
15. Sutapa Saryal, Women's Rights in India: Problems and Prospects, International Research Journal of Social Sciences, Vol. 3(7), 49-53, July (2014), pp. 48-53.
16. Ritu, Dhanoa, Violation of women human rights in India, Shiv Shakti: International Journal in Multidisciplinary and Academic Research, Vol. 1, No. 4, p. 2.
17. Sutapa Saryal, Women's Rights in India: Problems and Prospects, International Research Journal of Social Sciences, Vol. 3(7), 49-53, July (2014), pp. 48-53.
18. Women property rights: A comparative study of Hindu, Christian and Muslim, pp.155-158, Retrieved from http://shodhganga.inflibnet.ac.in/bitstream/10603/8148/8/08_chapter%204.pdf
19. Women's rights in the administration of Justice, p. 448, Retrieved from http://www.ohchr.org/Documents/Publications/training 9chapter11en.pdf
20. Term paper sample on women and their rights, Retrieved from http://www.thehankwilliamsmuseum.com/graded-term-paper-example-on-womens-rights
21. Mariko Hirata, Women rights Essay, Retrieved from http://www2.hawaii.edu/~sford/alternatv/sum05/news/mari_women.htm
22. Samita Sen, Toward a Feminist Politics? The Indian Women's Movement in Historical Perspective, Retrieved from http://siteresources.worldbank.org/INTGENDER/Resources/wp9.pdf
23. Women Rights in Conflict Zones: A Focus on India (2010), Retrieved from http://www.hrln.org/hrln/images/stories/pdf/Report%20-%20Women%20Rights%20in%20Conflict%20Zones%20-%20A%20Focus%20on%20India.pdf
24. Sheela Saravanan, Violence Against Women in India: A Literature Review, Retrieved from http://www.isst-india.org/pdf/violence%20against%20women%20india.pdf

4

Women Empowerment

> "Anyone who is steady in his determination for the advanced stage of spiritual realisation and can equally tolerate the onslaughts of distress and happiness is certainly a person eligible for liberation."
>
> —*The Bhagavad Gita*

Introduction

'Women empowerment is basically the creation of an environment where women can make independent decisions on their personal development as well as shine as equals in society. Women want to be treated as equals so much so that if a woman rises to the top of her field it should be a commonplace occurrence that draws nothing more than a raised eyebrow at the gender.'[1] 'The subject of empowerment of women has becoming a burning issue all over the world including India since last few decades. Many agencies of United Nations in their reports have emphasised that gender issue is to be given utmost priority. The position and status of women all over the world has risen incredibly in the twentieth century. For a long time women in India remained within the four walls of their household. Their dependence on men folk was total.'[2]

'Harnessing the power of innovation to transform the lives of women in the developing world is an idea whose time has come. Never before has the world experienced such dynamic change in technologies, economies and societies as it is today. An increasingly wide range of institutions from business, civil society and government have committed resources, rhetoric and political capital to promote women's empowerment. Recent developments in innovation thinking increasingly emphasise the opportunities that innovations can bring about to address development issues and spur wider social change. Innovations to change social norms can be catalytic because women's empowerment requires the transformation of inequitable gender attitudes, behaviours and harmful practices, such as child marriage, female genital cutting as well as restrictions on women's mobility and their rights to education, health, work and civic participation.'[3]

'For women's empowerment, the 1990s were an important time. The world conferences of the 1990s gives provided opportunities to mobilise and build a consensus among many actors around women's empowerment. This was crystallised in the 1995 Beijing Platform for Action (BPA) which remains the most comprehensive document of the world's commitment to women's rights. The changing political context at the international level, with the collapse of the Soviet Union and increasing democratisation in Latin America and other regions, allowed women to organise locally and transnationally and to use national and international political structures to highlight issues of gender inequality and to get commitment from leaders everywhere to acknowledge and address inequality.'[4]

Meaning of the Concept

'Women's empowerment is a process of personal and social change through which they gain power, meaningful choices and control over their lives. Empowerment is not something that can be done to or for women. Women are the agents of their empowerment. Women's empowerment has been a feature of development assistance since the 1990s. Given the continued resistance to 'gender issues' in some parts of the development community, this alone is an achievement. To contribute to progress on women's empowerment, the international community must support the political actions of women and their allies to change gender and other power hierarchies.'[5]

'Empowerment is an active process, which enables women to realise their identity and power in all aspects of life. It enables women to have more access to knowledge and resources, greater autonomy in decision-making, greater ability to plan their times, free them from the clutches of irrelevant customs built and practices.'[6] 'It is an active and multidimensional process that enables women to realise their identity and power in all aspects of life. It has three core dimensions: political empowerment, economic empowerment and control over one's body. In today's developed countries, the historic process of economic empowerment and to a lesser extent, control over the body, mostly preceded universal suffrage.'[7]

'Empowerment is now increasingly seen as a process by which the one's without power gain greater control over their lives. This means control over material assets, intellectual resources and ideology. It involves power to, power with and power within. Some define empowerment as a process of awareness and conscientisation, of capacity building leading to greater participation, effective decision-making power and control leading to transformative action.'[8]

Importance of Empowerment

'Women's empowerment is defined as women's ability to make strategic life choices where that ability had been previously denied them. Empowering women to participate fully in economic life across all sectors and throughout all levels of economic activity is essential to: (a) Build strong economies; (b) Establish more stable and just societies; (c) Achieve internationally agreed goals for development, sustainability and human rights; (d) Improve quality of life for women, men, families and communities; and (e) Propel businesses' operations and goals.'[9] 'Companies from around the world already furnish concrete examples of how they advance women's empowerment.

Efforts to improve productivity and earnings and increase the numbers of women in the workforce are important for women and the economy. Empower women have significant benefits for society. In addition, increases in employment and earnings benefit individual women by boosting their self-esteem and bargaining power at home, reducing domestic mistreatment and violence and delaying early marriage and pregnancy.

In addition to gains for individual women and the economy, income-enhancing interventions for women can help to change traditional gender norms that influence family spending on female children. Rising aspirations for girls, along with increased family spending on them, may be among the most consequential benefits of jobs for women.'[10]

'Women entrepreneurs are an untapped resource and leveraging women's strengths is a huge opportunity for the sector. Women are the fastest growing cohort of entrepreneurs and business owners in many developing countries. Today women in developing countries are more likely than those in developed countries to start or maintain businesses. Women's networks can open doors for new cooking product businesses and provide access to consumers in hard-to-reach markets. When women enter the marketplace as entrepreneurs, they have immense potential to spur economic growth. Furthermore, when a woman is given an opportunity to earn an income, it has positive impacts on many other areas of her life outside of the clean cooking sector.'[11]

'Women and girls are overrepresented among those who are food-insecure. Worldwide, an estimated 60 per cent of undernourished people are women or girls. By investing more in women using an approach that is empowering and enlarges their freedoms, the gains accrue to all of society. There is a mutually reinforcing relationship between expanding social and economic opportunities for women. This is particularly true of improving women's access to education and strengthening their role in decision-making within the household and within society. Greater economic autonomy improves the bargaining position of women within the household and increases their voice in public decision-making. Expanding the opportunities of women and girls is a duty of states, which ratified various human rights instruments on the human rights of women in general and the rights of women at work.'[12]

Missing Women

'The persistence of gender inequality is most starkly brought home in the phenomenon of missing women. The term was coined by Amartya Sen in a now classic article in the New York Review of Books (Sen, 1990) to capture the fact that the proportion of women is lower than what would be expected if girls and women throughout the developing world were born and died at the same rate, relative to boys and men, as they do in sub-Saharan Africa. Today, it is estimated that six million women are missing every year.'[13]

'The phenomenon of the missing women of Asia is a shortfall in the number of women in Asia relative to the number that would be expected if there were no sex-selective abortion and female infanticide and if the newborn of both sexes received similar levels of healthcare and nutrition. According to Sen, women allegedly make up the majority of the world's population, even though this is not the case throughout every country. While there are typically more women than men in European and North American countries, the sex ratio of developing countries in Asia, as well as the Middle East, is much lower. In China, the ratio of men to women is 1.06, far higher than most countries. Sen argued that the disparity in sex ratio across eastern Asian countries like India, China and Korea when compared to North America and Europe, as seen in 1992, could only be explained by deliberate nutritional and health deprivations against female children.

Sen suggests that the care and nutrition female children receive may be positively correlated to the outside earning power and sense of contribution of women when compared to men. Sen is hopeful that policies aimed to address education, women's property rights as well as economic rights and opportunities outside the home may improve the missing women situation and fight the stigma attached to female children. Sen originally based his calculations on the average sex ratio of Europe and North America in order to calculate the number of missing women, assuming that in these countries men and women receive equal care. Using population data from several countries and the disparity between their respective sex ratios and the standard he was able to conclude that over 100 million women were missing. Some have speculated that the disparity in the sex ratio may have an impact on the marriage market in such a way that may turn the tide of missing women. Since the advent of sex-selective abortions via ultrasound and other medical procedures in the 1980s, the gender discriminations that have caused the "missing women" have simultaneously produced cohorts of excess men. To combat runaway sex-ratio disparity, Hesketh recommends government policy to intervene by making sex selective abortion illegal and promoting awareness to fight son preference paradigms.'[14]

Women Empowerment in India

'India's poor performance on women's empowerment and gender equality is reflected in many indicators. In many parts of the country, sex ratio has dropped to fewer than 850 females per 1000 males. India is ranked 132 out of 148 countries on Gender Inequality Index as per the 2013 Global Human Development Report. Women from disadvantaged groups such as Scheduled Castes, Scheduled Tribes and minorities in particular face discrimination, exploitation and limited employment opportunities.'[15]

'Women's empowerment in India is heavily dependent on many different variables that include geographical location (urban/rural), educational status, social status (caste and class) and age. Social divisions among urban women also have a similar impact on empowerment indicators. Upper class and educated women have better access to health, education and economic opportunities, whereas lower class, less educated women in urban settings enjoy these rights significantly less. Empowerment for women in India requires a cross-cutting approach and one which addresses the diversity of social structures that govern women's lives. Women's security, decision-making power and mobility are three indicators for women's empowerment. In India and more so for rural and less educated women, these three indicators are significantly low.'[16]

'Ministry of Rural Development is implementing various poverty alleviation and rural development programmes. These programmes have special components for women. Major schemes, having women's component, implemented by the Ministry include the Mahatma Gandhi National Rural Employment Guarantee Act (MGNREGA), Swarnjayanti Gram Swarozgar Yojana (SGSY) now restructured as National Rural Livelihood Mission (NRLM) and the Indira Awaas Yojana (IAY). The implementation of these programmes is monitored specifically with reference to coverage of women. MGNREGA the programme guidelines stipulate certain provisions for creation of specific facilities at the worksites for the working women facilitating their participation in the programme.

Self Help Group (SHG), of 10-20 women in general (5-20 in difficult areas) is the primary building block of the NRLM institutional design. National Rural Livelihood Mission would promote SHGs with exclusive women membership. The SHGs and the federation of these SHGs at village and higher levels shall serve the purpose of providing women member's space for self-help, mutual cooperation and collective action for social and economic development. An important component of NRLM is the Mahila Kisan Sashaktikaran Pariyojana (MKSP) which aims at supporting women farmers. Primarily, MKSP aims to recognise women farmers, a hitherto unrecognised category, even though most of the farming activities are almost exclusively handled by the women.'[17]

'A recent legislation of the Central Government, the Hindu Succession Amendment Act, 2005 has also moved towards women's equality in property rights. It makes Hindu women's inheritance rights in agricultural land legally equal to those of men. All daughters including married daughters age Co-parceners in joint family property daughters now have the right to claim partition and to become 'Karta'. All daughters, married or unmarried can reside, seek partition of the parental dwelling place. This law of the centre well has the power to displace any conflicting laws of the state which are unequal to women. This is a far reaching message to assure women control over property. Government schemes could be seen as Relief policies like widow pension schemes.'[18]

Policies for Women Empowerment

'The principle of gender equality is enshrined in the Indian Constitution in its Preamble, Fundamental Rights, Fundamental Duties and Directive Principles. The Constitution not only grants equality to women, but also empowers the State to adopt measures of positive discrimination in favour of women. The National Commission for Women was set up by an Act of Parliament in 1990 to safeguard the rights and legal entitlements of women. The 73rd and 74th Amendments (1993) to the Constitution of India have provided for reservation of seats in the local bodies of Panchayats and Municipalities for women, laying a strong foundation for their participation in decision-making at the local levels.'[19] 'Resources and agency (in various forms and by various names, e.g., control, awareness, voice, power), were the two most common components.'[20]

Table 1: Commonly used dimensions of empowerment and potential operationalisation in the household, community and broader arenas

Dimension	*Household*	*Community*	*Broader Arenas*
Economic	Women's control over income; relative contribution to family support; access to and control of family resources	Women's access to employment; ownership of assets and land; access to credit; involvement and/or representation in local trade associations; access to markets	Women's representation in high paying jobs; women CEO's; representation of women's economic interests in macro-economic policies, state and federal budgets
Socio-cultural	Women's freedom of movement; lack of discrimination against daughters; commitment to educating daughters	Women's visibility in and access to social spaces; access to modern transportation; participation in extra-familial groups and social networks; shift in patriarchal norms (such as son preference); symbolic representation of the female in myth and ritual	Women's literacy and access to a broad range of educational options; Positive media images of women, their roles and contributions
Familial/ Interpersonal	Participation in domestic decision-making; control over sexual relations; ability to make childbearing decisions, use contraception, access abortion; control over spouse selection and marriage timing; freedom from domestic violence	Shifts in marriage and kinship systems indicating greater value and autonomy for women (e.g. later marriages, self selection of spouses, reduction in the practice of dowry; acceptability of divorce); local campaigns against domestic violence	Regional/national trends in timing of marriage, options for divorce; political, legal, religious support for (or lack of active opposition to) such shifts; systems providing easy access to contraception, safe abortion, reproductive health services
Legal	Knowledge of legal rights; domestic support for exercising right	Community mobilization for rights; campaigns for rights awareness; effective local enforcement of legal rights	Laws supporting women's rights, access to resources and options; Advocacy for rights and legislation; use of judicial system to redress rights violations
Political	Knowledge of political system and means of access to it; domestic support for political engagement; exercising the right to vote	Women's involvement or mobilisation in the local political system/campaigns; support for specific candidates or legislation; representation in local bodies of government	Women's representation in regional and national bodies of government; strength as a voting bloc; representation of women's interests in effective lobbies and interest groups
Psychological	Self-esteem; selfefficacy; psychological well-being	Collective awareness of injustice, potential of mobilisation	Women's sense of inclusion and entitlement; systemic acceptance of women's entitlement and inclusion

Source: http://siteresources.worldbank.org/INTGENDER/Resources/MalhotraSchulerBoender.pdf

'By incorporating gender-transformative activities in adaptation strategies at all levels, we actively strive to examine, question and change rigid gender norms and imbalances of power in order to increase people's resilience. Gender transformative activities encourage critical awareness among men and women of gender roles and norms; promote the position of women; challenge the distribution of resources and allocation of duties between men and women; and/or address power relationships between women and others in the community, such as service providers or traditional leaders.'[21]

'In an era characterised by growing global market competition, social protection is central to promoting inclusive growth. Social protection assists women and men to cope with and recover from, the various kinds of risks and insecurities associated with globalisation. In addition, social protection measures can be designed to address the risks and insecurities that are endemic to livelihoods in the informal economy where a disproportionate per centage of working women are concentrated. The empowerment potential of cash transfers could be enhanced if they are untied from women's reproductive responsibilities and combined with improved access to markets and the banking sector through, for example, smart cards, livelihoods training, information dissemination and business skills development to enhance their longer term employment prospects.'[22]

'Targeting adolescents is key to empowering women. As dependence on parents comes to a close during adolescence, there is a central tension between whether women choose to delay childbearing and pursue some form of career, or become dependent on men. This is the period when women become fertile and when human capital investments critical to careers are taking place, or not. A lack of future labour market opportunities can reduce the incentives for young girls to invest in their human capital, leading to early marriage and childbearing and potentially increasing their dependency on older men.'[23]

'The law is an essential tool for advancing women's and girls' rights and equality. A robust and effective legal system based on the rule of law is central to assisting women to become equal partners in decision-making and development. Over the last couple of decades, the international community has invested substantially in programmes aimed at strengthening the rule of law in developing countries. Despite this investment, the rule of law continues to mean very little for the vast majority of women and girls. Focusing on legal empowerment as a way to improve both access to justice and the quality of justice women receive, the study presents strategies and best practices in both formal and informal justice systems. Legal empowerment strategies can be successfully used to improve women's access to justice in both formal and informal systems. Legal empowerment strategies, through legal literacy programmes, legal aid or alternative dispute resolution mechanisms, can help create a 'culture of justice' among women and ensure that principles of equality and nondiscrimination are not only enshrined in law, but also translated into practice.'[24]

'Functional literacy to rural women should be provided. Strict government and social compulsion should be there for educating the girls. Training to rural women about income generating enterprises and it will engage them in self-employment. Reservation of women or girls is necessary in every area of development. Provisions should be made for maintaining equal status of women with that of men in the society.'[25] 'Gender equality concerns began to enter the mainstream of development policy, there were various attempts to conceptualise women's empowerment in ways that spoke to the mainstream policy discourse.'[26]

National Mission for Empowerment of Women

'The National Mission for Empowerment of Women (NMEW) was launched by the Government of India on International Women's Day in 2010 with the aim to strengthen overall processes that promote all-round development of women. It has the mandate to strengthen the inter-sector convergence; facilitate the process of coordinating all the women's welfare and socio-economic development programmes across ministries and departments. The Mission aims to provide a single window service for all programmes run by the government for women under aegis of various central ministries. The National Resource Center for Women has been set up which functions as a national convergence center for all schemes and programmes for women. It acts as a central repository of knowledge, information, research and data on all gender related issues and is the main body servicing the National and State Mission Authority.'[27]

Women's Empowerment Principles

'The Women's Empowerment Principles offer practical guidance to business and the private sector on how to empower women in the workplace, marketplace and community.'[28] 'The Women's Empowerment Principles offer practical guidance to business and the private sector on how to empower women in the workplace, marketplace and community. Developed through a partnership between UN Women and the United Nations Global Compact, the Principles are designed to support companies in reviewing existing policies and practices or establishing new ones to realise women's empowerment. Subtitled *Equality Means Business*, the Principles emphasise the business case for corporate action to promote gender equality and women's empowerment and are informed by real-life business practices and input gathered from across the globe.'[29]

'In the last two decades, there has been much progress in gender equality. In most developing countries MDGs show narrowing gaps, with rapid increases in girls' primary school enrollment and significant increases in female life expectancy. Significant gains have also been made globally with respect to women's economic participation, although there are variations in nature and degree.'[30]

Women Empowerment and Economic Development

'There is a bidirectional relationship between economic development and women's empowerment defined as improving the ability of women to access the constituents of development, in particular, health, education, earning opportunities, rights and political participation. Policy-makers and social scientists have tended to focus on one or the other of these two relationships. The Secretary General of the United Nations, Kofi Annan, for example, has argued that achieving gender equality is a "prerequisite" to achieving the other Millennium Development Goals, including eliminating poverty, reducing infant mortality, achieving universal education and eliminating the gender gap in education by 2015.'[31]

'Since the "UN Declaration of the Decade of Women" in 1975, attention and action on women's concerns have steadily increased and education, whether it be the form of consciousness-raising or skills acquisition, was one of the areas women's organisations, government agencies and international donor agencies focused on. Understanding that empowerment is a complex issue with varying interpretations in different societal, national and cultural contexts, the participants also came out with a tentative listing of indicators. Empowerment through education is ideally seen as a continuous holistic process with cognitive, psychological, economic and political dimensions in order to achieve emancipation.'[32]

'Gender equality and female empowerment are core development objectives, fundamental for the realisation of human rights and key to effective and sustainable development outcomes. No society can develop successfully without providing equitable opportunities, resources and life prospects for males and females so that they can shape their own lives and contribute to their families and communities. Gender equality and female empowerment are now universally recognised as core development objectives, fundamental for the realisation of human rights and key to effective and sustainable development outcomes.'[33] 'Evidence demonstrates that, in economies where gender equality is greater in terms of both opportunities and benefits, there is not only higher economic growth but also a better quality of life. Addressing gender inequalities and empowering women are vital to meeting the challenge of improving food and nutrition security and enabling poor rural people to overcome poverty.'[34]

'Economic empowerment is the capacity of women and men to participate in, contribute to and benefit from growth processes in ways which recognise the value of their contributions, respect their dignity and make it possible to negotiate a fairer distribution of the benefits of growth. Economic empowerment increases women's access to economic resources and opportunities including jobs, financial services, property and other productive assets, skills development and market information. Women's economic participation and empowerment are fundamental to strengthening women's rights and enabling women to have control over their lives and exert influence in society. The economic empowerment of women is a prerequisite for sustainable development, pro-poor growth and the achievement of all the Millennium Development Goals. Gender equality and empowered women are catalysts for multiplying development efforts. Investments in gender equality yield the highest returns of all development investments. Increasing the role of women in the economy is part of the solution to the financial and economic crises and critical for economic resilience and growth.'[35]

Women's Empowerment in Agriculture Index

'The Women's Empowerment in Agriculture Index (WEAI) measures the empowerment, agency and inclusion of women in the agriculture sector in an effort to identify ways to overcome those obstacles and constraints. The Index is a significant innovation in its field and aims to increase understanding of the connections between women's empowerment, food security and agricultural growth. It measures the roles and extent of women's engagement in the agriculture sector in five domains: (1) decisions about agricultural production, (2) access to and decision-making power over productive resources, (3) control over use of income, (4) leadership in the community and (5) time use. It also measures women's empowerment relative to men within their households.

It is an innovative new tool composed of two sub-indexes: one measure the five domains of empowerment for women and the other measure gender parity in empowerment within the household. It is an aggregate index reported at the country or regional level that is based on individual-level data on men and women within the same households.'[36]

Constrains before Women Empowerment

'Women are still at the lower end of the labour market in pay and authority. They typically occupy lower-paid and lower status jobs. Women's unemployment rate is higher than that of men and far more women than men work in the informal sector. In organised sector the number of women is significantly small even if they have the benefit of education and skills. Various factors are responsible for this like socio-cultural and traditional patriarchal society, which discourages women's working outside the house, perception that women have domestic managerial role to play leads to low female participation in formal employment, society's dictum of sparing females from being employed as wage labourers as social prestige.'[37]

'Political, social, cultural, economic and psychological barriers that obstruct women's access to justice and legal empowerment are found at every stage of the justice chain.'[38] 'Women's position in the household is impacted by a myriad of factors. These may include, varying in different contexts and often over-lapping: rights to property; inheritance and divorce; access to family planning and childcare; social and cultural norms related to childcare and paid and unpaid care work; social and cultural norms related to work; value placed on girls' education; intra-household dynamics and bargaining power; and burdens of unpaid productive or care work. In the wider society and economy, women's work may be constrained by discriminatory legal and regulatory barriers, limited access to financial and physical assets and market information, fewer social networks and business connections, limited access to education and skills development and weaker bargaining power in labour markets.'[39]

Conclusion

Women's empowerment is a process of personal and social change through which they gain power, meaningful choices and control over their lives. Empowerment is not something that can be done to or for women. Women's empowerment has been a feature of development assistance since the 1990s. The Women's Empowerment Principles offer practical guidance to business and the private sector on how to empower women in the workplace, marketplace and community. There is a bidirectional relationship between economic development and women's empowerment defined as improving the ability of women to access the constituents of development in particular health, education, earning opportunities, rights and political participation. Women's empowerment in India is heavily dependent on many different variables that include geographical location, educational status, social status and age. Social divisions among urban women also have a similar impact on empowerment indicators.

References

1. Women Empowerment in India – A Burning Issue, Retrieved from http://www.womenempowermentinindia.com/
2. Puja Mondal, Essay on Women Empowerment in India, Retrieved from http://www.yourarticlelibrary.com/essay/essay-on-women-

empowerment-in-india/31317/

3. See http://www.icrw.org/files/publications/Innovation-for-Womens-Empowerment.pdf
4. Manisha Desai, Hope in Hard Times: Women's Empowerment and Human Development, Human Development Research Paper 2010/14, pp. 1-2.
5. Tam O'Neil, Pilar Domingo and Craig Valters (2014), Progress on women's empowerment from technical fixes to political action, Retrieved from http://www.developmentprogress.org/sites/developmentprogress.org/files/case-study-report/progress_on_womens_empowerment_-_from_technical_fixes_to_political_action_final_-_20-11-14.pdf
6. Manmeet Kaur, B. Mishra, Prakash Singh, Archana Singh and Surya Rathore (2007), Empowerment of Rural Women: An Analysis of Constraints, Indian Res. J. Ext. Edu. 7 (2 and 3), May and September 2007, p. 90.
7. Oriana Bandiera, Niklas Buehren, Robin Burgess, Markus Goldstein Selim Gulesci, Imran Rasul and Munshi Sulaiman (2014), Women's Empowerment in Action: Evidence from a Randomised Control Trial in Africa, p.2, Retrieved from http://www.ucl.ac.uk/~uctpimr/research/ELA.pdf
8. Dr Rakesh Chandra, Women Empowerment in India: Milestones and challenges, Retrieved from http://en.wikieducator.org/images/2/2c/Women_empowerment.pdf
9. Women's empowering principles, Retrieved from http://www.unwomen.org/~/media/headquarters/attachments/sections/partnerships/businesses%20and%20foundations/women-s-empowerment-principles_en%20pdf.pdf
10. A roadmap for promoting women's economic empowerment, p. 12, Retrieved from http://www.womeneconroadmap.org/sites/default/files/WEE_Roadmap_Report_Final.pdf
11. Scaling Adoption of Clean Cooking Solutions through Women's Empowerment, p. 5, Retrieved from https://cleancookstoves.org/binary-data/RESOURCE/file/000/000/223-1.pdf
12. Gender Equality and Food Security—Women's Empowerment as a Tool against Hunger, p.1, Retrieved from http://www.fao.org/wairdocs/ar259e/ar259e.pdf
13. Esther Duflo, Women Empowerment and Economic Development, Journal of Economic Literature 2012, 50(4), 1051–1079.
14. Missing Women of Asia (2014), Retrieved from http://en.wikipedia.org/wiki/Missing_women_of_Asia

15. Women empowerment and inclusion, Retrieved from http://www.in.undp.org/content/india/en/home/ourwork/womenempowerment/overview.html
16. Reecha Upadhyay, Women's empowerment in India: An Analytical Overview, Retrieved from https://asiafoundation.org/resources/pdfs/womensempowermentindiabriefs.pdf
17. Empowerment of Women, chapter 8, Retrieved from http://rural.nic.in/sites/downloads/programmes-schemes/Empowerment%20of%20Women.pdf
18. Dr Rakesh Chandra, Women Empowerment in India: Milestones and challenges, Retrieved from http://en.wikieducator.org/images/2/2c/Women_empowerment.pdf
19. National Policy for Empowerment of Women, Retrieved from http://www.wcd.nic.in/empwomen.htm
20. Anju Malhotra, Sidney Ruth Schuler and Carol Boender, Measuring Women's Empowerment as a Variable in International Development, Retrieved from http://siteresources.worldbank.org/INTGENDER/Resources/MalhotraSchulerBoender.pdf
21. Adaptation, gender and women's empowerment, Retrieved from http://www.care.org/sites/default/files/documents/CC-2010-CARE_Gender_Brief.pdf
22. Paid work, women's empowerment and inclusive growth: Transforming the structures of constraint, p.11, Retrieved from http://www.lse.ac.uk/genderInstitute/about/resources NailaKabeer/kabeerEtAlPaidWorkWomens EmpowermentAndInclusiveGrowth.pdf
23. Oriana Bandiera, Niklas Buehren, Robin Burgess, Markus Goldstein, Selim, Gulesci, Imran Rasul and Munshi Sulaiman (2014), Women's Empowerment in Action: Evidence from a Randomised Control Trial in Africa, p. 2, Retrieved from http://www.ucl.ac.uk/~uctpimr/research/ELA.pdf
24. Accessing justice: Models, strategies and best practices on women's empowerment, Retrieved from http://www.cide.edu/docs/buenas-practicas/equidad-genero/WomenAccesstoJustice.pdf
25. Manmeet Kaur , B. Mishra , Prakash Singh, Archana Singh and Surya Rathore (2007), Empowerment of Rural Women: An Analysis of Constraints, Indian Res. J. Ext. Edu. 7 (2 and 3), May and September 2007, p. 93.
26. Professor Naila Kabeer (2012), Women's economic empowerment and inclusive growth: labour markets and enterprise development, Retrieved from http://www.idrc.ca/EN/Documents/NK-WEE-Concept-Paper.pdf

27. National Mission for Empowerment of Women (2015), Retrieved from http://www.nmew.gov.in/index.php
28. Women's Empowerment Principles, Retrieved from http://www.unwomen.org/en/partnerships/businesses-and-foundations/womens-empowerment-principles
29. Women's Empowerment Principles: Equality Means Business, See more at: http://www.unwomen.org/en/digital-library/publications/2011/10/women-s-empowerment-principles-equality-means-business#sthash.GsqH555k.dpuf
30. http://www.idrc.ca/EN/Documents/GrOW-Literature Review EN.pdf
31. Esther Duflo, Women Empowerment and Economic Development, Journal of Economic Literature 2012, 50(4): 1051–1079.
32. Carolyn Medel-Anonuevo (1995), Women, Education and Empowerment: Pathways towards Autonomy, Retrieved from http://www.unesco.org/education/pdf/283_102.pdf
33. USAID Gender equality and female empowerment policy (2012), Retrieved from http://www.usaid.gov/sites/default/files/documents/1860/Gender_Equality_Policy.pdf
34. Gender equality and women's empowerment Policy, p. 8, Retrieved from http://www.ifad.org/gender/policy/gender_e.pdf
35. Women's economic empowerment: The OECD DAC Network on Gender Equality, Retrieved from http://www.oecd.org/dac/povertyreduction/50157530.pdf
36. Women's Empowerment in Agriculture Index, Retrieved from http://www.ifpri.org/sites/default/files/publications/weai_brochure.pdf
37. Soumitro Chakravarty, Anant Kumar and Amar Nath Jha, Women's Empowerment in India: Issues, Challenges and Future Directions, International Review of Social Sciences and Humanities, Vol. 5, No. 1 (2013), p. 157.
38. Accessing justice: Models, strategies and best practices on women's empowerment, Retrieved from http://www.cide.edu/docs/buenas-practicas/equidad-genero/WomenAccesstoJustice.pdf
39. See http://www.idrc.ca/EN/Documents/GrOW-Literature ReviewEN.pdf

5

Women Entrepreneurship

> "A gift is pure when it is given from the heart to the right person at the right time and at the right place and when we expect nothing in return"
>
> —*The Bhagavad Gita*

Introduction

'Entrepreneurship is a multilevel and complex phenomenon that gained importance in the global economy as a result of changes in employee qualifications, work contents and psychological contracts in the employment field. It plays an important role in exploring the knowledge and utilising it to provide goods and services. The motivation for considering female entrepreneurship both in developing and developed countries derives from the increasing understanding of their important role in creating, running and developing businesses as a fundamental driver for economic growth.'[1] 'The origin of the basic word "entrepreneurship" is from a French word "Entree". The Oxford English dictionary 1897 defines the term "Entrepreneur" in similar way as the director or the manager of public musical institution, one who gets up entertainment arranged, especially musical performance.'[2]

'An entrepreneur is a person who combines capital and labour for production. According to Cantillion: Entrepreneur is the agent who buys means of production at certain prices, in order to sell at prices that are certain at the moment at which he commits himself to his cost. According to P.F Drucker: Entrepreneur is one who always (1) searches for change (2) responds to it (3) exploits it as an opportunity'.[3] 'Female entrepreneurship has attracted increasing attention in recent years in light of concrete evidence of the importance of new business creation for economic growth and development. There is indeed accumulating evidence suggesting that although the rate at which women are forming businesses has increased significantly, the rates of female entrepreneurial activity are significantly and systematically lower than those for males.'[4] 'The emergence and development of women entrepreneurship in the past 20 years, is closely linked to the process of equalisation of rights of men and women and with democratisation in general.'[5]

'Rural women's entrepreneurship can contribute to economic growth in developing countries and clearly represents an untapped potential. For many rural women, entrepreneurship is part of a broader livelihood strategy, often undertaken on a part-time basis and where it is difficult to separate production and reproduction tasks, as well as market and non-market work. Given that the factors limiting women's entrepreneurship are manifold and intertwined, integrated measures are needed to realise rural women entrepreneurs' potential.'[6] 'Women have made remarkable educational gains over the last few decades. Women now consistently outpace men in terms of college enrollment and receive 50 per cent more master's degrees than men do. Among the youngest workers, those eighteen to thirty-two, women are now far more likely to have bachelor's degrees than men are.'[7]

Meaning of the Concept

'Women entrepreneurs may be defined as a woman or a group of women, who initiate, organise and run a business enterprise. Government of India has defined women entrepreneurs based on women participation in equity and employment of a business enterprise. Accordingly, a woman run an enterprise is defined as an enterprise owned and controlled by a women having a minimum financial interest of 51 per cent of the capital and giving at least 51 per cent of the employment generated in the enterprise to women.'[8] 'Women's entrepreneurship is both about women's position in society and the role of entrepreneurship in the same society.

The ILO defined the women's enterprise as a small unit where one or more women entrepreneurs have not less than 50 per cent financial holdings. A woman entrepreneur is an adult who owns and runs an enterprise, especially a commercial one, often at personal financial risk. The concept of women entrepreneurship is becoming a global phenomenon playing a vital role in the business community.'[9]

Importance of Women Entrepreneurs

'Women entrepreneurship has been recognised as an important source of economic growth. Women entrepreneurs create new jobs for themselves and others and also provide society with different solutions to management, organisation and business problems. However, they still represent a minority of all entrepreneurs. Women's entrepreneurship can make a particularly strong contribution to the economic well-being of the family and communities, poverty reduction and women's empowerment, thus contributing to the Millennium Development Goals.'[10] 'Women's entrepreneurship needs to be studied separately for two main reasons. The first reason is that women's entrepreneurship has been recognised during the last decade as an important untapped source of economic growth. Women entrepreneurs create new jobs for themselves and others and by being different also provide society with different solutions to management, organisation and business problems as well as to the exploitation of entrepreneurial opportunities.'[11]

'Women and girls constitute three-fifths of the world's poor. Their poverty level is worse than that of men as clear gender disparities in education, employment opportunities and decision-making power exist. The "bottom-up growth strategy" focuses on the transformation and diversification of micro and small-scale enterprises to growth-oriented activities and on increasing the productive capacity in order to enable them to participate in the mainstream economy of the nation. Micro- and small-scale enterprises are affordable and manageable by rural people. They create a large number of non-farm employments and income opportunities in relatively poorly developed areas and require small capital and little sophisticated managerial and technical skills.'[12] 'Entrepreneurship is necessary to initiate the process of economic development of both developed and developing countries. It is also instrumental in sustaining the process of economic development.'[13]

Factors Influencing Women Entrepreneurs

'Factors can be divided in push factors and·pull factors. Push factors are elements of necessity such as insufficient family income, dissatisfaction with salaries job, difficulty in finding work and a need for flexible work schedule because of family responsibilities. These factors may have more importance for women than for men. Pull factors are factors that work as entrepreneurial drive factors relate to independence, self-fulfillment, entrepreneurial drive and desire for wealth, power and social status, co-operation and support of family members and a strong network of contacts.'[14]

'No single factor motivates women to become an entrepreneur. Family support, social perceptions and attitudes towards women entrepreneurship are just some of the factors influencing the decision to become a female entrepreneur. The growth of the business depends partially on the entrepreneur's motivation. Population growth has an impact on entrepreneurship among men and women in low income countries. Generally, good economic conditions are a supportive and encouraging factor for female entrepreneurship. In economies with high income rates, the correlation between unofficial economic activities and entrepreneurship is negative whilst in low income economies it is positive.'[15]

'The glass ceilings are shattered and women are found indulged in every line of business. The entry of women into business in India is traced out as an extension of their kitchen activities, mainly 3P's, Pickle, Powder and Pappad. But with the spread of education and passage of time women started shifting from 3P's to modern 3E's i.e., Energy, Electronics and Engineering. Skill, knowledge and adaptability in business are the main reasons for women to emerge into business ventures.'[16]

Women Empowerment: Global Perspectives[17]

'Women entrepreneurs, encompass approximately 1/3 of all entrepreneurs worldwide. Before the twentieth century, women were operating businesses as a way of supplementing income. Women became more involved in the business world only when the idea of women in business became palatable to the general public. During the mid eighteenth century, it was popular for women to own certain businesses like brothels, alehouses, taverns and retail shops, among others. Most of these businesses were not perceived with good reputations. In the 1900s, due to a more progressive way of thinking and the rise of feminism, female entrepreneurs began to be a widely accepted term and although these women entrepreneurs serviced mostly women consumers, they were making great strides. The 1980s and '90s were a time of reaping the benefits from the hard work of women who worked tirelessly for their rightful place in the workforce as employees and entrepreneurs.'[18] 'Today women in advance market economies own more than 25 per cent of all businesses and women owned business in Africa, Asia, Eastern Europe and Latin America are growing rapidly.'[19]

'The number of female-owned enterprises is growing at a faster pace than that of male counterparts with no evidence that women-owned enterprises fail at a faster rate. New, internationally comparable data on female entrepreneurship from countries belonging to the Organisation for Economic Cooperation and Development show that the birth rates of female-owned enterprises are higher than those of male-owned ones. Women-owned enterprises are well-positioned to enhance national prosperity and to contribute to economic growth and development.'[20] 'Female-run enterprises are steadily growing all over the world, contributing to household incomes and growth of national economies. However, women face time, human, physical and social constraints that limit their ability to grow their businesses.'[21]

'In most countries, regions and sectors, the majority of business owner/managers are male (from 65 per cent to 75 per cent). However, there is increasing evidence that more and more women are becoming interested in small business ownership and/or actually starting up in business. In addition, rates of self-employment among women are increasing in several EU countries.'[22] 'One characteristic of MSEs that contrasts to that of larger business is the relative larger presence of women as enterprise owners. In Tanzania, at least one-third of MSE operators are thought to be women. A wide range of donor and national government programmes has targeted these women and supported their entry into the sector.'[23]

'Whilst Europe does not have enough entrepreneurs following through on their ideas to set up in business, there are, disproportionately, even fewer women than men entrepreneurs. Europe's economy needs more entrepreneurs to take the plunge. The Commission is working with Member States to find ways to overcome the factors which particularly discourage women from taking up the option of entrepreneurship. Although there has been an encouraging upturn in women running businesses in the past decade or so, much more needs to be done to overcome the specific factors which discourage women, in particular, from starting or taking over small firms.

Today women entrepreneurs in Europe are only 30 per cent of all entrepreneurs. More importantly, we have to create an environment in which those women who do run a small business can more easily grow their firms. The European Network of Mentors for Women Entrepreneurs has been inaugurated in Warsaw, Poland under a Polish Presidency event on 15th November 2011. The European Network of Female Entrepreneurship Ambassadors was inaugurated on 5th October 2009 in Stockholm during the Swedish Presidency by Crown Princess Victoria of Sweden, Vladimir Spidla, the European Commissioner for Employment, Social Affairs and Equal Opportunities and Maud Olofsson Minister of Enterprise, Energy and Communications and Deputy Prime Minister of Sweden.'[24]

'Data published in an August 2013 report by Statistics Canada/Industry Canada show female business owners contributed to the creation of almost 10,000 jobs in 2011 alone.'[25] 'According to Statistics Canada's Labour Force Survey reports there were 950,000 self-employed women in Canada in 2012, accounting for 35.6 per cent of all self-employed persons. According to Industry Canada, 47 per cent are SME's were entirely or partly owned by women. In terms of employee growth rates, majority female-owned firms with growth intentions are significantly more active in hiring new employees than majority male-owned firms.'[26]

'Women in Latin America and the Caribbean (LAC) represent 42 per cent of the economically active population and

15 per cent of the region's high-growth entrepreneurs. The challenges LAC women entrepreneurs face in growing their businesses include lack of access to capital, coordinated support through networks and resources, education and training and a culture of entrepreneurship. Public-private partnerships are an important tool that can help women entrepreneurs, as well as entrepreneurs the world over, break down barriers and achieve success. Women entrepreneurs in Latin America and the Caribbean have the potential to contribute significantly to their countries' and the global economy. Public-private partnerships are a critical mechanism that can enable them to achieve their potential and make a lasting difference in their homes, communities and countries.'[27]

'Australia is the second best place in the world to be a female entrepreneur, according to international rankings. The Gender-Global Entrepreneur and Development Index, which was released at the Dell Women's Entrepreneur Network conference in the US, places Australia just behind the US as countries which encourage and foster female entrepreneurship and ahead of Germany, France, Mexico and the UK. The rankings are calculated based on three factors: the entrepreneurial environment in a country; the entrepreneurial ecosystem; and entrepreneurial aspirations. There are many factors contributing to the apparent low numbers of female entrepreneurs across the country, including cultural factors such as women not being involved in business for as long as men. There is a lack of access to funding and investment for female entrepreneurs. Many women start businesses with the goal to run a small business.'[28]

'Nowadays, the women entrepreneurs in China almost 25 per cent of the total, of which 60 per cent are successful entrepreneurs in recent 10 years, the largest number of women entrepreneurs is from 40 to 45 years. After China accession to WTO, the adjustment of industrial structure provide more opportunities for women entrepreneurs to success, but in the context of economic globalisation, the financial crisis will inevitably affect Chinese economic development and enterprise operation, it makes the women entrepreneurs enterprises have encountered unprecedented challenges. With the changes of period and the advance of the society, the women already got the high status in China. In fact, 50 per cent of the women entrepreneurs without specific business knowledge of trained or no management experience before starting a business, most of them are teacher, commercial retail staff, office assistant or secretary before starting a business.'[29]

'Entrepreneurial activity by women in the People's Republic of China has become more active in recent years with much greater attention being paid within and outside of China. In the late 1990s, several nationwide studies of female entrepreneurs were launched in China: Chinese Entrepreneurs Investigation System, the Association of Women Entrepreneurs in China and the All-China Women's Federation. Issued in 2001 and 2002 by the Association of Women Entrepreneurs, the Women Entrepreneurs Development Reports analysed China's Women entrepreneurs' developmental situations and the factors and trends from the macro-point of view.'[30]

Women Entrepreneurship in India

'In India, women entrepreneurship is a recent topic which started only after the 1970s with the introduction of the Women's Decade (1975 to 1985) and which mostly picked up in the late 70s.'[31] 'Increasingly female entrepreneurs are considered important for economic development. Not only do they contribute to employment creation and economic growth through their increasing numbers, they also make a contribution to the diversity of entrepreneurship in the economic process.'[32] 'Women entrepreneurs have been gravitating towards the natural and applied sciences, as well as business and finance-related occupations, such as advertising, business consulting and accounting, reflecting the improving educational credentials of women in recent years. Furthermore, technical and professional occupations in the health sector have become an important source of growth for self-employed women.'[33] 'The implementation of political reservations for women in India has been proven to affect many aspects of the economic, political and social lives of women.'[34]

'The 1991 Industrial Policy has envisaged special training programmes to support women entrepreneurs. Accordingly women entrepreneurs are receiving training through Entrepreneurship Development Programmes (EDPS) conducted by various institutions and organisations both at central and state levels. The Small Industries Development Organisation (SIDO), with its field offices all over the country has been carrying out development programmes for women entrepreneurs and is providing technical schemes for setting up of SSI units. In view of the changing outlook for the promotion of women enterprises, the SSI Board in 1991 revised the definition of women enterprises by omitting the condition of employing 50 per cent of women workers.'[35]

'There are several schemes of the government at central and state levels, which provide assistance for setting up training-cum-income generating activities for needy women to make them economically independent. Small Industries Development Bank of India (SIDBI) has also been implementing special schemes for women entrepreneurs. In addition to the special schemes for women entrepreneurs, various government schemes for MSMEs also provide certain special incentives and concessions for women entrepreneur. The efforts of government and its different agencies are supplemented by NGOs and associations that are playing an equally important role in facilitating women empowerment.'[36]

'Women operating in the informal economy lack the ability to accumulate the savings required for the start-up process, women with poor levels of education are less likely to have accumulated savings from previous employment.'[37] 'SIDBI has developed this fund for the entrepreneurial development of women especially in rural areas. Under Mahila Vikas Nidhi grants loan to women are given to start their venture in the field like spinning, weaving, knitting, embroidery products, block printing, handlooms handicrafts, bamboo products etc. In 1993, Rashtriya Mahila Kosh was set up to grant micro credit to poor women at reasonable rates of interest with very low transaction costs and simple procedures. Consortium of Women Entrepreneurs of India provides a platform to assist the women entrepreneurs to develop new, creative and innovative techniques of production, finance and marketing. There are different bodies such as NGOs, voluntary organisations, Self-help groups, institutions and individual enterprises from rural and urban areas which collectively help the women entrepreneurs in their activities.'[38]

'The scheme, Development of Women and Children in Rural Areas (DWCRA) launched in 1982-83 (presently called as SHGs), inaugurated an era for systematically organising women in groups for providing them opportunities of self-employment on a sustained basis. Several thousands of rural women from the length and breadth of the country participate in programme and they have taken up a number of trades under DWCRA banner. The programme is implemented by the District Rural Development Agency (DRDA) at the district level. SHG is the only programme of its kind, which aims at empowering the rural poor women by inculcating entrepreneurial skill. It seeks to encourage collective action in the form of group activities, which are known to work better than individual efforts.'[39]

'Many women in India have attained prominent or leadership positions, rising to the highest echelons in every walk of life, for example, as entrepreneurs, industrialists, civil servants, police officers, airline pilots, scientists and engineers. The Micro, Small and Medium Enterprises sector in particular, which plays a central role in the economic and social development of the country and is described as an "engine of growth" is attracting increasing policy attention. Women's entrepreneurship encompasses self-employment, income generation and the management of businesses/enterprises.'[40] 'In India, there are still many social and cultural restrictions on women. Hence, women participation in entrepreneurial activities is less than the requirement of the fast growth of India.'[41]

Successful Women Entrepreneurs in India of 21st Century[42]

1. Akhila Srinivasan, Managing Director, Shriram Investments Ltd
2. Chanda Kocchar, Executive Director, ICICI Bank
3. Ekta Kapoor, Creative Director, Balaji Telefilms Ltd
4. Jyoti Naik, President, Lijjat Papad
5. Kiran Mazumdar Shaw, Chairman and Managing Director, Biocon Ltd
6. Lalita D. Gupte, JMD, ICICI Bank
7. Naina Lal Kidwar, Deputy CEO, HBSE
8. Preetha Reddy, Managing Director, Apollo Hospitals

9. Priya Paul, Chairman, Apeejay Park Hotels
10. Rajshree Pathy, Chairman, Rajshree Sugars and Chemicals Ltd
11. Ranjana Kumar, Chairman, NABARD.

Challenges before Women Entrepreneurs

'Even though female entrepreneurship and the formation of women business networks are steadily rising, there are a number of challenges and obstacles that female entrepreneurs face. One major challenge that many women entrepreneurs face is the traditional gender-roles society may still have on women. Entrepreneurship is still considered as a male-dominated field and it may be difficult to surpass these conventional views. Other than dealing with the dominant stereotype, women entrepreneurs are facing several obstacles related to their businesses. In general, women have lower personal financial assets than men. Women entrepreneurs often face gender-based barriers to starting and growing their businesses, like discriminatory property; matrimonial and inheritance laws and/ or cultural practices; lack of access to formal finance mechanisms; limited mobility and access to information and networks, etc. Despite the fact that many women entrepreneurs face growth barriers, they are still able to achieve substantial firm growth.'[43]

'Women in the MSE sector face a number of serious obstacles. Among these are gender-blind or gender-insensitive macroeconomic policies; complex tax policies and compliance procedures; gender-based inequalities in employment policies and regulations; complex business registration and licensing procedures for the smallest micro-enterprises; lack of cultural acceptance for the role of entrepreneurship for women; limited access to appropriate business premises; lack of collateral due to property ownership practices; lack of access to term loans and sufficient working capital to meet their needs; and the limited organisational and management capacity among women's advocacy groups. In addition, women face a number of gender-related problems: a lack of property rights over assets; lack of confidence in women by bank officers; discouragement from men when starting or formalising businesses; social restrictions regarding networking with men in business; and suppliers sometimes insisting that they deal with the entrepreneur's husband when decisions are being made.'[44]

'Women in India are very emotionally attached to their families. They are supposed to attend to all the domestic work, to look after the children and other members of the family. They are over burden with family responsibilities like extra attention to husband, children and in-laws which take away a lots of their time and energy. Women in India are lagging far behind in the field of education. The traditions and customs prevailed in Indian societies towards women sometimes stand as an obstacle before them to grow and prosper. Usually women entrepreneurs employ low technology in the process of production. Women mobility in India is highly limited and has become a problem due to traditional values and inability to drive vehicles. Lack of entrepreneurial aptitude is a matter of concern for women entrepreneurs.'[45]

Federation of Indian Women Entrepreneurs

'Federation of Indian Women Entrepreneurs, a National-level organisation, founded in 1993 and registered under Society Act of India in May 1999, is one of India's Premier Institution for Women thoroughly devoted towards Entrepreneurship Development in the country. It has branches in different states of India with membership base of 15,000 individual members / professionals and more than 28 Member Associations spread throughout the country.'[46]

Conclusion

Women entrepreneurship has been recognised as an important source of economic growth. They create new jobs for themselves and others and also provide society with different solutions to management, organisation and business problems. Women and girls constitute three-fifths of the world's poor. Their poverty level is worse than that of men as clear gender disparities in education, employment opportunities and decision-making power exist. Women entrepreneurs, encompass approximately one-third of all entrepreneurs worldwide. Before the twentieth century, women were operating businesses as a way of supplementing income. Women became more involved in the business world only when the idea of women in business became palatable to the general public.

The 1991 Industrial Policy has envisaged special training programmes to support women entrepreneurs. There are several schemes of the government at central and state level, which provide assistance for setting up training-cum-income generating activities for needy women to make them economically independent. Small Industries Development Bank of India has also been implementing special schemes for women entrepreneurs. Even though female entrepreneurship and the formation of women business networks are steadily rising, there are a number of challenges and obstacles that female entrepreneurs face. One major challenge that many women entrepreneurs face is the traditional gender-roles society may still have on women.

References

1. Jacques Ascher, Female Entrepreneurship – An Appropriate Response to Gender Discrimination, Journal of Entrepreneurship, Management and Innovation (JEMI), Volume 8, Issue 4, 2012: 97-114.
2. Arakeri Shanta V., Women Entrepreneurship in India, Retrieved from http://www.abhinavjournal.com/images/Arts_&_Education/Mar12/1.pdf
3. Priyanka Sharma, Women Entrepreneurship Development in India, Global Journal of Management and Business Studies. Volume 3, Number 4 (2013), pp. 371-376.
4. Dima Jamali, Constraints and opportunities facing women entrepreneurs in developing countries: A relational perspective, Gender in Management: An International Journal, Vol. 24 No. 4, 2009, pp. 232-251.
5. Assessment of the environment for women entrepreneurship in Montenegro (2013), Retrieved from http://poslodavci.org/doc/WED_ Assessment %20of%20the %20environment %20for%20women%20entrepreneurship%20in%20MN.pdf
6. Rural women's entrepreneurship is "good business", Retrieved from http://www.fao.org/docrep/013/i2008e/i2008e03.pdf
7. Alicia Robb, Susan Coleman University of Hartford and Dane Stangler, Sources of Economic hopes: Women entrepreneurship, Retrieved from http://www.kauffman.org/~/media/kauffman_org/research%20reports%20and%20covers/2014/11/sources_of_economic_hope_womens_entrepreneurship.pdf
8. Ms. Yogita Sharma, Women Entrepreneur in India, IOSR Journal of Business and Management, Volume 15, Issue 3 (Nov. - Dec. 2013), pp. 9-14.

9. Sreenivasa Rao Behara and K. Niranjan, Rural Women Entrepreneurship in India, IJCEM International Journal of Computational Engineering and Management, Vol. 15 Issue 6, November 2012, p. 6.
10. Female entrepreneurs (2014), Retrieved from http://en.wikipedia.org/wiki/Female_entrepreneur
11. Women's Entrepreneurship: Issues and Policies (2004), p. 9, Retrieved from http://www.oecd.org/cfe/smes/31919215.pdf
12. A path out of poverty: Developing rural and women entrepreneurship (2003), Retrieved from https://www.unido.org/fileadmin/import/11092_RuralwomenEntrepreneurshipBrochure_April2003.2.pdf
13. Prof C.P. Kothawale, Women Entrepreneurship Development: Problems and Prospects, International Multidisciplinary Research Journal, Vol. 2, Issue I, May, 2013, p. 1.
14. Ms. Yogita Sharma, Women Entrepreneur in India, IOSR Journal of Business and Management, Volume 15, Issue 3 (Nov. - Dec. 2013), pp. 9-14.
15. Jacques Ascher, Female Entrepreneurship – An Appropriate Response to Gender Discrimination, Journal of Entrepreneurship, Management and Innovation (JEMI), Volume 8, Issue 4, 2012: 97-114.
16. Meenu Goyal and Jai Pakash, Women Entrepreneurship in India: Problems and Prospects, ZENITH: International Journal of Multidisciplinary Research, Vol. 1 Issue 5, September 2011, pp. 196-97.
17. Women entrepreneur (2014), Retrieved from http://smallb.sidbi.in/%20/fund-your-business%20/additional-benefits-msmes%20/women-entrepreneurship
18. Female entrepreneurs (2014), Retrieved from http://en.wikipedia.org/wiki/Female_entrepreneur
19. S. Mohan Kumara, H.S. Chandrika Mohana , Vijaya Ca and Lokeshwari N. (2013). The Role of Women Entrepreneurship in Modern World, International Journal of Current Engineering and Technology, p. 12.
20. Carmen Niethammer, Odebrecht, Women, Entrepreneurship and the Opportunity to Promote Development and Business, pp. 31-32, Retrieved from http://www.brookings.edu/~/media/research/files/reports/2013/09/private-sector-global-poverty-blum-roundtable/2013-bbr-women-entrepreneurship.pdf

21. Female Entrepreneurship: Program Guidelines and Case Studies, Retrieved from http://siteresources.worldbank.org/EXTGENDER/Resources/FemaleEntrepreneurshipResource Point041113.pdf

22. Young Women, Ethnic Minority and Co-Entrepreneurs, Retrieved from http://www.cartierwomensinitiative.com/docs/womenentrepreneurs_-_Europ_Com.pdf

23. Pat Richardson, Rhona Howarth and Gerry Finnegan, The Challenges of Growing Small Businesses: Insights from Women Entrepreneurs in Africa, SEED Working Paper No. 47, Retrieved from http://natlex.ilo.ch/wcmsp5/groups/public/—ed_emp/—emp_ent/documents/publication/wcms_111395.pdf

24. See http://ec.europa.eu/enterprise/policies/sme/promoting-entrepreneurship/women/

25. See http://business.financialpost.com/entrepreneur/fp-startups/canada-a-global-pace-setter-in-female-entrepreneurship-but-barriers-still-persist?__lsa=784a-0a6b

26. Facts and Figures on Canadian Women Entrepreneurs, Retrieved from http://www.owit-ottawa.ca/wp-content/uploads/2014/03/Facts-and-figures-on-women-entrepreneurs.pdf

27. See http://www.forbes.com/sites/ey/2014/10/17/realizing-the-potential-of-latin-american-women-entrepreneurs/

28. Australia ranked second best place to be a female entrepreneur, Retrieved from

29. Zhouqiaoqin, Xie Ying Ying, Zhang Lu, Suresh Kumah (2013), Factors that influence the success of women entrepreneur in China: a survey of women entrepreneurs in Beijing, IOSR Journal of Humanities and Social Science, pp. 83-85.

30. Ilan Alon, Shengliang Deng and Xu Wang (2001), Framework for female entrepreneurship in China, International Journal of Business and Emerging Markets 3 (1): 3-20.

31. See http://shodhganga.inflibnet.ac.in/bitstream/10603/6732/7/07_chapter%202.pdf

32. Ingrid Verheul, André van, Stel Roy Thurik and Zoetermeer (2004), Explaining female and male entrepreneurship across 29 countries, Retrieved from http://www.entrepreneurship-sme.eu/pdf-ez/N200403.pdf

33. Women Entrepreneurs: Leading the Charge, Retrieved from https://www.cibc.com/ca/pdf/women-entrepreneurs-en.pdf

34. Ejaz Ghani, William R. Kerr and Stephen D. O'Connell (2014), Retrieved from Political Reservations and Women's Entrepreneurship in India.

35. T. Vijayakumar and B. Naresh, Women entrepreneurship in India: Role of women in small and medium enterprises, TRANS Asian Journal of Marketing and Management Research, Vol. 2 Issue 7, July 2013, p. 16.

36. Women entrepreneur (2014), Retrieved from http://smallb.sidbi.in/%20/fund-your-business%20/additional-benefits-msmes%20/women-entrepreneurship

37. Ms. Yogita Sharma, Women Entrepreneur in India, IOSR Journal of Business and Management, Volume 15, Issue 3 (Nov. - Dec. 2013), pp. 9-14.

38. Ms. Yogita Sharma, Women Entrepreneur in India, IOSR Journal of Business and Management, Volume 15, Issue 3 (Nov. - Dec. 2013), pp. 9-14.

39. Ranbir Singh, Women Entrepreneurship Issues, Challenges and Empowerment through Self Help Groups: An Overview of Himachal Pradesh, International Journal of Democratic and Development Studies, 1 (1), pp. 54-55.

40. Hina Shah (2013), Creating an Enabling Environment for Women's Entrepreneurship in India, Retrieved from http://www.unescap.org/sites/default/files/ESCAP-SSWA-Development-Paper_1304_1.pdf

41. Vijay Kumar (2012), Some Critical Issues of Women Entrepreneurship in Rural India, European Academic Research, Volume 01, Issue 02, p. 186.

42. Anjali Singh, Role of Women Entrepreneurs in India: A SWOT Analysis, International Journal of Management and International Business Studies, Volume 4, Number 2 (2014), pp. 231-238.

43. Female entrepreneurs (2014), Retrieved from http://en.wikipedia.org/wiki/Female_entrepreneur

44. Lois Stevenson and Annette St-Onge (2005), Support for Growth-oriented Women Entrepreneurs in Tanzania, Retrieved from http://www.afdb.org/fileadmin/uploads/afdb/Documents/Policy-Documents/GOWE%20Tanzania.pdf

45. Ms. Yogita Sharma, Women Entrepreneur in India, IOSR Journal of Business and Management, Volume 15, Issue 3 (Nov. - Dec. 2013), pp. 09-14.

46. Federation of Indian Women Entrepreneurs (2014), Retrieved from http://www.fiwe.org/

6

Self-Help Group and Microfinance

> *"Any time women come together with a collective intention, it's a powerful thing. Whether it's sitting down making a quilt, in a kitchen preparing a meal, in a club reading the same book, or around the table playing cards, or planning a birthday party, when women come together with a collective intention, magic happens."*
>
> —***Phylicia Rashad***

Introduction

'Economic growth and development is taking place at a rapid pace since the middle of last century. Technological advances and globalisation have played a major role in propelling this advancement. One section of the global population has greatly benefitted through this development.'[1] 'Microfinance is a source of financial services for entrepreneurs and small businesses lacking access to banking and related services. The two main mechanisms for the delivery of financial services to such clients are: (1) relationship-based banking for individual entrepreneurs and small businesses; and (2) group-based models, where several entrepreneurs come together to apply for loans and other services as a group. It is a broad category of services, which includes microcredit. Microcredit is provision of credit services to poor clients. Microcredit is one of the aspects of microfinance and the two are often confused.'[2] A good definition of microfinance as provided by Robinson is, *'Microfinance refers to small-scale financial services for both credits and deposits that are provided to people who farm or fish or herd; operate small or microenterprises where goods are produced, recycled, repaired, or traded; provide services; work for wages or commissions; gain income from renting out small amounts of land, vehicles, draft animals, or machinery and tools; and to other individuals and local groups in developing countries, in both rural and urban areas'.*[3]

'Microfinance refers more widely to the provision of financial services to the same "unbanked" poor. This includes microcredit as well as savings, insurance, remittance, money transfer and leasing services. It refers to the provision of credit services to people who do not have access to traditional banking services, mostly because they cannot offer the expected collateral. This definition includes the historical forms of credit activity, such as money lending, pawn broking or consumption credit by shopkeepers. Microfinance institutions refer to structures that provide microfinance services to their customers.'[4] 'Microfinance in a post-conflict context is often described as a powerful tool to boost local economic development and to support post-conflict rehabilitation assistance.'[5] 'It has captured the imaginations of many people working to reduce poverty.'[6] 'Traditionally Banks and Lending Institutions do not lend money to low-income individuals.'[7]

'Typical microfinance clients have low incomes and are often self-employed in the informal economy, conditions that together typically deny them access to banks and other formal financial institutions. They commonly run small stores or street stalls, create and sell items they make in their homes and in rural areas, microfinance clients may be small-scale farmers and those who process or trade crops and goods.'[8] 'Although the exact location and date of the first microfinance effort has yet to be determined, scholars attribute the modern microcredit movement to the work of the Grameen Bank and Accion International. Both organisations developed independently of one another, but share a number of common characteristics.'[9]

What is Self-Help Group?

'Self-help group is a village-based financial intermediary committee usually composed of 10–20 local women or men. A mixed group is generally not preferred. They may be registered or unregistered. It typically comprises a group of micro entrepreneurs having homogeneous social and economic backgrounds; all voluntarily coming together to save regular small sums of money, mutually agreeing to contribute to a common fund and to meet their emergency needs on the basis of mutual help. The group members use collective wisdom and peer pressure to ensure proper end-use of credit and timely repayment.'[10] 'It is mainly concerned with the poor and it is for the people and of the people. Apart from inculcating socially desirable habits and ethics among members, SHGs serve the purpose of a moneylender, a development bank, a cooperative and a voluntary agency.'[11]

'Self Help Group is a homogeneous group of micro entrepreneurs with affinity among themselves, voluntarily formed to save whatever amount they can conveniently save out of their earnings and mutually agree to contribute to a common fund of the group from which small loans are given to the members for meeting their productive and emergent credit needs at such rate of interest, period of loan and other terms as the group may decide.'[12]

Features of Self-Help Group

'In a self-help group, the members share a common problem, often a common disease or addiction. Their mutual goal is to help each other to deal with, if possible to heal or to recover from, this problem. Self-help groups may exist separately or as part of larger organisations. They may operate informally or according to a format or programme. Through self-disclosure, members share their stories, stresses, feelings, issues and recoveries.'[13]

'The followings are some of essential characteristics of SHGs: (a) A group of persons of small means; (b) A group can be registered or unregistered; (c) Members of the group come together out of their volition; (d) The limit of members of the group is restricted in between 10-20; (e) Members contribute a part of their earnings regularly to a common fund; (f) There is frequent meeting of members to decide on terms and conditions on savings and loans; (g) Records maintained by the groups are membership register minute book, saving book and loan book;

and (h) There is the provision of borrowing from bank and use of borrowing for credit of its members.'[14]

'The group is not simply gathering of people in one place. In fact, the group has its own identity. It has a special strength and energy that plays on each member. In the self-help group, no one is obliged to speak. A person can be content to listen and find that the group brings a lot to him. Each person must decide for himself if he wants to speak or not. Moreover, the members of self-help group take part in the meetings for as long as they deem it useful.'[15] 'Micro-financial activities in the less developed countries in the world have a slightly different character: (a) Strong social feeling appearing by the expressive 'bottom-up' activity. The active attitude of the poor smallholders, fishermen, craftsmen, businessmen and other population of the very poor countryside in these countries; (b) Poverty in rural areas where all these people housekeep; and (c) Period in which micro- financial activities of the micro financial institutions become evident decidedly.'[16]

Microfinance Institution

'Microfinance institution is an organisation that provides microfinance services. MFIs range from small non-profit organisations to large commercial banks. There are three kinds of costs the MFI has to cover when it makes microloans. The first two, the cost of the money that it lends and the cost of loan defaults, are proportional to the amount lent.'[17] 'Microfinance institutions and other financial service providers have worked over the past decades to develop products and delivery methods to meet the diverse financial needs of low-income people. For example, unlike other forms of lending, microcredit loans use methodologies such as group lending and liability, pre-loan savings requirements and the gradually increase in loan sizes to evaluate clients' credit worthiness.'[18]

'Micro Finance Institutions (MFIs) around the world follow a variety of different methodologies. The focus of such service is women rather than men for the reason women are more judicious and economical to men. The following are major methodologies employed by MFIs for delivery of financial services to low income families.

(a) **Self Help Group:** The Self Help Groups (SHGs) is the dominant microfinance methodology in India. In this case the members of Self Help Group pool their small savings regularly at a prefixed amount on daily or weekly basis and SHGs provide loan to members for a period fixed. SHGs are essentially formal and voluntary association of 15 to 20 people formed to attain common objectives.

(b) **Individual Banking Programmes:** In Individual Banking Programmes (IBPs) there is provision by Microfinance institutions for lending to individual clients though they may sometimes be organised into joint liability groups, credit and saving cooperatives. This model is increasingly popular through cooperatives. In cooperatives, all borrowers are members of organisation directly or indirectly by being member of cooperative society.

(c) **Grameen Model:** Grameen Model was pioneered by Dr Mohammed Yunus of Grameen Bank of Bangladesh. It is perhaps the most well known and widely practiced model in the world. In Grameen Model the groups are formed voluntarily consisting of five borrowers each. According to the rules, if one member ever defaults, all in the group are denied subsequent loans.

(d) **Mixed Model:** Some MFIs started with the Grameen model but converted to the SHG model at a later stage. However, they did not completely do away with Grameen type lending and smaller groups. They are a mix of SHG and Grameen model.'[19]

Importance of Microfinance

'Microfinance can give unprivileged people enough capital stability, which gives them financial security from sudden monetary problems. Savings allow for improved nutrition, reduced illness, better living conditions and educational investment. Microcredit empowers women since they are the major beneficiaries. In the past, women were not able to participate in economic activities. Microfinance institutions now provide women with the capital they require to start business projects. This gives them more confidence and allows them to participate in decision-making; thereby encouraging gender equality.'[20] 'Microfinance improves the quality of life of families in the poorest countries in a sustainable way. Microfinance gives poor people the opportunity to establish an existence and to create a future with prospects. Microfinance permits an increasing number of families access to food, to medical care and to education for their children – now also for their daughters. Consequently, microfinance has an impact on the future generation.'[21]

'There's now plenty of evidence that access to financial services is a critical tool for both economic growth and human development. In many countries, poor and low-income people don't have access even to basic savings accounts, let alone more advanced financial services that could provide security, predictability and the seeds of economic growth for their household. An inclusive financial sector will support the full participation of lower income households in the financial system.'[22] 'The Rural Microenterprise Finance Project helped to reduce the dependence of participating households on other loans such as informal moneylenders and more expensive loans from financial institutions. In addition, the proportion of participating households with savings accounts increased, as did the amounts in these savings accounts. All these improved the consumption smoothing capabilities of participating households.'[23]

'Microfinance has a very important role to play in development according to proponents of microfinance. UNCDF (2004) states that studies have shown that microfinance plays three key roles in development. It helps very poor households meet basic needs and protects against risks. It is associated with improvements in household economic welfare. It helps to empower women by supporting women's economic participation and so promotes gender equity.'[24] 'Recognising that microfinance can be an important channel in poverty alleviation, Islamic microfinance is increasingly seen, especially in Muslim majority countries, as an alternative to conventional microfinance to alleviate the poor out of poverty. Islamic MFIs have been developed with the sole purpose of providing the poor which have little or no access to capital from the commercial banking sector with viable financial services that are in accordance with Islamic principles.'[25]

Grameen Bank in Bangladesh

'In 1972, Yunus returned to Bangladesh after eight years as a student and professor in the US and became a professor of economics. He had no intentions of becoming a banker. Bangladesh had been devastated by its War of Liberation and a famine followed shortly thereafter. He wanted desperately to be helpful. In the nearby village of Jobra, he set up a cooperative with farmers and landowners to grow rice more efficiently. The yield at the end of the season was high but he discovered the farmers had robbed him of his share of the profits. Seeking another way to help the poor, Yunus took groups of his students and colleagues for numerous field trips to Jobra to learn about poverty. One day he lent some small amounts of money, less than twenty-seven dollars in all, to forty-two impoverished villagers. To his surprise, they paid him back. He discovered over the next months and years that not only do the poor pay back their loans even without any collateral, but also they pay back at rates far higher than the 60 per cent rate that was typical of commercial banks. This was the defining moment for Yunus. In 1983, after years of negotiating with skeptical bankers and haggling reluctant government officials, the Bangladesh government recognised his organisation, now called the Grameen (village) Bank as an independent bank.'[26]

'This bank originated in 1976 as an experiment in a research project of Muhammad Yunus, Professor of Economics at Chittagong University in Bangladesh. The GB was chartered to operate as a national bank in 1983, with 75 branches spread in five districts of the country. The extremely poor can get small loans at GB if they form groups of five people. Each member of the group receives an individual loan; however, they are mutually responsible for all five credits. The bulk of GB's borrowers are women who constitute the weakest social group among the rural poor. Lending money to women has largely enhanced recoverability for GB's loans.'[27] 'The aim of Grameen Bank is to reduce poverty in both rich and poor countries. It gives loan to those people whom the government or any commercial bank will not give loan facility. Both rich and poor countries of the world microfinance tries to improve access to loans and to saving services for low-income, low-wealth people which is the fastest-growing and best-known tool to combat poverty.'[28]

'The Grameen Bank of Bangladesh has triumphed against long odds to help spark an international movement that heralds new approaches to poverty alleviation. The movement emphasises market-based institutions that provide credit to poor households to generate new opportunities through self-employment. Until recently, Grameen has reported repayment rates of 98 per cent and modest profits while serving over two million functionally landless borrowers.'[29] 'Grameen Bank targets the poorest of the poor, with a particular emphasis on women, who receive 95 per cent of the bank's loans. Women represent a suitable clientele because, given that they have less access to alternatives, such as traditional credit lines and salaries, they are more likely to be credit constrained and they have an inequitable share of power in household decision-making. Grameen Bank maintains its own regulation system outside the purview of the Central Bank of Bangladesh and relies heavily on social pressure among the group members to keep default rates low.'[30]

Microfinance in India

'The microfinance industry in India is in the midst of the most severe crisis in its 25 years history. The genesis of the crisis lies with the actions taken by the government of the southern state of Andhra Pradesh in October 2010, when it passed legislation effectively shutting down all private sector microfinance institutions operating in the state. Microfinance in India can trace its origins back to the early 1970s when the Self Employed Women's Association (SEWA) of the state of Gujarat formed an urban cooperative bank, called the Shri Mahila SEWA Sahakari Bank, with the objective of providing banking services to poor women employed in the unorganised sector in Ahmedabad City, Gujarat. According to recent RBI estimates, there are over 450 million "unbanked people" in India, most of who live in rural areas. The term "unbanked" refers to people who have no access to formal financial services, but rather must rely on either family, or informal providers of finance, such as the village moneylender. Microfinance in India is currently being provided by three sectors: the government, the private sector and charities. These three sectors, as large as they are, have only a small fraction of the capital and geographic scale required to meet the overwhelming need for finance amongst India's rural poor.'[31]

'In India, the history of microfinance dates back to establishment of Syndicate Bank in 1921 in private sector. During the early years, Syndicate Bank concentrated on raising micro deposits in the form of daily/weekly basis and sanctioned micro loans to its clients for shorter period of time. But microfinance came to limelight only when Dr Yunus gave it a mass movement in Grameen Bank experiment. After intervention of National Bank for Agriculture and Rural Development in 1992 in the field of microcredit, the movement of microfinance got a boost in India. In India, around 70 per cent of landless and marginal farmers did not have a bank account and 87 per cent of poor had no access to credit from a formal source. Now the microfinance service providers include apex institutions like National Bank for Agriculture and Rural Development, Small Industries Development Bank of India and Rashtriya MahilaKosh. At the lower level we have Commercial Banks, Regional Rural Banks and cooperatives to provide microfinance services.'[32]

'The steady increase in the NPA against loans to SHGs continued unabated during the current year as well with overall NPA against loans to SHGs increased by 26 per cent to 2,787 crore by March 2013 against 2,213 crore a year earlier. In per centage terms NPA (gross) increased from 6.09 per cent last year to 7.08 per cent during the current year. Among the regions, Southern region with a NPA of 5.11 per cent (4.98 per cent) was the lowest while Central region with an alarming 17.3 per cent (13.2 per cent last year) was the highest. What cause grave concern are the high NPAs in major states like Madhya Pradesh (21.16 per cent), Uttar Pradesh (18.22 per cent), Odisha (18.27 per cent), Tamil Nadu (10.81 per cent) and Kerala (12.38 per cent). NABARD had also introduced a scheme of 'Bulk Lending to NGOs' in 1993 for on-lending to small, micro household enterprises un-reached by banks. This was termed as Revolving Fund Assistance [RFA] and was primarily provided to NGOs and MFIs to experiment various credit delivery innovations. Under this approach select NGOs, which act as financial intermediaries were provided longer-term lendable funds with service charges in the range of 6.5 to 9.0 per cent p.a. In the initial 10 years of operation i.e. upto 2004, about 31 NGOs, MFIs were assisted.

NABARD continued with its role as the main facilitator and mentor of microfinance initiatives in the country, particularly the SHG-BLP initiative. Its focus was on bringing in various stakeholders on a common platform and build capacity among them to take the SHG-BLP movement forward while extending 100 per cent refinance to all banks participating in the programme. NABARD has been extending 100 per cent refinance to banks for their lending to SHGs since the SHG-BLP was launched. Initially, this was intended at concessional rates to encourage the banks to actively participate in the programme. The Micro-finance Development and Equity Fund (MFDEF) continued to be utilised for promotion of various micro-finance activities. During 2012-13, 33.50 crore was utilised for various promotional activities like promotion, capacity building and other interventions. With large number of on-going promotional projects with 3700 NGO and other partners, NABARD had committed expenses ruling in the range of 200 crore. Besides, the SHG-BLP, NABARD has been supporting formation of informal groups like Joint Liability Groups (JLGs) with 4-10 members. NABARD has been supporting and organising training programmes on SHG-BLP for various stakeholders for quite sometime.'[33]

'The growth in SHG loan outstanding (8.4 per cent) during 2012–13 is almost four times that in the number of SHGs having outstanding loans with banks (2.2 per cent). This gap, it is apprehended, could in part be the result of increased non-performing assets of SHG loans with banks. Annual growth rates of the major indicators of physical and financial progress of SBLP for the three-year period since 2010, the year of the crisis in Andhra Pradesh, confirm the impression of stagnation and decline. The number of SHGs savings-linked with the banking system grew steadily since 2008 and had peaked at 7.96 million groups in March 2012. The number declined to 7.32 million as at the end of March 2013. Among the financing agencies, commercial banks had the leading share (56 per cent) in the number of groups with savings accounts, while RRBs had 28 per cent of accounts and cooperative banks 16 per cent. There has been no significant change in these shares. Commercial banks accounted for two-thirds of the amount saved by SHGs as on 31 March 2013. If the regional picture is considered, the shares of the southern and eastern regions in loans outstanding have remained virtually unchanged between 2009 and 2013.'[34]

Success Story of Microfinance

'Success in microfinance refers to measures which when adopted will significantly improve the life and operations of the institutions though many authors have different views on what constitute success. The imperatives have been used to scan success of microfinance institutions are acquiring more clients, effective and efficient loan processing, effective record keeping, increased savings, external and internal audits, level of staff remuneration and staff turnover rate.'[35]

'The Grameen Bank model has been a case of exceptional success in Bangladesh. It turns out that many organisations in India have adopted the Grameen Bank model with little variations and good success. Some of the significant features of Grameen Bank model are low transaction costs, no collateral (peer pressure is sufficient), repayment of loans in small and short interval and quick loan sanctions with little or no paper works and no formalities.'[36] 'The principal microfinance service providers in Bangladesh are usually categorised into four major groups: MF-NGOs, specialised institutions, commercial banks with microfinance programmes and administrative ministries or divisions.'[37]

'The evidence of the impact of microcredit can be assessed from two interrelated angles. First, who does credit reach and second, how does it affect the welfare of different groups of individuals and households. Land ownership, occupational criteria and asset valuations are standard targeting tools used by microcredit providers in Bangladesh in order to direct resources to the rural poor. These indicators have been shown to be relatively accurate correlates of poverty by programme administrators who do not have the time, resources, or expertise to carry out more sophisticated calculations of poverty for each household in their targeted area. There is strong evidence that microcredit contributes to reducing household vulnerability. Asset creation is important to reduce household vulnerability to various livelihood risks. Another pathway by which microfinance appears to reduce vulnerability is through the emergency assistance provided by many microfinance organisations during acute natural disasters, such as the recent floods in Bangladesh. The impact of credit on women's empowerment, or reducing female vulnerability, has also received considerable attention.'[38]

'The Latin American context has most of the common features of Microfinance around the world, but also has its very distinct characteristics. Assessing the performance indicators of the region as a whole, one could note the great accomplishments of Latin America. The total number of customers amounts to nine million borrowers. Because of the growing demand for financial services and also the need for more complex products, Latin America has pioneered a whole new way of approaching Microfinance, a new methodology that has produced a shift in the Microfinance Paradigm. The MFIs of South America have created a few of the most important microfinance business strategies and also provided valuable lessons for all the other countries and regions to follow.'[39] 'Success factors are factors that contribute to the sustainability and growth of microfinance businesses around the world. Some leading microfinance businesses like the Grameen Bank have been tested and proven overtime. It has withstood the test of time. Therefore, most microfinance businesses look up to the Grameen Bank as a role model of microfinance and to follow its success factors.'[40]

'Agricultural production, reduction in food insecurity and rural poverty and improvement in the lives of rural women represent three important reasons for MFIs to expand into rural areas and agriculture. Many MFIs emphasise serving poor women so they have an advantage compared to other financial institutions in improving gender balance in access to finance.'[41] 'The establishment of long-lasting microfinance institutions serving a large number of poor people has been a crucial element of Ethiopia's development strategy. Within the last decade the number of microfinance institutions that serves poor people in Ethiopia has reached twenty six and the scale of outreach of these organisations has also been expanding. Among the microfinance institutions that are found in Ethiopia, ACSI is the most popular and it operates in all the ten administrative zones of the Amhara region.'[42]

Poverty Eradication

'Microfinance refers to a range of financial services such as savings, credit and insurance for the poor. In 1980s and early 1990s, a more popular term was microcredit to emphasise the main service, i.e. credit to the poor though small savings has always been an integral part of microcredit programs.'[43] 'In the last two decades, substantial progress has been made in developing techniques to deliver financial services to the poor on a sustainable basis. Most donor interventions have concentrated on one of these services, microcredit. For microcredit to be appropriate however, the clients must have the capacity to repay the loan under the terms by which it is provided. Otherwise, clients may not be able to benefit from credit and risk being pushed into debt problems.'[44] 'Poverty alleviation or reduction is an ultimate goal of most MFIs, with either direct or indirect links to immediate objectives. Objectives are in turn determined by the organisationís ideological outlook, in particular how the organisation perceives the relationship between poverty alleviation and access to credit.'[45]

'Microfinance is not a panacea for poverty and related development challenges, but rather an important tool in the mission of poverty eradication. Poverty is a multidimensional problem, embedded in a complex and interconnected political, economic, cultural and ecological system. Owing to poverty's large scope and multiplicity of actors, there is no single guaranteed approach to its eradication. As microfinance becomes more widely accepted and moves into the mainstream, the supply of services to the poor may likewise increase, improving efficiency and outreach, while lowering costs. This, in turn, can have a multiplier effect on people's standard of living. Perhaps the greatest contribution of microfinance is that it empowers people, providing them with confidence, self-esteem and the financial means to play a larger role in their development.'[46]

Women Empowerment

'Microfinance programmes have generally targeted poor women. By providing access to financial services only through women-making women responsible for loans, ensuring repayment through women, maintaining savings accounts for women, providing insurance coverage through women-microfinance programmes send a strong message to households as well as to communities.'[47] 'Women are typically targeted for microfinance initiatives around the globe because studies indicate that involving women in microfinance ventures often plays a role in increasing gender equality within a country. Efforts to reduce gender inequality can be linked to positive effects within a country. When women have greater access to financial resources and services, they obtain greater decision-making power regarding money and their households. Where this power lies may have significant implications for families and communities.'[48]

'In addition to borrowing and savings services, the poor need insurance to protect themselves from uncertainty. In the absence of insurance, the poor often avoid risky but potentially profitable economic activities and enter into informal insurance arrangements or rely on precautionary savings. Some microfinance institutions have begun to offer insurance products. The Bangladesh Rural Advancement Committee offers life insurance contracts to women who live below the poverty line and Nirdhan, a group-based microfinance institution in Nepal, provides livestock insurance to those who borrow to finance livestock investment. Perhaps the most important factor to consider in increasing access to financial services to the poor is that programmes must fit the specific context of a particular area and its population.'[49]

'Micro-finance programmes have significant potential for contributing to women's economic, social and political empowerment. Access to savings and credit can initiate or strengthen a series of interlinked and mutually reinforcing 'virtuous spirals' of empowerment. The 1980s saw the emergence of poverty-targeted micro-finance institutions like Grameen Bank. Many of these programmes see themselves as empowerment-oriented.'[50] 'Microfinance has come to play a major role in many gender and development strategies because of its direct relationship to both poverty alleviation and to the empowerment of women. Women are the most crucial elements of the social fabric and are playing a pivotal role in the socioeconomic scenario of Rajasthan. Microfinance programmes like the SHGs in India have been promoted for their positive economic impact and the belief that they empower women.'[51]

'Micro-finance and SHGs are effective in reducing poverty, empowering women and creating awareness which finally results in sustainable development of the nation. The main aim of microfinance is to empower women. Microfinance is the provision of financial services to low-income clients, including consumers and the self-employed, who traditionally lack access to banking and related service. Micro-finance programmes not only give women and men access to savings and credit, but reach millions of people worldwide bringing them together regularly in organised groups. Majority of microfinance programmes focus women with a view to empower them. There are varying underlying motivations for pursuing women empowerment. Some argue that women are amongst the poorest and the most vulnerable of the underprivileged and thus helping them should be a priority.'[52]

Shortcoming of Microfinance

'Nonetheless, micro financing raises important questions with respect to its application and the heavy burden it places on the borrowers. Micro financing particularly faces two urgent issues undermining its popularity worldwide. The first of these issues concerns microfinance institutions. The second problem facing micro financing surfaced in the form of increased commercialisation. MFIs have increasingly gained a commercial nature with investment banks obtaining a larger share of the microcredit sector. Both of these problems, the lack of financial sustainability of MFIs and the commercialisation of micro financing, point to a serious issue at the very foundation of micro financing: interest-based credits. The interest-based mechanics of micro financing and by association its commercialisation, have become an effective mechanism for integrating the poor into the global financial system.'[53]

Conclusion

Self Help Group is a homogeneous group of micro entrepreneurs with affinity among themselves, voluntarily formed to save whatever amount they can conveniently save out of their earnings and mutually agree to contribute to a common fund of the group from which small loans are given to the members for meeting their productive and emergent credit needs at such rate of interest, period of loan and other terms as the group may decide. Such groups may exist separately or as part of larger organisations. They may operate informally or according to a format or program. Microfinance institution is an organisation that provides microfinance services. MFIs range from small non-profit organisations to large commercial banks. Micro Finance Institutions around the world follow a variety of different methodologies. The focus of such service is women rather than men for the reason women are more judicious and economical to men.

References

1. The Self Help Group Approach - a Manual, Retrieved from http://www.self-help-approach.com/doc/shg_manual.pdf
2. Microfinance (2015), Retrieved from http://en.wikipedia.org/wiki/Microfinance
3. R. Srinivasan and M.S. Sriram, Microfinance: An Introduction, Retrieved from http://www.mssriram.in/sites/mssriram.in/files/microfinance-RT_0.pdf
4. Prof Ulrich Steger, Alexander Schwandt and Matthieu Perissé (2007), Sustainable Banking with the Poor: Evolution, Status Quo and Prospects, Retrieved from https://www.imd.org/research/publications/upload/CSM_Steger_Schwandt_ Perisse_ WP_ 2007_12_level_1.pdf
5. Pascal Marino, Beyond Economic Benefits: The contribution of microfinance to post conflict recovery in Asia and the Pacific, Retrieved from http://www.gdrc.org/icm/country/fdc-afgan.pdf
6. Jonathan Morduch (1998), Does Microfinance Really Help the Poor? New Evidence from Flagship Programs in Bangladesh, Retrieved from http://www.nyu.edu/projects/morduch/documents/microfinance/Does_Microfinance_Really_Help.pdf
7. Introduction to Microfinance, Retrieved from http://www.cse.iitb.ac.in/~cs671/web07/web06/web05/submissions/portal/Microfinance_Portal.pdf
8. See http://www.microfinancegateway.org/what-is-microfinance
9. Cindy Dyar, Patrice Harduar, Cynthia Koenig and Gabriela Reyes (2006), Microfinance and Gender Inequality in China, Retrieved from http://www.umich.edu/~ipolicy/IEDP/2006china/10%29%20Microfinance%20and%20Gender%20 Inequality%20in%20China.pdf
10. Self-help group (2014), Retrieved from http://en.wikipedia.org/wiki/Self-help_group_%28finance%29
11. Group characteristics of self help groups, Journal of Tropical Agriculture 39 (2001): 84-86.
12. Self-help group (2015), Retrieved from http://www.unionbankofindia.co.in/RABD_Other_SelfHelpGroups.aspx
13. Kate S. Ahmadi (2013), What is self-help group? Retrieved from http://psychcentral.com/lib/what-is-a-self-help-group/0001280

14. What are the main essential characteristics of self-help groups (SHGs)? Retrieved from http://www.publishyourarticles.net/eng/articles/what-are-the-main-essential-characteristics-of-self-help-groups-shgs.html

15. Characteristics of a self-help relationship, Retrieved from http://www.capsante-outaouais.org/content/characteristics-self-help-relationship

16. K. Srnec, E. Svobodova (2009), Microfinance in less developed countries: history, progress, present – charity or business?, pp.467-68, Retrieved from http://www.agriculturejournals.cz/publicFiles/12074.pdf

17. About microfinance (2014), Retrieved from http://www.kiva.org/about/microfinance

18. See http://www.microfinancegateway.org/what-is-microfinance

19. Status of microfinance in India: A Review, International Journal of Marketing, Financial Services and Management Research, Vol.1 Issue 11, November 2012, Retrieved from http://indianresearchjournals.com/pdf/IJMFSMR/2012/November/13.pdf

20. Benefits of Microfinance (2014), Retrieved from http://benefitof.net/benefits-of-microfinance/

21. http://www.visionmicrofinance.com/en/vision-microfinance/social-benefit/

22. Dr Vinita K. Pimpale (2012), An introductory overview of microfinance in India: An inquiry into future prospects, IRJC: International Journal of Marketing, Financial Services and Management Research, Vol. 1, Issue 9, p. 180.

23. Effect of Microfinance Operations on Poor Rural Households and the Status of Women, Retrieved from http://www.oecd.org/countries/bangladesh/39503711.pdf

24. Micro finance: Literature Review, Retrieved from http://www.dochas.ie/Shared/Files/2/MicroFinance_ literature_review.pdf

25. Scaling up Islamic Microfinance in Bangladesh through the Private Sector: Experience of Islami Bank Bangladesh Limited (IBBL), Retrieved from http://www.undp.org/content/dam/undp/library/Poverty%20Reduction/Participatory% 20Local%20Development/Bangladesh_D10_web.pdf

26. Katharine Esty (2011), Lessons from Muhammad Yunus and the Grameen Bank, Retrieved from http://c.ymcdn.com/sites/www.odnetwork.org/resource/resmgr/364.pdf

27. M. Kabir Hassan and Luis Renteria-Guerrero, The experience of the Grameen Bank of Bangladesh in community development, International Journal of Social Economics, Retrieved from http://www.1stethical.com/wp-content/uploads/2010/07/The_experience_of_the_Grameen_Bank_of_ Bangladesh_ in_community_development.pdf

28. Jamal Nazrul Islam, Haradhan Kumar Mohajan and Rajib Datta (2002), Aspects of microfinance system of Grameen Bank of Bangladesh, Retrieved from http://www.ijeronline.com/documents/volumes/Vol%203%20Iss%204/ijerv3i4JuAu2012%286%29.pdf

29. Jonathan Morduch (1999), The role of subsidies in microfinance: evidence from the Grameen Bank, Journal of Development Economics Vol. 60, 1999, 229–248.

30. Evaristus Mainsah, Schuyler R. Heuer and Qiulin Zhang, Grameen Bank: Taking Capitalism to the Poor, Retrieved from https://www0.gsb.columbia.edu/mygsb/faculty/research/pubfiles/848/Grameen_Bank_v04.pdf

31. Microfinance in India: A crisis at the bottom of the pyramid, Retrieved from http://www.legatum.org/attachments/MicrofinanceCrisis.pdf

32. Status of micro finance in India: A Review, International Journal of Marketing, Financial Services and Management Research, Vol.1 Issue 11, November 2012, Retrieved from http://indianresearchjournals.com/pdf/IJMFSMR/2012/November/13.pdf

33. Status of microfinance in India 2012-13, Retrieved from https://www.nabard.org/Publication/Status_of_Microfinance_in_India_2012-13.pdf

34. Tara Nair and Ajay Tankha (2014), Microfinance India State of the Sector Report 2013, Retrieved from http://inclusivefinanceindia. org/uploads/news_attachments/20141007121437_sos-report-2013.pdf

35. F. K. Aveh, P. S. Dadzie and R. Y. Krah, Success of Microfinance Institutions: The Ghanaian Experience, International Business and Management Vol. 6, No. 2, 2013, pp. 91-97.

36. Sibghatullah Nasir (2013), Microfinance in India: Contemporary Issues and Challenges, Middle-East Journal of Scientific Research 15 (2): 191-199.

37. David Pine (2010), The microfinance sector in Bangladesh: Innovation or Stagnation, Retrieved from http://www.cmf.uzh.ch/publications/david_pine.pdf

38. Hassan Zaman, Microfinance in Bangladesh: Growth, Achievements and Lessons, Retrieved from http://info.worldbank.org/etools/docs/reducingpoverty/case/108/fullcase/Bangladesh%20Microfinance%20Full%20Case.pdf

39. Petra Dacheva, Commercialisation in Microfinance – A Study of Profitability, Outreach and Success Factors within the Latin American Context, Retrieved from http://www.sbc.edu/sites/default/files/Honors/PDacheva.pdf

40. Irene Akuamoah Boateng and Albert Agyei (2013), Microfinance in Ghana: Development, Success Factors and Challenges, International Journal of Academic Research in Accounting, Finance and Management Sciences, Vol. 3, No. 4, p. 155.

41. Richard L. Meyer, Microcredit and Agriculture: Challenges, Successes and Prospects, Retrieved from https://www.incofin.com/sites/default/files/attachments/publications/Micro finance%20and%20agriculture.pdf

42. A Lesson of Success in Microfinance in Africa: the Experience of ACSI in Ethiopia (2009), Submitted to: The Organising Committee of the First European International Conference on Microfinance, Brussels, July 2-4, Retrieved from https://smartech.gatech.edu/bitstream/handle/1853/36657/Conference%20 Paper%20on%20ACSI%20March%202009.pdf

43. State of Microfinance in Bangladesh (2009), Retrieved from http://www.inm.org.bd/publication/state_of_micro/Bangladesh.pdf

44. About microfinance (2014), Retrieved from http://www.kiva.org/about/microfinance

45. David Hulme and Karen Moore (2006), Why has microfinance been a policy success in Bangladesh? Retrieved from http://www.gprg.org/pubs/workingpapers/pdfs/gprg-wps-041.pdf

46. Microfinance in Africa: Combining the Best Practices of Traditional and Modern Microfinance Approaches towards Poverty Eradication, Retrieved from http://www.un.org/esa/africa/microfinanceinafrica.pdf

47. About microfinance (2014), Retrieved from http://www.kiva.org/about/microfinance

48. Cindy Dyar, Patrice Harduar, Cynthia Koenig and Gabriela Reyes (2006), Microfinance and Gender Inequality in China, Retrieved from http://www.umich.edu/~ipolicy/IEDP/2006china/10%29%2 0Microfinance%20and%20Gender%20Inequality%20in%20 China.pdf

49. Banking on the poor: Unleashing the Benefits of Microfinance, Retrieved from http://www.ifpri.org/sites/default/files/publications/ib12.pdf

50. Dr Jyotish Prakash Basu, Microfinance and Women Empowerment An Empirical Study with special reference to West Bengal, Retrieved from http://www.igidr.ac.in/money/mfc_10/Jyotish%20Prakash%20Basu_submission_55.pdf

51. Dr Dhiraj Jain and Ms. Bhagyashree Jain, Does microfinance empower rural women? ; a empirical study in Udaipur district, Rajasthan, Journal of Arts, Science and Commerce, Retrieved from http://www.researchersworld.com/vol3/issue2/vol3_issue2_1/Paper_09.pdf

52. Dr Shuchi Loomba, Role of microfinance of women empowerment in India, Retrieved from http://jaipuria.edu.in/pgdm/wp-content/uploads/2013/07/Role-of-microfinane-in-women-empowerment-in-india.pdf

53. A. Kadir Yildirim (2009), Microfinance for the Poor: Burden or Blessing? Retrieved from http://www.fountainmagazine.com/Issue/detail/Microfinance-for-the-Poor-Burden-or-Blessing

7

Human Rights

> "Women have always been the strong ones of the world. The men are always seeking from women a little pillow to put their heads down on. They are always longing for the mother who held them as infants."
>
> —*Coco Chanel*

Introduction

'The doctrine of human rights has been highly influential within international law, global and regional institutions. Many of the basic ideas that animated the human rights movement developed in the aftermath of the Second World War. The philosophy of human rights attempts to examine the underlying basis of the concept of human rights and critically looks at its content and justification. Several theoretical approaches have been advanced to explain how and why human rights have become a part of social expectations. Human rights can be classified and organised in a number of different ways. At an international level the most common categorisation of human rights has been to split them into civil and political rights and economic, social and cultural rights.

Human rights advocates agree that, sixty years after its issue, the Universal Declaration of Human Rights is still more a dream than reality. Violations exist in every part of the world.'[1]

'Human Rights are the minimum rights which are compulsorily obtainable by every individual as he/she is a member of human society. But it has been found that each and every right of the women is being violated in one or another way. The crimes against women in India are increasing at a very fast pace.

The term human rights was mentioned seven times in the UN's founding Charter, making the promotion and protection of human rights a key purpose and guiding principle of the Organisation. In 1948, the Universal Declaration of Human Rights brought human rights into the realm of international law. Since then, the Organisation has diligently protected human rights through legal instruments and on-the-ground activities. The Office of the UN High Commissioner for Human Rights (OHCHR) has lead responsibility in the UN system for the promotion and protection of human rights. The High Commissioner for Human Rights regularly comments on human rights situations in the world and has the authority to investigate situations and issue reports on them. The Human Rights Council, established in 2006, replaced the 60-year old UN Commission on Human Rights as the key independent UN intergovernmental body responsible for human rights. The human rights treaty bodies are committees of independent experts that monitor implementation of the core international human rights treaties. The UN Development Group's Human Rights Mainstreaming Mechanism (UNDG-HRM) advances human rights mainstreaming efforts within the UN development system.'[2]

Meaning of the Concept

'Human rights are rights inherent to all human beings, whatever our nationality, place of residence, sex, national or ethnic origin, colour, religion, language, or any other status. We are all equally entitled to our human rights without discrimination. All human rights are indivisible, whether they are civil and political rights, such as the right to life, equality before the law and freedom of expression; economic, social and cultural rights, such as the rights to work, social security and education, or collective rights, such as the rights to development and self-determination, are indivisible, interrelated and interdependent. The improvement of one right facilitates advancement of the others. Likewise, the deprivation of one right adversely affects the others. Human rights entail both rights and obligations. States assume obligations and duties under international law to respect, to protect and to fulfill human rights. The obligation to respect means that States must refrain from interfering with or curtailing the enjoyment of human right.'[3]

'Human rights are basic rights and freedoms that all people are entitled to regardless of nationality, sex, national or ethnic origin, race, religion, language, or other status. Human rights include civil and political rights, such as the right to life, liberty and freedom of expression; and social, cultural and economic rights including the right to participate in culture, the right to food and the right to work and receive an education. Human rights are protected and upheld by international and national laws and treaties.'[4]

'The Universal Declaration of Human Rights (UDHR), 1948, defines human rights as "rights derived from the inherent dignity of the human person." Human rights when they are guaranteed by a written constitution are known as "Fundamental Rights" because a written constitution is the fundamental law of the state.'[5] 'Rights for all members of the human family were first articulated in 1948 in the United Nations' Universal Declaration of Human Rights. Following the horrific experiences of the Holocaust and World War II and amid the grinding poverty of much of the world's population, many people sought to create a document that would capture the hopes, aspirations and protections to which every person in the world was entitled and ensure that the future of humankind would be different.'[6] 'Some examples of human rights include:

- The right to life.
- The right to liberty and freedom.
- The right not to be prosecuted from your thoughts.
- The right to be free from prejudice on the basis of race, gender, national origin, colour, age or sex.
- The right to grow old.
- The right to a fair trial and due process of the law.
- The right to the pursuit of happiness.
- The right to live your life free of discrimination.

- The right to control what happens to your own body and to make medical decisions for yourself.
- The right to freely exercise your religion and practice your religious beliefs without fear of being prosecuted for your beliefs.
- The right to be free from slavery.
- The right to freedom of speech.
- The right to freely associate with whomever you like and to join groups of which you'd like to be a part.
- The right to freedom of thought.
- The right to be free from cruel and unusual punishment.
- The right to be free from torture.'[7]

Importance of Human Rights

'Since its conception, Human Rights and value for life is a universal doctrine grounded on comprehensive high moral and intellectual values. Probably, rights and values are best reflected in our nation when the crusader's objective based on their ideologies marries with their level of interest. There has been a sight of beneficial debates over the politicisation of human rights arena. Human rights and its values, elements are more or less part of every social and political ideology (left, right or centre). It's the strategical and tactical use of these values and elements to attain higher political objective, irrespective of political formation, which is circumscribing the actual strength of human right movement in India.'[8]

'Human rights are conferred on an individual due to the very nature of his existence. In the absence of human rights, the moral, physical, social and spiritual welfare of an individual is impossible. Human rights are essential as they provide suitable conditions for material and moral upliftment of the people. It is applied to those conditions which are essential for the fulfillment of this purpose. The values such as divinity, dignity and equality which form the basis of these rights are inherent in human nature. Human rights go on expanding with socio-eco-cultural and political developments within the State. Human rights imply that every individual has legitimate claims upon his or her society for certain freedom and benefits.'[9]

'The basic rights and freedoms to which all humans are considered to be entitled, often held to include the rights to life, liberty, equality and a fair trial, freedom from slavery and torture, freedom of thought and expression.[9] Human rights empower people with a framework for action when those minimum standards are not met, for people still have human rights even if the laws or those in power do not recognise or protect them. Human rights are held by all persons equally, universally and forever. Human rights are inalienable, indivisible and interdependent.'[10] 'Human rights are important. No matter where people come from, or what their age, culture, religion or income may be, they tend to talk about their concerns in terms of human rights. Human rights issues are often seen as national or international in scope, but human rights are equally relevant at an individual and community level.'[11]

'Rights are related to the values that societies live by. These values have their origins in the world's great religions and philosophies. Since the end of the Second World War, there has been a concerted attempt by the nations of the world to work together to identify what human rights exist and how they can best be promoted and protected.'[12] 'Equality and human rights is core to achieving national and local performance outcomes which aim to improve the quality of life and opportunities for all people. The consideration of human rights and equality issues will assist in improving performance in delivering high quality public services as efficiently, effectively and economically as possible as they will ensure they are responsive to people's individual circumstances at the point of delivery.'[13]

National Human Rights Commission

'Human Rights Commission is a body set up to investigate, promote or protect human rights. National and sub-national human rights commissions have been established in a number of countries for the promotion and protection of their citizens' human rights and most commissions are public bodies but with some degree of independence from the state. In other countries the ombudsman performs that role. The National Human Rights Commission of India is an autonomous public body constituted on 12 October 1993 under the Protection of Human Rights Ordinance of 28 September 1993. It was given a statutory basis by the Protection of Human Rights Act, 1993. Sections 3 and 4 of TPHRA lay down the rules for appointment to the NHRC.'[14]

Universal Declaration of Human Rights

'The Universal Declaration of Human Rights is a declaration adopted by the United Nations General Assembly on 10th December, 1948 at the Palais de Chaillot, Paris. The Declaration consists of thirty articles which have been elaborated in subsequent international treaties, regional human rights instruments, national constitutions and other laws. The Declaration was commissioned in 1946 and was drafted over two years by the Commission on Human Rights. The Commission consisted of 18 members from various nationalities and political backgrounds. The Universal Declaration of Human Rights Drafting Committee was chaired by Eleanor Roosevelt, who was known for her human rights advocacy. On 10th December 1948, the Universal Declaration was adopted by the General Assembly by a vote of 48 in favour, none against and eight abstentions (the Soviet Union, Ukrainian SSR, Byelorussian SSR, People's Federal Republic of Yugoslavia, People's Republic of Poland, Union of South Africa, Czechoslovakia and the Kingdom of Saudi Arabia). The adoption of the Universal Declaration is a significant international commemoration marked each year on 10th December and is known as Human Rights Day or International Human Rights Day.'[15]

Universal Declaration of Human Rights

Article 1: All human beings are born free and equal in dignity and rights. They are endowed with reason and conscience and should act towards one another in a spirit of brotherhood.

Article 2: Everyone is entitled to all the rights and freedoms set forth in this Declaration, without distinction of any kind, such as race, colour, sex, language, religion, political or other opinion, national or social origin, property, birth or other status. Furthermore, no distinction shall be made on the basis of the political, jurisdictional or international status of the country or territory to which a person belongs, whether it be independent, trust, non-self-governing or under any other limitation of sovereignty.

Article 3: Everyone has the right to life, liberty and security of person.

Article 4: No one shall be held in slavery or servitude; slavery and the slave trade shall be prohibited in all their forms.

Article 5: No one shall be subjected to torture or to cruel, inhuman or degrading treatment or punishment.

Article 6: Everyone has the right to recognition everywhere as a person before the law.

Article 7: All are equal before the law and are entitled without any discrimination to equal protection of the law. All are entitled to equal protection against any discrimination in violation of this Declaration and against any incitement to such discrimination.

Article 8: Everyone has the right to an effective remedy by the competent national tribunals for acts violating the fundamental rights granted him by the constitution or by law.

Article 9: No one shall be subjected to arbitrary arrest, detention or exile.

Article 10: Everyone is entitled in full equality to a fair and public hearing by an independent and impartial tribunal, in the determination of his rights and obligations and of any criminal charge against him.

Article 11: (1) Everyone charged with a penal offence has the right to be presumed innocent until proved guilty according to law in a public trial at which he has had all the guarantees necessary for his defence. (2) No one shall be held guilty of any penal offence on account of any act or omission which did not constitute a penal offence, under national or international law, at the time when it was committed. Nor shall a heavier penalty be imposed than the one that was applicable at the time the penal offence was committed.

Article 12: No one shall be subjected to arbitrary interference with his privacy, family, home or correspondence, nor to attacks upon his honour and reputation. Everyone has the right to the protection of the law against such interference or attacks.

Article 13: (1) Everyone has the right to freedom of movement and residence within the borders of each state. (2) Everyone has the right to leave any country, including his own and to return to his country.

Article 14: (1) Everyone has the right to seek and to enjoy in other countries asylum from persecution. (2) This right may not be invoked in the case of prosecutions genuinely arising from non-political crimes or from acts contrary to the purposes and principles of the United Nations.

Article 15: (1) Everyone has the right to a nationality. (2) No one shall be arbitrarily deprived of his nationality nor denied the right to change his nationality.

Article 16: (1) Men and women of full age, without any limitation due to race, nationality or religion, have the right to marry and to found a family. They are entitled to equal rights as to marriage, during marriage and at its dissolution. (2) Marriage shall be entered into only with the free and full consent of the intending spouses. (3) The family is the natural and fundamental group unit of society and is entitled to protection by society and the State.

Article 17: (1) Everyone has the right to own property alone as well as in association with others. (2) No one shall be arbitrarily deprived of his property.

Article 18: Everyone has the right to freedom of thought, conscience and religion; this right includes freedom to change his religion or belief and freedom, either alone or in community with others and in public or private, to manifest his religion or belief in teaching, practice, worship and observance.

Article 19: Everyone has the right to freedom of opinion and expression; this right includes freedom to hold opinions without interference and to seek, receive and impart information and ideas through any media and regardless of frontiers.

Article 20: (1) Everyone has the right to freedom of peaceful assembly and association. (2) No one may be compelled to belong to an association.

Article 21: (1) Everyone has the right to take part in the government of his country, directly or through freely chosen representatives. (2) Everyone has the right of equal access to public service in his country. (3) The will of the people shall be the basis of the authority of government; this will shall be expressed in periodic and genuine elections which shall be by universal and equal suffrage and shall be held by secret vote or by equivalent free voting procedures.

Article 22: Everyone, as a member of society, has the right to social security and is entitled to realisation, through national effort and international co-operation and in accordance with the organisation and resources of each State, of the economic, social and cultural rights indispensable for his dignity and the free development of his personality.

Article 23: (1) Everyone has the right to work, to free choice of employment, to just and favourable conditions of work and to protection against unemployment. (2) Everyone, without any discrimination, has the right to equal pay for equal work. (3) Everyone who works has the right to just and favourable remuneration ensuring for himself and his family an existence worthy of human dignity and supplemented, if necessary, by other means of social protection. (4) Everyone has the right to form and to join trade unions for the protection of his interests.

Article 24: Everyone has the right to rest and leisure, including reasonable limitation of working hours and periodic holidays with pay.

Article 25: (1) Everyone has the right to a standard of living adequate for the health and well-being of himself and of his family, including food, clothing, housing and medical care and necessary social services and the right to security in the event of unemployment, sickness, disability, widowhood, old age or other lack of livelihood in circumstances beyond his control. (2) Motherhood and childhood are entitled to special care and assistance. All children, whether born in or out of wedlock, shall enjoy the same social protection.

Article 26: (1) Everyone has the right to education. Education shall be free, at least in the elementary and fundamental stages. Elementary education shall be compulsory. Technical and professional education shall be made generally available and higher education shall be equally accessible to all on the basis of merit. (2) Education shall be directed to the full development of the human personality and to the strengthening of respect for human rights and fundamental freedoms. It shall promote understanding, tolerance and friendship among all nations, racial or religious groups and shall further the activities of the United Nations for the maintenance of peace. (3) Parents have a prior right to choose the kind of education that shall be given to their children.

Article 27: (1) Everyone has the right freely to participate in the cultural life of the community, to enjoy the arts and to share in scientific advancement and its benefits. (2) Everyone has the right to the protection of the moral and material interests resulting from any scientific, literary or artistic production of which he is the author.

Article 28: Everyone is entitled to a social and international order in which the rights and freedoms set forth in this Declaration can be fully realised.

Article 29: (1) Everyone has duties to the community in which alone the free and full development of his personality is possible. (2) In the exercise of his rights and freedoms, everyone shall be subject only to such limitations as are determined by law solely for the purpose of securing due recognition and respect for the rights and freedoms of others and of meeting the just requirements of morality, public order and the general welfare in a democratic society. (3) These rights and freedoms may in no case be exercised contrary to the purposes and principles of the United Nations.

Article 30: Nothing in this Declaration may be interpreted as implying for any State, group or person any right to engage in any activity or to perform any act aimed at the destruction of any of the rights and freedoms set forth herein.

Source: http://www.un.org/en/documents/udhr/#atop

International Covenant on Civil and Political Rights

'The International Covenant on Civil and Political Rights (ICCPR) is a multilateral treaty adopted by the United Nations General Assembly on 16 December 1966 and in force from 23rd March, 1976. The ICCPR is part of the Declaration on the Granting of Independence to Colonial Countries and Peoples, International Bill of Human Rights, along with the International Covenant on Economic, Social and Cultural Rights (ICESCR) and the Universal Declaration of Human Rights (UDHR). The ICCPR is monitored by the United Nations Human Rights Committee (a separate body to the United Nations Human Rights Council), which reviews regular reports of States parties on how the rights are being implemented.

The ICCPR has its roots in the same process that led to the Universal Declaration of Human Rights. There are two Optional Protocols to the Covenant. The First Optional Protocol establishes an individual complaints mechanism, allowing individuals to complain to the Human Rights Committee about violations of the Covenant. The Second Optional Protocol abolishes the death penalty; however, countries were permitted to make a reservation allowing for use of death penalty for the most serious crimes of a military nature, committed during wartime. The International Covenant on Civil and Political Rights has 167 states parties, 67 by signature and ratification and the remainder by accession or succession. Another five states have signed but have yet to ratify the treaty.'[16]

PART 1

Article 1: All peoples have the right of self-determination. By virtue of that right they freely determine their political status and freely pursue their economic, social and cultural development. All peoples may, for their own ends, freely dispose of their natural wealth and resources without prejudice to any obligations arising out of international economic co-operation, based upon the principle of mutual benefit and international law. In no case may a people be deprived of its own means of subsistence. The States Parties to the present Covenant, including those having responsibility for the administration of Non-Self-Governing and Trust Territories, shall promote the realisation of the right of self-determination and shall respect that right, in conformity with the provisions of the Charter of the United Nations.

PART II

Article 2: Each State Party to the present Covenant undertakes to respect and to ensure to all individuals within its territory and subject to its jurisdiction the rights recognised in the present Covenant, without distinction of any kind, such as race, colour, sex, language, religion, political or other opinion, national or social origin, property, birth or other status. Where not already provided for by existing legislative or other measures, each State Party to the present Covenant undertakes to take the necessary steps, in accordance with its constitutional processes and with the provisions of the present Covenant, to adopt such laws or other measures as may be necessary to give effect to the rights recognised in the present Covenant. Each State Party to the present Covenant undertakes: (a) To ensure that any person whose rights or freedoms as herein recognised are violated shall have an effective remedy, notwithstanding that the violation has been committed by persons acting in an official capacity; (b) To ensure that any person claiming such a remedy shall have his right thereto determined by competent judicial, administrative or legislative authorities, or by any other competent authority provided for by the legal system of the State and to develop the possibilities of judicial remedy; To ensure that the competent authorities shall enforce such remedies when granted.

Article 3: The States Parties to the present Covenant undertake to ensure the equal right of men and women to the enjoyment of all civil and political rights set forth in the present Covenant.

Article 4: In time of public emergency which threatens the life of the nation and the existence of which is officially proclaimed, the States Parties to the present Covenant may take measures derogating from their obligations under the present Covenant to the extent strictly required by the exigencies of the situation, provided that such measures are not inconsistent with their other obligations under international law and do not involve discrimination solely on the ground of race, colour, sex, language, religion or social origin. Any State Party to the present Covenant availing itself of the right of derogation shall immediately inform the other States Parties to the present Covenant, through the intermediary of the Secretary-General of the United Nations, of the provisions from which it has derogated and of the reasons by which it was actuated. A further communication shall be made, through the same intermediary, on the date on which it terminates such derogation.

Article 5: Nothing in the present Covenant may be interpreted as implying for any State, group or person any right to engage in any activity or perform any act aimed at the destruction of any of the rights and freedoms recognised herein or at their limitation to a greater extent than is provided for in the present Covenant. There shall be no restriction upon or derogation from any of the fundamental human rights recognised or existing in any State Party to the present Covenant pursuant to law, conventions, regulations or custom on the pretext that the present Covenant does not recognise such rights or that it recognises them to a lesser extent.

PART III

Article 6: Every human being has the inherent right to life. This right shall be protected by law. No one shall be arbitrarily deprived of his life. In countries which have not abolished the death penalty, sentence of death may be imposed only for the most serious crimes in accordance with the law in force at the time of the commission of the crime and not contrary to the provisions of the present Covenant and to the Convention on the Prevention and Punishment of the Crime of Genocide. This penalty can only be carried out pursuant to a final judgement rendered by a competent court. When deprivation of life constitutes the crime of genocide, it is understood that nothing in this article shall authorise any State Party to the present Covenant to derogate in any way from any obligation assumed under the provisions of the Convention on the Prevention and Punishment of the Crime of Genocide. Anyone sentenced to death shall have the right to seek pardon or commutation of the sentence. Amnesty, pardon or commutation of the sentence of death may be granted in all cases. Sentence of death shall not be imposed for crimes committed by persons below eighteen years of age and shall not be carried out on pregnant women. Nothing in this article shall be invoked to delay or to prevent the abolition of capital punishment by any State Party to the present Covenant.

Article 7: No one shall be subjected to torture or to cruel, inhuman or degrading treatment or punishment. In particular, no one shall be subjected without his free consent to medical or scientific experimentation.

Article 8: No one shall be held in slavery; slavery and the slave-trade in all their forms shall be prohibited.

Article 9: Everyone has the right to liberty and security of person. No one shall be subjected to arbitrary arrest or detention. No one shall be deprived of his liberty except on such grounds and in accordance with such procedure as are established by law. Anyone who is arrested shall be informed, at the time of arrest, of the reasons for his arrest and shall be promptly informed of any charges against him. Anyone arrested or detained on a criminal charge shall be brought promptly before a judge or other officer authorised by law to exercise judicial power and shall be entitled to trial within a reasonable time or to release. It shall not be the general rule that persons awaiting trial shall be detained in custody, but release may be subject to guarantees to appear for trial, at any other stage of the judicial proceedings and, should occasion arise, for execution of the judgement. Anyone who is deprived of his liberty by arrest or detention shall be entitled to take proceedings before a court, in order that that court may decide without delay on the lawfulness of his detention and order his release if the detention is not lawful. Anyone who has been the victim of unlawful arrest or detention shall have an enforceable right to compensation.

Article 10: All persons deprived of their liberty shall be treated with humanity and with respect for the inherent dignity of the human person. Accused persons shall, save in exceptional circumstances, be segregated from convicted persons and shall be subject to separate treatment appropriate to their status as unconvicted persons. Accused juvenile persons shall be separated from adults and brought as speedily as possible for adjudication. The penitentiary system shall comprise treatment of prisoners the essential aim of which shall be their reformation and social rehabilitation. Juvenile offenders shall be segregated from adults and be accorded treatment appropriate to their age and legal status.

Article 11: No one shall be imprisoned merely on the ground of inability to fulfil a contractual obligation.

Article 12: Everyone lawfully within the territory of a State shall, within that territory, have the right to liberty of movement and freedom to choose his residence. Everyone shall be free to leave any country, including his own. The above-mentioned rights shall not be subject to any restrictions except those which are provided by law, are necessary to protect national security, public order (ordre public), public health or morals or the rights and freedoms of others and are consistent with the other rights recognised in the present Covenant. No one shall be arbitrarily deprived of the right to enter his own country.

Article 13: An alien lawfully in the territory of a State Party to the present Covenant may be expelled there from only in pursuance of a decision reached in accordance with law and shall, except where compelling reasons of national security otherwise require, be allowed to submit the reasons against his expulsion and to have his case reviewed by and be represented for the purpose before, the competent authority or a person or persons especially designated by the competent authority.

Article 14: All persons shall be equal before the courts and tribunals. In the determination of any criminal charge against him, or of his rights and obligations in a suit at law, everyone shall be entitled to a fair and public hearing by a competent, independent and impartial tribunal established by law. The press and the public may be excluded from all or part of a trial for reasons of morals, public order (ordre public) or national security in a democratic society, or when the interest of the private lives of the parties so requires, or to the extent strictly necessary in the opinion of the court in special circumstances where publicity would prejudice the interests of justice; but any judgement rendered in a criminal case or in a suit at law shall be made public except where the interest of juvenile persons otherwise requires or the proceedings concern matrimonial disputes or the guardianship of children.

Article 15: No one shall be held guilty of any criminal offence on account of any act or omission which did not constitute a criminal offence, under national or international law, at the time when it was committed. Nor shall a heavier penalty be imposed than the one that was applicable at the time when the criminal offence was committed. If, subsequent to the commission of the offence, provision is made by law for the imposition of the lighter penalty, the offender shall benefit thereby. Nothing in this article shall prejudice the trial and punishment of any person for any act or omission which, at the time when it was committed, was criminal according to the general principles of law recognised by the community of nations.

Article 16: Everyone shall have the right to recognition everywhere as a person before the law.

Article 17: No one shall be subjected to arbitrary or unlawful interference with his privacy, family, home or correspondence, nor to unlawful attacks on his honour and reputation. Everyone has the right to the protection of the law against such interference or attacks.

Article 18: Everyone shall have the right to freedom of thought, conscience and religion. This right shall include freedom to have or to adopt a religion or belief of his choice and freedom, either individually or in community with others and in public or private, to manifest his religion or belief in worship, observance, practice and teaching. No one shall be subject to coercion which would impair his freedom to have or to adopt a religion or belief of his choice. Freedom to manifest one's religion or beliefs may be subject only to such limitations as are prescribed by law and are necessary to protect public safety, order, health, or morals or the fundamental rights and freedoms of others. The States Parties to the present Covenant undertake to have respect for the liberty of parents and, when applicable, legal guardians to ensure the religious and moral education of their children in conformity with their own convictions.

Article 19: Everyone shall have the right to hold opinions without interference. Everyone shall have the right to freedom of expression; this right shall include freedom to seek, receive and impart information and ideas of all kinds, regardless of frontiers, either orally, in writing or in print, in the form of art, or through any other media of his choice. The exercise of the rights provided for in paragraph 2 of this article carries with it special duties and responsibilities.

Article 20: Any propaganda for war shall be prohibited by law. Any advocacy of national, racial or religious hatred that constitutes incitement to discrimination, hostility or violence shall be prohibited by law.

Article 21: The right of peaceful assembly shall be recognised. No restrictions may be placed on the exercise of this right other than those imposed in conformity with the law and which are necessary in a democratic society in the interests of national security or public safety, public order (ordre public), the protection of public health or morals or the protection of the rights and freedoms of others.

Article 22: Everyone shall have the right to freedom of association with others, including the right to form and join trade unions for the protection of his interests. No restrictions may be placed on the exercise of this right other than those which are prescribed by law and which are necessary in a democratic society in the interests of national security or public safety, public order (ordre public), the protection of public health or morals or the protection of the rights and freedoms of others. This article shall not prevent the imposition of lawful restrictions on members of the armed forces and of the police in their exercise of this right. Nothing in this article shall authorise States Parties to the International Labour Organisation Convention of 1948 concerning Freedom of Association and Protection of the Right to Organise to take legislative measures which would prejudice, or to apply the law in such a manner as to prejudice, the. guarantees provided for in that Convention.

Article 23: The family is the natural and fundamental group unit of society and is entitled to protection by society and the State. The right of men and women of marriageable age to marry and to found a family shall be recognised. No marriage shall be entered into without the free and full consent of the intending spouses. States Parties to the present Covenant shall take appropriate steps to ensure equality of rights and responsibilities of spouses as to marriage, during marriage and at its dissolution. In the case of dissolution, provision shall be made for the necessary protection of any children.

Article 24: Every child shall have, without any discrimination as to race, colour, sex, language, religion, national or social origin, property or birth, the right to such measures of protection as are required by his status as a minor, on the part of his family, society and the State. Every child shall be registered immediately after birth and shall have a name. Every child has the right to acquire a nationality.

Article 25: Every citizen shall have the right and the opportunity, without any of the distinctions mentioned in Article 2 and without unreasonable restrictions: (a) To take part in the conduct of public affairs, directly or through freely chosen representatives; (b) To vote and to be elected at genuine periodic elections which shall be by universal and equal suffrage and shall be held by secret ballot, guaranteeing the free expression of the will of the electors; (c) To have access, on general terms of equality, to public service in his country.

Article 26: All persons are equal before the law and are entitled without any discrimination to the equal protection of the law. In this respect, the law shall prohibit any discrimination and guarantee to all persons equal and effective protection against discrimination on any ground such as race, colour, sex, language, religion, political or other opinion, national or social origin, property, birth or other status.

Article 27: In those States in which ethnic, religious or linguistic minorities exist, persons belonging to such minorities shall not be denied the right, in community with the other members of their group, to enjoy their own culture, to profess and practise their own religion, or to use their own language.

PART IV

Article 28: There shall be established a Human Rights Committee (hereafter referred to in the present Covenant as the Committee). It shall consist of eighteen members and shall carry out the functions hereinafter provided. The Committee shall be composed of nationals of the States Parties to the present Covenant who shall be persons of high moral character and recognised competence in the field of human rights, consideration being given to the usefulness of the participation of some persons having legal experience. The members of the Committee shall be elected and shall serve in their personal capacity.

Article 29: The members of the Committee shall be elected by secret ballot from a list of persons possessing the qualifications prescribed in Article 28 and nominated for the purpose by the States Parties to the present Covenant. Each State Party to the present Covenant may nominate not more than two persons. These persons shall be nationals of the nominating State. A person shall be eligible for renomination.

Article 30: The initial election shall be held no later than six months after the date of the entry into force of the present Covenant. At least four months before the date of each election to the Committee, other than an election to fill a vacancy declared in accordance with Article 34, the Secretary-General of the United Nations shall address a written invitation to the States Parties to the present Covenant to submit their nominations for membership of the Committee within three months. The Secretary-General of the United Nations shall prepare a list in alphabetical order of all the persons thus nominated, with an indication of the States Parties which have nominated them and shall submit it to the States Parties to the present Covenant no later than one month before the date of each election. Elections of the members of the Committee shall be held at a meeting of the States Parties to the present Covenant convened by the Secretary General of the United Nations at the Headquarters of the United Nations. At that meeting, for which two-thirds of the States Parties to the present Covenant shall constitute a quorum, the persons elected to the Committee shall be those nominees who obtain the largest number of votes and an absolute majority of the votes of the representatives of States Parties present and voting.

Article 31: The Committee may not include more than one national of the same State. In the election of the Committee, consideration shall be given to equitable geographical distribution of membership and to the representation of the different forms of civilisation and of the principal legal systems.

Article 32: The members of the Committee shall be elected for a term of four years. They shall be eligible for re-election if renominated. However, the terms of nine of the members elected at the first election shall expire at the end of two years; immediately after the first election, the names of these nine members shall be chosen by lot by the Chairman of the meeting referred to in Article 30, paragraph 4.

Article 33: If, in the unanimous opinion of the other members, a member of the Committee has ceased to carry out his functions for any cause other than absence of a temporary character, the Chairman of the Committee shall notify the Secretary-General of the United Nations, who shall then declare the seat of that member to be vacant. In the event of the death or the resignation of a member of the Committee, the Chairman shall immediately notify the Secretary-General of the United Nations, who shall declare the seat vacant from the date of death or the date on which the resignation takes effect.

Article 34: When a vacancy is declared in accordance with Article 33 and if the term of office of the member to be replaced does not expire within six months of the declaration of the vacancy, the Secretary-General of the United Nations shall notify each of the States Parties to the present Covenant, which may within two months submit nominations in accordance with Article 29 for the purpose of filling the vacancy. The Secretary-General of the United Nations shall prepare a list in alphabetical order of the persons thus nominated and shall submit it to the States Parties to the present Covenant. The election to fill the vacancy shall then take place in accordance with the relevant provisions of this part of the present Covenant. A member of the Committee elected to fill a vacancy declared in accordance with Article 33 shall hold office for the remainder of the term of the member who vacated the seat on the Committee under the provisions of that article.

Article 35: The members of the Committee shall, with the approval of the General Assembly of the United Nations, receive emoluments from United Nations resources on such terms and conditions as the General Assembly may decide, having regard to the importance of the Committee's responsibilities.

Article 36: The Secretary-General of the United Nations shall provide the necessary staff and facilities for the effective performance of the functions of the Committee under the present Covenant.

Article 37: The Secretary-General of the United Nations shall convene the initial meeting of the Committee at the Headquarters of the United Nations. After its initial meeting, the Committee shall meet at such times as shall be provided in its rules of procedure. The Committee shall normally meet at the Headquarters of the United Nations or at the United Nations Office at Geneva.

Article 38: Every member of the Committee shall, before taking up his duties, make a solemn declaration in open committee that he will perform his functions impartially and conscientiously.

Article 39: The Committee shall elect its officers for a term of two years. They may be re-elected. The Committee shall establish its own rules of procedure, but these rules shall provide, inter alia, that: (a) Twelve members shall constitute a quorum; Decisions of the Committee shall be made by a majority vote of the members present.

Article 40: The States Parties to the present Covenant undertake to submit reports on the measures they have adopted which give effect to the rights recognised herein and on the progress made in the enjoyment of those rights: (a) Within one year of the entry into force of the present Covenant for the States Parties concerned; (b) Thereafter whenever the Committee so requests. All reports shall be submitted to the Secretary-General of the United Nations, who shall transmit them to the Committee for consideration. Reports shall indicate the factors and difficulties, if any, affecting the implementation of the present Covenant. The Secretary-General of the United Nations may, after consultation with the Committee, transmit to the specialised agencies concerned copies of such parts of the reports as may fall within their field of competence. The Committee shall study the reports submitted by the States Parties to the present Covenant. It shall transmit its reports and such general comments as it may consider appropriate, to the States Parties. The Committee may also transmit to the Economic and Social Council these comments along with the copies of the reports it has received from States Parties to the present Covenant. The States Parties to the present Covenant may submit to the Committee observations on any comments that may be made in accordance with paragraph 4 of this article.

Article 41: A State Party to the present Covenant may at any time declare under this article that it recognises the competence of the Committee to receive and consider communications to the effect that a State Party claims that another State Party is not fulfilling its obligations under the present Covenant. Communications under this article may be received and considered only if submitted by a State Party which has made a declaration recognising in regard to itself the competence of the Committee.

Article 42: If a matter referred to the Committee in accordance with Article 41 is not resolved to the satisfaction of the States Parties concerned, the Committee may, with the prior consent of the States Parties concerned, appoint an ad hoc Conciliation Commission (hereinafter referred to as the Commission). The good offices of the Commission shall be made available to the States Parties concerned with a view to an amicable solution of the matter on the basis of respect for the present Covenant. The Commission shall consist of five persons acceptable to the States Parties concerned. If the States Parties concerned fail to reach agreement within three months on all or part of the composition of the Commission, the members of the Commission concerning whom no agreement has been reached shall be elected by secret ballot by a two-thirds majority vote of the Committee from among its members.

Article 43: The members of the Committee and of the ad hoc conciliation commissions which may be appointed under Article 42, shall be entitled to the facilities, privileges and immunities of experts on mission for the United Nations as laid down in the relevant sections of the Convention on the Privileges and Immunities of the United Nations.

Article 44: The provisions for the implementation of the present Covenant shall apply without prejudice to the procedures prescribed in the field of human rights by or under the constituent instruments and the conventions of the United Nations and of the specialised agencies and shall not prevent the States Parties to the present Covenant from having recourse to other procedures for settling a dispute in accordance with general or special international agreements in force between them.

Article 45: The Committee shall submit to the General Assembly of the United Nations, through the Economic and Social Council, an annual report on its activities.

PART V

Article 46: Nothing in the present Covenant shall be interpreted as impairing the provisions of the Charter of the United Nations and of the constitutions of the specialised agencies which define the respective responsibilities of the various organs of the United Nations and of the specialised agencies in regard to the matters dealt with in the present Covenant.

Article 47: Nothing in the present Covenant shall be interpreted as impairing the inherent right of all peoples to enjoy and utilise fully and freely their natural wealth and resources.

PART VI

Article 48: The present Covenant is open for signature by any State Member of the United Nations or member of any of its specialised agencies, by any State Party to the Statute of the International Court of Justice and by any other State which has been invited by the General Assembly of the United Nations to become a Party to the present Covenant. The present Covenant is subject to ratification. Instruments of ratification shall be deposited with the Secretary-General of the United Nations.

Article 49: The present Covenant shall enter into force three months after the date of the deposit with the Secretary-General of the United Nations of the thirty-fifth instrument of ratification or instrument of accession. For each State ratifying the present Covenant or acceding to it after the deposit of the thirty-fifth instrument of ratification or instrument of accession, the present Covenant shall enter into force three months after the date of the deposit of its own instrument of ratification or instrument of accession.

Article 50: The provisions of the present Covenant shall extend to all parts of federal States without any limitations or exceptions.

Article 51: Any State Party to the present Covenant may propose an amendment and file it with the Secretary-General of the United Nations. The Secretary-General of the United Nations shall thereupon communicate any proposed amendments to the States Parties to the present Covenant with a request that they notify him whether they favour a conference of States Parties for the purpose of considering and voting upon the proposals. In the event that at least one third of the States Parties favours such a conference, the Secretary-General shall convene the conference under the auspices of the United Nations. Any amendment adopted by a majority of the States Parties present and voting at the conference shall be submitted to the General Assembly of the United Nations for approval. Amendments shall come into force when they have been approved by the General Assembly of the United Nations and accepted by a two-thirds majority of the States Parties to the present Covenant in accordance with their respective constitutional processes. 3. When amendments come into force, they shall be binding on those States Parties which have accepted them, other States Parties still being bound by the provisions of the present Covenant and any earlier amendment which they have accepted.

Article 52: Irrespective of the notifications made under Article 48, paragraph 5, the Secretary-General of the United Nations shall inform all States referred to in paragraph I of the same article of the following particulars: (a) Signatures, ratifications and accessions under Article 48; (b) The date of the entry into force of the present Covenant under Article 49 and the date of the entry into force of any amendments under Article 51.

Article 53: The present Covenant, of which the Chinese, English, French, Russian and Spanish texts are equally authentic, shall be deposited in the archives of the United Nations. The Secretary-General of the United Nations shall transmit certified copies of the present Covenant to all States referred to in article 48.

International Covenant on Economic, Social and Cultural Rights

'The International Covenant on Economic, Social and Cultural Rights (ICESCR) is a multilateral treaty adopted by the United Nations General Assembly on 16th December 1966 and in force from 3rd January 1976. The Covenant is monitored by the UN Committee on Economic, Social and Cultural Rights. It commits its parties to work toward the granting of economic, social and cultural rights (ESCR) to the Non-Self-Governing and Trust Territories and individuals, including labour rights and the right to health, the right to education and the right to an adequate standard of living. The Committee on Economic, Social and Cultural Rights is a body of human rights experts tasked with monitoring the implementation of the Covenant. It consists of 18 independent human rights experts, elected for four-year terms, with half the members elected every two years.'[17]

Article 1: All peoples have the right of self-determination. By virtue of that right they freely determine their political status and freely pursue their economic, social and cultural development. All peoples may, for their own ends, freely dispose of their natural wealth and resources without prejudice to any obligations arising out of international economic co-operation, based upon the principle of mutual benefit and international law. In no case may a people be deprived of its own means of subsistence. The States Parties to the present Covenant, including those having responsibility for the administration of Non-Self-Governing and Trust Territories, shall promote the realisation of the right of self-determination and shall respect that right, in conformity with the provisions of the Charter of the United Nations.

Article 2: Each State Party to the present Covenant undertakes to take steps, individually and through international assistance and co-operation, especially economic and technical, to the maximum of its available resources, with a view to achieving progressively the full realisation of the rights recognised in the present Covenant by all appropriate means, including particularly the adoption of legislative measures. The States Parties to the present Covenant undertake to guarantee that the rights enunciated in the present Covenant will be exercised without discrimination of any kind as to race, colour, sex, language, religion, political or other opinion, national or social origin, property, birth or other status. Developing countries, with due regard to human rights and their national economy, may determine to what extent they would guarantee the economic rights recognised in the present Covenant to non-nationals.

Article 3: The States Parties to the present Covenant undertake to ensure the equal right of men and women to the enjoyment of all economic, social and cultural rights set forth in the present Covenant.

Article 4: The States Parties to the present Covenant recognise that, in the enjoyment of those rights provided by the State in conformity with the present Covenant, the State may subject such rights only to such limitations as are determined by law only in so far as this may be compatible with the nature of these rights and solely for the purpose of promoting the general welfare in a democratic society.

Article 5: Nothing in the present Covenant may be interpreted as implying for any State, group or person any right to engage in any activity or to perform any act aimed at the destruction of any of the rights or freedoms recognised herein, or at their limitation to a greater extent than is provided for in the present Covenant. No restriction upon or derogation from any of the fundamental human rights recognised or existing in any country in virtue of law, conventions, regulations or custom shall be admitted on the pretext that the present Covenant does not recognise such rights or that it recognises them to a lesser extent.

Article 6: The States Parties to the present Covenant recognise the right to work, which includes the right of everyone to the opportunity to gain his living by work which he freely chooses or accepts and will take appropriate steps to safeguard this right. The steps to be taken by a State Party to the present Covenant to achieve the full realisation of this right shall include technical and vocational guidance and training programmes, policies and techniques to achieve steady economic, social and cultural development and full and productive employment under conditions safeguarding fundamental political and economic freedoms to the individual.

Article 7: The States Parties to the present Covenant recognise the right of everyone to the enjoyment of just and favourable conditions of work which ensure, in particular: (a) Remuneration which provides all workers, as a minimum; (b) Safe and healthy working conditions; (c) Equal opportunity for everyone to be promoted in his employment to an appropriate higher level, subject to no considerations other than those of seniority and competence; (d) Rest, leisure and reasonable limitation of working hours and periodic holidays with pay, as well as remuneration for public holidays.

Article 8: The States Parties to the present Covenant undertake to ensure: (a) The right of everyone to form trade unions and join the trade union of his choice, subject only to the rules of the organisation concerned, for the promotion and protection of his economic and social interests. No restrictions may be placed on the exercise of this right other than those prescribed by law and which are necessary in a democratic society in the interests of national security or public order or for the protection of the rights and freedoms of others; (b) The right of trade unions to establish national federations or confederations and the right of the latter to form or join international trade-union organisations; (c) The right of trade unions to function freely subject to no limitations other than those prescribed by law and which are necessary in a democratic society in the interests of national security or public order or for the protection of the rights and freedoms of others; (d) The right to strike, provided that it is exercised in conformity with the laws of the particular country. This article shall not prevent the imposition of lawful restrictions on the exercise of these rights by members of the armed forces or of the police or of the administration of the State. 3. Nothing in this article shall authorise States Parties to the International Labour Organisation Convention of 1948 concerning Freedom of Association and Protection of the Right to Organise to take legislative measures which would prejudice, or apply the law in such a manner as would prejudice, the guarantees provided for in that Convention.

Article 9: The States Parties to the present Covenant recognise the right of everyone to social security, including social insurance.

Article 10: The States Parties to the present Covenant recognise that: (a) The widest possible protection and assistance should be accorded to the family, which is the natural and fundamental group unit of society, particularly for its establishment and while it is responsible for the care and education of dependent children. Marriage must be entered into with the free consent of the intending spouses; (b) Special protection should be accorded to mothers during a reasonable period before and after childbirth. During such period working mothers should be accorded paid leave or leave with adequate social security benefits; (c) Special measures of protection and assistance should be taken on behalf of all children and young persons without any discrimination for reasons of parentage or other conditions. Children and young persons should be protected from economic and social exploitation. Their employment in work harmful to their morals or health or dangerous to life or likely to hamper their normal development should be punishable by law. States should also set age limits below which the paid employment of child labour should be prohibited and punishable by law.

Article 11: The States Parties to the present Covenant recognise the right of everyone to an adequate standard of living for himself and his family, including adequate food, clothing and housing and to the continuous improvement of living conditions. The States Parties will take appropriate steps to ensure the realisation of this right, recognising to this effect the essential importance of international cooperation based on free consent. The States Parties to the present Covenant, recognising the fundamental right of everyone to be free from hunger, shall take, individually and through international co-operation, the measures, including specific programmes, which are needed: (a) To improve methods of production, conservation and distribution of food by making full use of technical and scientific knowledge, by disseminating knowledge of the principles of nutrition and by developing or reforming agrarian systems in such a way as to achieve the most efficient development and utilisation of natural resources; (b) Taking into account the problems of both food-importing and food-exporting countries, to ensure an equitable distribution of world food supplies in relation to need.

Article 12: The States Parties to the present Covenant recognise the right of everyone to the enjoyment of the highest attainable standard of physical and mental health. The steps to be taken by the States Parties to the present Covenant to achieve the full realisation of this right shall include those necessary for: (a) The provision for the reduction of the stillbirth-rate and of infant mortality and for the healthy development of the child; (b) The improvement of all aspects of environmental and industrial hygiene; (c) The prevention, treatment and control of epidemic, endemic, occupational and other diseases; (d) The creation of conditions which would assure to all medical service and medical attention in the event of sickness.

Article 13: The States Parties to the present Covenant recognise the right of everyone to education. They agree that education shall be directed to the full development of the human personality and the sense of its dignity and shall strengthen the respect for human rights and fundamental freedoms. They further agree that education shall enable all persons to participate effectively in a free society, promote understanding, tolerance and friendship among all nations and all racial, ethnic or religious groups and further the activities of the United Nations for the maintenance of peace.

Article 14: Each State Party to the present Covenant which, at the time of becoming a Party, has not been able to secure in its metropolitan territory or other territories under its jurisdiction compulsory primary education, free of charge, undertakes, within two years, to work out and adopt a detailed plan of action for the progressive implementation, within a reasonable number of years, to be fixed in the plan, of the principle of compulsory education free of charge for all.

Article 15: The States Parties to the present Covenant recognise the right of everyone: (a) To take part in cultural life; (b) To enjoy the benefits of scientific progress and its applications; (c) To benefit from the protection of the moral and material interests resulting from any scientific, literary or artistic production of which he is the author. The steps to be taken by the States Parties to the present Covenant to achieve the full realisation of this right shall include those necessary for the conservation, the development and the diffusion of science and culture. The States Parties to the present Covenant undertake to respect the freedom indispensable for scientific research and creative activity. The States Parties to the present Covenant recognise the benefits to be derived from the encouragement and development of international contacts and co-operation in the scientific and cultural fields.

Article 16: The States Parties to the present Covenant undertake to submit in conformity with this part of the Covenant reports on the measures which they have adopted and the progress made in achieving the observance of the rights recognised herein.

Article 17: The States Parties to the present Covenant shall furnish their reports in stages, in accordance with a programme to be established by the Economic and Social Council within one year of the entry into force of the present Covenant after consultation with the States Parties and the specialised agencies concerned.

Article 18: Pursuant to its responsibilities under the Charter of the United Nations in the field of human rights and fundamental freedoms, the Economic and Social Council may make arrangements with the specialised agencies in respect of their reporting to it on the progress made in achieving the observance of the provisions of the present Covenant falling within the scope of their activities. These reports may include particulars of decisions and recommendations on such implementation adopted by their competent organs.

Article 19: The Economic and Social Council may transmit to the Commission on Human Rights for study and general recommendation or, as appropriate, for information the reports concerning human rights submitted by States in accordance with articles 16 and 17 and those concerning human rights submitted by the specialised agencies in accordance with article 18.

Article 20: The States Parties to the present Covenant and the specialised agencies concerned may submit comments to the Economic and Social Council on any general recommendation under article 19 or reference to such general recommendation in any report of the Commission on Human Rights or any documentation referred to therein.

Article 21: The Economic and Social Council may submit from time to time to the General Assembly reports with recommendations of a general nature and a summary of the information received from the States Parties to the present Covenant and the specialised agencies on the measures taken and the progress made in achieving general observance of the rights recognised in the present Covenant.

Article 22: The Economic and Social Council may bring to the attention of other organs of the United Nations, their subsidiary organs and specialised agencies concerned with furnishing technical assistance any matters arising out of the reports referred to in this part of the present Covenant which may assist such bodies in deciding, each within its field of competence, on the advisability of international measures likely to contribute to the effective progressive implementation of the present Covenant.

Article 23: The States Parties to the present Covenant agree that international action for the achievement of the rights recognised in the present Covenant includes such methods as the conclusion of conventions, the adoption of recommendations, the furnishing of technical assistance and the holding of regional meetings and technical meetings for the purpose of consultation and study organised in conjunction with the governments concerned.

Article 24: Nothing in the present Covenant shall be interpreted as impairing the provisions of the Charter of the United Nations and of the constitutions of the specialised agencies which define the respective responsibilities of the various organs of the United Nations and of the specialised agencies in regard to the matters dealt with in the present Covenant.

Article 25: Nothing in the present Covenant shall be interpreted as impairing the inherent right of all peoples to enjoy and utilise fully and freely their natural wealth and resources.

Article 26: The present Covenant is open for signature by any State Member of the United Nations or member of any of its specialised agencies, by any State Party to the Statute of the International Court of Justice and by any other State which has been invited by the General Assembly of the United Nations to become a party to the present Covenant.

Article 27: The present Covenant shall enter into force three months after the date of the deposit with the Secretary-General of the United Nations of the thirty-fifth instrument of ratification or instrument of accession. For each State ratifying the present Covenant or acceding to it after the deposit of the thirty-fifth instrument of ratification or instrument of accession, the present Covenant shall enter into force three months after the date of the deposit of its own instrument of ratification or instrument of accession.

Article 28: The provisions of the present Covenant shall extend to all parts of federal States without any limitations or exceptions.

Article 29: Any State Party to the present Covenant may propose an amendment and file it with the Secretary-General of the United Nations. The Secretary-General shall thereupon communicate any proposed amendments to the States Parties to the present Covenant with a request that they notify him whether they favour a conference of States Parties for the purpose of considering and voting upon the proposals. In the event that at least one-third of the States Parties favours such a conference, the Secretary-General shall convene the conference under the auspices of the United Nations. Any amendment adopted by a majority of the States Parties present and voting at the conference shall be submitted to the General Assembly of the United Nations for approval.

Article 30: Irrespective of the notifications made under Article 26, paragraph 5, the Secretary-General of the United Nations shall inform all States referred to in paragraph I of the same article of the following particulars: (a) Signatures, ratifications and accessions under Article 26; (b) The date of the entry into force of the present Covenant under Article 27 and the date of the entry into force of any amendments under Article 29.

Article 31: The present Covenant, of which the Chinese, English, French, Russian and Spanish texts are equally authentic, shall be deposited in the archives of the United Nations.

Convention on the Elimination of all Forms of Discrimination against Women

'The Convention on the Elimination of all Forms of Discrimination against Women (CEDAW) is an international treaty adopted in 1979 by the United Nations General Assembly. Described as an international bill of rights for women, it was instituted on 3rd September 1981 and has been ratified by 189 states. The Convention defines discrimination against women in the following terms: "*Any distinction, exclusion or restriction made on the basis of sex which has the effect or purpose of impairing or nullifying the recognition, enjoyment or exercise by women, irrespective of their marital status, on a basis of equality of men and women, of human rights and fundamental freedoms in the political, economic, social, cultural, civil or any other field.*" It also establishes an agenda of action for putting an end to sex-based discrimination. States must take measures to seek to eliminate prejudices and customs based on the idea of the inferiority or the superiority of one sex or on stereotyped role for men and women. The six UN member states that have not ratified or acceded to the convention are Iran, Palau, Somalia, Sudan, Tonga and the United States.'[18]

International Convention on the Elimination of All Forms of Racial Discrimination

'It is a United Nations convention. A third-generation human rights instrument, the Convention commits its members to the elimination of racial discrimination and the promotion of understanding among all races. The Convention includes an individual complaints mechanism, effectively making it enforceable against its parties. This has led to the development of a limited jurisprudence on the interpretation and implementation of the Convention. The convention was adopted and opened for signature by the United Nations General Assembly on 21 December 1965. The Convention is monitored by the Committee on the Elimination of Racial Discrimination. A number of parties have made reservations and interpretative declarations to their application of the Convention.'[19]

Convention on the Rights of Persons with Disabilities

'The Convention on the Rights of Persons with Disabilities is an international human rights treaty of the United Nations intended to protect the rights and dignity of persons with disabilities. Parties to the Convention are required to promote, protect and ensure the full enjoyment of human rights by persons with disabilities and ensure that they enjoy full equality under the law. The text was adopted by the United Nations General Assembly on 13th December 2006 and opened for signature on 30th March 2007. Following ratification by the 20th party, it came into force on 3rd May 2008. The Convention is monitored by the Committee on the Rights of Persons with Disabilities. The Convention defines reasonable accommodation to be necessary and appropriate modification and adjustments not imposing a disproportionate or undue burden, where needed in a particular case, to ensure to persons with disabilities the enjoyment or exercise on an equal basis with others of all human rights and fundamental freedoms" at the Article 2 and demands this all aspects of life including inclusive education.

The Convention states that persons with disabilities should be guaranteed the right to inclusive education at all levels, regardless of age, without discrimination and on the basis of equal opportunity. Article 26 of the Convention affirms that *"States Parties shall take effective and appropriate measures, including through peer support, to enable persons with disabilities to attain and maintain maximum independence, full physical, mental, social and vocational ability and full inclusion and participation in all aspects of life."* The Convention on the Right of Persons with Disabilities recognised that disability results from the interaction between persons with impairments and attitudinal and environmental barriers that hinders their full and effective participation in society on an equal basis with others and that persons with disabilities continue to face barriers in their participation as equal members of society.'[20]

Convention on the Rights of Persons with Disabilities and Optional Protocol

Article 1. Purpose: The purpose of the present Convention is to promote, protect and ensure the full and equal enjoyment of all human rights and fundamental freedoms by all persons with disabilities and to promote respect for their inherent dignity. Persons with disabilities include those who have long-term physical, mental, intellectual or sensory impairments which in interaction with various barriers may hinder their full and effective participation in society on an equal basis with others.

Article 2. Definitions: For the purposes of the present Convention: "Communication" includes languages, display of text, Braille, tactile communication, large print, accessible multimedia as well as written, audio, plain-language, human-reader and augmentative and alternative modes, means and formats of communication, including accessible information and communication technology; "Language" includes spoken and signed languages and other forms of non-spoken languages."Discrimination on the basis of disability" means any distinction, exclusion or restriction on the basis of disability which has the purpose or effect of impairing or nullifying the recognition, enjoyment or exercise, on an equal basis with others, of all human rights and fundamental freedoms in the political, economic, social, cultural, civil or any other field. It includes all forms of discrimination, including denial of reasonable accommodation; "Reasonable accommodation" means necessary and appropriate modification and adjustments not imposing a disproportionate or undue burden, where needed in a particular case, to ensure to persons with disabilities the enjoyment or exercise on an equal basis with others of all human rights and fundamental freedoms; "Universal design" means the design of products, environments, programmes and services to be usable by all people, to the greatest extent possible, without the need for adaptation or specialised design. "Universal design" shall not exclude assistive devices for particular groups of persons with disabilities where this is needed.

Article 3. General principles: The principles of the present Convention shall be: (*a*) Respect for inherent dignity, individual autonomy including the freedom to make one's own choices and independence of persons; (*b*) Non-discrimination; (*c*) Full and effective participation and inclusion in society; (*d*) Respect for difference and acceptance of persons with disabilities as part of human diversity and humanity; (*e*) Equality of opportunity; (*f*) Accessibility; (*g*) Equality between men and women; (*h*) Respect for the evolving capacities of children with disabilities and respect for the right of children with disabilities to preserve their identities.

Article 4. General obligations: States Parties undertake to ensure and promote the full realisation of all human rights and fundamental freedoms for all persons with disabilities without discrimination of any kind on the basis of disability. With regard to economic, social and cultural rights, each State Party undertakes to take measures to the maximum of its available resources and, where needed, within the framework of international cooperation, with a view to achieving progressively the full realisation of these rights, without prejudice to those obligations contained in the present Convention that are immediately applicable according to international law. In the development and implementation of legislation and policies to implement the present Convention and in other decision-making processes concerning issues relating to persons with disabilities, States Parties shall closely consult with and actively involve persons with disabilities, including children with disabilities, through their representative organisations. The provisions of the present Convention shall extend to all parts of federal States without any limitations or exceptions.

Article 5. Equality and non-discrimination: States Parties recognise that all persons are equal before and under the law and are entitled without any discrimination to the equal protection and equal benefit of the law. States Parties shall prohibit all discrimination on the basis of disability and guarantee to persons with disabilities equal and effective legal protection against discrimination on all grounds. In order to promote equality and eliminate discrimination, States Parties shall take all appropriate steps to ensure that reasonable accommodation is provided. Specific measures which are necessary to accelerate or achieve de facto equality of persons with disabilities shall not be considered discrimination under the terms of the present Convention.

Article 6. Women with disabilities: States Parties recognise that women and girls with disabilities are subject to multiple discrimination and in this regard shall take measures to ensure the full and equal enjoyment by them of all human rights and fundamental freedoms. States Parties shall take all appropriate measures to ensure the full development, advancement and empowerment of women, for the purpose of guaranteeing them the exercise and enjoyment of the human rights and fundamental freedoms set out in the present Convention.

Article 7. Children with disabilities: States Parties shall take all necessary measures to ensure the full enjoyment by children with disabilities of all human rights and fundamental freedoms on an equal basis with other children. In all actions concerning children with disabilities, the best interests of the child shall be a primary consideration. States Parties shall ensure that children with disabilities have the right to express their views freely on all matters affecting them, their views being given due weight in accordance with their age and maturity, on an equal basis with other children and to be provided with disability and age-appropriate assistance to realise that right.

Article 8. Awareness-raising: States Parties undertake to adopt immediate, effective and appropriate measures: (*a*) To raise awareness throughout society, including at the family level, regarding persons with disabilities and to foster respect for the rights and dignity of persons with disabilities; (*b*) To combat stereotypes, prejudices and harmful practices relating to persons with disabilities, including those based on sex and age, in all areas of life; (*c*) To promote awareness of the capabilities and contributions of persons with disabilities. Measures to this end include: (*a*) Initiating and maintaining effective public awareness campaigns designed: (i) To nurture receptiveness to the rights of persons with disabilities; (ii) To promote positive perceptions and greater social awareness towards persons with disabilities; (iii) To promote recognition of the skills, merits and abilities of persons with disabilities and of their contributions to the workplace and the labour market; (*b*) Fostering at all levels of the education system, including in all children from an early age, an attitude of respect for the rights of persons with disabilities; (*c*) Encouraging all organs of the media to portray persons with disabilities in a manner consistent with the purpose of the present Convention; (d) Promoting awareness-training programmes regarding persons with disabilities and the rights of persons with disabilities.

Article 9. Accessibility: To enable persons with disabilities to live independently and participate fully in all aspects of life, States Parties shall take appropriate measures to ensure to persons with disabilities access, on an equal basis with others, to the physical environment, to transportation, to information and communications, including information and communications technologies and systems and to other facilities and services open or provided to the public, both in urban and in rural areas. These measures, which shall include the identification and elimination of obstacles and barriers to accessibility, shall apply to, inter alia: (*a*) Buildings, roads, transportation and other indoor and outdoor facilities, including schools, housing, medical facilities and workplaces; (*b*) Information, communications and other services, including electronic services and emergency services. States Parties shall also take appropriate measures: (*a*) To develop, promulgate and monitor the implementation of minimum standards and guidelines for the accessibility of facilities and services open or provided to the public; (*b*) To ensure that private entities that offer facilities and services which are open or provided to the public take into account all aspects of accessibility for persons with disabilities; (*c*) To provide training for stakeholders on accessibility issues facing persons with disabilities; (*d*) To provide in buildings and other facilities open to the public signage in Braille and in easy to read and understand forms; (*e*) To provide forms of live assistance and intermediaries, including guides, readers and professional sign language interpreters, to facilitate accessibility to buildings and other facilities open to the public; (*f*) To promote other appropriate forms of assistance and support to persons with disabilities to ensure their access to information; (*g*) To promote access for persons with disabilities to new information and communications technologies and systems, including the Internet; (*h*) To promote the design, development, production and distribution of accessible information and communications technologies and systems at an early stage, so that these technologies and systems become accessible at minimum cost.

Article 10. Right to life: States Parties reaffirm that every human being has the inherent right to life and shall take all necessary measures to ensure its effective enjoyment by persons with disabilities on an equal basis with others.

Article 11. Situations of risk and humanitarian emergencies: States Parties shall take, in accordance with their obligations under international law, including international humanitarian law and international human rights law, all necessary measures to ensure the protection and safety of persons with disabilities in situations of risk, including situations of armed conflict, humanitarian emergencies and the occurrence of natural disasters.

Article 12. Equal recognition before the law: States Parties reaffirm that persons with disabilities have the right to recognition everywhere as persons before the law. States Parties shall recognise that persons with disabilities enjoy legal capacity on an equal basis with others in all aspects of life. States Parties shall take appropriate measures to provide access by persons with disabilities to the support they may require in exercising their legal capacity. States Parties shall ensure that all measures that relate to the exercise of legal capacity provide for appropriate and effective safeguards to prevent abuse in accordance with international human rights law. Such safeguards shall ensure that measures relating to the exercise of legal capacity respect the rights, will and preferences of the person, are free of conflict of interest and undue influence, are proportional and tailored to the person's circumstances, apply for the shortest time possible and are subject to regular review by a competent, independent and impartial authority or judicial body. The safeguards shall be proportional to the degree to which such measures affect the person's rights and interests. Subject to the provisions of this article, States Parties shall take all appropriate and effective measures to ensure the equal right of persons with disabilities to own or inherit property, to control their own financial affairs and to have equal access to bank loans, mortgages and other forms of financial credit and shall ensure that persons with disabilities are not arbitrarily deprived of their property.

Article 13. Access to justice: States Parties shall ensure effective access to justice for persons with disabilities on an equal basis with others, including through the provision of procedural and age-appropriate accommodations, in order to facilitate their effective role as direct and indirect participants, including as witnesses, in all legal proceedings, including at investigative and other preliminary stages. In order to help to ensure effective access to justice for persons with disabilities, States Parties shall promote appropriate training for those working in the field of administration of justice, including police and prison staff.

Article 14. Liberty and security of person: States Parties shall ensure that persons with disabilities, on an equal basis with others: (*a*) Enjoy the right to liberty and security of person; (*b*) Are not deprived of their liberty unlawfully or arbitrarily and that any deprivation of liberty is in conformity with the law and that the existence of a disability shall in no case justify a deprivation of liberty. States Parties shall ensure that if persons with disabilities are deprived of their liberty through any process, they are, on an equal basis with others, entitled to guarantees in accordance with international human rights law and shall be treated in compliance with the objectives and principles of the present Convention, including by provision of reasonable accommodation.

Article 15. Freedom from torture or cruel, inhuman or degrading treatment or punishment: No one shall be subjected to torture or to cruel, inhuman or degrading treatment or punishment. In particular, no one shall be subjected without his or her free consent to medical or scientific experimentation. States Parties shall take all effective legislative, administrative, judicial or other measures to prevent persons with disabilities, on an equal basis with others, from being subjected to torture or cruel, inhuman or degrading treatment or punishment.

Article 16. Freedom from exploitation, violence and abuse: States Parties shall take all appropriate legislative, administrative, social, educational and other measures to protect persons with disabilities, both within and outside the home, from all forms of exploitation, violence and abuse, including their gender-based aspects. States Parties shall also take all appropriate measures to prevent all forms of exploitation, violence and abuse by ensuring, inter alia, appropriate forms of gender- and age-sensitive assistance and support for persons with disabilities and their families and caregivers, including through the provision of information and education on how to avoid, recognise and report instances of exploitation, violence and abuse. States Parties shall ensure that protection services are age-, gender- and disability-sensitive. In order to prevent the occurrence of all forms of exploitation, violence and abuse, States Parties shall ensure that all facilities and programmes designed to serve persons with disabilities are effectively monitored by independent authorities. States Parties shall take all appropriate measures to promote the physical, cognitive and psychological recovery, rehabilitation and social reintegration of persons with disabilities who become victims of any form of exploitation, violence or abuse, including through the provision of protection services. Such recovery and reintegration shall take place in an environment that fosters the health, welfare, self-respect, dignity and autonomy of the person and takes into account gender- and age-specific needs. States Parties shall put in place effective legislation and policies, including women- and child-focused legislation and policies, to ensure that instances of exploitation, violence and abuse against persons with disabilities are identified, investigated and, where appropriate, prosecuted.

Article 17. Protecting the integrity of the person: Every person with disabilities has a right to respect for his or her physical and mental integrity on an equal basis with others.

Article 18. Liberty of movement and nationality: States Parties shall recognise the rights of persons with disabilities to liberty of movement, to freedom to choose their residence and to a nationality, on an equal basis with others, including by ensuring that persons with disabilities: (a) Have the right to acquire and change a nationality and are not deprived of their nationality arbitrarily or on the basis of disability; (b) Are not deprived, on the basis of disability, of their ability to obtain, possess and utilise documentation of their nationality or other documentation of identification, or to utilise relevant processes such as immigration proceedings, that may be needed to facilitate exercise of the right to liberty of movement; (c) Are free to leave any country, including their own; (d) Are not deprived, arbitrarily or on the basis of disability, of the right to enter their own country. Children with disabilities shall be registered immediately after birth and shall have the right from birth to a name, the right to acquire a nationality and, as far as possible, the right to know and be cared for by their parents.

Article 19. Living independently and being included in the community: States Parties to the present Convention recognise the equal right of all persons with disabilities to live in the community, with choices equal to others and shall take effective and appropriate measures to facilitate full enjoyment by persons with disabilities of this right and their full inclusion and participation in the community, including by ensuring that: (a) Persons with disabilities have the opportunity to choose their place of residence and where and with whom they live on an equal basis with others and are not obliged to live in a particular living arrangement; (b) Persons with disabilities have access to a range of in-home, residential and other community support services, including personal assistance necessary to support living and inclusion in the community and to prevent isolation or segregation from the community; (c) Community services and facilities for the general population are available on an equal basis to persons with disabilities and are responsive to their needs.

Article 20. Personal mobility: States Parties shall take effective measures to ensure personal mobility with the greatest possible independence for persons with disabilities, including by: (a) Facilitating the personal mobility of persons with disabilities in the manner and at the time of their choice and at affordable cost; (b) Facilitating access by persons with disabilities to quality mobility aids, devices, assistive technologies and forms of live assistance and intermediaries, including by making them available at affordable cost; (c) Providing training in mobility skills to persons with disabilities and to specialist staff working with persons with disabilities; (d) Encouraging entities that produce mobility aids, devices and assistive technologies to take into account all aspects of mobility for persons with disabilities.

Article 21. Freedom of expression and opinion and access to information: States Parties shall take all appropriate measures to ensure that persons with disabilities can exercise the right to freedom of expression and opinion, including the freedom to seek, receive and impart information and ideas on an equal basis with others and through all forms of communication of their choice, as defined in Article 2 of the present Convention, including by: (a) Providing information intended for the general public to persons with disabilities in accessible formats and technologies appropriate to different kinds of disabilities in a timely manner and without additional cost; (b) Accepting and facilitating the use of sign languages, Braille, augmentative and alternative communication and all other accessible means, modes and formats of communication of their choice by persons with disabilities in official interactions; (c) Urging private entities that provide services to the general public, including through the Internet, to provide information and services in accessible and usable formats for persons with disabilities; (d) Encouraging the mass media, including providers of information through the Internet, to make their services accessible to persons with disabilities; (e) Recognising and promoting the use of sign languages.

Article 22. Respect for privacy: No person with disabilities, regardless of place of residence or living arrangements, shall be subjected to arbitrary or unlawful interference with his or her privacy, family, home or correspondence or other types of communication or to unlawful attacks on his or her honour and reputation. Persons with disabilities have the right to the protection of the law against such interference or attacks. States Parties shall protect the privacy of personal, health and rehabilitation information of persons with disabilities on an equal basis with others.

Article 23. Respect for home and the family: States Parties shall take effective and appropriate measures to eliminate discrimination against persons with disabilities in all matters relating to marriage, family, parenthood and relationships, on an equal basis with others, so as to ensure that: (*a*) The right of all persons with disabilities who are of marriageable age to marry and to found a family on the basis of free and full consent of the intending spouses is recognised; (*b*) The rights of persons with disabilities to decide freely and responsibly on the number and spacing of their children and to have access to age-appropriate information, reproductive and family planning education are recognised and the means necessary to enable them to exercise these rights are provided; (c) Persons with disabilities, including children, retain their fertility on an equal basis with others. States Parties shall ensure the rights and responsibilities of persons with disabilities, with regard to guardianship, wardship, trusteeship, adoption of children or similar institutions, where these concepts exist in national legislation; in all cases the best interests of the child shall be paramount. States Parties shall render appropriate assistance to persons with disabilities in the performance of their child-rearing responsibilities. States Parties shall ensure that children with disabilities have equal rights with respect to family life. With a view to realising these rights and to prevent concealment, abandonment, neglect and segregation of children with disabilities, States Parties shall undertake to provide early and comprehensive information, services and support to children with disabilities and their families. States Parties shall ensure that a child shall not be separated from his or her parents against their will, except when competent authorities subject to judicial review determine, in accordance with applicable law and procedures, that such separation is necessary for the best interests of the child. In no case shall a child be separated from parents on the basis of a disability of either the child or one or both of the parents. States Parties shall, where the immediate family is unable to care for a child with disabilities, undertake every effort to provide alternative care within the wider family and failing that, within the community in a family setting.

Article 24. Education: States Parties recognise the right of persons with disabilities to education. In realising this right, States Parties shall ensure that: (a) Persons with disabilities are not excluded from the general education system on the basis of disability and that children with disabilities are not excluded from free and compulsory primary education, or from secondary education, on the basis of disability; (b) Persons with disabilities can access an inclusive, quality and free primary education and secondary education on an equal basis with others in the communities in which they live; (c) Reasonable accommodation of the individual's requirements is provided; (d) Persons with disabilities receive the support required, within the general education system, to facilitate their effective education; (e) Effective individualised support measures are provided in environments that maximise academic and social development, consistent with the goal of full inclusion. States Parties shall enable persons with disabilities to learn life and social development skills to facilitate their full and equal participation in education and as members of the community. To this end, States Parties shall take appropriate measures, including: (a) Facilitating the learning of Braille, alternative script, augmentative and alternative modes, means and formats of communication and orientation and mobility skills and facilitating peer support and mentoring; (b) Facilitating the learning of sign language and the promotion of the linguistic identity of the deaf community; (c) Ensuring that the education of persons and in particular children, who are blind, deaf or deaf blind, is delivered in the most appropriate languages and modes and means of communication for the individual and in environments which maximise academic and social development. In order to help ensure the realisation of this right, States Parties shall take appropriate measures to employ teachers, including teachers with disabilities, who are qualified in sign language and/or Braille and to train professionals and staff who work at all levels of education. Such training shall incorporate disability awareness and the use of appropriate augmentative and alternative modes, means and formats of communication, educational techniques and materials to support persons with disabilities. States Parties shall ensure that persons with disabilities are able to access general tertiary education, vocational training, adult education and lifelong learning without discrimination and on an equal basis with others. To this end, States Parties shall ensure that reasonable accommodation is provided to persons with disabilities.

Article 25. Health: States Parties recognise that persons with disabilities have the right to the enjoyment of the highest attainable standard of health without discrimination on the basis of disability. States Parties shall take all appropriate measures to ensure access for persons with disabilities to health services that are gender-sensitive, including health-related rehabilitation. In particular, States Parties shall: (a) Provide persons with disabilities with the same range, quality and standard of free or affordable healthcare and programmes as provided to other persons, including in the area of sexual and reproductive health and population-based public health programmes; (b) Provide those health services needed by persons with disabilities specifically because of their disabilities, including early identification and intervention as appropriate and services designed to minimise and prevent further disabilities, including among children and older persons. (c) Provide these health services as close as possible to people's own communities, including in rural areas; (d) Require health professionals to provide care of the same quality to persons with disabilities as to others, including on the basis of free and informed consent by, inter alia, raising awareness of the human rights, dignity, autonomy and needs of persons with disabilities through training and the promulgation of ethical standards for public and private healthcare; (e) Prohibit discrimination against persons with disabilities in the provision of health insurance and life insurance where such insurance is permitted by national law, which shall be provided in a fair and reasonable manner; (f) Prevent discriminatory denial of healthcare or health services or food and fluids on the basis of disability.

Article 26. Habilitation and rehabilitation: States Parties shall take effective and appropriate measures, including through peer support, to enable persons with disabilities to attain and maintain maximum independence, full physical, mental, social and vocational ability and full inclusion and participation in all aspects of life. To that end, States Parties shall organise, strengthen and extend comprehensive habilitation and rehabilitation services and programmes, particularly in the areas of health, employment, education and social services, in such a way that these services and programmes: (a) Begin at the earliest possible stage and are based on the multidisciplinary assessment of individual needs and strengths; (b) Support participation and inclusion in the community and all aspects of society, are voluntary and are available to persons with disabilities as close as possible to their own communities, including in rural areas. States Parties shall promote the development of initial and continuing training for professionals and staff working in habilitation and rehabilitation services. States Parties shall promote the availability, knowledge and use of assistive devices and technologies, designed for persons with disabilities, as they relate to habilitation and rehabilitation.

Article 27. Work and employment: States Parties recognise the right of persons with disabilities to work, on an equal basis with others; this includes the right to the opportunity to gain a living by work freely chosen or accepted in a labour market and work environment that is open, inclusive and accessible to persons with disabilities. States Parties shall safeguard and promote the realisation of the right to work, including for those who acquire a disability during the course of employment, by taking appropriate steps, including through legislation, to, inter alia: (a) Prohibit discrimination on the basis of disability with regard to all matters concerning all forms of employment, including conditions of recruitment, hiring and employment, continuance of employment, career advancement and safe and healthy working conditions; (b) Protect the rights of persons with disabilities, on an equal basis with others, to just and favourable conditions of work, including equal opportunities and equal remuneration for work of equal value, safe and healthy working conditions, including protection from harassment and the redress of grievances; (c) Ensure that persons with disabilities are able to exercise their labour and trade union rights on an equal basis with others; (d) Enable persons with disabilities to have effective access to general technical and vocational guidance programmes, placement services and vocational and continuing training; (e) Promote employment opportunities and career advancement for persons with disabilities in the labour market, as well as assistance in finding, obtaining, maintaining and returning to employment; (f) Promote opportunities for self-employment, entrepreneurship, the development of cooperatives and starting one's own business; (g) Employ persons with disabilities in the public sector; (h) Promote the employment of persons with disabilities in the private sector through appropriate policies and measures, which may include affirmative action programmes, incentives and other measures; (i) Ensure that reasonable accommodation is provided to persons with disabilities in the workplace; (j) Promote the acquisition by persons with disabilities of work experience in the open labour market; (k) Promote vocational and professional rehabilitation, job retention and return-to-work programmes for persons with disabilities. States Parties shall ensure that persons with disabilities are not held in slavery or in servitude and are protected, on an equal basis with others, from forced or compulsory labour.

Article 28. Adequate standard of living and social protection: States Parties recognise the right of persons with disabilities to an adequate standard of living for themselves and their families, including adequate food, clothing and housing and to the continuous improvement of living conditions and shall take appropriate steps to safeguard and promote the realisation of this right without discrimination on the basis of disability. States Parties recognise the right of persons with disabilities to social protection and to the enjoyment of that right without discrimination on the basis of disability and shall take appropriate steps to safeguard and promote the realisation of this right, including measures: (a) To ensure equal access by persons with disabilities to clean water services and to ensure access to appropriate and affordable services, devices and other assistance for disability-related needs; (b) To ensure access by persons with disabilities, in particular women and girls with disabilities and older persons with disabilities, to social protection programmes and poverty reduction programmes; (c) To ensure access by persons with disabilities and their families living in situations of poverty to assistance from the State with disability related expenses, including adequate training, counselling, financial assistance and respite care; (d) To ensure access by persons with disabilities to public housing programmes; (e) To ensure equal access by persons with disabilities to retirement benefits and programmes.

Article 29. Participation in political and public life: States Parties shall guarantee to persons with disabilities political rights and the opportunity to enjoy them on an equal basis with others and shall undertake: (a) To ensure that persons with disabilities can effectively and fully participate in political and public life on an equal basis with others, directly or through freely chosen representatives, including the right and opportunity for persons with disabilities to vote and be elected, inter alia, by: (i) Ensuring that voting procedures, facilities and materials are appropriate, accessible and easy to understand and use; (ii) Protecting the right of persons with disabilities to vote by secret ballot in elections and public referendums without intimidation and to stand for elections, to effectively hold office and perform all public functions at all levels of government, facilitating the use of assistive and new technologies where appropriate; (iii) Guaranteeing the free expression of the will of persons with disabilities as electors and to this end, where necessary, at their request, allowing assistance in voting by a person of their own choice. To promote actively an environment in which persons with disabilities can effectively and fully participate in the conduct of public affairs, without discrimination and on an equal basis with others and encourage their participation in public affairs, including: (a) Participation in non-governmental organisations and associations concerned with the public and political life of the country and in the activities and administration of political parties; (b) Forming and joining organisations of persons with disabilities to represent persons with disabilities at international, national, regional and local levels.

Article 30. Participation in cultural life, recreation, leisure and sport: States Parties recognise the right of persons with disabilities to take part on an equal basis with others in cultural life and shall take all appropriate measures to ensure that persons with disabilities: (a) Enjoy access to cultural materials in accessible formats; (b) Enjoy access to television programmes, films, theatre and other cultural activities, in accessible formats; (c) Enjoy access to places for cultural performances or services, such as theatres, museums, cinemas, libraries and tourism services and, as far as possible, enjoy access to monuments and sites of national cultural importance. States Parties shall take appropriate measures to enable persons with disabilities to have the opportunity to develop and utilise their creative, artistic and intellectual potential, not only for their own benefit, but also for the enrichment of society. States Parties shall take all appropriate steps, in accordance with international law, to ensure that laws protecting intellectual property rights do not constitute an unreasonable or discriminatory barrier to access by persons with disabilities to cultural materials. Persons with disabilities shall be entitled, on an equal basis with others, to recognition and support of their specific cultural and linguistic identity, including sign languages and deaf culture.With a view to enabling persons with disabilities to participate on an equal basis with others in recreational, leisure and sporting activities, States Parties shall take appropriate measures: (a) To encourage and promote the participation, to the fullest extent possible, of persons with disabilities in mainstream sporting activities at all levels; (b) To ensure that persons with disabilities have an opportunity to organise, develop and participate in disability-specific sporting and recreational activities and, to this end, encourage the provision, on an equal basis with others, of appropriate instruction, training and resources; (c) To ensure that persons with disabilities have access to sporting, recreational and tourism venues; (d) To ensure that children with disabilities have equal access with other children to participation in play, recreation and leisure and sporting activities, including those activities in the school system; (e) To ensure that persons with disabilities have access to services from those involved in the organisation of recreational, tourism, leisure and sporting activities.

Article 31. Statistics and data collection: States Parties undertake to collect appropriate information, including statistical and research data, to enable them to formulate and implement policies to give effect to the present Convention. The process of collecting and maintaining this information shall: (a) Comply with legally established safeguards, including legislation on data protection, to ensure confidentiality and respect for the privacy of persons with disabilities; (b) Comply with internationally accepted norms to protect human rights and fundamental freedoms and ethical principles in the collection and use of statistics. The information collected in accordance with this article shall be disaggregated, as appropriate and used to help assess the implementation of States Parties' obligations under the present Convention and to identify and address the barriers faced by persons with disabilities in exercising their rights. States Parties shall assume responsibility for the dissemination of these statistics and ensure their accessibility to persons with disabilities and others.

Article 32. International cooperation: States Parties recognise the importance of international cooperation and its promotion, in support of national efforts for the realisation of the purpose and objectives of the present Convention and will undertake appropriate and effective measures in this regard, between and among States and, as appropriate, in partnership with relevant international and regional organisations and civil society, in particular organisations of persons with disabilities. Such measures could include, inter alia: (a) Ensuring that international cooperation, including international development programmes, is inclusive of and accessible to persons with disabilities; (b) Facilitating and supporting capacity-building, including through the exchange and sharing of information, experiences, training programmes and best practices; Facilitating cooperation in research and access to scientific and technical knowledge; Providing, as appropriate, technical and economic assistance, including by facilitating access to and sharing of accessible and assistive technologies and through the transfer of technologies. The provisions of this article are without prejudice to the obligations of each State Party to fulfill its obligations under the present Convention.

Article 33. National implementation and monitoring: States Parties, in accordance with their system of organisation, shall designate one or more focal points within government for matters relating to the implementation of the present Convention and shall give due consideration to the establishment or designation of a coordination mechanism within government to facilitate related action in different sectors and at different levels. States Parties shall, in accordance with their legal and administrative systems, maintain, strengthen, designate or establish within the State Party, a framework, including one or more independent mechanisms, as appropriate, to promote, protect and monitor implementation of the present Convention. When designating or establishing such a mechanism, States Parties shall take into account the principles relating to the status and functioning of national institutions for protection and promotion of human rights. Civil society, in particular persons with disabilities and their representative organisations shall be involved and participate fully in the monitoring process.

Article 34. Committee on the Rights of Persons with Disabilities: There shall be established a Committee on the Rights of Persons with Disabilities, which shall carry out the functions hereinafter provided. The Committee shall consist, at the time of entry into force of the present

Convention, of twelve experts. After an additional sixty ratifications or accessions to the Convention, the membership of the Committee shall increase by six members, attaining a maximum number of eighteen members. The members of the Committee shall serve in their personal capacity and shall be of high moral standing and recognised competence and experience in the field covered by the present Convention. When nominating their candidates, States Parties are invited to give due consideration to the provision set out in Article 4, paragraph 3, of the present Convention. The members of the Committee shall be elected by States Parties, consideration being given to equitable geographical distribution, representation of the different forms of civilisation and of the principal legal systems, balanced gender representation and participation of experts with disabilities. The members of the Committee shall be elected by secret ballot from a list of persons nominated by the States Parties from among their nationals at meetings of the Conference of States Parties. At those meetings, for which two-thirds of States Parties shall constitute a quorum, the persons elected to the Committee shall be those who obtain the largest number of votes and an absolute majority of the votes of the representatives of States Parties present and voting. The initial election shall be held no later than six months after the date of entry into force of the present Convention. At least four months before the date of each election, the Secretary-General of the United Nations shall address a letter to the States Parties inviting them to submit the nominations within two months. The Secretary-General shall subsequently prepare a list in alphabetical order of all persons thus nominated, indicating the State Parties which have nominated them and shall submit it to the States Parties to the present Convention. The members of the Committee shall be elected for a term of four years. They shall be eligible for re-election once. However, the term of six of the members elected at the first election shall expire at the end of two years; immediately after the first election, the names of these six members shall be chosen by lot by the chairperson of the meeting referred to in paragraph 5 of this article. The election of the six additional members of the Committee shall be held on the occasion of regular elections, in accordance with the relevant provisions of this article. If a member of the Committee dies or resigns or declares that for any other cause she or he can no longer perform her or his duties, the State Party which nominated the member shall appoint another expert possessing the qualifications and meeting the requirements set out in the relevant provisions of this article, to serve for the remainder of the term. The Committee shall establish its own rules of procedure. The Secretary-General of the United Nations shall provide the necessary staff and facilities for the effective performance of the functions of the Committee under the present Convention and shall convene its initial meeting. With the approval of the General Assembly of the United Nations, the members of the Committee established under the present Convention shall receive emoluments from United Nations resources on such terms and conditions as the Assembly may decide, having regard to the importance of the Committee's responsibilities. The members of the Committee shall be entitled to the facilities, privileges and immunities of experts on mission for the United Nations as laiddown in the relevant sections of the Convention on the Privileges and Immunities of the United Nations.

Article 35. Reports by States Parties: Each State Party shall submit to the Committee, through the Secretary-General of the United Nations, a comprehensive report on measures taken to give effect to its obligations under the present Convention and on the progress made in that regard, within two years after the entry into force of the present Convention for the State Party concerned. Thereafter, States Parties shall submit subsequent reports at least every four years and further whenever the Committee so requests. The Committee shall decide any guidelines applicable to the content of the reports. A State Party which has submitted a comprehensive initial report to the Committee need not, in its subsequent reports, repeat information previously provided. When preparing reports to the Committee, States Parties are invited to consider doing so in an open and transparent process and to give due consideration to the provision set out in Article 4, paragraph 3, of the present Convention. Reports may indicate factors and difficulties affecting the degree of fulfillment of obligations under the present Convention.

Article 36. Consideration of reports: Each report shall be considered by the Committee, which shall make such suggestions and general recommendations on the report as it may consider appropriate and shall forward these to the State Party concerned. The State Party may respond with any information it chooses to the Committee. The Committee may request further information from States Parties relevant to the implementation of the present Convention. If a State Party is significantly overdue in the submission of a report, the Committee may notify the State Party concerned of the need to examine the implementation of the present Convention in that State Party, on the basis of reliable information available to the Committee, if the relevant report is not submitted within three months following the notification. The Committee shall invite the State Party concerned to participate in such examination. Should the State Party respond by submitting the relevant report, the provisions of paragraph 1 of this article will apply. The Secretary-General of the United Nations shall make available the reports to all States Parties. States Parties shall make their reports widely available to the public in their own countries and facilitate access to the suggestions and general recommendations relating to these reports. The Committee shall transmit, as it may consider appropriate, to the specialised agencies, funds and programmes of the United Nations and other competent bodies, reports from States Parties in order to address a request or indication of a need for technical advice or assistance contained therein, along with the Committee's observations and recommendations, if any, on these requests or indications.

Article 37. Cooperation between States Parties and the Committee: Each State Party shall cooperate with the Committee and assist its members in the fulfillment of their mandate. In its relationship with States Parties, the Committee shall give due consideration to ways and means of enhancing national capacities for the implementation of the present Convention, including through international cooperation.

Article 38. Relationship of the Committee with other bodies: In order to foster the effective implementation of the present Convention and to encourage international cooperation in the field covered by the present Convention: (a) The specialised agencies and other United Nations organs shall be entitled to be represented at the consideration of the implementation of such provisions of the present Convention as fall within the scope of their mandate. The Committee may invite the specialised agencies and other competent bodies as it may consider appropriate to provide expert advice on the implementation of the Convention in areas falling within the scope of their respective mandates. The Committee may invite specialised agencies and other United Nations organs to submit reports on the implementation of the Convention in areas falling within the scope of their activities; The Committee, as it discharges its mandate, shall consult, as appropriate, other relevant bodies instituted by international human rights treaties, with a view to ensuring the consistency of their respective reporting guidelines, suggestions and general recommendations and avoiding duplication and overlap in the performance of their functions.

Article 39. Report of the Committee: The Committee shall report every two years to the General Assembly and to the Economic and Social Council on its activities and may make suggestions and general recommendations based on the examination of reports and information received from the States Parties. Such suggestions and general recommendations shall be included in the report of the Committee together with comments, if any, from States Parties.

Article 40. Conference of States Parties: The States Parties shall meet regularly in a Conference of States Parties in order to consider any matter with regard to the implementation of the present Convention. No later than six months after the entry into force of the present

Convention, the Conference of States Parties shall be convened by the Secretary-General of the United Nations. The subsequent meetings shall be convened by the Secretary-General biennially or upon the decision of the Conference of States Parties.

Article 41. Depositary: The Secretary-General of the United Nations shall be the depositary of the present Convention.

Article 42. Signature: The present Convention shall be open for signature by all States and by regional integration organisations at United Nations Headquarters in New York as of 30 March 2007.

Article 43. Consent to be bound: The present Convention shall be subject to ratification by signatory States and to formal confirmation by signatory regional integration organisations. It shall be open for accession by any State or regional integration organisation which has not signed the Convention.

Article 44. Regional integration organisations: "Regional integration organisation" shall mean an organisation constituted by sovereign States of a given region, to which its member States have transferred competence in respect of matters governed by the present Convention. Such organisations shall declare, in their instruments of formal confirmation or accession, the extent of their competence with respect to matters governed by the present Convention. Subsequently, they shall inform the depositary of any substantial modification in the extent of their competence. References to "States Parties" in the present Convention shall apply to such organisations within the limits of their competence. For the purposes of Article 45, paragraph 1 and Article 47, paragraphs 2 and 3, of the present Convention, any instrument deposited by a regional integration organisation shall not be counted. Regional integration organisations, in matters within their competence, may exercise their right to vote in the Conference of States Parties, with a number of votes equal to the number of their member States that are Parties to the present Convention. Such an organisation shall not exercise its right to vote if any of its member States exercises its right and vice versa.

Article 45. Entry into force: The present Convention shall enter into force on the thirtieth day after the deposit of the twentieth instrument of ratification or accession. For each State or regional integration organisation ratifying, formally confirming or acceding to the present Convention after the deposit of the twentieth such instrument, the Convention shall enter into force on the thirtieth day after the deposit of its own such instrument.

Article 46. Reservations: Reservations incompatible with the object and purpose of the present Convention shall not be permitted. Reservations may be withdrawn at any time.

Article 47. Amendments: Any State Party may propose an amendment to the present Convention and submit it to the Secretary-General of the United Nations. The Secretary-General shall communicate any proposed amendments to States Parties, with a request to be notified whether they favour a conference of States Parties for the purpose of considering and deciding upon the proposals. In the event that, within four months from the date of such communication, at least one-third of the States Parties favour such a conference, the Secretary-General shall convene the conference under the auspices of the United Nations. Any amendment adopted by a majority of two-thirds of the States Parties present and voting shall be submitted by the Secretary-General to the General Assembly of the United Nations for approval and thereafter to all States Parties for acceptance. An amendment adopted and approved in accordance with paragraph 1 of this article shall enter into force on the thirtieth day after the number of instruments of acceptance deposited reaches two-thirds of the number of States Parties at the date of adoption of the amendment. Thereafter, the amendment shall enter into force for any State Party on the thirtieth day following the deposit of its own instrument of acceptance. An amendment shall be binding only on those States Parties which have accepted it. If so decided by the Conference of States Parties by consensus, an amendment adopted and approved in accordance with paragraph 1 of this article which relates exclusively to Articles 34, 38, 39 and 40 shall enter into force for all States Parties on the thirtieth day after the number of instruments of acceptance deposited reaches two-thirds of the number of States Parties at the date of adoption of the amendment.

Article 48. Denunciation: A State Party may denounce the present Convention by written notification to the Secretary-General of the United Nations. The denunciation shall become effective one year after the date of receipt of the notification by the Secretary-General.

Article 49. Accessible format: The text of the present Convention shall be made available in accessible formats.

Article 50. Authentic texts: The Arabic, Chinese, English, French, Russian and Spanish texts of the present Convention shall be equally authentic. IN WITNESS THEREOF the undersigned plenipotentiaries, being duly authorised thereto by their respective Governments, have signed the present Convention.

Source: http://www.un.org/disabilities/documents/convention/convoptprot-e.pdf

United Nations Convention against Torture

'It is an international human rights treaty, under the review of the United Nations that aims to prevent torture and other acts of cruel, inhuman, or degrading treatment or punishment around the world. The Convention requires states to take effective measures to prevent torture in any territory under their jurisdiction and forbids states to transport people to any country where there is reason to believe they will be tortured. The Committee against Torture (CAT) is a body of human rights experts that monitors implementation of the Convention by State parties. The Committee is one of eight UN-linked human rights treaty bodies. All state parties are obliged under the Convention to submit regular reports to the CAT on how rights are being implemented. Upon ratifying the Convention, states must submit a report within one year, after which they are obliged to report every four years. The CAT usually meets in April/May and November each year in Geneva.'[21]

International Convention on the Protection of the Rights of All Migrant Workers and Members of Their Families

'It is a United Nations multilateral treaty governing the protection of migrant workers and families. Signed on 18 December 1990, it entered into force on 1st July 2003 after the threshold of 20 ratifying States was reached in March 2003. The United Nations Convention constitutes a comprehensive international treaty regarding the protection of migrant workers' rights. It emphasises the connection between migration and human rights, which is increasingly becoming a crucial policy topic worldwide. The Convention aims at protecting migrant workers and members of their families; its existence sets a moral standard and serves as a guide and stimulus for the promotion of migrant rights in each country. The Convention proposes that actions be taken to eradicate clandestine movements, notably through the fight against misleading information inciting people to migrate irregularly and through sanctions against traffickers and employers of undocumented migrants.'[22]

Convention on the Rights of the Child

'The United Nations Convention on the Rights of the Child is a human rights treaty which sets out the civil, political, economic, social, health and cultural rights of children. The Convention deals with the child-specific needs and rights. It requires that states act in the best interests of the child. The Convention acknowledges that every child has certain basic rights, including the right to life, his or her own name and identity, to be raised by his or her parents within a family or cultural grouping and to have a relationship with both parents, even if they are separated. The Convention obliges states to allow parents to exercise their parental responsibilities. The Convention also acknowledges that children have the right to express their opinions and to have those opinions heard and acted upon when appropriate, to be protected from abuse or exploitation and to have their privacy protected and it requires that their lives not be subject to excessive interference. The Convention forbids capital punishment for children. The Convention also obliges signatory states to provide separate legal representation for a child in any judicial dispute concerning their care and asks that the child's viewpoint be heard in such cases.'[23]

Conclusion

Human Rights are the minimum rights which are compulsorily obtainable by every individual as he/she is a member of human society. But it has been found that each and every right of the women is being violated in one or another way. Human rights are rights inherent to all human beings, whatever our nationality, place of residence, sex, national or ethnic origin, colour, religion, language, or any other status. The crimes against women in India are increasing at a very fast pace. In 1948, the Universal Declaration of Human Rights brought human rights into the realm of international law. Since then, the Organisation has diligently protected human rights through legal instruments and on-the-ground activities. The Office of the UN High Commissioner for Human Rights has lead responsibility in the UN system for the promotion and protection of human rights. Since its conception, Human Rights and value for life is a universal doctrine grounded on comprehensive high moral and intellectual values. Probably, rights and values are best reflected in our nation when the crusader's objective based on their ideologies marries with their level of interest.

References

1. See http://www.humanrights.com/what-are-human-rights/violations-of-human-rights/article-3.html
2. Protect the human rights, Retrieved from http://www.un.org/en/sections/what-we-do/protect-human-rights/index.html
3. See http://www.ohchr.org/EN/Issues/Pages/WhatareHuman Rights.aspx
4. Human rights basics, Retrieved from http://www.amnestyusa.org/research/human-rights-basics
5. Human rights: Nature and constituents, Retrieved from http://www.mu.ac.in/myweb_test/SYBA%20Study%20Material/fc.pdf
6. What are human rights? Retrieved from http://www1.umn.edu/humanrts/edumat/hreduseries/hereandnow/Part-1/whatare.htm
7. See http://examples.yourdictionary.com/examples-of-human-rights.html
8. http://indiaopines.com/cases-human-rights-violation-oblivious-india/
9. See http://www.thefreedictionary.com/human+rights

10. What are human rights? Retrieved from http://www1.umn.edu/humanrts/edumat/hreduseries/hereandnow/Part-1/whatare.htm
11. Commission Website: Information for Students - Human Rights Essentials - Resource Sheet: What are Human Rights? Retrieved from https://www.humanrights.gov.au/commission-website-information-students-human-rights-essentials-resource-sheet-what-are-human-rights
12. Information for Students: Human Rights Essentials - Important info you should know about human rights, Retrieved from https://www.humanrights.gov.au/information-students-human-rights-essentials-important-info-you-should-know-about-human-rights
13. The importance of equality and human rights to your organisation, Retrieved from http://www.scottishhumanrights.com/eqhria/eqhriatrainingimporg
14. National Human Rights Commission (2014), Retrieved from http://en.wikipedia.org/wiki National_Human_ Rights_ Commission_ of_India
15. Universal Declaration of Human Rights (2014), Retrieved from http://en.wikipedia.org/wiki/Universal_Declaration_of_Human_Rights
16. International Covenant on Civil and Political Rights (2014), Retrieved from http://en.wikipedia.org/wiki/International_Covenant_on_Civil_and_Political_Rights
17. International Covenant on Economic, Social and Cultural Rights (2014), Retrieved from http://en.wikipedia.org/wiki/International_Covenant_on_Economic,_Social_and_Cultural_Rights
18. Convention on the Elimination of all Forms of Discrimination Against Women (2014), Retrieved from http://en.wikipedia.org/wiki/Convention_on_the_Elimination_of_All_Forms_of_Discrimination_ Against_Women
19. International Convention on the Elimination of All Forms of Racial Discrimination (2014), Retrieved from http://en.wikipedia.org/wiki/International_Convention_on_the_ Elimination_of_All_Forms_of_Racial_Discrimination
20. Convention on the Rights of Persons with Disabilities (2014), Retrieved from http://en.wikipedia.org/wiki/Convention_on_the_ Rights_of_ Persons_with_Disabilities
21. United Nations Convention against Torture (2014), Retrieved from http://en.wikipedia.org/wiki/United_Nations_ Convention_against_Torture

22. International Convention on the Protection of the Rights of All Migrant Workers and Members of Their Families (2014), Retrieved from http://en.wikipedia.org/wiki/International_Convention_on_the_Protection_of_the_Rights_of_All_ Migrant_Workers_and_Members_of_Their_Families

23. Convention on the Rights of the Child (2015), Retrieved from http://en.wikipedia.org/wiki/Convention_on_ the_ Rights_of_the_Child

Part II: Violation of Women Rights

8

Force Marriage

"A woman has two smiles that an angel might envy, the smile that accepts a lover before words are uttered and the smile that lights on the first born babe and assures it of a mother's love."

—*Thomas Chandler Haliburton*

Introduction

'Birth, marriage and death are the key events in most people's lives. But only one, marriage is a matter of choice. Customs surrounding marriage, including the desirable age and the way in which a spouse is selected, depend on a society's view of the family – its role, structure, pattern of life and the individual and collective responsibilities of its members. The idea and function of 'family' varies across the world and is in a state of constant evolution. Early marriage is one way to ensure that a wife is 'protected', or placed firmly under male control; that she is submissive to her husband and works hard for her in-laws' household; that the children she bears are 'legitimate'; and that bonds of affection between couples do not undermine the family unit. Poverty is one of the major factors underpinning early marriage.'[1]

'According to wikipedia, marriage is a socially or ritually recognised union or legal contract between spouses that establishes rights and obligations between them. Individuals may marry for several reasons, including legal, social, libidinal, emotional, financial, spiritual and religious purposes. It can be recognised by a state, an organisation, a religious authority, a tribal group, a local community or peers. Since the late twentieth century, major social changes in Western countries have led to changes in the demographics of marriage, with the age of first marriage increasing, fewer people marrying and more couples choosing to cohabit rather than marry. Cohabitation is an arrangement where two people who is not married live together in an emotionally and/or sexually intimate relationship on a long-term or permanent basis.

Marriage can be classified in various ways. Monogamy is a form of marriage in which an individual has only one spouse during their lifetime or at any one time. Governments that support monogamy may allow easy divorce. Polygamy is a marriage which includes more than two partners. When a man is married to more than one wife at a time, the relationship is called polygyny and there is no marriage bond between the wives; and when a woman is married to more than one husband at a time, it is called polyandry and there is no marriage bond between the husbands. If a marriage includes multiple husbands and wives, it can be called group marriage. In many Western cultures, marriage usually leads to the formation of a new household comprising the married couple, with the married couple living together in the same home, often sharing the same bed, but in some other cultures this is not the tradition.'[2]

Meaning of the Concept

'Forced marriage is a marriage in which one or both of the parties are married without his or her consent or against his or her will. It is a form of child/domestic abuse and violence against women; it should form part of existing child and adult protection structures, policies and procedures. As defined in the Children Acts 1989 and 2004, child means a person who has not reached their eighteenth birthday. This includes young people aged 16 and 17 who are living independently; their status and entitlement to services and protection under the Children Act 1989 is not altered by the fact that they are living independently.

A forced marriage is a marriage in which one or both spouses do not consent to the marriage and duress is involved. Duress can include physical, psychological, financial, sexual and emotional pressure.'[3] 'An arranged marriage is not the same as a forced marriage. In an arranged marriage, the families take a leading role in choosing the marriage partner, but the choice of whether to enter the marriage is left to both people. The pressure put on people to marry against their will can be physical (including threats, actual physical violence and sexual violence) or emotional and psychological (for example, when someone is made to feel like they're bringing shame on their family. Financial abuse (taking your wages or not giving you any money) can also be a factor.'[4]

Types of Forced Marriage

1. *Forced Marriage by Parents, Families and Communities:* The most common type of forced marriage occurs when parents or other family members force one or both of the participants into the marriage. This type of forced marriage is usually supported by the surrounding community, making it difficult to avoid or escape.
2. *Forced Marriage by Religious Leaders:* In this type of forced marriage, one or both of the participants to the marriage are forced into it by religious leaders, supported by their religious community.
3. *Forced Marriage in Conflict Zones:* In the upheaval of war and conflict, with the breakdown of law and government, women and girls may be forced to marry men on either side of the conflict. This has occurred recently in places such as Sierra Leone, Uganda and the Democratic Republic of Congo.
4. *Trafficking for the Purpose of Forced Marriage:* There is a growing trade in the trafficking of women and girls for the purpose of forced marriage.
5. *Kidnapping for the Purpose of Forced Marriage:* In many cases women are kidnapped by the man who wishes to marry them, often with the help of a group of his friends.
6. *Adoption for the Purpose of Forced Marriage:* In a number of reported cases, girls have been adopted from abroad to serve as second or third wives in polygamous marriages.
7. *Forced Marriage Through Hereditary Slavery:* In these cases, a

slave owner forces the slaves he inherits into marriages of the slave owner's choosing.

8. *Forced Marriage by Partner:* In these cases, an abusive partner forces the other partner into marriage through the use of violence or threat of violence.[5]

Arrange Marriage

'Arranged marriages are an age-old tradition in India, generally one can define them as marriages in which neither the brides nor the grooms actively look for their future spouses. Instead, in most cases it is the father who feels called upon to choose a partner for his child. Important criteria for selection are caste, religion, star sign, age, skin colour and character attributes.'[6] 'Even among the educated middle classes in modern, urban India, marriage is as much a concern of the families as it is of the individuals. So customary is the practice of arranged marriage that there is a special name for a marriage which is. In a society where divorce is still a scandal and where, in fact, the divorce rate is exceedingly low, an arranged marriage is the beginning of a lifetime relationship not just between the bride and groom but between their families as well.'[7]

Reasons of Force Marriage

'Parents who force their children to marry often justify their behaviour as protecting their children, building stronger families and preserving cultural or religious traditions. They often do not see anything wrong in their actions. Often parents believe that they are upholding the cultural traditions of their home country when in fact, practices and values there may have changed. Some parents come under significant pressure from their extended families to get their children married. Women and girls may have an increased risk of forced marriage if they have disclosed sexual abuse. Parents may feel that this has brought shame on the woman or girl and that ensuring that she is married may restore honour to the family. Isolation is one of the biggest problems facing those trapped in, or under threat of, a forced marriage.

Forced marriage is not an issue that is specific to any religion, ethnic group or culture. It occurs in many different communities and types of families. It is sometimes interpreted as a religious practice but it cannot be justified on religious grounds: every major faith condemns it and freely given consent is a prerequisite of Christian, Jewish, Hindu, Muslim and Sikh marriages. There are several different motivations for forced marriage. For women, forced marriage is usually used to control their sexuality including in cases of unplanned pregnancy but also encompassing 'unsuitable' boyfriends or the family's interpretation of her dress or behaviour as immodest. Similarly, for the 15 per cent of forced marriage victims who are male, many are forced into marriage because their families know or suspect they are gay. Other reasons can include strengthening family links, interpretation of religious position, exchanging land/property or for the provision of care where one party has a disability.'[8]

'According to the Forced Marriage Unit's handbook *Multi-Agency Practice Guidelines: Handling Cases of Forced Marriage* some of the key motives of forced marriage are to: (a) control unwanted behaviour and sexuality, particularly the behaviour and sexuality of women; (b) control unwanted behaviour, for example, alcohol and drug use, wearing make-up or behaving in what is perceived to be a "westernised manner"; (c) prevent "unsuitable" relationships, e.g. outside the ethnic, cultural, religious or caste group; (d) protect family honour or *Izzat*; (e) respond to peer group or family pressure; (f) attempt to strengthen family links; (g) achieve financial gain; (h) ensure that land, property and wealth remain within the family; (i) protect perceived cultural ideals; (j) protect perceived religious ideals which are misguided; (k) ensure care for a child or adult with special needs when parents or existing carers are unable to fulfill that role and (l) to maintain long-standing family commitments.'[9]

Force Marriage: Global Perspectives

'According to wikipedia, Forced marriage is still practised in various cultures across the world, particularly in parts of South Asia and Africa. In South Africa, Ukuthwala is the practice of abducting young girls and forcing them into marriage, often with the consent of their parents. The girls who are involved in this practice are frequently under-aged, including some as young as eight. It is common in Niger. Girls who attempt to leave forced marriages are most often rejected by their families and are often forced to enter prostitution in order to survive. It is prevalent in Madagascar. Forced marriage is very common in Afghanistan and sometimes women resort to suicide to escape these marriages. As in other parts of South Asia, girls in Nepal are often seen as an economic burden to the family, due to dowry. Parents often compel young girls to marry, because older and more educated men can demand a higher dowry. It can be made because of family pride, the wishes of the parents, or social obligation. Forced marriage is practiced among immigrant communities in Canada.'[10]

'In South Asia, UNICEF estimates that among women ages 15 to 24; 48 per cent were married before the age of 18. In Bangladesh, 27.3 per cent of women ages 15 to 19 were married by the age of 15 and 65.3 per cent of women ages 20 to 24 were married before the age of 18. In Africa, 42 per cent of women ages 15 to 24 were married before the age of 18. In Niger, 27.3 per cent of women ages 15 to 19 were married before the age of 15 and 76.6 per cent of women ages 20 to 24 were married before the age of 18. Within North America, in 2000, approximately four per cent of women aged 15 to 19 were married.'[11] 'The controversial and hidden nature of forced marriage makes statistics of incidence difficult to compile. Conservative estimates suggest that 1,000 women in the UK are annually subjected to forced marriage, either within the UK or during a visit to India, Bangladesh, or Pakistan under the guise of a vacation or visiting a sick relative.'[12]

Force Marriage in India

'For some Indians, the conundrum is exacerbated by the fact that our parents had no choice for a partner; the only choice was how hard they have work to be happy. My father saw my mother once before they got married. For Indians, there's no way to escape thinking about marriage, eventually. It would not be a stretch to say that *shaadi*, the word for marriage in many Indian languages, is the first word a child understands after *mummy* and *papa*.'[13] 'Arranged marriages have been an integral part of the Indian society since ages. In older times, the bride and the groom were neither asked for their consent, nor were they informed about the partner. However, with the evolution of time, the society has undergone a significant change.

Nowadays, in arranged marriages both the girl and the boy are asked for their consent. The marriage ceremony is highly formal is case of an arranged marriage, with the groom's family playing to the gallery.'[14]

'In South Asian communities, ensuring that son or daughter is married is an important duty as a parent and is sometimes handled through the process of arranging the marriage. In such cases, marriage is a practice that is meant to ensure the continuity of cultural or religious traditions and strengthens family ties. In these cases marriage may be viewed as not only a union between two individuals, but a union between two families, preferably with a shared ethnicity, faith, caste and/or class. According to UNICEF, 48 per cent of women in South Asia are forced to marry before they are 18. The average age different in an arranged marriage is that the male is 4.5 years older. This means that nearly half of women in India and other South Asian countries are marrying while they are in the teens to men older than they are. Approximately 18 per cent of girls (nearly one in five) are married before they are 15 years old.'[15]

Effects of Force Marriage

'Forced marriages are often related to violence, both in regard to violence perpetrated inside the marriage (domestic violence) and in regard to violence inflicted in order to force an unwilling participant to accept the marriage, or to punish a refusal. Forced and early marriage deprives women and young girls of their basic human rights. Forced marriage describes a marriage that takes place without the free or valid consent of one or both of the partners and involves either physical or emotional duress. Early marriage is related to forced marriage because minors are deemed incapable of giving informed consent. Forced and early marriages are recognised as human rights violations. Numerous international and regional legal instruments condemn the practices of forced and early marriage.'[16]

'Young people, particularly girls, forced to marry or those who may be forced to marry, are frequently withdrawn from education, restricting their educational and personal development. Women forced to marry may find it very difficult to initiate any action to end the marriage and may be subjected to repeated rape (sometimes until they become pregnant) and ongoing domestic abuse within the marriage. Both men and women facing forced marriage may become anxious, depressed and emotionally withdrawn with low self-esteem. For many people, especially women, it may be their first experience of travelling overseas. If they are being held against their will and forced to marry there are various difficulties they may encounter if they want to return.'[17]

'Forced marriage is an extremely complex issue and often involves parties that are young and vulnerable and their families. There are significant impacts and effects of being forced into a marriage and these impacts often occur over a sustained period of time.'[18] 'It is specifically recognised as an abuse of human rights in a number of UN treaties and other international instruments. It is generally viewed as encompassing child and early marriage because minors are deemed incapable of giving informed consent.'[19] 'It is part of broader range of issues related to authoritarian upbringing, control and violence. The term "honour-related violence" is often used when referring to this form of violence because it is linked to certain societies' notions of honour and shame.'[20]

'Forced marriage has been seen as a form of child abuse, with young girls disproportionately experiencing the negative consequences of such marriages. Harmful outcomes include sexual assault and health risks associated with early pregnancy, high maternal and child mortality and increased risk of sexually transmitted diseases.'[21] 'Forced marriage is one of the ways honour-based violence can be manifested.'[22]

Legal Mechanism

'Marriage is not considered directly in the Convention on the Rights of the Child (CRC). Practitioners look other rights (e.g. health, education, life, development and survival) or the CRC general principles (best interests of the child, non-discrimination, respect for the views of the child) for guidance on this. The 2005 Council of Europe study, Forced Marriage in Council of Europe Member States, uses a very broad definition according to which forced marriage constitutes an: umbrella term covering marriage as slavery, arranged marriage, traditional marriage, marriage for reasons of custom, expediency of perceived respectability, child marriage, early marriage, fictitious, bogus or shame marriage, marriage of convenience, consummated marriage, putative marriage, marriage to acquire nationality and undesirable marriage – in all of which the concept of consent to marriage is at issue.'[23]

'In 2000, the Foreign and Commonwealth Office agreed a Joint Action Plan with the Home Office in response to the forced marriage report 'A Choice by Right'. In 2005, this was followed by a national consultation and the creation of the Forced Marriage Unit and The Forced Marriage (Civil Protection) Act 2007, (which came into force November 2008). The Act aims to 'make provision for protecting individuals against being forced to enter into marriage without their free and full consent and for protecting individuals who have been forced to enter into marriage without such consent; and for connected purposes. The Act gives the courts a wide discretion to deal flexibly with each individual case, employing civil remedies that offer protection to victims without criminalising family members. The Act has powers to ensure a Forced Marriage Protection Order, require family members to reveal a person's whereabouts, prevent a forced marriage from occurring, to hand over all passports (where there is dual nationality) and birth certificates and not to apply for a new passport, stop someone from being taken abroad, facilitate or enable a person to return to the UK within a given time period.'[24]

'Rights relating to marriage, including dissolution of marriage, guardianship and custody of children and related issues are governed by various religious personal laws, which vary depending on religious community or affiliation. So, for example, The Hindu Marriage Act 1956 (HMA) lays down the various requirements of marriage for Hindus. Muslim personal laws on marriage are not similarly codified (except for the Muslim Personal Law (Shariat Application) Act, 1937, the Dissolution of Muslim Marriages Act, 1939 and the Muslim Women (Protection of Rights on Divorce) Act, 1986). The laws applicable to Christians include the Indian Christian Marriage Act, 1872 (CMA) and the Divorce Act 1869 (as amended 2001) (DA). Civil marriages, particularly between persons belonging to different religions, are contracted under the Special Marriage Act, 1956 (SMA) and marriages contracted under other laws may also be registered under it.'[25]

'Various courts continue to uphold the customary practices and personal laws of different religious communities, which govern family matters. Only the Hindu Marriage Act, 1955 changed with time to bring the age criteria in consonance with the Child Marriage Restraint Act (CMRA). Absence of a uniform civil code allows differential treatment of children resulting in discrimination. Some victims of child marriage are thus entitled to better legal protection under the national law while their peers may remain out of this protective net. Under the Hindu Marriage Act, 1955, the parties to the marriage must have the capacity to consent and a marriage where consent is obtained through force is voidable and can be annulled by a decree of nullity.'[26]

'This law governs all Hindus, Sikhs, Jains and also Buddhists. Under the Islamic law, both the bride and groom must consent to the marriage and also express the same verbally and in writing. Under the Indian Christian Marriage Act, 1872, if a party to a marriage is a minor, the consent of father if living, or if the father is dead, the consent of the guardian of the person of such minor or if there is no guardian, then that of the mother, is essential before marriage. A marriage of minor without such consent is not valid.'[27] 'The Special Marriages Act, 1954, which allows inter-caste and interreligious marriage, contains provisions similar to the Hindu Marriage Act.'[28] 'The Registration of Births and Deaths (Amendment) Bill, 2012 was introduced in the Rajya Sabha on May 7, 2012 after a series of efforts being made since 2007 primarily to include the registration of marriages within its purview.'[29]

Constitutional and Legal Provisions

'The Constitution of India 1950 ('the Constitution') in Part III guarantees a range of fundamental rights, including the rights to life (Article 21), freedom of expression and movement (Article 19) and equality and non-discrimination. Article 14 encompasses a negative injunction prohibiting the State from denying any person equality before the law or the equal protection of laws. Article 15 prohibits discrimination against any person on the grounds of religion, race, caste, sex or place of birth. This provision also empowers the State to take affirmative action for the benefit of historically disadvantaged sections of the population and for women and children. The Constitution provides for specific remedies, including *habeas corpus* petitions and applications for enforcement of fundamental rights, which often prove useful in cases on choice in marriage. Civil laws applicable to all communities which are relevant in the context of forced marriage include the Prohibition of Child Marriage Act, 2006 (PCMA), the Guardians and Wards Act 1890 (G and WA), the Majority Act, 1875, the Family Courts Act, 1984 (FCA) and the Family Courts Rules as laid down in various states as well as the recent Protection of Women from Domestic Violence Act, 2005.'[30]

Conclusion

Marriage is a socially recognised union or legal contract between spouses that establishes rights and obligations between them. Forced marriage is a marriage in which one or both of the parties are married without his or her consent or against his or her will. It is a form of child/domestic abuse and violence against women. Parents who force their children to marry often justify their behaviour as protecting their children, building stronger families and preserving cultural or religious traditions. Such marriage is still practised in various cultures across the world, particularly in parts of South Asia and Africa. In South Asian communities, ensuring that your son or daughter is married is an important duty as a parent and is sometimes handled through the process of arranging the marriage as discussed earlier. Forced marriages are often related to violence, both in regard to violence perpetrated inside the marriage and in regard to violence inflicted in order to force an unwilling participant to accept the marriage, or to punish a refusal.

References

1. Early marriage: child spouses (2001), Retrieved from http://www.unicef-irc.org/publications/pdf/digest7e.pdf
2. Marriage (2015), Retrieved from http://en.wikipedia.org/wiki/Marriage
3. Multi-agency practice guidelines: Handling cases of Forced Marriage, Retrieved fromhttps://www.gov.uk/government/uploads/system/uploads/attachment_data/file/35530/forced-marriage-guidelines09.pdf
4. What is a forced marriage? Retrieved from https://www.gov.uk/government/uploads/system/uploads/attachment_data/file/35527/what-is-forced-marriage.pdf

5. Introduction to Forced Marriage, Retrieved from http://www.fmp-acsa.ca/wp-content/uploads/2013/03/FMP_SPT_Intro_to_Forced-Marriage.pdf
6. The Idea of Arranged Marriages in India Then and Now, Retrieved from http://www.certilingua.net/wp-content/uploads/arranged-marriage.pdf
7. Serena Nanda, Arranging a Marriage in India, Retrieved from http://www.anthroProforg/documents/docs102/102articles/india20.pdf
8. Policy briefing on Forced Marriage, Retrieved from http://www.avaproject.org.uk/media/62277/forced%20marriage%20briefing.pdf
9. Debjani Roy (2011), An Introduction to Forced Marriage in the South Asian Community in the United States, Manavi Occasional Paper No. 9, Retrieved from http://www.manavi.org/documents/Manavi_paper9_pass-6.26.12.pdf
10. Forced marriage (2014), Retrieved from http://en.wikipedia.org/wiki/Forced_marriage
11. Cheryl Thomas (2009), Forced and early marriage: A focus on central and eastern Europe and former Soviet Union countries with selected laws in other countries, Retrieved from http://www.un.org/womenwatch/daw/egm/vaw_legislation_2009/Expert%20Paper% 20EGMGPLHP%20_ Cheryl%20Thomas%20revised_.pdf
12. Forced marriage, Retrieved from http://www.soas.ac.uk/honourcrimes/resources/file55689.pdf?filename= Forced+Marriage
13. Anita Jain, Is Arranged Marriage Really Any Worse Than Craigslist? Retrieved from http://nymag.com/nymetro/news/culture/features/11621/
14. Arrange marriage, Retrieved from http://www.culturalindia.net/weddings/arranged-marriage.html
15. See http://www.triplepundit.com/podium/reality-early-forced-marriages-india/
16. Cheryl Thomas (2009), Forced and early marriage: A focus on central and eastern Europe and former Soviet Union countries with selected laws in other countries, Retrieved from http://www.un.org/womenwatch/daw/egm/vaw_legislation_2009/Expert%20Paper%20EGMG PLHP%20_Cheryl%20Thomas%20revised_.pdf

17. Multi-agency practice guidelines: Handling cases of Forced Marriage, Retrieved fromhttps://www.gov.uk/government/uploads/system/uploads/attachment_data/file/35530/forced-marriage-guidelines09.pdf
18. Forced marriage in New Zealand, Retrieved from http://www.immigration.govt.nz/NR/rdonlyres/A34EFD89-CB2B-4809-B6EB-2B92DAE072A0/0/MultiAgencyStatementCollaborativeResponsetoPotentialandActualForcedMarriagePDFdocpd.pdf
19. Child, Early and Forced Marriage: A Multi-Country Study: A Submission to the UN Office of the High Commissioner on Human Rights (OCHCR) (2013), Retrieved from http://www.wluml.org/sites/wluml.org/files/UN%20report%20final.pdf
20. Action Plan against Forced Marriage, Retrieved from https://www.politi.no/vedlegg/skjema/Vedlegg_673.pdf
21. Geetanjali Gangoli and Melanie McCarry, Child Marriage or Forced Marriage?, South Asian Communities in North East England, Children and Society, 23, 2009, pp. 418-29.
22. Forced marriage and honour based violence: Screening toolkit, Retrieved from http://www.resolution.org.uk/site_content_files/files/forcedmarriage_toolkit_layout_1.pdf
23. Child, Early and Forced Marriage: A Multi-Country Study: A Submission to the UN Office of the High Commissioner on Human Rights (OCHCR) (2013), Retrieved from http://www.wluml.org/sites/wluml.org/files/UN%20report%20final.pdf
24. Policy briefing on Forced Marriage, Retrieved from http://www.avaproject.org.uk/media/62277/forced%20marriage%20briefing.pdf
25. Sara Hossain and Lynn Welchman (2014), Remedies for Forced Marriage: A handbook for lawyers, Retrieved from http://www.interights.org/userfiles/Chapter_4.pdf
26. Section 5 and Section 12 of the Hindu Marriage Act, 1955 (as amended in 1978), Available at: http://indiankanoon.org/doc/590166/
27. Section 19 and 22 of the Indian Christian Marriage Act, 1872, Available at: http://indiankanoon.org/doc/1166543/
28. Section 5 and Section 12 of the Special Marriage Act, 1954, Available at: http://indiankanoon.org/doc/4234/
29. Enakshi Ganguly Thukral and Bharti Ali, Child Marriage in India: Achievements, Gaps and Challenges, Retrieved from http://www.ohchr.org/Documents/Issues/Women/WRGS/ForcedMarriage/NGO/HAQCentreForChildRights1.pdf
30. Sara Hossain and Lynn Welchman (2014), Remedies for Forced Marriage: A handbook for lawyers, Retrieved from http://www.interights.org/userfiles/Chapter_4.pdf

9

Dowry

> "From birth to age 18 a girl needs good parents. From 18 to 35 she needs good looks. From 35 to 55 she needs a good personality. From 55 on, she needs good cash."
>
> —*Sophie Tucker*

Introduction

'In the early days dowry was an institution in which gifts and presents were given to a girl at the time of her marriage when she was required to leave her parents' home and join her husband's household. The problem of dowry has become a serious social evil among the upper castes and middle classes both in towns and villages. Dowry has become a symbol of prestige for both the dowry-givers and the dowry-takers. In north India, it is considered as a gift or *dahej*. The giving of gifts and help to a daughter was quite a normal activity in ancient India. Mahatma Gandhi writes: Any young man who makes dowry a condition for marriage discredits his education and his country and dishonours womanhood. Young men who soil their fingers with such ill-gotten gold should be excommunicated from society.'[1]

'Dowry system is the one of the worst problem in Indian Society. It does not only affect the individual victims, the brides, but the entire social fabric which was created to help realise the aspirations of both the individuals and the collective. The brides as sacrificial goats only show the canker that spreads all over this social fabric. Dowry system has its root in the attitude of Indian society towards women.'[2]

What is Dowry?

'Dowry is the transfer of parental property to a daughter at her marriage rather than at the owner's death. A dowry establishes a type of conjugal fund, the nature of which may vary widely. This fund may provide an element of financial security in widowhood or against a negligent husband and may eventually go to provide for her sons and daughters. Locally, dowry is called *dahej* in Hindi.'[3] 'The modern definition of the Dowry System in India is as follows: This menace of Dowry has become a social menace in modern India leading to the oppression on women, physical violence on the bride, causing a financial and emotional stress on the parents of the bride, marital conflict and so on. This menace exists even today in the society even though it is a criminal offence to take Dowry during marriage.'[4]

Reasons of Dowry

'Various reasons have been suggested as cause of dowry practice in India. These include economic factors and social factors. There are many economic factors that contribute towards the system of dowry. Some of these include inheritance systems and the bride's economic status. Dowry gave, at least in theory, women economic and financial security in their marriage in the form of movable goods. This helped prevent family wealth break-up and provided security to the bride at the same time. The structure and kinship of marriage in parts of India contributes to dowry. In addition to marriage customs that may influence dowry, social customs or rituals and parents expectations of dowry are important factors to consider. Dowry in India is not limited to any specific religion. It is widespread among Hindus and other religions.'[5]

Advantages and Disadvantages of Dowry System[6]

'Although government implemented Acts for removing such system, but still it prevail. Some of the arguments in favour of dowry by the supporters of this system are: (a) Dowry, money, utensils and other household articles that a bride brings at the time of marriage help the newly married couple to establish their new home; (b) Dowry makes the marriage of ugly looking, uneducated and aged girl to found suitable bridegroom for the bride; (c) Dowry solves the financial problem of poor young bachelors; (d) Girl earring with her huge amount of dowry feels confident while entering her in-laws house and is given greater attention and importance in-laws family; (e) It helps to find a suitable bridegroom from other caste, religion or form other state; and (f) Dowry acts as a provident fund for the girls to face many financial hazards in future.

There are some demerits of such system, such as: (a) Dowry has become a great economic burden to the middle and lower class families; (b) Many parents develop their corrupt attitude to collect money for paying dowry; (c) Each marriage of daughters leads the drainage of money from brides' side; (d) A girl is considered a liability in her own natal home due to prevalence of the custom of dowry practice; (e) Parent of poor families kill their daughter from their vary birth or at the stage of fetuses in their mother's womb; and (f) Many marriages breakdown due to dowry practice and increases the tension of both parents and daughters.'

Dowry in Marriage: Global Perspectives

'From wikipedia, Dowry is a common practice in many parts of the world, especially in South Asia and several Middle East and North African countries. It is most common in nations with inadequate male-biased inheritance laws and patrilineal societies, which expect women to live with or near their husband's family. An unusual exception to the dowry custom in South Asia is found in Bhutan. The dowry system does not exist in Bhutan. The original custom in Bangladesh was the bride price, called *pawn*, where the groom's family makes a payment to the bride's parents. Bangladesh has seen a rise in the expected size of dowries in recent decades, as its middle class has grown and there has been an accompanying rise in the rate of "dowry deaths". In Pakistan, dowry is called *Jahez* in Arabic. Pakistan has seen a rise in the values of dowries in recent decades, as in other South Asian countries. However, in Pakistan it is still expected that a bride will bring some kind of dowry with her to a marriage, whether she is Muslim, Hindu, or Christian.

The practice of dowry is common in Nepal and dowry-related violence is increasingly becoming a problem. Nepali people of the Madhesi society still freely welcome dowry as a right to the groom's side. Even highly educated people living in the Terai of Nepal accept dowry without any second thoughts. The payment of dowry in Sri Lanka has a strong tradition and has been connected to family violence. A large dowry is sometimes expected and given in Afghanistan; some houses are almost emptied so that the daughter may make a grand show at the wedding. Items included in a dowry depend on the resources of the bride's family and the demands made by the groom's family. In Egypt, dowry is known as *Gehaz*. This is the property a bride is expected to bring with her at marriage and it is different from the dower (*Mahr*) paid by the groom to the bride per requirements of Sharia.'[7]

Dowry System in India

'In India, dowry refers to the durable goods, cash and real or movable property that the bride's family gives to the bridegroom, his parents, or his relatives as a condition of the marriage. Dowry is a payment of cash or gifts from the bride's family to the bridegroom's family upon marriage. It may include cash, jewellery, electrical appliances, furniture, bedding, crockery, utensils and other household items that help the newlyweds set up their home. When dowry evolved in the Vedic period, it was essentially followed by the upper castes to benefit the bride, who was unable to inherit property under Hindu law. Since marriages in India are a time for big celebrations in each family, they tend to be very lavish. Accordingly, Indian weddings usually involve considerable expenditure and accompanying wedding presents from relatives in both sides of the family.'[8]

'The dowry system is so deeply rooted in Indian culture, that sometimes one feels that there's going to be no way out - at least not for another century. Even modern, well-educated families start saving up money for their daughter's dowry as soon as she is born. Dowry is an evil, evil system and all of us, at some level, condone it and even contribute to it. When demands for dowry are not met, the bride is subject to torture and often even killed. Come festivals like Diwali or Holi and the parents of the daughter flood her in-laws with gifts.'[9]

'The giving of gifts or money to a groom on behalf of the bride's family is common practice in India, a marital tradition which dates back centuries. The dowry buys into people's pride and desire to "save face" and the system has substantial consequences for families and women in general. The origins of the dowry system in India have been greatly debated. One theory is that historically parents of the bride nominally provided gifts such as jewellry and everyday household items to the bride which evolved over time to providing a sum of money to the groom's family. Another, more patriarchal view, alleges that daughters were given away and that grooms were offered gifts (and eventually money) as somewhat of a bribe to ensure the fair treatment of the woman.'[10] 'The Indian police say that they receive over 2,500 reports of bride-burning alone every year while the number of dowry deaths is about 9000. These numbers increase at a rate of one to two per cent every year. It is also a reason why many parents do not want to have daughters, because of the dowry they will have to shell out at her marriage and the stress they go through due to never-ending demands from her in-laws. In fact, dowry deaths of a newly married bride are regularly in the news.'[11]

'Dowry-related domestic abuse is still prevalent in India, despite years of feminist campaigning. Dowry is the exchange of money and/or goods from the bride's family to the groom's at the point of marriage. Families give as much as possible, that in some cases will involve selling land and homes or taking out loans. Women's organisations in India have moved away from anti-dowry campaigning and focused more on increasing women's independence through better access to healthcare and advice, education and employment and encouraging women to take on political roles. Most of the younger women interviewed saw dowry as one of the main problems faced by women, but also had no intention of stopping the practice. Those who had experienced mental or physical abuse linked to their dowry still intended to give a dowry when their daughter married, as they feared negative repercussions if they did not do this.'[12]

Dowry Death in India

'From the article "Rising number of dowry deaths in India: NCRB, that published in *The Hindu* (August 7, 2014), the NCRB statistics show that 91,202 dowry deaths were reported in the country from January 1, 2001 to December 31 2012. Out of that 84,013 were charged and sent for trial and the rest were either withdrawn by the government during the course of investigation or not investigated. Of this, 5,081 cases were reported to be false after investigations. While 6,851 dowry deaths were reported in the country in 2001, the figure reached 7,618 in 2006 and touched 8,233 in 2012. While 6,539 cases were charged and 6,060 sent for trail in 2001, in 2012, the number of cases charged was 8,022 and 7,537 of that sent for trial. 21,922 dowry death cases were pending trial from the previous year in 2001 and the figure touched 29,669 in 2012. In 2001, the total number of cases on trial was 27,969 and at the end of that year 22,697 cases were pending trial. The corresponding figures for 2012 were 37,206 and 31,888 respectively. A total of 1,389 cases were withdrawn for various reasons after coming up for trial during the 12-year period. 44,668 cases were convicted during the period.

A State-wise break-up provided in the statistics show that the highest incidence of dowry deaths was in Uttar Pradesh and Bihar. During the period, 23,824 dowry deaths were reported in U.P. and 19,702 sent for trial. In Bihar 13,548 cases were reported during the period and 9,984 sent for trial. The conviction rate was always in the vicinity of 50 per cent in U.P. and in the vicinity of less than 30 per cent in Bihar. In fact, the number of dowry death cases acquitted was always much higher than those convicted in all the States. In Maharashtra, the incidence of dowry cases getting acquitted was seen to be very high. Out of a total of 3,485 cases for which trial was completed during the 12-year period, 3,066 were acquitted. In U.P., the dowry death figure was above 2,000 during most of the years of statistics period and in Bihar, it was above 1,000 for the majority of the years. In Madhya Pradesh, it was above 600 during the early years of the statistics period and later climbed to 800 plus. 1,582 dowry deaths were reported in Delhi during the 12-year period. Nagaland is the only State and Lakshadweep the only Union Territory where no dowry deaths were reported during the period.'[13]

'Official figures from India's National Crime Records Bureau reveal that 8,233 young women, many of them new brides, were killed in so-called 'dowry deaths' in 2012. The report comes amid growing concern over the level of violence against women following the Delhi gang rape case December 2012. The number of deaths is marginally less than in 2011, but reflects a broader increase in gender violence. While dowry deaths fell slightly from 8618 to 8233, the number of cases of cruelty committed by husbands and their relatives increased significantly from 99,135 in 2011 to 106,527 in 2012. Many of the cruelty cases are believed to be dowry-related and many dowry killings are preceded by cruelty by the husband and in-laws. Although the payment of dowries for marriage is illegal in India, they remain widespread across caste, class and educational divides. In recent years demands have become more insistent and expensive.'[14]

Effects of Dowry

'Dowry system is an insult to our society. It reduces the position of both man and woman. Many educated men are demanding dowry. Dowry system is an insult to our education and culture. Poor people cannot afford dowry. Many good-looking and brilliant girls remain unmarried because they are poor. Even after marriage, some brides are tortured and forced to bring more and more dowry from their parents' house. If they fail, they are tortured and finally killed.'[15] 'There have been horrible, true stories of the groom's family agreeing to one dowry and after the bride is married demanding more from the bride's parents. Threats of divorce are often used to entice the bride's parents to give more dowries. In a country where shame is brought down on the divorcee, parents of the bride will do whatever they can to save their daughters this shame.'[16] 'In India and particularly in Delhi and other metropolis, dowry murders and suicides have become a matter of great concern. In Delhi alone, a bride was burnt to death every twelve hours.

The custom of dowry has become widespread. The rate of dowry changes according to the qualification of the boy. There are "rates" fixed for I.A.S., I.P.S., P.C.S., I.E.S. officers and qualified engineers and doctors. In fact, a regular marriage cannot be held and a marriage without dowry is almost unthinkable. Even before the marriage, the amount to be given as dowry is discussed and settled with the change of time. In India, many of the traditional customs have been given up, but the custom of dowry has not only continued, but flourished over the years.'[17]

'Dowry can be a source of violence. This often starts with the parents-in-law, seeing as if dowry is not sent; they might start being violent towards their daughter-in-law. In the absence of dowry gifts, the daughter-in-law is subject to verbal and emotional abuse. Mother-in-law and sister-in-law will taunt daughter-in-law for not bringing dowry. If a wife does not bring dowry, sometimes the in-laws will not accept her into the family. She will sometimes be treated like a servant, expected to do all house chores and sexually satisfy her husband to gain her respectable place within the family. Physical and mental violence can cause the wife serious psychological problems and even require hospitalisation. Lack of dowry, or parents-in-law dissatisfaction with the amount of dowry, can be a reason for them to be violent against their daughter-in-law and in extreme cases causing her death by burning and try to stage it as suicide.'[18]

Dowry Prohibition Act 1961

'The payment of dowries was prohibited in India in 1961. Subsequently, the Indian Penal Code was amended to make it easier for a wife to seek redress from harassment by the husband's family. Section 2 of the *Dowry Prohibition Act 1961* defines "dowry" as any property or valuable security given or agreed to be given either directly or indirectly: (a) by one party to a marriage to the other party to the marriage; or (b) by the parents of either party to a marriage or by any other person, to either party to the marriage or to any other person, at or before (1) [or any time after the marriage] (2) [in connection with the marriage of the said parties, but does not include] dower or *mahr* in the case of persons to whom the Muslim Personal Law (Shariat) applies.

The *Dowry Prohibition Act 1961* prohibits the request, payment or acceptance of a dowry "as consideration for the marriage", where "dowry" is defined as a gift demanded or given as a precondition for a marriage. Gifts given without a precondition are not considered dowry and are legal, per Section 3(2). Asking for or giving of dowry can be punished by imprisonment of up to six months, a fine of up to Rs 15000 or the amount of dowry (whichever is higher), or imprisonment up to five years. It replaced several pieces of anti-dowry legislation that had been enacted by various Indian states.'[19]

Protection of Women from Domestic Violence Act 2005

'The Protection of Women from Domestic Violence Act 2005 is an Act of the Parliament of India enacted to protect women from domestic violence. It was brought into force by the Indian government from 26th October 2006. The Act was passed by the Parliament in August 2005 and assented to by the President on 13th September 2005. The Protection of Women from Domestic Violence Act 2005 differs from the earlier law, Section 498A of the Indian Penal Code, in that it explicitly defines domestic violence in addition to dowry-related cruelty. Primarily meant to provide protection to the wife or female live-in partner from domestic violence at the hands of the husband or male live-in partner or his relatives, the law also extends its protection to women living in a household such as sisters, widows or mothers. Domestic violence under the act includes actual abuse or the threat of abuse whether physical, sexual, verbal, emotional or economic.'[20]

Conclusion

Dowry is the transfer of parental property to a daughter at her marriage rather than at the owner's death. There are many economic factors contribute dowry. Some of these include inheritance systems and the bride's economic status. Dowry gave, at least in theory, women economic and financial security in their marriage in the form of movable goods. This helped prevent family wealth break-up and provided security to the bride at the same time. The Indian police say that they receive over 2,500 reports of bride-burning alone every year while the number of dowry deaths is about 9000. These numbers increase at a rate of one to two per cent every year. The highest incidence of dowry deaths was in Uttar Pradesh and Bihar. There have been horrible, true stories of the groom's family agreeing to one dowry and after the bride is married demanding more from the bride's parents. Threats of divorce are often used to entice the bride's parents to give more dowries. The Protection of Women from Domestic Violence Act 2005 is an Act of the Parliament of India enacted to protect women from domestic violence. It was brought into force by the Indian government from 26th October 2006.

References

1. Puja Mondal, Dowry System in India: Problems, Social Dimensions and Other Details, Retrieved from http://www.yourarticlelibrary.com/society/dowry/dowry-system-in-india-problems-social-dimensions-and-other-details/35175/
2. Problem of dowry system in India, Retrieved from http://www.importantindia.com/10609/problem-of-dowry-system-in-india/
3. Dowry (2014), Retrieved from http://en.wikipedia.org/wiki/Dowry
4. See http://www.hitxp.com/articles/history/origin-dowry-system-bride-woman-india-british/
5. Dowry system in India (2014), Retrieved from http://en.wikipedia.org/wiki/Dowry_system_in_India
6. Shuani (2014), Dowry System in India: Advantages and Disadvantages, Retrieved from http://www.yourarticlelibrary.com/society/dowry/dowry-system-in-india-advantages-and-disadvantages/47642/
7. Dowry (2014), Retrieved from http://en.wikipedia.org/wiki/Dowry
8. Dowry system in India (2014), Retrieved from http://en.wikipedia.org/wiki/Dowry_system_in_India
9. The Dowry System (2014), Retrieved from http://www.indiaparenting.com/womens-issues/177_662/the-dowry-system.html
10. The dowry system (2014), Retrieved from http://en.reset.org/knowledge/dowry-system
11. Vineeta Chawla (2010), Dowry System in India: Then and Now, Retrieved from http://www.youthkiawaaz.com/2010/12/dowry-system-in-india-then-and-now/
12. Dowry and abuse still a problem in India (2013), Retrieved from http://www.port.ac.uk/uopnews/2013/11/19/dowry-and-abuse-still-a-problem-in-india/
13. From the article "Rising number of dowry deaths in India" NCRB, that published in The Hindu (August 07, 2014), Retrieved from http://www.thehindu.com/news/national/rising-number-of-dowry-deaths-in-india-ncrb/article4995677.ece
14. The Telegraph (Sep 02, 2013), Woman killed over dowry 'every hour' in India, Retrieved from http://www.telegraph.co.uk/news/worldnews/asia/india/10280802/Woman-killed-over-dowry-every-hour-in-India.html

15. Mili, Short Essay on Dowry System in India, Retrieved from http://www.preservearticles.com/201104306067/short-essay-on-dowry-system-in-india.html

16. Arranged Marriages and Dowry, Retrieved from http://www.pardesiservices.com/tradition/arrangedmarg.asp

17. An essay on evils of dowry system in India, Retrieved from http://www.infipark.com/content/589-Essay-on-Dowry-System-in-India

18. Tazeen Saeed Ali Gunnhildur Árnadóttir, Asli Kulane, Dowry practices and their negative consequences from a female perspective in Karachi, Pakistan–A qualitative study, Vol. 5, No. 7A4, 84-91 (2013), pp. 87-89.

19. Dowry law in India (2014), Retrieved from http://en.wikipedia.org/wiki/Dowry_law_in_India

20. Protection of Women from Domestic Violence Act 2005, Retrieved from http://en.wikipedia.org/wiki/Protection_of_Women_from_Domestic_ Violence_Act_2005

10

Women Trafficking

> "Girls have an unfair advantage over men: if they can't get what they want by being smart, they can get it by being dumb."
>
> —*Yul Brynner*

Introduction

'Human trafficking is considered as one of the most problematic issues in today world's society. Since this problem happens throughout the world, it is necessary to deal with it globally. Traffickers can be involved in various functions and in various activities during the different stages of the process. Women play a role during the recruitment and exploitation phases.'[1] 'Human migration has been and still is intimately connected with the transformations of the world economy. Mass migrations were a common phenomenon in pre-modern world politics in which they shaped the fates of empires and entire civilisations'.[2] 'The forces of globalisation have often been connected to the rising levels of migration around the world as well as an increasing prevalence of abusive and irregular forms of migration, among them trafficking. Like migration, trafficking is not a new phenomenon, but rapidly changing structures and circumstances in the global arena have led to a continuous development of new forms, purposes, routes and sources of trafficking.'[3]

'Trafficked persons point towards economic and other oppressive conditions, as well as lack of opportunities in their own countries as the main reasons of why they felt the need to migrate for employment and thus risk being used and exploited by trafficker. Amidst poverty and limited prospects, many individuals are willing to take risks in order to seize opportunities abroad. The oppression of women and children within patriarchal family and social structures, in which women are subordinated to men, is of the main reasons why they fall prey to traffickers.'[4] 'It is a multi-dimensional threat: it deprives people of their human rights and freedoms, it is a global health risk and it fuels the growth of organised crime. It has a devastating impact on individual victims, who often suffer physical and emotional abuse, rape, threats against self and family, passport theft and even death. But the impact of human trafficking goes beyond individual victims; it undermines the safety and security of all nations it touches.'[5]

Meaning of the Concept

'Human trafficking is the trade of humans, most commonly for the purpose of sexual slavery, forced labour or commercial sexual exploitation for the trafficker or others. It can occur within a country or trans-nationally. It is a crime against the person because of the violation of the victim's rights of movement through coercion and because of their commercial exploitation. Trafficking of women involves the recruitment, transportation, transfer, harbouring, or receipt of children for the purpose of exploitation. The commercial sexual exploitation of children can take many forms, including forcing a child into prostitution or other forms of sexual activity or pornography.'[6]

'The first internationally agreed upon definition of trafficking is embodied in the UN Protocol to Prevent, Suppress and Punish Trafficking in Persons, Especially Women and Children, Supplementing the UN Convention Against Transnational Organised Crime (2000),[7] as follows: *[...] the recruitment, transportation, transfer, harbouring or receipt of persons, by means of threat or use of force or other forms of coercion, of abduction, of fraud, of deception, of the abuse of power or of a position of vulnerability or of the giving or receiving of payments or benefits to achieve the consent of a person having control over another person, for the purpose of exploitation. Exploitation shall include, at a minimum, the exploitation of the prostitution of others or other forms of sexual exploitation, forced labour or services, slavery or practices similar to slavery, servitude or the removal, manipulation or implantation of organs.*'[8]

'The definition of trafficking in human beings contains three elements, namely: 1. The activity: the recruitment, transport, transfer, harbouring or receipt of a person; 2. The means: threat or use of force or other forms of coercion, of abduction, of fraud, of deception, of the abuse of power or of a position of vulnerability or of the giving or receiving of payments or benefits to achieve the consent of a person having control over another person; 3. The purpose: the exploitation of the prostitution of others or other forms of sexual exploitation, forced labour or services, slavery or practices similar to slavery, servitude or the removal of organs.'[9] 'The nature of globalisation has also exacerbated the demand for human trafficking all over the world. Globalisation with its inherent global technology has further contributed to the enslavement and total exploitation of people across the worlds. Most of these exploitations have usually gone unnoticed due to the subtle nature of their operation.'[10]

Reasons of Trafficking

'The root causes of trafficking are various and often differ from one country to another. Some of the common factors are local conditions that make populations want to migrate in search of better conditions: poverty, oppression, lack of human rights, lack of social or economic opportunity, dangers from conflict or instability and similar conditions. Political instability, militarism, civil unrest, internal armed conflict and natural disasters may result in an increase in trafficking. War and civil strife may lead to massive displacements of populations, leaving orphans and street children extremely vulnerable to trafficking. The rapid expansion of broadcast and telecommunication media, including the Internet, across the developing world may have increased the desire to migrate to developed countries and, with it, the vulnerability of would-be migrants to traffickers.'[11]

'In general root causes of human trafficking world-wide include those which are economic, those that stem from social exclusion and gender discrimination and those which are political, legal or result from conflict.'[12] 'The lack of adequate legislation, properly functioning administrative machinery and an effective judiciary are the most obvious causes of human trafficking in this category. The main "buyers" of trafficked persons include sex tourists, pornography producers, brothel owners, sex customers and employers of all types looking for cheap labour both for domestic and industrial purposes. The main destinations are developed countries in the West, the Middle East as well as big cities, conflict zones, military bases and mining areas in developing countries themselves.'[13]

'The growing demand for a wide variety of exploitable sex workers and cheap labour has become a primary reason for trafficking. Prostitution in religious pilgrimage sites, sex tourism and child sexual abuse are some of the alarming trends that have emerged in recent years. The HIV/AIDS pandemic has also increased the demand for young virgins by HIV positive men who believe sex with a virgin will cure them of AIDS.'[14]

Women Trafficking: Global Perspectives

'Human trafficking is a modern-day form of slavery. Victims are young children, teenagers, men and women. Victims of human trafficking are subjected to force, fraud, or coercion to compel them to engage in commercial sex or involuntary labour.'[15] 'It has received increasing global attention over the past decade. Initially, trafficking of women and girls for forced sex work and, to a lesser extent, domestic servitude, were the sole focus of advocacy and assistance. Today, there is recognition that women, children and men are trafficked into many different forms of labour and for sexual exploitation.'[16] 'Trafficking is the second largest and fastest growing crime industry in the world and its success is largely dependent on a lack of awareness by the community.'[17]

'Most countries are confronting the problem of migrant trafficking for labour and for sexual exploitation. Trafficking has become a transnational and intra-national industry that affects mostly all countries, although not all equally. Governments have viewed transnational trafficking as a crime of illegal migration in which trafficked women are often treated as the criminals.'[18]

'Human trafficking, child and forced labour and the global capitalist enterprise are inextricably connected phenomena in Africa. Victims of human trafficking usually end up as forced labourers on the continent or abroad. Female victims, especially young girls, typically find themselves involuntarily working in the capacity of domestic servants or sex slaves. Boys often wind up in forced labour camps on agricultural plantations and mining areas.'[19] 'In West and Central Africa the different perceptions of human trafficking combined with different socio-economic and political situations in the various countries have created a mixture of policy responses. The first wave of trafficking in adult women from West Africa to Western Europe began in the 1980s and continued through the 1990s. Children are trafficked into a variety of exploitative situations including commercial sex, domestic service, armed conflict, service industries like bars and restaurants; or into hazardous forms of work in factories, mines, agriculture and fishing, construction; also begging.'[20]

'UNODC finds that there is significant intraregional trafficking in West, Central and South Africa. Victims of the West and Central Africa region are trafficked to other neighbouring countries such as Benin, Cote d'Ivoire, Gabon, Ghana, Nigeria, Liberia and Togo but also internally trafficked within the border. In Southern Africa, the victims identified by the state authorises are from Mozambique, Malawi, the Democratic Republic of the Congo (DRC), Zambia and Zimbabwe as well as from East, South-East and South Asia. In West and Central Africa, children are trafficked for forced labour, such as slavery, domestic servitude, street begging and as camel jockeys. In Southern Africa, human trafficking forms include sexual exploitation, forced labour, slavery and domestic servitude.'[21]

'Incidences of human trafficking are often affected by migration flows, particularly when those flows are illegal and unregulated. In recent years, several factors have influenced emigration flows from Latin America and the Caribbean. Primary destination countries for Latin American immigrants have included the United States, Spain, Italy, Canada, the Netherlands and Britain. These countries, many with low birth rates and aging populations, came to rely on migrant labourers from Latin America in recent decades to fill low-paying jobs in agriculture, construction, manufacturing and domestic service.'[22] 'While trafficking for forced labour is a serious problem in Latin America and the Caribbean, trafficking for sexual exploitation has been perceived as a more widespread and pressing regional problem. Most victims are trafficked for prostitution, but others are used for pornography and stripping. Every year thousands of undocumented Haitians flock to the Dominican Republic lured by false promises from recruiters of profits to be made in the sugarcane fields. Both individual factors and outside circumstances may account for the rise of human trafficking within and from Latin America and the Caribbean. Individual risk factors include poverty, unemployment, illiteracy, history of physical or sexual abuse, homelessness, drug use and gang membership.'[23]

'During the past decade, trafficking has become an issue of growing concern in South-East Asia. It has been conservatively estimated that at least 200-225,000 women and children from South-East Asia are trafficked annually, a figure representing nearly one-third of the global trafficking trade. Of the estimated 45-50,000 women and children estimated to be trafficked into the US each year, 30,000 are believed to come from South-East Asia. Trafficking is not a new problem for South-East Asia and many initiatives have been developed to combat the problem by NGOs, inter-governmental organisations, government ministries, national and international bodies, human rights organisations and lobby network.'[24]

'In South-East Asia, trafficking is predominantly for forced labour. With its wide economic, social and political impacts, trafficking is a significant development issue in South-East Asia. One of the reasons for such high numbers of people trafficked or in forced labour in Asia is that many ASEAN countries are at the bottom of a lot of the world's supply chains, including for food, garments and technology. Yet few countries in the region have adequate laws for addressing corporate responsibility for human trafficking, including in their supply chains. Similarly, the bias towards the sex sector in the anti-trafficking response to date has left law enforcement officials ill-equipped to recognise and lacking familiarity with indicators of labour trafficking.'[25]

Women Trafficking in South Asia

'Trafficking has been viewed with increasing concern in South Asia as a region and by individual South Asian countries as well. Bangladesh is a major country of origin and transit for men, women and children subjected to 20 trafficking in persons, especially forced labour and forced prostitution. A large proportion of cross-border trafficking in Bangladesh is due to migration in search of employment. Many Bangladeshi men and women migrate willingly to countries other than India, such as Saudi Arabia, Bahrain, Kuwait, the United Arab Emirates (UAE), Qatar, Iraq, Lebanon and Malaysia for work under formal contracts. Recruiting agencies acting as middlemen in such cases often charge exorbitantly and there have been a number of cases of recruitment fraud where such migrants are misled about the terms of employment including payment.'[26]

'Over the last five years at least 13,220 children are reported as being trafficked out of the country and it was possible to rescue only 4,700 of them. It is believed that about 4,500 women and children from Bangladesh are trafficked to Pakistan annually. On the other hand, Bangladesh boys in the ages between 4-12 years are trafficked for camel racing in the Gulf; sexual exploitation of these boys by the employers in not uncommon.'[27] 'Bangladeshi children and adults are trafficked internally for commercial sexual exploitation, domestic servitude and forced and bonded labour, including forced begging. In some instances, children are sold into bondage by their parents, while others are induced into labour or commercial sexual exploitation through fraud and physical coercion. Internationally, women and children from Bangladesh are trafficked to India and Pakistan for commercial sexual exploitation or forced labour. Some Rohingyan refugees from Burma have been subjected to human trafficking in Bangladesh. Many brothel owners and pimps coerce Bangladeshi girls to take steroids to make them more attractive to clients, with devastating side effects; the drug is reported to be used by 90 per cent of girls and women between the ages of 15 and 35 in Bangladeshi brothels.'[28]

'The Constitution of Bangladesh deals specifically with two forms of trafficking - labour and commercial sexual exploitation. In Article 34(1), all forms of forced labour are prohibited and Article 18(2) places a duty upon the State to prevent prostitution. Trafficking for purposes of labour or sexual exploitation, thus, are dealt with in the Constitution. Article 31 of the Constitution guarantees every citizen the right to enjoy the protection of law wherever they may be. Bangladesh's Women and Children Repression Prevention Act, 2000, is a fairly recent law which was enacted for the sole purpose of dealing with violence against women and children, including for commercial sexual exploitation.'[29]

'Bhutan is beginning to feel the nudges of organised crime with more number of human trafficking cases being reported over the past few years. Since 2007, National Commission for Women and Children (NCWC) has recorded cases of young boys and girls who have been trafficked from Thimphu, Dagana and other parts of Bhutan to India and then sometimes further to Nepal. Indian women from West Bengal and Assam have also been trafficked into Bhutanese border towns of Phuentsholing, Gelephug and Samdrup Jongkhar, mostly for sexual exploitation.'[30]

'Human trafficking in Nepal is a serious concern. Nepal is mainly a source country for men, women and children subjected to forced labour and sex trafficking. Trafficking victims often are taken to locations within Nepal, often from rural areas to the urban centers. Mainly young girls and women are trafficked for sexual exploitation in places such as cabin/dance restaurants, massage parlours and other places within tourism sector. The trafficking of girls from Nepal into India for forced prostitution is perhaps one of the busiest slave trafficking routes anywhere in the world; with estimated 5,000-10,000 Nepali women and girls trafficked to India each year. Victims, especially girls and women, are trafficked to Saudi Arabia, Malaysia, Hong Kong, Russia, Pakistan, the United Arab Emirates and other Gulf states. The majority of trafficking victims are women and girls, who are especially vulnerable due to limited economic opportunities, illiteracy or low education and low socioeconomic and cultural status.'[31]

'Nepal is a party to several international instruments to curb trafficking. These include the Convention on the Suppression of Trafficking and the Exploitation of the Prostitution of Others, 1949, Convention on the Elimination of all Form of Discrimination against Women, 1979 and the Convention of Rights of Child, 1990, among others. At present, about three-dozen NGOs, INGOs and UN agencies are involved in various ways in the struggle against trafficking. Their major areas of concern include awareness raising, advocacy, lobbying, prevention, rescue and reintegration. In spite of such efforts, the rate of trafficking continues to rise. Much has to be done to bolster the implementation aspect of such endeavours. Widespread poverty, lack of education, deep-rooted patriarchal norms and values that exist in all sections of society and are discriminatory to women make them very vulnerable to trafficking.'[32]

'Trafficking of girls/women in entertainment sector and their exploitation has been documented since 2000. The magnitude of women/girls working in the entertainment sectors is not known in Kathmandu valley. However, the FGD participants (girls/ women working in the entertainment sectors) reported that the number of girls/women working in this sector is on decline because either close of restaurants or recession in business due to the government's order not to drive while one has taken alcohol. Trafficking of Nepali young women for the purpose of marriage to Korea is reported widely through media. One source reported that there are about 500-600 Nepali girls went to Korea for the purpose of marriage. In late 2009, it estimated nearly 300 people in Kavre district were the victims of illegal extraction of kidney. Sources said that trafficking is managed by criminal racket- extending its network from villages to Kathmandu and Kathmandu to Indian cities. Kidneys are sold in India up to Rs 150,000 by the Nepali brokers while the Indian brokers can sell it from Rs 700,000 to Rs 1,800,000.'[33]

'Pakistan is a source, transit and destination country for men, women and children subjected to trafficking in persons, specifically forced labour and prostitution. The largest human trafficking problem is bonded labour, concentrated in the Sindh and Punjab provinces in agriculture and brick making and to a lesser extent in mining and carpet-making. Many Pakistani women and men migrate voluntarily to the Persian Gulf States, Iran, Turkey, South Africa, Uganda, Greece and other European countries for low-skilled employment such as domestic work, driving or construction work; once abroad, some become victims of labour trafficking.'[34]

'Sri Lanka is a source and destination country for men and women trafficked for the purposes of involuntary servitude and commercial sexual exploitation. Sri Lankan men and women migrate willingly to Kuwait, Jordan, Saudi Arabia, Qatar, Lebanon, Singapore, Hong Kong, Malaysia and South Korea to work as construction workers, domestic servants, or garment factory workers. Government prohibits all forms of trafficking through an April 2006 amendment to its penal code. Trafficking offenses are punishable by up to 20 years' imprisonment; these penalties are commensurate with those assigned for other grave crimes. In August 2007, the Bureau of Foreign Employment (BFE) began requiring that all overseas employment contracts be signed in the presence a BFE official to ensure that migrant workers understand the contracts' terms.'[35]

'The Sri Lankan Constitution is a written Constitution which contains two provisions specifically on trafficking. Both provisions are on trafficking of children. The Constitution of Sri Lanka places an obligation on the State to protect children and to take concrete action to ensure such protection. Details of punishing trafficking are dealt with by legislation and are covered subsequently. Children under Article 27(13) of the Constitution of Sri Lanka must be protected against all harm, including by implication trafficking. Article 12(4) further implies that the State must take action in order to ensure such protection to children. The Constitution places emphasis on the duty of the State to actively protect children. Although there is an Act in Sri Lanka which is specifically on trafficking, though limited to women and children in prostitution, it has not yet been notified and cannot be used in cases of trafficking.'[36]

'The Maldives is primarily a destination country for migrant workers from Bangladesh and, to a lesser extent, India, some of whom are subjected to trafficking in persons, specifically forced labour. A small number of women from Sri Lanka, Thailand, India, China, the Philippines, Eastern Europe and former Soviet Union countries are recruited for forced prostitution in Male, the capital. Diplomatic sources estimate that half of the 35,000 Bangladeshis in the Maldives went there illegally and that most of these workers are probably victims of trafficking.'[37]

'Trafficking within Afghanistan is more prevalent than transnational trafficking and the majority of victims are children. Afghan boys are subjected to forced prostitution and forced labour in the drug smuggling industry in Pakistan and Iran. NGOs indicate that families sometimes make cost-benefit analyses regarding how much debt they can incur based on their tradable family members. Women and girls from Iran, Tajikistan and possibly Uganda and China are forced into prostitution in

Afghanistan. Some international security contractors may have been involved in the sex trafficking of these women. Brothels and prostitution rings are sometimes run by foreigners, sometimes with links to larger criminal networks.'[38]

'Internal displacement due to the conflict has left many Afghanis without a home, exposing them to the dangers of trafficking. Widespread poverty and lack of legitimate economic opportunities have increased the instances of child labour and child trafficking. The cultural treatment of women makes them especially susceptible to violence, including forced marriage. Afghanistan does not have a specific anti-trafficking law and does not explicitly criminalise trafficking in persons in its penal code. However, other laws can be used to address trafficking in persons and related crimes. The constitution of Afghanistan guarantees the equality of all Afghani citizens, whether male or female, before the law as well as the liberty and human dignity of any human being. The constitution also specifies that Afghanistan shall abide by the United Nations Charter, international treaties and the Universal Declaration of Human Rights. The Ministry of Women's Affairs (MoWA) was established under the Bonn Agreement in late 2001. MoWA focuses on advocacy and gender equality, aims at ensuring that the specific needs of women are reflected in national policy, develops projects targeting vulnerable women, promotes gender awareness among the public, collaborates with nongovernmental organisations on advocacy and monitors government action on the development and implementation of national policies affecting women.'[39]

Women Trafficking in India

'India is a destination for women and girls from Nepal and Bangladesh trafficked for the purpose of commercial sexual exploitation. Indian women are trafficked to the Middle East for commercial sexual exploitation. Indian migrants who migrate willingly every year to the Middle East and Europe for work as domestic servants and low-skilled labourers may also end up part of the human-trafficking industry.'[40] 'In India, a large number of children are trafficked not only for the sex 'trade' but also for other forms of non-sex based exploitation that includes servitude of diverse kinds, as industrial labour, domestic labour, agricultural labour, organ trade begging and false marriage.'[41]

'Trafficking patterns and routes are often highly complex, ranging from trafficking within one country and cross-border flows between neighbouring countries to inter-continental and globalised trade. Routes are usually divided into origin, transit and destination points; some reports also mention collection and dispersal points. Correspondingly, countries are categorised as sending, transit or destination countries. India is a destination country for persons from Bangladesh and Nepal and a bulk of those trafficked from these countries is women and children. In both cases, the initial migration, legal or illegal, may be voluntary and subsequently migrants may be trafficked. The numbers are very large, though precise figures are lacking and need to be tackled urgently.'[42]

'In the September of 2006, the Indian government created an anti-trafficking law enforcement nodal cell. It is a central department comprising two officials responsible for accumulating and analysing data relating to trafficking in persons in the country. Its duty also includes the action taken by the central and state governments to combat the evil of trafficking. In 2007, three state governments established anti-trafficking police units, the first of this kind in the India. The Central Government, in 2007, banned the employment of child labour in domestic work. The Constitution of India, the supreme law of the land from which all laws originate, guarantees equality and freedom to all citizens by virtue of fundamental rights vested in them. Trafficking is explicitly forbidden as it is opposed to these basic tenants of the Constitution. Article 23 (1) of the Indian Constitution explicitly forbids traffic in human beings, beggar and all other forms of forced labour.'[43]

'The Government of India signed the Trafficking Protocol on 12 December 2002. This is a huge step forward in advancing the human rights of trafficked people as it not only prevents and protects the victims of trafficking but also punishes the traffickers. Further, the 1949 Convention for the Suppression of the Traffic of Persons and of the Exploitation of the Prostitution of Others, the Convention on the Elimination of All Forms of Discrimination Against Women and the Convention on the Rights of the Child (CRC), have been ratified by the Government of India.'[44]

Effects of Women Trafficking

'Women who have been trafficked may suffer from serious health problems, including physical health, reproductive health and mental health problems. Trafficking victims often suffer from serious physical abuse and physical exhaustion, as well as starvation. Typical injuries can include broken bones, concussion, bruising or burns, as well as other injuries consistent with assault.[45] Women are beaten when they disobey the pimp or try to escape. There are countless reports of victims subjected to emotional abuse, in addition to physical battery and rape.'[46]

'Human trafficking deprives people of their human rights and freedoms, it is a global health risk and it fuels the growth of organised crime. But the impact of human trafficking goes beyond individual victims; it undermines the safety and security of all nations it touches. It has a devastating impact on individual victims, who often suffer physical and emotional abuse, rape, threats against self and family, passport theft and even death.'[47] 'Several social and human costs to development are attributable to trafficking in persons. Victims of trafficking could hardly care for the elderly and their children. In several cases, the forced absence of women leads to the breakdown of families and neglect of children. Both human trafficking and HIV greatly threaten human development and food security.'[48] 'The trauma associated with trafficking and its psychological effects can be devastating and, if left unaddressed, can undermine victims' recovery and potentially contribute to vulnerability to re-victimisation. Because traffickers dehumanise and objectify their victims, victims' innate sense of power, visibility and dignity often become obscured.'[49]

'Health issues seen in trafficking victims include the following: (a) Sexually transmitted diseases, HIV/AIDS, pelvic pain, rectal trauma and urinary difficulties from working in the sex industry; (b) Pregnancy, resulting from rape or prostitution; (c) Infertility from chronic untreated sexually transmitted infections or botched or unsafe abortions; (d) Infections or mutilations causes by unsanitary and dangerous medical procedures performed by the trafficker's so-called 'doctor';

(e) Chronic back, hearing, cardiovascular or respiratory problems from endless days toiling in dangerous agriculture, sweatshop or construction conditions; (f) Weak eyes and other eye problems from working in dimly lit sweatshops; (g) Malnourishment and serious dental problems; (h) Infectious diseases like tuberculosis; (i) Undetected or untreated diseases, such as diabetes or cancer; (j) Bruises, scars and other signs of physical abuse and torture; (k) Substance abuse problems or addictions either from being coerced into drug use by their traffickers or by turning to substance abuse to help cope with or mentally escape their desperate situations.'[50]

United Nations Global Initiative to Fight Human Trafficking

'The United Nations Global Initiative to Fight Human Trafficking (UN.GIFT) was born out of a renewed commitment by world leaders in the battle against human trafficking to end this crime, one of the most egregious violations of human rights in the world today.[51] UN.GIFT was launched in March 2007 by the International Labour Organisation (ILO), the Office of the United Nations High Commissioner for Human Rights (OHCHR), the United Nations Children's Fund (UNICEF), the United Nations Office on Drugs and Crime (UNODC), the International Organisation for Migration (IOM) and the Organisation for Security and Cooperation in Europe (OSCE). The Global Initiative is based on a simple principle: human trafficking is a crime of such magnitude and atrocity that it cannot be dealt with successfully by any government alone. This global problem requires a global, multi-stakeholder strategy that builds on national efforts throughout the world.'[52]

'The UN.GIFT alliance is composed of the six major international organisations providing technical know-how and expertise to governments and non-governmental entities in addressing the human trafficking challenge. The UN.GIFT Steering Committee, comprising representatives from the six founding members and the main donor to UN.GIFT, coordinates anti-trafficking efforts of its members and their respective networks and alliances. The UN.GIFT Steering Committee provides a unique opportunity to increase the impact of anti-trafficking responses supported by the UN and other organisations and to create synergies to ensure the most efficient and effective delivery of anti-trafficking activities.'[53]

International Conventions

'The UN General Assembly defines human trafficking as "The illicit and clandestine movement of persons across national borders with the end goal of forcing women, girls and children into sexually oppressive and exploitative situations for profit for recruiters, traffickers and crime syndicate, as well as other illegal activities related to trafficking such as forced domestic labour, false marriages, clandestine employment and false adoption." The eight major forms of trafficking as stated in the United Nations (UN) Protocol against trafficking 2000 are forced labour, sex trafficking, bonded labour, debt bondage among migrant labourers, involuntary servitude, forced child labour, child soldiers and child sex trafficking.'[54]

'On 15th November 2000, the United Nations General Assembly adopted the United Nations Convention Against Organised Crime, which came into force on 23rd September 2003. To supplement the Convention, the Protocol to Prevent, Suppress and Punish Trafficking in Persons, Especially Women and Children, also known as the Palermo Protocol, was adopted. The Palermo Protocol defines Trafficking in Persons as: *the recruitment, transportation, transfer, harbouring or receipt of persons, by means of the threat or use of force or other forms of coercion, of abduction, of fraud, of deception, of the abuse of power or of a position of vulnerability or of the giving or receiving of payments or benefits to achieve the consent of a person having control of another person, for the purpose of exploitation. Exploitation shall include, at a minimum, the exploitation of the prostitution of others or other forms of sexual exploitation, forced labour or services, slavery or practices similar to slavery, servitude or the removal of organs.*'[55]

'Of the 79 ACP countries, 52 States signed and ratified and 19 accessed to the Palermo Protocol that entered into force in 2003 (UN, 2011). Almost all ACP countries ratified the 1930 ILO Convention No. 29 concerning Forced or Compulsory Labour, the 1957 ILO Convention No. 105 concerning the Abolition of Forced Labour and the 1999 ILO Convention No. 182 on the Prohibition and Elimination of the Worst Forms of Child Labour.

The United Nations Convention against Transnational Organised Crime, adopted by General Assembly resolution 55/25 of 15th November 2000, is the main international instrument in the fight against transnational organised crime. It opened for signature by Member States at a High-level Political Conference convened for that purpose in Palermo, Italy, on 12-15 December 2000 and entered into force on 29th September 2003. The Convention is further supplemented by three Protocols, which target specific areas and manifestations of organised crime: the Protocol to Prevent, Suppress and Punish Trafficking in Persons, Especially Women and Children; the Protocol against the Smuggling of Migrants by Land, Sea and Air; and the Protocol against the Illicit Manufacturing of and Trafficking in Firearms, their Parts and Components and Ammunition. The Convention represents a major step forward in the fight against transnational organised crime and signifies the recognition by Member States of the seriousness of the problems posed by it, as well as the need to foster and enhance close international cooperation in order to tackle those problems. The Protocol against the Illicit Manufacturing of and Trafficking in Firearms, their Parts and Components and Ammunition was adopted by General Assembly resolution 55/255 of 31st May 2001.'[56]

'Instruments that have dealt with human trafficking date back to the abolition of slavery. They include provisions within the Slavery Convention (1926) and the Supplementary Convention on the Abolition of Slavery, the Slave Trade and Institutions and Practices Similar to Slavery (1956). Additional tools of international law that include segments against the trafficking of persons include: the Universal Declaration of Human Rights (1948), the International Covenants on Civil and Political Rights (1966), The United Nations Convention for the Suppression of the Traffic in Persons and of the Exploitation of the Prostitution of Others (1949) and the Convention on the Elimination of all Forms of Discrimination Against Women (1979). Anti-trafficking laws are problematic to enforce because victims of trafficking are hesitant to identify traffickers for fear of repercussion. Furthermore, trafficking is a crime that transcends borders and therefore jurisdictions.'[57]

Conclusion

Human trafficking is the trade of humans for sexual slavery, forced labour or commercial sexual exploitation for the trafficker or others. It can occur within a country or trans-nationally. The root causes of trafficking are various and often differ from one country to another. Some of the common factors are local conditions that make populations want to migrate in search of better conditions: poverty, oppression, lack of human rights, lack of social or economic opportunity, dangers from conflict or instability and similar conditions. Human trafficking is a modern-day form of slavery. Victims are young children, teenagers, men and women. Victims of human trafficking are subjected to force, fraud, or coercion to compel them to engage in commercial sex or involuntary labour. Trafficking has been viewed with increasing concern in South Asia as a region and by individual South Asian countries as well. India is a destination for women and girls from Nepal and Bangladesh trafficked for the purpose of commercial sexual exploitation. Trafficking victims often suffer from serious physical abuse and physical exhaustion, as well as starvation. Typical injuries can include broken bones, concussion, bruising or burns, as well as other injuries consistent with assault.

References

1. Investigating Human trafficking types causes and effects, Retrieved from http://www.ukessays.com/essays/criminology/investigating-human-trafficking-types-causes-and-effects-criminology-essay.php
2. Gudetu Wakgari, Causes and Consequences of Human Trafficking in Ethiopia: The case of Women in the Middle East, International Journal of Gender and Women's Studies, June 2014, Vol. 2, No. 2, pp. 233-246.
3. Combating Trafficking in South-East Asia: A Review of Policy and Programme Responses, Retrieved from http://www.unesco.org/most/migration/ctsea.pdf
4. Gabriel Temesgen, Root causes and solutions to Human trafficking in Ethiopia, Retrieved from http://aigaforum.com/articles/root-causes-and-solutions-to-human-trafficking-in-Ethiopia.pdf
5. Facts about the human trafficking, Retrieved from http://2001-2009.state.gov/documents/organisation/33216.pdf
6. Human trafficking (2014), Retrieved from http://en.wikipedia.org/wiki/Human_trafficking

7. See http://unesdoc.unesco.org/images/0014/001478/147844e.pdf
8. Johannes Koettl (2009), Human Traffi cking, Modern Day Slavery and Economic Exploitation, Retrieved from http://siteresources.worldbank.org/SOCIALPROTECTION/Resources/SP-Discussion-papers/Labor-Market-DP/0911.pdf
9. Violation of Women's Rights: A cause and consequence of trafficking in women (2008), Retrieved from http://lastradainternational.org/lsidocs/431%20LSI-%20violation%20of%20womens%20rights.pdf
10. Majeed A. Rahman, Human Trafficking in the era of Globalisation: The case of Trafficking in the Global Market Economy, Transcience Journal Vol. 2, No. 1 (2011), p. 80.
11. Addressing the root causes of trafficking, Retrieved from http://www.unodc.org/documents/human-trafficking/Toolkit-files/08-58296_tool_9-2.pdf
12. Root Causes of Human Trafficking, Retrieved from http://www.ipjc.org/links/USCSAHT%20-%20HT%20and%20Root%20Causes%20module.pdf
13. Gabriel Temesgen, Root causes and solutions to Human trafficking in Ethiopia, Retrieved from http://aigaforum.com/articles/root-causes-and-solutions-to-human-trafficking-in-Ethiopia.pdf
14. Migration Challenges in the Indian Ocean Littoral, Retrieved from http://www.stimson.org/images/uploads/research-pdfs/ruchira.pdf
15. Child victims of human trafficking, Retrieved from http://www.law.washington.edu/AsianLaw/HumanTrafficking/child_victims.pdf
16. Human trafficking: Understanding and addressing violence against women, Retrieved from http://apps.who.int/iris/bitstream/10665/77394/1/WHO_RHR_12.42_eng.pdf
17. Erin Weaver (2014), Human trafficking has wide-reaching social impact, Retrieved from http://www.montgomerynews.com/articles/2014/01/21/souderton_independent/news/doc52d735fdbe3eb165162138.txt
18. A Comparative Study of Women Trafficked in the Migration Process, Retrieved from http://www.oas.org/atip/Migration/Comparative%20study%2 0of%20women%20trafficked%20in%20migration%20process.pdf
19. Ambe J. Njoh and Elizabeth N.M. Ayuk-Etang, Combating Forced Labour and Human Trafficking in Africa: The Role of Endogenous and Exogenous Forces, African Review of Economics and Finance, Vol. 4, No. 1, Dec. 2012.

20. Thanh-Dam Truong and Maria Belen Angeles (2005), Searching for Best Practices to Counter Human Trafficking in Africa: A Focus on Women and Children, Report Commissioned by United Nations Educational, Scientific and Cultural Organisation.
21. Human Trafficking: A Brief Overview, Retrieved from http://siteresources.worldbank.org/EXTSOCIALDEVELOPMENT/Resources/244362-1239390842422/6012763-1239905793229/Human_Trafficking.pdf
22. Clare Ribando Seelke (2015), Trafficking in Persons in Latin America and the Caribbean, Retrieved from https://www.fas.org/sgp/crs/row/RL33200.pdf
23. Clare Ribando (2005), Trafficking in Persons in Latin America and the Caribbean, Retrieved from http://www.oas.org/atip/Latin%20America/CRS%20Dec%202005.pdf
24. Combating Trafficking in South-East Asia: A Review of Policy and Programme Responses (2000), Retrieved from http://www.unesco.org/most/migration/ctsea.pdf
25. Human Trafficking in South-East Asia | Overview, Retrieved from http://www.afppd.org/files/1113/8206/9530/Policy_Brief.pdf
26. Responses to Human Trafficking in Bangladesh, India, Nepal and Sri Lanka, Retrieved from http://www.unodc.org/documents/human-trafficking/2011/Responses_to_Human_Trafficking_in_Bangladesh_India_Nepal_and_Sri_Lanka.pdf
27. Ruh Afza Ruhi, Human trafficking in Bangladesh: An Overview, Asian Affairs, Vol. 25, No. 4 : 45-56, October-December, 2003.
28. Mohammad Barad Hossain Chowdhury, Human trafficking in persons in Bangladesh, Retrieved from http://www.unafei.or.jp/english/pdf/RS_No89/No89_PA_Chowdhury.pdf
29. Responses to Human Trafficking in Bangladesh, India, Nepal and Sri Lanka, Retrieved from http://www.unodc.org/documents/human-trafficking/2011/Responses_to_Human_ Trafficking_in_Bangladesh_India_Nepal_and_Sri_Lanka.pdf
30. Bhutan: Working against human trafficking - focusing on rights, not on numbers, Retrieved from http://www.unodc.org/southasia//frontpage/2013/April/bhutan-working-against-human-trafficking-focussing-on-rights-not-on-numbers.html
31. Human trafficking in Nepal (2014), Retrieved from http://en.wikipedia.org/wiki/Human_trafficking_in_Nepal
32. Nayan B. Khatri. Nepal: The problem of trafficking in women and children, Retrieved from http://www.asiapacificforum.net/about/

annual-meetings/7th-india-2002/downloads/thematic-issues/nepal_trafficking.pdf

33. Trafficking in persons especially on women and children in Nepal (2011), Retrieved from http://www.nhrcnepal.org/nhrc_new/doc/newsletter/National%20Report%20on%20Traffiking%20in%20Persons%20%20Especially%20%20on%20women%20and%20Children%20in%20Nepal%20-%202012.pdf
34. Human trafficking in Pakistan (2014), Retrieved from http://en.wikipedia.org/wiki/Human_trafficking_in_Pakistan
35. Human trafficking in Sri Lanka (2014), Retrieved from http://en.wikipedia.org/wiki/Human_trafficking_in_Sri_Lanka
36. Responses to Human Trafficking in Bangladesh, India, Nepal and Sri Lanka, Retrieved from http://www.unodc.org/documents/human-trafficking/2011/Responses_to_Human_Trafficking _in_Bangladesh_India_ Nepal_and_Sri_Lanka.pdf
37. Human trafficking in Maldives (2014), Retrieved from http://en.wikipedia.org/wiki/Human_trafficking_in_the_Maldives
38. Human trafficking in Afghanistan (2014), Retrieved from http://en.wikipedia.org/wiki/Human_trafficking_in_Afghanistan
39. A Human Rights Report on Trafficking in Persons, Especially Women and Children, Retrieved from http://www.protection project. org/wp-content/uploads/2010/09/Afghanistan.pdf
40. Human trafficking in India (2014), Retrieved from http://en.wikipedia.org/wiki/Human_trafficking_in_India
41. Eira Mishra, Combating Human Trafficking: A Legal Perspective with Special Reference to India, Sociology and Anthropology 1(4): 172-179, 2013.
42. Responses to Human Trafficking in Bangladesh, India, Nepal and Sri Lanka, Retrieved from http://www.unodc.org/documents/human-trafficking/2011/Responses_to_Human_Trafficking_in_Bangladesh_India_Nepal_and_Sri_Lanka.pdf
43. Eira Mishra, Combating Human Trafficking: A Legal Perspective with Special Reference to India, Sociology and Anthropology 1(4): 172-179, 2013.
44. See http://www.protectionproject.org/wp-content/uploads/2010/11/NAP-Draft-India_2006.pdf
45. Effects and consequences of trafficking in women, Retrieved from http://www1.umn.edu/humanrts/svaw/trafficking/explore/4effects.htm
46. Erin Weaver (2014), Human trafficking has wide-reaching social impact, Retrieved from http://www.montgomerynews.com/

articles/2014/01/21/souderton_independent/news/doc52d735fdbe3eb165162138.txt

47. Impact of Human Trafficking on Victims, Retrieved from http://www.justice.gov/usao-ndia/human-trafficking-response-team/impact-human-trafficking-victims

48. Gabriel Temesgen, Root causes and solutions to Human trafficking in Ethiopia, Retrieved from http://aigaforum.com/articles/root-causes-and-solutions-to-human-trafficking-in-Ethiopia.pdf

49. See http://www.state.gov/documents/organisation/194931.pdf

50. Human Trafficking - Medical effects on victims, Retrieved from https://ec.europa.eu/anti-trafficking/sites/antitrafficking/files/forum_magazine_on_medical_effects_1.pdf

51. An Introduction to Human Trafficking: Vulnerability, Impact and Action, Retrieved from http://www.unodc.org/documents/human-trafficking/An_Introduction_to_Human_Trafficking_-_Background_Paper.pdf

52. See http://www.ungift.org/knowledgehub/en/about/index.html

53. United Nations Global Initiative to Fight Human Trafficking (2014), Retrieved from http://en.wikipedia.org/wiki/United_Nations_Global_Initiative_to_Fight_Human_Trafficking

54. Internal Trafficking of Women and Girls in Pakistan (2012), Retrieved from http://www.af.org.pk/gep/Research%20Studies%20%28Gender%20Based%20Violence%29/study%20on%20trafficking%20final.pdf

55. Human trafficking in Eastern Africa: Research Assessment and Baseline Information in Tanzania, Kenya, Uganda and Burundi (2008), International Organisation for Migration.

56. United Nations Convention against Transnational Organised Crime and the Protocols Thereto, Retrieved from http://www.unodc.org/unodc/treaties/CTOC/

57. Lindsey King, International Law and Human Trafficking, Retrieved from http://endslavery.salvos.org.au/wp-content/uploads/2014/09/10.-InternationalLaw.pdf

11

Marital Rape

> "Clearly older women and especially older women who have led an active life or elder women who successfully maneuver through their own family life have so much to teach us about sharing, patience and wisdom."
>
> —*Alice Walker*

Introduction

'Marriage in Indian society is considered to be a sacred institution. It is the very foundation of a stable family and a civilised society. However, such institution veils acts like sexual cruelty and other forms of brutality in the household. Marital rape is one such brutality. Among all the crimes against the women, marital rape seems to be the most under reported crimes in the country. Indian society can still be considered to be a conservative society, where the woman is restricted from discussing her sexual as well as her personal life with anyone.'[1] 'In his *History of the Pleas of the Crown* (1736), Sir Matthew Hale made the following pronouncement: But the husband cannot be guilty of a rape committed by himself upon his lawful wife, for by their mutual matrimonial consent and contract the wife hath given up herself in this kind unto her husband which she cannot retract.'[2]

'Typically the screening criteria include caste, ancient Indian astrological signs and sub-caste. Instead of two people who want to spend their life together getting married, it's a situation where society mandates that the match two families have decided be accepted by the new husband and wife. Arranged marriage is almost inevitably tied to the dowry system and the woman's family paying for the incredibly expensive marriage festivals. Society forces this and very often the woman's parents take huge loans and go broke. This happens throughout the Indian class spectrum. The arranged marriage system is indirectly responsible for perpetuating the caste system and almost certainly one of the major reasons this marital rape law will not get passed anytime soon.'[3]

'The International Centre for Women (ICRW) and United Nations Population Fund's (UNPFA) new study provides some insight into societal expectations of masculinity, son preference and the impact on violence against women. Among the findings is some data on sexual violence within relationships. The data assumes more importance since household-level data on the nature of human relationships is rare in India and the National Family Health Survey being famously delayed.'[4]

Meaning of the Concept

'Marital rape is non-consensual sex in which the perpetrator is the victim's spouse. It is a form of partner rape, of domestic violence and of sexual abuse. The issues of sexual and domestic violence within marriage and the family unit and more generally, the issue of violence against women, have come to growing international attention from the second half of the twentieth century onwards. The reluctance to criminalise and prosecute marital rape has been attributed to traditional views of marriage, to interpretations of religious doctrines, to ideas about male sexuality and female sexuality and to cultural expectations of subordination of a wife to her husband.'[5]

'Marital rape is rape within a marriage, where consent to sexual intercourse is not given. According to wikipedia, which defines it rather succinctly, marital rape, also known as spousal rape, is non-consensual sex in which the perpetrator is the victim's spouse.'[6] 'As such, it is a form of partner rape, of domestic violence and of sexual abuse. Once widely condoned or ignored by law, spousal rape is now repudiated by international conventions and increasingly criminalised. Still, in many countries, spousal rape either remains legal, or is illegal but widely tolerated and accepted as a spouse's prerogative.'[7]

'Marital rape is the term used to describe nonconsensual sexual acts between spouses, ex-spouses, or intimate long-term partners. These sexual acts can include: intercourse, anal or oral sex, forced sexual behaviour with other individuals and other unwanted, painful and humiliating sexual activities. It is rape if your partner uses force, threats, or intimidation to get you to submit to sexual acts. Marital rape occurs when your spouse forces you to take part in certain sex acts without your consent. It is a form of intimate partner violence, i.e., an abuse of power by which one spouse attempts to establish dominance and control over the other. While every state has its own laws on the subject, broadly defined, marital rape includes any unwanted intercourse or penetration (vaginal, anal, or oral) obtained by force, threat of force, or when the wife is unable to consent.'[8] 'One of the difficulties in addressing the issue of wife rape, as is the case with rape in general, is defining what behaviours should be considered rape.'[9]

Types of Marital Rape

'The following three kinds of marital rape are identified by legal scholars as generally prevalent in the society.

(a) *Battering Rape*: In battering rapes, women experience both physical and sexual violence in the relationship and they experience this violence in various ways.

(b) *Force-only Rape*: In what is called force-only rape, husbands use only the amount of force necessary to coerce their wives; battering may not be characteristic of these relationships.

(c) *Obsessive Rape:* Other women experience what has been labelled sadistic or obsessive rape; these assaults involve torture and/or perverse sexual acts and are often physically violent.'[10]

Reasons of Marital Rape

'The essential feature of marital rape is the relationship of husband and wife between the man and woman; this makes the issue more socially relevant. Like in rape, in marital rape also there is no consent of the women and there is use of force by the man for sexual intercourse. The reasons of marital rape can be many such as sexual perversion of husband; desire to assert superiority of men over women; petty domestic issues; attempt of women to demand her right in marital relationship etc. Also, one of the reasons is the role traditionally assigned to married women in our society. The role as defined by society to married women is of *pativratastri* means pure, faithful and obliging women. Thus, a married woman is supposed to follow her husband's directions fully and fulfill all his demands without any questioning. Economic dependence over her husband and in-laws is also one of the reasons that married women are unable to protect themselves from frequent practice of marital rape and are bound to bear the violence. Another reason is the absence of legal provisions recognising marital rape as an offence.'[11]

Marital Rape: Global Perspectives

'Marital rape is illegal in 18 American States, three Australian States, New Zealand, Canada, Israel, France, Sweden, Denmark, Norway, Soviet Union, Poland and Czechoslovakia.'[12] 'Malaysia changed its laws to that effect in 2007; Turkey in 2005; and Bolivia earlier in 2012. The United States began criminalising marital rape in 1970s and most European countries in the 1990s.'[13] 'China, Afghanistan, Pakistan and Saudi Arabia are some of the countries that do not criminalise marital rape.'[14]

According to wikipedia, countries which were early to criminalise marital rape include the Soviet Union (1922/1960), Poland (1932), Czechoslovakia (1950), some other members of the Communist Bloc, Sweden (1965) and Norway (1971). Slovenia, then a republic within federal Yugoslavia, criminalised marital rape in 1977. The Israeli Supreme Court affirmed that marital rape is a crime in a 1980 decision, citing law based on the Talmud (at least sixth century). Criminalisation in Australia began with the state of New South Wales in 1981, followed by all other states from 1985 to 1992. Several formerly British-ruled countries followed suit: Canada (1983), New Zealand (1985) and Ireland (1990). Marital rape was criminalised in Austria in 1989.

In Switzerland marital rape became a crime in 1992. Marital rape was made illegal in the Netherlands in 1991. Cyprus criminalised marital rape in 1994. Marital rape was made illegal in Macedonia in 1996. Croatia marital rape was criminalised in 1998. Liechtenstein made marital rape illegal in 2001. In Colombia, marital rape was criminalised in 1996, in Chile in 1999. Thailand outlawed marital rape in 2007. Papua New Guinea criminalised marital rape in 2003. Namibia outlawed marital rape in 2000. Recent countries to criminalise marital rape include Zimbabwe (2001), Turkey (2005), Cambodia (2005), Liberia (2006), Nepal (2006), Mauritius (2007), Ghana (2007), Malaysia (2007), Thailand (2007), Rwanda (2009), Suriname (2009), Nicaragua (2012), Sierra Leone (2012), South Korea (2013), Bolivia (2013), Samoa (2013).'[15]

Marital Rape in India

'The marital rape exemption can be traced to statements by Sir Mathew Hale, Chief Justice in England, during the 1600s. He wrote, "The husband cannot be guilty of a rape committed by himself upon his lawful wife, for by their mutual matrimonial consent and contract, the wife hath given herself in kind unto the husband, whom she cannot retract." In the present day, studies indicate that between 10 and 14 per cent of married women are raped by their husbands: the incidents of marital rape soars to one-third to half among clinical samples of battered women. Sexual assault by one's spouse accounts for approximately 25 per cent of rapes committed.'[16] 'Statistics paint a disturbing picture about the condition of married women in our country. According to the UN Population Fund, more than two-thirds of married women in India, aged between 15 to 49, have been beaten, raped or forced to provide sex.'[17]

'A new study has revealed 26 per cent of women in Pune, 23 per cent in Bhubaneswar and 16 per cent in Jaipur often have sex with husbands against their desire. The findings by International Institute of Population Sciences (IIPS), Mumbai, show drinking to be the biggest reason for rampant and large-scale victimisation of urban poor women in marriages. This is marital rape. Overall, two per cent of women in Bhubaneswar and six per cent in Jaipur and Pune said their last sexual intercourse had some component of alcohol. The use of alcohol was three times higher in slum areas as compared to non-slum areas in cities. Twelve per cent of women in Pune slums, five per cent in Bhubaneswar and nine per cent in Jaipur slums reported use of alcohol during their last intercourse, said S K Singh, who headed the research. The figures are always higher in slum areas. In Pune, for instance, 31 per cent of women living in slums said their husbands were often drunk as compared to 12 in non-slum areas. Alcoholism is an important factor in violence against women by their husbands. A women's leader in Pune said there was a high per centage of alcoholism among men.'[18]

'A number of studies and statistics prove that marital rape is a reality in India. But laws that do not acknowledge this are another reality that a large number of married women are forced to live with. Any marriage counsellor, family lawyer, women's rights activist or victim will tell you that marital rape is a reality in India. That laws do not acknowledge it is another reality that a large number of married women are forced to live with. Accounts of domestic violence are often accompanied with accounts of sexual violence against the wife. A 2014 research, titled "Masculinity, Intimate Partner Violence and Son Preference in India", by the International Center for Research on Women and United Nations Population Fund conducted on men and women aged 18-49 in seven states across India investigated the prevalence of sexual violence within marriage.'[19] 'Marital rape is a common but it is only un-reported crime. A study conducted by the Joint Women Programme, an NGO found that one out of seven married women had been raped by their husband at least once. They frequently do not report these rapes because the law does not support them.'[20]

Effects of Marital Rape

'Women who are raped by their partners are likely to suffer severe psychological consequences as well. Some of the short-term effects of marital rape include anxiety, shock, intense fear, depression, suicidal ideation and post-traumatic stress. Long-term effects often include disordered eating, sleep problems, depression, problems in establishing trusting relationships and increased negative feelings about themselves. Psychological effects are likely to be long-lasting.'[21]

'Sexual violence is a serious intrusion of sexual and reproductive autonomy, bodily and psychological integrity and when it occurs in intimate relationships, it is also a breach of trust and can be a serious risk factor for femicide. Women experiencing spousal violence are far more likely than men to be fearful, depressed, or suffer anxiety attacks. For Indigenous women and perhaps other women as well, sexual violence may also be seen as a threat to health and security of the entire community. Poverty, social inequalities and the lack of available services may make it difficult for women to leave violent relationships, thus putting them at risk of further violence and harm. There are few specific statistics available on the incidence of sexual violence in intimate relationships.'[22]

'Victims of rape are impacted in many ways. In addition to suffering physical injury they suffer great distress living with the memory of what happened to them, worrying about the risk of pregnancy and disease and living with feelings of guilt, shame and self-loathing. Victims often blame themselves for succumbing to the rape. Jewish law prohibits emotional assault and abuse.'[23] 'Women who have been raped by their partners experience pain, humiliation and distress. Marital rape causes public health problems including poor maternal and child health, repeat-infections with Sexually-Transmitted Infections (STIs) and long-term exposure to the risk of HIV infection. Marital rape prevents individuals from being able to take control of their own sexual and reproductive health. Marital rape is one of the under-reported violent crimes because it is socially tolerated. Some abused women are afraid to report the violence because they rely financially on their husbands for their upkeep and children's maintenance.'[24]

'Research indicates that wife rape victims are more likely to be raped multiple times when compared with stranger and acquaintance rape victims and women who experience wife rape suffer long lasting physical and psychological injuries which are as severe or more severe than stranger rape victims. Women raped by a partner are being violated by someone with whom they share their lives, homes and possibly children. In addition to the violation of their bodies, they are faced with a betrayal of trust and intimacy. Sadly, victims of wife rape are not likely to see what is being done to them as a violation of their rights.'[25]

Legal Mechanism

'Under the Indian Penal Code (IPC), rape is defined as

sexual intercourse with a woman against her will or without her consent. By this definition, rape can and often is committed within a marriage. Besides cases that reach counsellors, family courts, NGOs and activists, there are studies to establish this. Section 375 of the IPC - the law governing rape makes an exception when forced sex is with a wife of over 15 years of age and says that this does not amount to rape.'[26] 'In India, marital rape can come under cruelty clauses of Section 498A of Indian Penal Code. Cruelty, though not specifically defined, covers physical and mental harassment. Punishment is maximum three years with fine. Another section of law, 375 IPC defines rape, but says it is not rape if it is intercourse between husband and wife and when such wife is not younger than 15.'[27]

' In *Bodhisattwa Gautam vs. Subhra Chakraborty* the Supreme Court said that "rape is a crime against basic human rights and a violation of the victim's" most cherished of fundamental rights, namely, the right to life enshrined in Article 21 of the Constitution. Yet it negates this very pronouncement by not recognising marital. Women who experience and wish to challenge sexual violence from their husbands are currently denied State protection as the Indian law in Section 375 of the Indian Penal Code, 1860 has a general marital rape exemption.'[28]

'The department of legal affairs has drafted the Criminal Law (Amendment) Bill based on recommendations of the women and child development ministry (WCD) and the National Commission for Women (NCW) to amend certain sections of the Indian Penal Code (IPC), the Code of Criminal procedure, 1973; and the Indian Evidence Act, 1872, to recognise new categories of sexual assault besides redefining rape by including sexual assault in any form in its definition. While women groups say that marital rape is a worldwide phenomenon and almost 50 per cent of women face forced sex by their husbands, men's organisations said the changes in law would essentially damage the fabric of a family system.

However, the proposed new law, besides terming sexual relationship of a man with a wife under the age of 18 as rape, also specifies under section 376 (1) that if a man commits sexual assault even on his wife, who is above 18 years of age, shall be punished with imprisonment which may extend to three years and shall be liable for a fine. The other proposals include making punishment for molestation more stringent. An additional section 354 (A) will be added saying: whoever strips a woman, attempts or abets to strip a woman in public place, shall be punishable for a term not less than one year, which may be extended up to seven years of rigorous imprisonment.'[29]

'Recently, after a student was raped and murdered in Delhi, former Indian Supreme Court chief justice J.S. Verma headed a committee that made recommendations for improving India's rape laws.'[30] 'Criminalising marital rape was also among the suggestions of the Verma Committee, a three-member panel appointed to suggest amendments to India's sexual assault laws. The government rejected this proposed change, leaving it out of the draft bill it then presented to Parliament. A panel of lawmakers who opposed the move argued it has the potential of destroying the institution of marriage, according to a report submitted to Parliament. "If marital rape is brought under the law, the entire family system will be under great stress," adds the report. Supporters of the government's decision, including the police, claim it is hard to prosecute marital rape, because unlike an unmarried victim, evidence of penetration is not considered sufficient evidence for rape. The law, they argue, could be misused by couples.

Some activists acknowledge it is hard to prove rape among married women, but argue this is not a good enough reason to deny women a legal framework to fight sexual abuse. Some legal experts believe the government is reluctant to criminalise marital rape because it would require them to tweak laws based on religious practices, including the Hindu Marriage Act 1955, which says a wife is duty-bound to have sex with her husband.'[31] 'The Law Commission of India did not recommend criminalisation of marital rape by amending the exception to Section 375 of the Indian Penal Code and hence presently there is no proposal to bring any amendment to the IPC in this regard.'[32] *"It is considered that the concept of marital rape, as understood internationally, cannot be suitably applied in the Indian context due to various factors, including level of education, illiteracy, poverty, myriad social customs and values, religious beliefs, mindset of the society to treat the marriage as a sacrament,"* Home Minister Haribhai Parathibhai Chaudhary said.'[33]

Declaration on the Elimination of Violence against Women

'In December 1993, the United Nations High Commissioner for Human Rights published the Declaration on the Elimination of Violence against Women and declared marital rape as a human rights violation. Similarly, the Council of Europe Convention, in force since 2014 August, declared non-consensual sexual acts committed against a spouse or partner as illegal. This convention is legally binding in Europe. Other countries where marital rape is illegal include the US, UK, Canada, Australia, New Zealand, Israel, Sweden, Russia, Poland and many more.'[34]

'The marital rape exemption or defense became more widely viewed as inconsistent with the developing concepts of human rights and equality. Feminists worked systematically since the 1960s to overturn the marital rape exemption and criminalise marital rape. In 2006, the UN Secretary-General's. In-depth study on all forms of violence against women stated that "Marital rape may be prosecuted in at least 104 States. Of these, 32 have made marital rape a specific criminal offence, while the remaining 74 do not exempt marital rape from general rape provisions. Marital rape is not a prosecutable offence in at least 53 States. Four States criminalise marital rape only when the spouses are judicially separated. Four States are considering legislation that would allow marital rape to be prosecuted."[35]

Conclusion

Marital rape is non-consensual sex in which the perpetrator is the victim's spouse. It is a form of partner rape, of domestic violence and of sexual abuse. It is the term used to describe nonconsensual sexual acts between spouses, ex-spouses, or intimate long-term partners. These sexual acts can include: intercourse, anal or oral sex, forced sexual behaviour with other individuals and other unwanted, painful and humiliating sexual activities. Women who are raped by their partners are likely to suffer severe psychological consequences as well.

Some of the short-term effects of marital rape include anxiety, shock, intense fear, depression, suicidal ideation and post-traumatic stress. Long-term effects often include disordered eating, sleep problems, depression, problems in establishing trusting relationships and increased negative feelings about themselves. Recently, after a student was raped and murdered in Delhi, former Indian Supreme Court chief justice J.S. Verma headed a committee that made recommendations for improving India's rape laws. Criminalising marital rape was also among the suggestions of the Verma Committee, a three-member panel appointed to suggest amendments to India's sexual assault laws.

References

1. Udisha Ghosh (2015), Marital Rape: The Need for Criminalisation in India, Retrieved from http://www.lawctopus.com/academike/marital-rape-need-criminalisation-india/
2. The possibility of rape within marriage, Retrieved from http://cw.routledge.com/textbooks/9780415639989/downloads/rape-marriage.pdf
3. https://www.reddit.com/r/worldnews/comments/34lvfl/indian_governments_reasoning_for_not/
4. The Hindu (November 12, 2014), Marital rape: the numbers don't lie, Retrieved from http://www.thehindu.com/data/statistics-on-marital-rape/article6586829.ece
5. Marital rape (2015), Retrieved from http://en.wikipedia.org/wiki/Marital_rape
6. Rape in Marriage, http://texaslawhelp.org/files/685E99A9-A3EB-6584-CA74-137E0474AE2C/attachments/BFA48673-8514-441E-8BC3-40625F79CC9C/rapeinmarriage.pdf
7. Vibha Yadav, Marital rape, Retrieved from http://ujala.uk.gov.in/files/ch19.pdf
8. https://www.rainn.org/public-policy/sexual-assault-issues/marital-rape
9. Patricia Mahoney and Linda M. Williams, Sexual Assault in Marriage: Prevalence, Consequences and Treatment of Wife Rape, Retrieved from http://www.janedoe.org/site/assets/docs/Curriculum_SA_IP/Sexual_Assault_in_Marriage.pdf
10. Udisha Ghosh (2015), Marital Rape: The Need for Criminalisation in India, Retrieved from http://www.lawctopus.com/academike/marital-rape-need-criminalisation-india/
11. Marital rape in India, Retrieved from http://www.india celebrating.com/social-issues/marital-rape/
12. Marital Rape and the Indian legal scenario, Retrieved from http://www.indialawjournal.com/volume2/issue_2/article_by_priyanka.html
13. Preetika Rana (2012), Why India Still Allows Marital Rape, Retrieved from http://blogs.wsj.com/indiarealtime/2013/03/26/why-india-allows-men-to-rape-their-wives/
14. http://blogs.wsj.com/indiarealtime/2015/04/30/modi-

governments-reasons-why-marital-rape-is-not-a-crime/

15. Marital rape (2014), Retrieved from http://en.wikipedia.org/wiki/Marital_rape
16. Marital Rape and the Indian legal scenario, Retrieved from http://www.indialawjournal.com/volume2/issue_2/article_by_priyanka.html
17. The Times of India (March 5, 2014), Treat marital sexual abuse as rape: Court, Retrieved from http://timesofindia.indiatimes.com/india/Treat-marital-sexual-abuse-as-rape-Court/articleshow/31434943.cms
18. The Indian Express (April 30, 2013), Marital rape is an ugly reality, Retrieved from http://archive.indianexpress.com/news/marital-rape-is-an-ugly-reality/1109618/
19. No rape in marriage? (2015), Retrieved from http://www.rediff.com/news/report/no-rape-in-marriage/20150509.htm
20. Dr Mukesh Garg and Dr Nareshlata Singla (2013), Marital rape under Indian law: A Study, International Journal in Management and Social Science, Vol. 1, Issue 2, (June, 2013), p. 63.
21. Business Standard (May 9, 2015), No rape in marriage, Retrieved from http://www.business-standard.com/article/beyond-business/no-rape-in-marriage-115050801423_1.html
22. Jennifer Koshan (2010), The Legal Treatment of Marital Rape and Women's Equality: An Analysis of the Canadian Experience, Retrieved from http://theequalityeffect.org/pdfs/maritalrapecanadexperience.pdf
23. Rabbi Mark Dratch (2006), Sexual Abuse and Marital Rape, Retrieved from http://www.jsafe.org/pdfs/pdf_032206_2.pdf
24. Marital Rape and its Impacts, Retrieved from http://www.realising-rights.org/docs/newsletter/Marital%20Rape%20Policy%20Brief%20for%20MPs.pdf
25. See http://www.crisisconnectioninc.org/domesticviolence/marital_rape_information.htm
26. Business Standard (May 9, 2015), No rape in marriage, Retrieved from http://www.business-standard.com/article/beyond-business/no-rape-in-marriage-115050801423_1.html
27. See http://www.ndtv.com/opinion/the-sordid-reality-of-marital-rape-760245
28. Saurabh Mishra and Sarvesh Sing, Marital Rape — Myth, Reality

and Need for Criminalisation, Retrieved from http://www.ebc-india.com/lawyer/articles/645.htm

29. Vineeta Pandey (2010), Husbands can't get away with marital rape: Government, Retrieved from http://www.dnaindia.com/india/report-husbands-can-t-get-away-with-marital-rape-government-1356512
30. http://thehigherlearning.com/2014/05/14/a-judge-in-india-just-confirmed-that-marital-rape-is-totally-legal-there/
31. Preetika Rana (2012), Why India Still Allows Marital Rape, Retrieved from http://blogs.wsj.com/indiarealtime/2013/03/26/why-india-allows-men-to-rape-their-wives/
32. http://www.ndtv.com/india-news/marriage-sacred-in-india-so-marital-rape-does-not-apply-government-759219
33. http://idiva.com/opinion-work-life/marital-rape-not-applicable-in-india-because-marriage-is-sacred-says-government/15043035
34. See http://www.ndtv.com/opinion/the-sordid-reality-of-marital-rape-760245
35. Marital rape (2015), Retrieved from http://en.wikipedia.org/wiki/Marital_rape

12

Acid Attack

> "Women have always been courageous... They are always fearless when protecting their children and in the last century they have been fearless in the fight for their rights."
>
> —*Isabel Allende*

Introduction

'Acid is a chemical substance whose aqueous solutions are characterised by a sour taste. There are numerous uses for acids. It often used to remove rust and other corrosion from metals in a process known as pickling. They may be used as an electrolyte in a wet cell battery, such as sulfuric acid in a car battery. Strong acids, sulfuric acid in particular, are widely used in mineral processing. In the chemical industry, acids react in neutralisation reactions to produce salts. Acids are used as additives to drinks and foods, as they alter their taste and serve as preservatives. Certain acids are used as drugs. Many biologically important molecules are acids.'[1]

'Sulfuric acid is one of the most important compounds made by the chemical industry. It is used to make, literally, hundreds of compounds needed by almost every industry. By far the largest amount of sulfuric acid is used to make phosphoric acid, it use to prepare the phosphate fertilisers, calcium dihydrogen phosphate and the ammonium phosphates. It is also used to make ammonium sulfate, which is a particularly important fertiliser in sulfur-deficient.'[2]

Acid throwers mainly use sulfuric or nitric acid which are two of the strongest acids and can eat through the skin, muscle and even bones of humans. Sulfuric acid is very common because it is used in car and motorcycle batteries. Nitric acid is used by goldsmiths to purify gold, separating it from silver and other metals. Another type of acid, hydrochloric, may also be used by acid throwers but not so commonly.[3]

Reasons of Acid Attack

The most common and obvious reason for such attacks can be referred to as "lover rejection", in which the proposer of the marriage, love or sex is rejected by the victim. When a woman refuses a man, it is seen as hampering his reputation and honour and he seeks to restore it by means of acid attacks. Men throw acid on women's faces as a mark of their masculinity and superiority, to keep women in their place. Another prominent reason for such attacks may be related to dowry and other marital disputes. Dowry is the system of giving money to the husband and his family at the time of marriage by the bride's family.[4]

'Acid throwing is usually an act of revenge, motivated by jealousy or hatred, because of a personal relationship problem such as a broken love affair or marriage, unfaithfulness, or rejection. The perpetrator blames the victim for the problem and wants to inflict as much physical and mental suffering as possible. The acid is usually thrown at the victim's face. The perpetrator wants to destroy the face and make the victim look like a monster, so nobody will love the victim ever again. Other reasons for acid attacks, in some cases, have included robbery or disputes between neighbours.'[5]

Effects of Acid Attack

'Medical effects of the acid attacks are extensive and the severity depends on the concentration of the acid and the time taken to thoroughly wash off the acid with water or to neutralise with a neutralising agent. It affects all organs of the body affecting from skull, ear, eyelids, nose, mouth and even causing respiratory problems and renal failure.'[6] 'The most notable effect of an acid attack is the lifelong bodily disfigurement. Consequently, the victim is faced with physical challenges, which require long-term surgical treatment, as well as psychological challenges, which require in-depth intervention from psychologists and counselors at each stage of physical recovery.'[7]

'Victims face a lifetime of discrimination from society and they become lonely. They are embarrassed that people may stare or laugh at them and may hesitate to leave their homes fearing an adverse reaction from the outside world. Victims who are not married are not likely to get married and those victims who have got serious disabilities because of an attack, like blindness, will not find jobs and earn a living. Inhalation of acid vapours can create breathing problems in two ways: i.e. by causing a poisonous reaction in the lungs or by swelling the neck, which constricts the airway and strangles the victim. When the burns from an acid attack heal, they form thick scars which pull the skin very tight and can cause disfigurements.'[8]

'After becoming an acid victim, the survivors were undervalued by their peers, colleague and friends and also from the community. Besides they had to struggle to get the earlier environment at their institutions or school/college. Even in some cases, they could not get the family and community support as they wanted. Sometimes the employer was not satisfied to survivors because of their disfigured outlooking/face.'[9] 'Lifelong disfiguration and disabilities are results in severe emotional and psychologic trauma for the survivor. The majority of the survivors had to give up their education or lose their job because of lengthy treatment period and disfigurements that take place.'[10]

'The victims who are not married are likely not to get married as they suffer from many disabilities like blindness, deafness and many others and our societies mindset is not that broad enough to accept a disabled person as their better half. They even do not get a job in spite of being qualified as they cannot meet up to the expectation of their employers as not having the personality. Some of the psychological problems which the victims suffer are insomnia, nightmares, depression, fear of facing the world, headache, tiredness, fear of other acid attacks. They also feel depressed and worried as they think themselves boycotted and castaway from the society.'[11]

'Acid violence is physically destructive and can require multiple surgeries and physical therapy to minimise damage and disability. Because the acid used in attacks is usually industrial-grade hydrochloric or nitric acid, the intensity of the burns can be extremely severe if not properly treated. Common injuries include melted tissue, exposed bone and damage to eyes and ears. However, the scars left by acid are not just skin deep. The initial shock of the attack leaves the victim in a very vulnerable position. The economic burden of seeking health treatment puts immense pressure on survivors and their families. Majority of acid victims come from low socio-economic status and they lack the financial and social supports to enable them to deal with such a crisis. Specialised hospital care is essential to recovery of burn injuries. Burn care involves high expense for wound management materials, staffing, equipment and long-term scar management products. There are also common long-term issues for acid victims resulting from the initial trauma, consequential scars and other social factors such as economic and social vulnerability, on-going legal procedures and fear of stigmatisation and social exclusion.'[12]

Acid Attack: Global Perspectives

'Pakistan, Bangladesh and Cambodia have seen a rising number of cases where not only have men been attacked, but also cases where women have been the attackers. In India too, there are reports of men being attacked with acid. Pakistan and Bangladesh have specific statues on acid crimes. In Bangladesh, the Acid Control Act of 2002 and the Acid Crime Control Act of 2002 are gender neutral, i.e. the attacker and the victim are 'person' and not him/her in specific. Similarly, Pakistan's Acid Control and Acid Crime Prevention Act, 2010 provisions are gender neutral.'[13] Historically, acid attacks were also widespread in France, the United Kingdom and other parts of Europe from the eighteenth century onwards. Today, in addition to acid attacks in Cambodia, Bangladesh and India, they are also reported widely in other parts of South East and South Asia; the Middle East; Central and Northern Africa; and, to a lesser extent acid attacks also occur in North America and Europe.

With regards to Bangladesh, recorded data suggests that the first attack in this country occurred in 1967 and that attacks have steadily been on the rise and similar to Cambodia, peaked in the late 1990s and the early years of 2000.'[14] 'From 496 in 2002 to under 100 in 2011, this is a 75 per cent reduction.'[15] 'The acid attacks, which began in late 2014 in the Iranian city of Isfahan, involved unidentified men flinging acid into the faces of women with whom they had no history of personal grudges. At least fourteen attacks have been reported and eyewitnesses have reported that the assailants proclaimed they were defending hijab during the assaults. No one has been charged in any of the attacks.'[16] 'More than 8,500 acid attacks, forced marriages and other forms of violence against women were reported in Pakistan in 2011, according to The Aurat Foundation, a women's rights organisation. Because the group relied mostly on media reports, the figure is likely an undercount.'[17]

Acid Attack in India

'Some 1,500 acid attacks are reported worldwide every year, according to the London-based charity Acid Survivors Trust International. The group says the actual figure is likely to be far higher because so many victims are too scared to speak out. India has no official statistics on the matter, but reports of acid attacks appear regularly in the media. Attackers often target the head and face in order to maim, disfigure and blind their victims, often because of spurned sexual advances.'[18] 'The year 2014 saw a never-before 309 acid attack incidents being reported from across the country. This is almost 300 per cent more than the average number of such cases witnessed during the preceding three years. The years 2011, 2012 and 2013 witnessed 83, 85 and 66 cases being reported respectively, but this number shot up to 309 in 2014 – almost four times the average number of acid attack cases in the preceding years.'[19]

'The Union home ministry has asked all states and Union territories to ensure quicker investigation of acid attack cases, leading to the timely arrest and trial of perpetrators under the new, stringent provisions of the criminal law. This, it said in an advisory sent to all state chief secretaries and UT administrators, would not only have a deterrent effect but also provide solace to the victims and their families. Batting for timely justice against acid attack perpetrators, the home ministry told the states that "the issue of apprehending the culprits and fast-tracking of justice needs to be seriously considered". Underlining how "the whole objective of stringent punishment provisions (Section 326A and 326B) in the Criminal Law (Amendment) Act 2013 is to increase the deterrent value against perpetrators of such crimes", the ministry requested the states and UTs to take proactive measures to expedite investigation and trial of acid attack cases and bring them under a definite timeframe.

The advisory also cited Section 357C of the Criminal Procedure Code to underline that no acid attack victim should be denied treatment by any hospital, whether public or private. Stating that it was for the administrative machinery of the states/ UTs to ensure full and free treatment of acid attack victims, 'health' being a 'state' subject, the home ministry said "it is relevant to mention that, in case of acid attack victims, treatment and compensation are to be treated separately". As per the advisory, "while treatment of the victim should be the primary consideration, the disbursal of compensation should also be expedited within the timeframe as stipulated by the Supreme Court". This means that the state/UT administrations will not only have to ensure full and free treatment of victims, but also separately provide them Rs 3 lakh under the Victim Compensation Scheme.'[20] Let discuss some renowned incidences of acid attacks:

'In 2003, Sonali Mukherjee was a 17-year-old college student when three men attacked her because she had rejected their sexual advances. On the night of April 22, they poured acid over her face while she was sleeping in her home in Dhanbad city. The acid melted away her face, leaving her partially deaf and blind and completely disfigured. While her father had to sell his land, jewellery and cattle to pay for 22 surgeries, the accused men were released on bail and Mukherjee received no state funding for her treatment. She even begged the government to allow euthanasia, which is illegal in India, to end her life to stop the suffering.

In 2012, Mukherjee burst into the national spotlight after she appeared on Kaun Banega Crorepati, hosted by Bollywood superstar Amitabh Bachchan, in a bid to win money for funding her treatment. The 27-year-old won 2.5 million rupees along with her celebrity partner former Miss Universe Lara Dutta. In 2014, Sonali Mukherjee was reportedly given a job in a government school in Bokaro. Sonali Mukherjee, an acid attack survivor, who fell in love with Chittaranjan Tiwari, an electrical engineer.'[21] 'An acid attack victim Sonali Mukherjee, who inspired Bollywood megastar Amitabh Bachchan on KBC with her courage, tied the knot with an electrical engineer. Her husband Chittaranjan Tiwari hails from Jamshedpur and works at a plant in Odisha. He learnt about Sonali after she appeared in the media demanding a job from the government and also shared the screen with Amitabh Bachchan on Kaun Banega Crorepati.'[22]

'Laxmi, now 24, whose story of courage in the face of extreme adversity was highlighted in a series on acid attack victims by Hindustan Times on July 21, 2013, has found a partner for life. Kanpur-based social activist Alok Dixit, 25, who runs a campaign on the social media against acid attacks, Spot of Shame, said he was bowled over by Laxmi's spirit.'[23] 'In 2005, when Delhi resident Laxmi was 15 years old, she turned down a marriage proposal from a 32 year old man. Slighted by her rejection, the man (with help from a friend) attacked Laxmi while she was out shopping one day. They poured acid on her face and arms.'[24] 'Meanwhile in 2013, the Supreme Court ruled in favour of Laxmi and Rupa's plea, thereby creating a fresh set of restrictions on the sale of acid. Under the new regulations, acid could not be sold to any individual below the age of 18 years. One is also required to furnish a photo identity card before buying acid. Laxmi claims that not much has changed on the ground, despite all the regulations.

US First Lady Michelle Obama has felicitated Indian acid attack victim Laxmi after she won the International Women of Courage Award for successfully leading the campaign against acid attacks on women in India. Michelle Obama and the large crowd at the US State Department auditorium was moved and touched when Laxmi, a standard-bearer of the movement to end acid attacks, recited a poem recounting her experience on the occasion. "You haven't thrown acid on my face; you threw it on my dreams. You didn't have love in your heart; you had acid in it," Laxmi recited soon after receiving the prestigious award along with several other women from different parts of the world including Afghanistan and Fiji. Recognition for her effort through this award, is a great encouragement and motivation for the girls and women of India, many of whom still are not able to speak out against the atrocities inflicted upon them, Laxmi said soon after receiving the award.

"There was never any love in your eyes. They burn me with caustic glance. I am sad that your corrosive name will always be the part of my identity that I carry with this face. Time will not come to my rescue. Every Thursday will remind me of you," Laxmi said reciting her poem with the First Lady and other top US officials on the dais."When we see these women raise their voices and move their feet and empower others to create change, we need to realise that each of us has that same power and that same obligation," the First Lady said in her speech. "And as I learned about this year honourees and I thought about how we could support their work, I realised that for most of these women, there is a common foundation for their efforts. It's a foundation of education," she said. "But after her attack, Laxmi became a tireless campaigner against acid attacks. Thanks to her hard work and tremendous diligence, Laxmi was successful in petitioning the Supreme Court to order the Indian government to regulate the sale of acid and to make prosecutions of acid attacks easier to pursue. And she continues to push for progress still today," she said.[25]

'A teenage girl in Haryana, who is a state-level volleyball player, was hospitalised with serious injuries after two motorcycle-borne men threw acid on her while she was going for practice. The men managed to escape from the spot after the attack near the crowded Prem Nagar Chowk, the police said. Rohtak is around 70 km from New Delhi and is the home town of Haryana Chief Minister Bhupinder Singh Hooda. Ritu's family says they have no idea on who would want to attack her like that. 'She was going to practice when boys on a bike with acid in a glass bottle threw it on her," explained her brother Lalit Saini.'[26] 'Police have arrested two youths, Pradeep, a college boy and Neeraj who were allegedly hired by the main accused Ram Niwas Saini (28) of Jamni village in Jind district for Rs 1.25 lakh to throw acid on the victim Ritu Saini. Cyber cell of the police helped investigating officers to reach out to the two at their residence in Jamni village. Call details from the phones of the victim as well as Ram Niwas helped police crack the case. Sources said Ram Niwas roped in two youths for Rs 1.25 lakh.

Police had come under heavy criticism after the incident, as it was also unable to crack another similar case occurred a year ago in Sector 1, when two youths attacked three minor schoolgirls with acid. Dissatisfied with the police investigation, the victims had approached the Punjab and Haryana High Court, which had referred the case to CBI.'[27]

'Ritu had suffered serious burns on her face, arms and chest in the incident. After being treated for 90 per cent burns in several hospitals, she has been undergoing reconstructive plastic surgeries in Delhi. In 2013, the Haryana Government had also sanctioned Rs 20 lakh for her treatment. The incident, forced her to drop out of school and give up her volleyball practice. Holding all the three accused guilty of the crime, the court of Sandeep Duggal convicted them to life imprisonment. Two other accused in the case were sentenced to 10 years in imprisonment.'[28]

'The 33-year-old former dancing girl who was allegedly attacked by her then-husband, an ex-lawmaker and son of a political powerhouse jumped from the sixth floor of a building in Rome, where she had been living and receiving treatment. Pakistani acid attack victim Fakhra Younus had endured more than three dozen surgeries over more than a decade to repair her severely damaged face and body when she finally decided life was no longer worth living. Her death came less than a month after a Pakistani filmmaker won the country's first Oscar for a documentary about acid attack victims. Younus' story highlights the horrible mistreatment many women face in Pakistan's conservative, male-dominated culture and is a reminder that the country's rich and powerful often appear to operate with impunity.

Younus was a teenage dancing girl working in the red light district of the southern city of Karachi when she met her future husband, the son of Ghulam Mustafa Khar, a former governor of Pakistan's largest province, Punjab. The unusual pairing was the younger Khar's third marriage. He was in his mid-30s at the time. The couple was married for three years, but Younus eventually left him because he allegedly physically and verbally abused her. She claimed that he came to her mother's house while she was sleeping in May 2000 and poured acid all over her in the presence of her five-year-old son from a different man.'[29]

'British model Katie Piper was raised in a small English village by a loving family. At 22, she moved out on her own to London to further her career as a television presenter.'[30] 'Katie Piper, 26, was a model and aspiring television presenter when she was splashed in the face with sulfuric acid by a stranger on the London streets in March 2008. Police moved quickly on the trail of her assailant. At least three separate security cameras captured the vicious incident and the hunt led to 19-year-old Stefan Sylvestre — who they found with acid burns on his hands. Sylvestre eventually told authorities he had been commissioned to throw the acid at Piper by Danny Lynch, a man Piper had started dating just two weeks before the attack. Lynch was a 33-year-old martial arts enthusiast who likely first saw Piper when she was working at martial arts matches as a ring girl. Piper said they initially met online. "The first initial contact was on Facebook, where he messaged me...his profile picture was him in a martial arts outfit. And then, the next few days we carried on, talking online and eventually swapped numbers," she said.' [31]

Assistance to Victims

'Acid attack violence is an act of intimate terrorism that involves the premeditated throwing of sulphuric, nitric, or hydrochloric acid onto another person. The media, medical agencies and human rights organisations working with acid attack survivors have compiled the predominant body of work on this issue.'[32] 'Many non-governmental organisations have been formed in the areas with the highest occurrence of acid attacks to combat such attacks. Bangladesh has its Acid Survivors Foundation, which offers acid victims legal, medical, counselling and monetary assistance in rebuilding their lives. NGOs provide rehabilitation services for survivors while acting as advocates for social reform, hoping to increase support and awareness for acid assault. Treatment for burn victims remains inadequate in many developing nations where incidence is high. Medical underfunding has resulted in very few burn centers available for victims in countries such as Uganda, Bangladesh and Cambodia.'[33]

'In the community, the perpetrators were threatening the survivors for withdrawing the cases against them. Sometimes, it was found that the survivor and their family had been attacked more than one time because of continuing acid case. Moreover, due to lower social status and economic power of the survivors, they faced trouble to survive at their locality by ignoring the threat of the perpetrator. Sometimes due to the threat from the perpetrators the victims might also lose their homes and shelter.'[34] 'After becoming an acid victim, he/she could not meet their family demand. Sometime the survivors had to depend on external support for their survival. Bivariate analysis also reiterated the strong relationship between domestic violence and poverty.'[35]

Legal Mechanism

'Acid violence can only be addressed if all enabling mechanisms are eliminated and the judicial system is the key interface for addressing acid violence. In Bangladesh, acid violence arises from a combination of three main factors: gender inequality and discrimination in a patriarchal social structure, the easy availability of acid and deficits in effectively punishing perpetrators.'[36] 'India does not have a separate law to tackle the crime of acid violence and Indian Penal Code also remains silent as far as defining acid attack is concerned. Hence most of the cases are registered under different sections of grievous hurt ranging from Sec. 320, Sec. 322, Sec. 325 and Sec. 326 of IPC. Law Commission17 headed by Justice A. R. Lakshmanan in 2008, proposed a new section 326A to be added to IPC. As per Sec. 326 A, there is a minimum imprisonment of ten years which is extendable upto imprisonment for life and fine. The offence is cognisable and non-bailable in nature and triable by Court of Session which is non-compoundable.'[37]

'The Supreme Court has directed the states and union territories to issue licenses to retailers selling acid after the government said it will categorise acid as poison. The court said anyone under the age of 18 will not be able to purchase acids like hydrochloric, sulfuric and nitric. Shops will have to keep details like the quantity sold and the addresses of buyers, who will need to present photo identification to purchase acids." Over the counter sale of acid is completely prohibited unless the seller maintains a log/register recording the sale of acid," the Supreme Court said."[38] 'Though Government passed the Criminal Law Amendment Act, 2013, a stronger legislation to combat violence against women wherein, the law defines acid attack as a separate Indian Penal Code offence and proposes punishment of not less than 10 years to a maximum of life imprisonment for perpetrators and fine that could go upto Rs 10 lakh under Sec. 326 A and for attempt to commit acid attack, imprisonment not less than five years but which may extend to seven years and shall also be liable to fine under Sec. 326 B.'[39]

'Now under Article 253 of the Indian Constitution, the Parliament has the power to make laws to give effect to international agreements. Hence India is under an obligation to curb the menace of acid attack. Now it is seen that the definition of grievous hurt as given under Section 322 of the Indian Penal Code is not inclusive of certain circumstances of acid attack as the definition clearly states the injuries that constitute grievous hurt. Therefore, if the perpetrator causes only skin damage to the victim of acid attack, with no substantial damage to other organs, it would not come under the ambit of grievous hurt.'[40]

Conclusion

Acid throwing is usually an act of revenge, motivated by jealousy or hatred, because of a personal relationship problem such as a broken love affair or marriage, unfaithfulness, or rejection. The perpetrator wants to destroy the face and make the victim look like a monster, so nobody will love the victim ever again. Other reasons for acid attacks, in some cases, have included robbery or disputes between neighbours. Medical effects of the acid attacks are extensive and the severity depends on the concentration of the acid and the time taken to thoroughly wash off the acid with water or to neutralise with a neutralising agent. It affects all organs of the body affecting from skull, ear, eyelids, nose, mouth and even causing respiratory problems and renal failure. Acid violence is physically destructive and can require multiple surgeries and physical therapy to minimise damage and disability. Pakistan, Bangladesh and Cambodia have seen a rising number of cases of acid attack.

References

1. Acid (2015), Retrieved from http://en.wikipedia.org/wiki/Acid
2. Sulfuric acid (2014), Retrieved from http://www.essentialchemicalindustry.org/chemicals/sulfuric-acid.html
3. Living in the Shadows: Acid attacks in Cambodia (2003), Retrieved from http://www.licadho-cambodia.org/reports/files/41acid%20report%20English.pdf
4. Parvathi Menon and Sanjay Vashishtha, Vitriolage and India - The Modern Weapon of Revenge, International Journal of Humanities and Social Science Invention, Volume 2, Issue 10, October 2013, pp. 1-9.
5. Living in the Shadows: Acid attacks in Cambodia, Retrieved from http://www.licadho-cambodia.org/reports/files/41acid%20report%20English.pdf
6. See http://jsslawcollege.in/wp-content/uploads/2013/12/ACID-ATTACK-ON-WOMEN-REPERCUSSIONS-AND-NEED-FOR-LAW.pdf
7. Acid throwing: A cause of concern, Punjab Acad Forensic Med Toxicol 2013;13(2), Retrieved from http://medind.nic.in/jbc/t13/i2/jbct13i2p60.pdf
8. Dr Ambika R Nair, Acid attract: violence against women, Journal of Innovative Research and Solution, 1(1), pp.117-15.
9. Biplob Kanti Mondal and Siddiqur Rube (2013), Causes and consequences of acid violence: A case of Bangladesh, Bangladesh research publication journals, Volume 9, Issue 2, pp. 97-102.
10. Anowar Ara Begum, Acid Violence: A Burning Issue of Bangladesh —Its Medicolegal Aspects, http://www.kln.ac.lk/medicine/depts/forensic/images/stories/ques_1/acid_violence.pdf
11. Ms. Nargis Yeasmeen, Acid Attack in the Back Drop of India and Criminal Amendment Act, 2013, International Journal of Humanities and Social Science Invention, Volume 4, Issue 1, January 2015, pp. 6-13
12. http://www.acidsurvivors.org/images/frontImages/Annual_Report-2012.pdf
13. See http://pldindia.org/wp-content/uploads/2013/03/PLD-notes-on-acid-attack.pdf
14. Chapel Hill (2009), It was like burning in hell: A comparative exploration of acid attract violence, See http://cgi.unc.edu/uploads/media_items/it-was-like-burning-in-hell-a-comparative-exploration-of-acid-attack-violence.original.pdf

15. See http://www.acidviolence.org/
16. Vigilante Violence: The Acid Attacks against Women in Iran and the State's Assault on Women's Rights, Retrieved from http://www.iranhumanrights.org/2015/03/vigilante-violence-report/
17. http://news.yahoo.com/prominent-pakistani-acid-victim-commits-suicide-063149605.html
18. http://www.dailymail.co.uk/news/article-2522422/Indian-government-doing-stop-acid-attacks-women-say-victims-believe-new-law-ignored.html
19. The Indian Express (April 10, 2015), 309 acid attack cases in '14, 300% rise in 3 yrs, Retrieved from http://indianexpress.com/article/india/india-others/309-acid-attack-cases-in-14-300-rise-in-3-yrs/
20. The Times of India (April 23, 2015), Home ministry asks all states and UTs to ensure quicker investigation of acid attack cases, Retrieved from http://timesofindia.indiatimes.com/india/Home-ministry-asks-all-states-and-UTs-to-ensure-quicker-investigation-of-acid-attack-cases/articleshow/47025915.cms
21. Acid Attack Survivor Sonali Mukherjee Marries Electrical Engineer in Jharkhand (2015), Retrieved from http://www.huffingtonpost.in/2015/04/17/sonali-mukherjee_n_ 7087402.html
22. Acid attack victim Sonali Mukherjee ties the knot with Facebook friend, Retrieved from http://www.news18.com/news/jharkhand/acid-attack-victim-sonali-mukherjee-ties-the-knot-with-facebook-friend-720021.html
23. http://www.hindustantimes.com/stopacidattacks/acid-attack-survivor-laxmi-s-spirit-wins-her-a-partner-for-life/article1-1170630.aspx
24. https://www.youtube.com/watch?v=CSxGqXbMby8
25. The Times of India (March 5, 2014), Michelle Obama felicitates Indian acid attack victim Laxmi, Retrieved from http://timesofindia.indiatimes.com/world/us/Michelle-Obama-felicitates-Indian-acid-attack-victim-Laxmi/articleshow/31459557.cms
26. See http://www.ndtv.com/india-news/acid-attack-on-volleyball-player-in-rohtak-485093
27. The Times of India (May 29, 2012), Acid attack: Two youths hired by cousin arrested, Retrieved from http://timesofindia.indiatimes.com/india/Acid-attack-Two-youths-hired-by-cousin-arrested/articleshow/13621197.cms

28. The Hindu (Dec 24, 2014), Three get lifer in acid attack case, Retrieved from http://www.thehindu.com/news/national/other-states/three-get-lifer-in-acid-attack-case/article6721570.ece

29. http://news.yahoo.com/prominent-pakistani-acid-victim-commits-suicide-063149605.html

30. See http://abcnews.go.com/2020/slideshow?id=9477095& imageid= 9476963

31. http://abcnews.go.com/2020/KatiePiper/secret-drives-katie-piper-boyfriend-sulfuric-acid-attack/story?id=9490538

32. Chapel Hill (2009), It was like burning in hell: A comparative exploration of acid attract violence, See http://cgi.unc.edu/uploads/media_items/it-was-like-burning-in-hell-a-comparative-exploration-of-acid-attack-violence.original.pdf

33. Acid throwing: A cause of concern, J Punjab Acad Forensic Med Toxicol 2013;13(2), Retrieved from http://medind.nic.in/jbc/t13/i2/jbct13i2p60.pdf

34. Biplob Kanti Mondal and Siddiqur Rube (2013), Causes and consequences of acid violence: A case of Bangladesh, Bangladesh research publication journals, Volume 9, Issue 2, pp. 97-102.

35. Biplob Kanti Mondal and Siddiqur Rube (2013), Causes and consequences of acid violence: A case of Bangladesh, Bangladesh research publication journals, Volume 9, Issue 2, pp. 97-102.

36. http://www.acidsurvivors.org/images/frontImages/Annual_Report-2012.pdf

37. Acid attract on women: Repercussions and need for law, Retrieved from http://jsslawcollege.in/wp-content/uploads/2013/12/ACID-ATTACK-ON-WOMEN-REPERCUSSIONS-AND-NEED-FOR-LAW.pdf

38. Acid throwing: A cause of concern, J Punjab Acad Forensic Med Toxicol 2013;13(2), Retrieved from http://medind.nic.in/jbc/t13/i2/jbct13i2p60.pdf

39. Acid attract on women: Repercussions and need for law, Retrieved from http://jsslawcollege.in/wp-content/uploads/2013/12/ACID-ATTACK-ON-WOMEN-REPERCUSSIONS-AND-NEED-FOR-LAW.pdf

40. Nargis Yeasmeen, Acid Attack in the Back Drop of India and Criminal Amendment Act 2013, International Journal of Humanities and Social Science Invention, Volume 4 Issue 1, January, 2015, pp. 6-13.

13
Domestic Violence

"Women are naturally secretive and they like to do their own secreting."

—*Arthur Conan Doyle*

Introduction

'The European Union defines violence against women as any act of gender-based violence that results in, or is likely to result in, physical, sexual or psychological harm or suffering to women, including threats of such acts, coercion or arbitrary deprivation of liberty, whether occurring in public or in private life.'[1] 'Domestic violence can occur regardless of ethnicity, religion, class, age, sexuality, disability or lifestyle. It can occur in a range of relationships including heterosexual, gay, lesbian, bisexual and transgender relationships. Abusers come from all walks of life. They can come from any ethnic group, religion, class or neighbourhood. They may be older or younger. However, whilst they may also be any gender, the majority of perpetrators are men and the effects of the violence are markedly more severe for women.'[2]

'According to the Merriam-Webster dictionary definition, domestic violence is the inflicting of physical injury by one family or household member on another; also a repeated / habitual pattern of such behaviour. Domestic violence can be physical, mental or verbal abuse, deprivation of basic rights or amenities, economic injury etc.'[3] 'Violence is perpetrated on women both inside and outside her home. Domestic violence comprises all acts of intimidation and aggression which forces a woman to seek redressal by breaking the silence imposed on her by a patriarchal culture.'[4]

'Domestic violence can take place in heterosexual or same-sex relationships. It can take a number of forms including physical, emotional, verbal, economic and sexual abuse, which can range from subtle, coercive forms to marital rape and to violent physical abuse that result in disfigurement or death. It often occurs because abuser believes that abuse is justified and acceptable and may produce intergenerational cycles of abuse that condone violence. Awareness, perception, definition and documentation of domestic violence differ widely from country to country. The term Intimate Partner Violence is often used synonymously with domestic abuse or domestic violence. Traditionally, domestic violence was mostly associated with physical violence.'[5]

Meaning of the Concept

'Domestic violence is control by one partner over another in a dating, marital or live-in relationship. The means of control include physical, sexual, emotional and economic abuse, threats and isolation.'[6] 'The definition of domestic violence varies depending on the context in which the term is used. A clinical or behavioural definition is a pattern of assaultive and/or coercive behaviours, including physical, sexual and psychological attacks, as well as economic coercion, that adults or adolescents use against their intimate partners.'[7] 'Domestic violence includes harassment, maltreatment, brutality or cruelty and even the threat of assault - intimidation. It includes physical injury, as well as willfully or knowingly placing or attempting to place a spouse in fear of injury and compelling the spouse by force or threat to engage in any conduct or act, sexual or otherwise, from which the spouse has a right to abstain.'[8]

'The term 'domestic violence' refers to interpersonal violence which takes place in domestic settings, family relationships and intimate relationships and is most commonly applied to violence by a man to his wife, female sexual partner or ex-partner. Domestic violence can take many different forms including intimidation, coercion or isolation, emotional, physical, sexual, financial and spiritual abuse.'[9] 'Domestic violence is a form of gender-based violence, intended at subordinating women. The United Nations Declaration on the Elimination of Violence against Women, 1993, defines violence against women as any act of gender-based violence that results in, or is likely to result in, physical, sexual or psychological harm or suffering to women, including threats of such acts, coercion or arbitrary deprivation of liberty, whether occurring in public or in private life.'[10]

Forms of Domestic Violence

'Violence against women can be physical, sexual, psychological and threat of physical or sexual violence. Physical violence includes acts of physical aggression such as slapping, hitting, kicking and beating. The common sexual abuses women endure are forced intercourse and other forms of sexual coercion. Psychological abuse includes acts like intimidation, constant belittling, humiliating, nagging and various controlling behaviours such as isolating a person from their family and friends, monitoring their movements and restricting their access to information or assistance.'[11] 'Under the Protection of Women from Domestic Violence Act, 2005 (PWDVA), domestic violence includes actual abuse or the threat of abuse whether physical, sexual, verbal, emotional or economic. It also covers harassment for dowry or any other unlawful demand.'[13]

'Physical abuse is abuse involving contact intended to cause pain, injury, or other physical suffering or bodily harm. It includes hitting, slapping, punching, choking, pushing, throwing objects, burning and other types of contact that result in physical injury to the victim. Sexual violence is defined by World Health Organisation as any sexual act, attempt to obtain a sexual act, unwanted sexual comments or advances, or acts to traffic, or otherwise directed, against a person's sexuality using coercion, by any person regardless of their relationship to the victim. Emotional abuse can include verbal abuse and is defined as any behaviour that threatens, intimidates, undermines the victim's self-worth or self-esteem, or controls the victim's freedom. Emotional abuse can include threatening the victim with injury or harm, telling the victim that they will be killed if they ever leave the relationship, isolating them from others and public humiliation. Verbal abuse is a form of emotionally abusive behaviour involving the use of language, which can involve threats, name-calling, blaming, ridicule, disrespect and criticism. Economic abuse is a form of abuse when one intimate partner has control over the other partner's access to economic resources.'[14]

Reasons of Domestic Violence

'Domestic violence can happen anywhere but certain factors seem to increase its likelihood. These include the age of the mother, poverty and unemployment and alcohol and substance abuse.'[15] 'The most common causes for women stalking and battering include dissatisfaction with the dowry and exploiting women for more of it, arguing with the partner, refusing to have sex with him, neglecting children, going out of home without telling the partner, not cooking properly or on time, indulging in extra-marital affairs, not looking after in-laws etc.'[16]

'Acceptability of violence as a means to resolve conflict is the major reason of violence against women. Victims generally feel that it is better to suffer in silence than to be separated from their loved ones. Another important factor that contributes to the violence against women is the economic and financial dependence of women on men. Improper and inadequate laws and legal status of women is the primary cause for domestic violence. The isolation of women from communities and less participation in the field of politics also contribute to more of violence on women.'[17]

Domestic Violence: Global Perspectives

'Domestic violence is a global problem of enormous proportions. Although men are sometimes victims, the vast majority are women. At least one in every three women globally has been beaten, coerced into sex, or abused in some other way – most often by someone she knows, including by her husband or another male family member. One woman in four has been abused during her pregnancy.'[18] 'Violence against women is present in every country, cutting across boundaries of culture, class, education, income, ethnicity and age. Even though most societies proscribe violence against women, the reality is that violations against women's human rights are often sanctioned under the garb of cultural practices and norms, or through misinterpretation of religious tenets.'[19]

'Gender-based violence is regarded as one of the forms of violating human rights. Domestic violence is a global phenomenon without national, economic, religious, geographic and cultural borders. Violence on woman is mostly performed in her direct social environment affecting the physical and mental health of the woman. Violence has negative consequences for social welfare, children, families and community. Domestic violence restricts the woman's right to be involved in social life.'[20] 'The World Health Organisation estimates that over one in three women globally will be beaten, raped or otherwise abused in her lifetime. Violence against women is a world-wide problem that affects women in all countries, of all faiths and economic backgrounds.'[21]

Domestic Violence in India

'The status of women in India has been subject to many great changes over the past few millennia. From equal status with men in ancient times through the low points of the medieval period, to the promotion of equal rights by many reformers, the history of women in India has been eventful.'[22] 'Marriage in India is a voluntary union for life of one man and one woman to the exclusion of all others. It is a social association where the husband has the responsibility to take care of and maintain his wife and not to neglect his duties. But in relation to this great institution, the problem of the "dowry" still persists. Women are ill-treated, harassed, killed or divorced for the simple reason that they do not get a dowry or do not get a sufficiently large one.'[23]

'Violence against women is a serious problem in India. Overall, one-third of women age 15-49 have experienced physical violence and about 1 in 10 has experienced sexual violence.'[24] 'Newspapers and periodicals of all hues in India often carry reports about violence against women. These include among others incidents of young brides being burnt for bringing insufficient dowry, women dieing in abnormal circumstances, rape on hapless women and molestation of young girls.'[25] 'In India, one in every ten women reported facing sexual violence by their husbands during their lifetime. Feminists and women's organisations in India have been fighting against sexual and physical violence against women for a long time. They have been agitating for both legal and social changes, with some successes.'[26]

'There is a tremendous rise in the officially claimed number of crimes committed against women and particularly wives in matrimonial homes in India. Violence against wives is found in all societies across all economic and age groups. Consequently, sexual violence appears to be an intrinsic part of women's lives.'[27] 'Violence against women is widely recognised as an important public health problem. A substantial number of women across several countries have reported abuse by intimate partner at some point in their lives.'[28] 'At least 170 million women in India are victims of domestic violence. Despite this widespread prevalence domestic violence is not customarily acknowledged and has remained largely invisible. The social construct of the divide between public and private underlies the hidden nature of domestic violence against women.'[29]

'Domestic violence is prevalent in all castes, socioeconomic classes, religious groups and regions except North Sentinel Island and the Jarawa reserve. The northern state of Uttar Pradesh experiences relatively high rates of domestic violence and gender disparities. Domestic violence often happens in India as a result of dowry demands. There are strong links between domestic violence and dowry, a cultural practice deeply rooted in many Indian communities. There is widespread hesitancy amongst most Indian women who experience domestic violence to report or prosecute against such crimes. Other factors outside culture that demonstrate differences in domestic violence prevalence and gender disparities in India include socioeconomic class, educational level and family structure beyond the patriarchal framework. The 2012 National Crime Records Bureau report of India states a reported crime rate of 46 per 100,000, rape rate of 2 per 100,000, dowry homicide rate of 0.7 per 100,000 and the rate of domestic cruelty by husband or his relatives as 5.9 per 100,000.'[30]

Effects of Domestic Violence

'Domestic violence can lead to common emotional traumas such as depression, anxiety, panic attacks, substance abuse and post-traumatic stress disorder. Abuse can trigger suicide attempts, psychotic episodes, homelessness and slow recovery from mental illness. Children exposed to domestic violence are at risk for developmental problems, psychiatric disorders, school difficulties, aggressive behaviour and low self-esteem.'[31] 'Generally women in domestic and family violence situations do not enter a relationship believing it will become violent. Although sometimes women will choose to make a long-term relationship commitment when there is abuse occurring, often believing marriage or moving in together will put a stop to his extreme jealousy and possessiveness.'[32]

'There has been increase in acknowledgement that a child who is exposed to domestic abuse during his upbringing will suffer in his development and psychological welfare. Among victims who are still living with their perpetrators, high amounts of stress, fear and anxiety are commonly reported. Bruises, broken bones, head injuries, lacerations and internal bleeding are some of the acute effects of a domestic violence incident that require medical attention and hospitalisation.'[33]

Domestic Violence Legislation in India

'The Indian Government has enacted legislation to provide women with a range of remedies and protections from domestic violence. In 1983, India's Parliament added Section 498A to the Indian Penal Code (IPC), which allows women to file criminal complaints against their husbands and husbands' relatives for any cruelty suffered at their hands. In 2005, the Parliament passed the Protection of Women from Domestic Violence Act, a wide-ranging law that protects women from various types of violence (physical, sexual, verbal and economic) and imposes positive obligations on the state to protect women from violence.'[34]

'In 1983, domestic violence was recognised as a specific criminal offence by the introduction of Section 498-A into the Indian Penal Code. This section deals with cruelty by a husband or his family towards a married woman. Four types of cruelty are dealt with by this law: (a) conduct that is likely to drive a woman to suicide, (b) conduct which is likely to cause grave injury to the life, limb or health of the woman, (c) harassment with the purpose of forcing the woman or her relatives to give some property, or (d) harassment because the woman or her relatives is unable to yield to demands for more money or does not give some property. The punishment is imprisonment for upto three years and a fine. The complaint against cruelty need not be lodged by the person herself. Any relative may also make the complaint on her behalf. Section 498-A of the Indian Penal Code covers dowry-related harassment. As with other provisions of criminal law, a woman can use the threat of going to court to deter this kind of harassment. The Indian Penal Code also addresses dowry deaths in Section 304-B. If a woman dies of unnatural causes within seven years of marriage and has been harassed for dowry before her death, the Courts will assume that it is a case of dowry death. The husband or in-laws will then have to prove that their harassment was not the cause of her death.'[35]

'The Protection of Women from Domestic Violence Act 2005 is an Act of the Parliament of India enacted to protect women from domestic violence. It was brought into force by the Indian government from 26th October 2006. The Act was passed by the Parliament in August 2005 and assented to by the President on 13th September 2005. Primarily meant to provide protection to the wife or female live-in partner from domestic violence at the hands of the husband or male live-in partner or his relatives, the law also extends its protection to women living in a household such as sisters, widows or mothers. Domestic violence under the act includes actual abuse or the threat of abuse whether physical, sexual, verbal, emotional or economic. The salient features of the Protection from Domestic Violence Act, 2005 are as follows:

(a) The Act seeks to cover those women who are or have been in a relationship with the abuser where both parties have lived together in a shared household and are related by consanguinity, marriage or a relationship in the nature of marriage, or adoption; in addition relationship with family members living together as a joint family are also included. Even those women who are sisters, widows, mothers, single women, or living with the are entitled to get legal protection under the proposed Act.

(b) "Domestic violence" includes actual abuse or the threat of abuse that is physical, sexual, verbal, emotional and economic. Harassment by way of unlawful dowry demands to the woman or her relatives would also be covered under this definition.

(c) One of the most important features of the Act is the woman's right to secure housing. The Act provides for the woman's right to reside in the matrimonial or shared household, whether or not she has any title or rights in the household. This right is secured by a residence order, which is passed by a court. These residence orders cannot be passed against anyone who is a woman.

(d) The other relief envisaged under the Act is that of the power of the court to pass protection orders that prevent the abuser from aiding or committing an act of domestic violence or any other specified act, entering a workplace or any other place frequented by the abused, attempting to communicate with the abused, isolating any assets used by both the parties and causing violence to the abused, her relatives and others who provide her assistance from the domestic violence.

(e) The draft Act provides for appointment of Protection Officers and NGOs to provide assistance to the woman w.r.t. medical examination, legal aid, safe shelter, etc.

(f) The Act provides for breach of protection order or interim protection order by the respondent as a cognisable and non-bailable offence punishable with imprisonment for a term which may extend to one year or with fine which may extend to twenty thousand rupees or with both. Similarly, non-compliance or discharge of duties by the Protection Officer is also sought to be made an offence under the Act with similar punishment.'[36]

Human Rights Violations

'One of the most prevalent human rights violations in the world is violence against women and girls. The United Nations Population Fund says that, worldwide one in three women will experience physical or sexual abuse in her lifetime. The United Nations Declaration on the Elimination of Violence against Women (1993) states that *"violence against women is a manifestation of historically unequal power relations between men and women, which has led to domination over and discrimination against women by men and to the prevention of the full advancement of women and that violence against women is one of the crucial social mechanisms by which women are forced into a subordinate position compared with men".* The Declaration on the Elimination of Violence against Women classifies violence against women into three categories: that occurring in the family that occurring within the general community and that perpetrated or condoned by the State. Violence against women is increasingly considered not only a human rights violation, but also a form of discrimination against women.'[37]

Management of Domestic Violence

'Management of domestic violence may take place through medical services, law enforcement, counseling and other forms of prevention and intervention. Law enforcement may be called in response to intimate partner violence. Counselling is another means of managing the effects of domestic violence. For the victim of abuse, counselling may include an assessment of the presence. Counselling may be used by offenders to minimise the risk of future domestic violence. Prevention and intervention includes ways to prevent domestic violence by offering safe shelter, crisis intervention, advocacy and education and prevention programmes. Media should bring women issues to public domain in a forceful manner. They can play an important role in spreading awareness. They can provide a platform to speakers and panelists from different fields, eminent personalities responsible for decision-making to share their views and conduct an in-depth study on various gender issues and view it holistically touching various aspects of the problem.'[38]

Conclusion

Domestic violence is control by one partner over another in a dating, marital or live-in relationship. It can happen anywhere but certain factors seem to increase its likelihood. These include the age of the mother, poverty and unemployment and alcohol and substance abuse. It is a global problem of enormous proportions. It can lead to other common emotional traumas such as depression, anxiety, panic attacks, substance abuse and post-traumatic stress disorder. Abuse can trigger suicide attempts, psychotic episodes, homelessness and slow recovery from mental illness. In 1983, India's Parliament added Section 498A to the Indian Penal Code, which allows women to file criminal complaints against their husbands and husbands' relatives for any "cruelty" suffered at their hands. In 2005, the Parliament passed the Protection of Women from Domestic Violence Act, a wide-ranging law that protects women from various types of violence (physical, sexual, verbal and economic) and imposes positive obligations on the state to protect women from violence.

References

1. Domestic Violence against Women Report (2010), Retrieved from http://ec.europa.eu/public_opinion/archives/ebs/ebs_344_en.pdf
2. Domestic Violence: Frequently Asked Questions Factsheet 2004/05, Retrieved from http://www.womensaid.org.uk/downloads/FAQs.pdf
3. Vaidehi Subramani (2012), Domestic Violence, Retrieved from http://www.dsw.gnu.ac.in/UserFiles/File/UTTHAN_ MARCH_ 2012.pdf
4. K.N. Tiwari (2012), Violence Against Women in India, Retrieved from http://www.dishain.org/custom/docs/violence-against-women-in-india.pdf
5. Domestic violence (2015), Retrieved from http://en.wikipedia.org/wiki/Domestic_violence
6. Domestic Violence (2014), Retrieved from http://www.soc.iastate.edu/sapp/DomesticViolence.pdf
7. Definitions of Domestic Violence (2013), Retrieved from https://www.childwelfare.gov/pubPDFs/defdomvio.pdf
8. Waghamode R.H., Desai Bhavana and Kalyan J.L. (2013), Domestic Violence against Women: An Analysis, International Research Journal of Social Sciences, Vol. 2(1), 34-37, p. 35.
9. Family and domestic violence, Retrieved from http://www.whiteribbon.org.au/uploads/media/updated_ factsheets_ Nov_ 13/Factsheet_6_Family_ and_ domestic_ violence. pdf
10. Vrinda Grover, Addressing domestic violence through law, Retrieved from http://www.ngo-marg.org/wp-content/uploads/2011/01/DV-BOOK-ENG.pdf
11. Sudha Chaudhary, Domestic violence in India, Journal of Indian Research, Retrieved from http://mujournal.mewaruniversity.in/JIR2/21.pdf

12. See http://www.prajnya.in/gvr09.pdf

13. Domestic violence (2015), Retrieved from http://en.wikipedia.org/wiki/Domestic_violence

14. See http://www.unicef.org/protection/files/BehindClosedDoors.pdf

15. Vaidehi Subramani, Domestic Violence, Retrieved from http://www.dsw.gnu.ac.in/UserFiles/File/UTTHAN_ MARCH_2012.pdf

16. Ms Nargis Yeasmeen, Domestic Violence In India (Socio-Legal Aspects) With Special Reference to Protection Officer Under Dvp, Act – How Far They are Successful in Providing Solace to the Victims? IOSR Journal of Humanities and Social Science, Volume 19, Issue 10, Ver. IV (Oct. 2014), pp. 8-14.

17. See http://www.unicef.org/protection/files/BehindClosedDoors.pdf

18. Domestic violence against women and girls, Retrieved from http://www.unicef-irc.org/publications/pdf/digest6e.pdf

19. Prof Marine Chitashvili, Prof Nino Javakhishvili, Assoc. Prof Luiza Arutiunov, Assoc. Prof Lia Tsuladze and Ms Sophio Chachanidze (2010), National research on domestic violence against women in Georgia, Retrieved from http://www2.ohchr.org/english/bodies/cedaw/docs/Advance Versions/ GeorgiaAnnexX.pdf

20. Violence Against Women – Case Studies, Retrieved from http://www.soroptimistinternational.org/assets/media/documents/violence_against_women_-_case_studies.pdf

21. Sunil S. Kadam and Vinod A. Chaudhar, Domestic Violence against Woman: Past, Present, Future, J Indian Acad Forensic Med. July-September 2011, Vol. 33, No. 3. p. 261.

22. B Suresh Kumar Shetty, P P Jagadish Rao and Aditi Suresh Shetty, Legal Terrorism in Domestic Violence – An Indian Outlook, Medico-Legal Journal (2012) Vol. 80 Part 1, 33–38.

23. Domestic Violence, Retrieved from http://hetv.org/india/nfhs/nfhs3/NFHS-3-Domestic-Violence.pdf

24. KN Tiwari, Violence Against Women In India, Retrieved from http://www.dishain.org/custom/docs/violence-against-women-in-india.pdf

25. Aashish Gupta (2014), Reporting an incidence of violence against women in India, Retrieved from http://riceinstitute.org/wordpress/wp-content/uploads/downloads/2014/10/Reporting-and-incidence-of-violence-against-women-in-India-working-paper-final.pdf

26. Biswajit Ghosh and Tanima Choudhuri (2011), Legal Protection Against Domestic Violence in India: Scope and Limitations, J Fam Viol (2011) 26:319–330, Retrieved from http://www.researchgate.net/profile/Biswajit_Ghosh/publication/225125399_Legal_ Protection_Against_Domestic_ Violence_in_India_Scope_ and_Limitations/links/02bfe5139eede 8a003000000.pdf
27. Bontha V Babu and Shantanu K Kar, Abuse against women in pregnancy: a population-based study from Eastern India, Retrieved from http://www.searo.who.int/publications/journals/seajph/media/2012/seajph_v1n2/whoseajphv1i2p133.pdf
28. See http://www.dasra.org/pdf/no_private_matter-domestic-violence-report.pdf
29. Domestic violence in India (2015), Retrieved from http://en.wikipedia.org/wiki/Domestic_violence_in_India
30. Domestic Violence, Retrieved from http://www.soc.iastate.edu/sapp/DomesticViolence.pdf
31. See http://www.domesticviolence.com.au/files/pdf/Info-Book-Final.pdf
32. Dr S. Prescila Sharon, Domestic Violence Against Women in India: A Family Menace, Retrieved from http://www.theglobaljournals.com/ijar/special_file. php?val=December_2014_ 1418821458__48.pdf
33. Rehan Abeyratne and Dipika Jain (2012), Domestic Violence Legislation in India: The Pitfalls of a Human Rights Approach to Gender Equality, Journal of Gender, Social Policy and the Law, 21 (2), p. 337.
34. Laws against domestic violence and abuse, Retrieved from http://indiatogether.org/manushi/issue137/laws.htm
35. Protection of Women from Domestic Violence Act 2005, Retrieved from http://en.wikipedia.org/wiki/Protection_of_Women_from_Domestic_Violence_Act_2005
36. Domestic violence (2015), Retrieved from http://en.wikipedia.org/wiki/Domestic_violence
37. *Ibid.*

14

Sexual Harassment

"All women should know how to take care of children. Most of them will have a husband some day."

—*Franklin P. Jones*

Introduction

'Sexual harassment is bullying or coercion of a sexual nature, or the unwelcome or inappropriate promise of rewards in exchange for sexual favours. Harassment can include sexual harassment or unwelcome sexual advances, requests for sexual favours and other verbal or physical harassment of a sexual nature. The term *sexual harassment* was used in 1973 in *"Saturn's Rings"*, a report authored by Mary Rowe to the then President and Chancellor of MIT about various forms of gender issues.'[1] 'Sexual harassment is not limited to offices and work arenas. Increasingly, sexual harassment is being displayed in our nation's schools.'[2]

'The relationship between the sexes in many countries around the world includes a considerable amount of violence against women. Violence by men against women exists in the workplace, as it does in other settings. Focusing on the economics of men's work and women's work exposes sexual harassment as a way for the men who harass women to express their resentment and try to reassert control when they view women as their economic competitor.'[3] 'The problem of sexual harassment is increasingly coming out of the closet. A relationship between two consenting adults would usually not be harassment. Yet, if the one party has far more power than the other and abuses this in the work situation to coerce the other, it could still be a case of harassment. If unwelcome attentions are repeated although they have been declined, or if the person is victimised because of having turned down such advances, the situation becomes worse.'[4]

'The Code of Good Practice on the Handling of Sexual Harassment Cases in the Workplace defines sexual harassment as an unwanted conduct of a sexual nature that violates the rights of an employee and constitutes a barrier to equity in the workplace. In terms of this Code, sexual harassment may include physical conduct, verbal conduct and non-verbal conduct. This Code is not legally binding, but it provides useful guidance in the manner in which an employer should deal with allegations of sexual harassment and encourages the development and implementation of policies and procedures to prevent sexual discrimination.'[5]

Meaning of the Concept

'Generally, international instruments define sexual harassment broadly as a form of violence against women and as discriminatory treatment, while national laws focus more closely on the illegal conduct. At the national level, the United States was one of the first countries to define sexual harassment, as a prohibited form of sex discrimination that violates Title VII of the Civil Rights Act, a federal law. Sex-based conduct in the workplace is unwelcome when (1) an employee does not solicit or initiate the conduct; and (2) when the employee regards the conduct as undesirable and offensive.'[6] 'The law defines sexual harassment as unwelcome sexual conduct at the workplace that causes an employee to lose his or her job or a promotion, or creates a workplace that is hostile, offensive or intimidating.'[7]

'Unwelcome sexual advances, requests for sexual favours and other verbal or physical conduct of a sexual nature constitute sexual harassment when this conduct explicitly or implicitly affects an individual's employment, unreasonably interferes with an individual's work performance, or creates an intimidating, hostile, or offensive work environment.'[8] 'It is unlawful to harass a person (an applicant or employee) because of that person's sex. Harassment can include sexual harassment or unwelcome sexual advances, requests for sexual favours and other verbal or physical harassment of a sexual nature.'[9] 'Using crude or sexually inappropriate language can be considered sexual harassment if it creates an uncomfortable environment for someone else. Sexual harassment may also include offensive jokes, comments, greetings, verbal teasing, or inappropriate name-calling, such as Hey babe, Hot stuff, or Big stud. Students often sexually harass others by calling them fag, homo, or other degrading terms that refer to sexual orientation.'[10]

'The EEOC has defined sexual harassment in its guidelines as: Unwelcome sexual advances, requests for sexual favours and other verbal or physical conduct of a sexual nature when: (a) Submission to such conduct is made either explicitly or implicitly a term or condition of an individual's employment, or; (b) Submission to or rejection of such conduct by an individual is used as a basis for employment decisions affecting such individual, or; (c) Such conduct has the purpose or effect of unreasonably interfering with an individual's work performance or creating an intimidating, hostile, or offensive working environment.'[11] 'Sexual harassment can take many different forms: it can be obvious or indirect, physical or verbal, repeated or one-off and perpetrated by males and females against people of the same or opposite sex.

Sexual harassment may include: Staring or leering; unnecessary familiarity, such as deliberately brushing up against you or unwelcome touching; Suggestive comments or jokes; Insults or taunts of a sexual nature; Intrusive questions or statements about your private life; Displaying posters, magazines or screen savers of a sexual nature; Sending sexually explicit e-mails or text messages; Inappropriate advances on social networking sites; Accessing sexually explicit internet sites; Requests for sex or repeated unwanted requests to go out on date; Behaviour that may also be considered to be an offence under criminal law, such as physical assault, indecent exposure, sexual assault, stalking or obscene communications.'[12]

Types of Sexual Harassment

Sexual harassment can take a variety of forms. It includes both physical violence and more subtle forms of violence such as coercion or the creation of a hostile work environment. A hostile work environment includes situations, for example, when the victim is not appointed to important committees, does not receive information about training opportunities or is not considered for promotion because of family responsibilities. This type of sexual harassment is difficult to document but still can significantly affect women's work and career paths.

U.S. law describes two different forms of sexual harassment: (1) *quid pro quo* and (2) hostile work environment. *Quid pro quo* sexual harassment occurs when employment decisions and conditions are based upon whether as employee is willing to grant sexual favours. Hiring, promotions, salary increases, shift or work assignments and performance expectation are some of the working benefits that can be made conditional on sexual favours. A hostile work environment is one in which unwelcome conduct of a sexual nature creates an uncomfortable work environment for some employees. Examples of this conduct include sexually explicit talk, sexually provocative photographs, foul or hostile language or inappropriate touching.[13]

'The several types of sexual harassment are the following:

1. **Verbal or Written:** This type includes comments about attire, personality, or physical appearance; sexual jokes; requesting sexual favours; constantly asking someone out; sexual insinuation; starting rumors about personal aspects or sexuality; threatening a person with sexual advances.
2. **Physical:** Sexual advances of the physical nature include assault; obstructing movement; improper and unwanted touching; kissing; hugging; patting; stroking.
3. **Nonverbal:** Sexual cues that are nonverbal include staring at someone body parts; hand gestures or facial expressions that are sexual; following a person or stalking.
4. **Visual:** This type includes sexually explicit drawings, pictures, posters, e-mails and any other images that depict unwanted sexual fixations.
5. **Non-sexual:** There is harassment that is not in a sexual manner, but is considered sexual harassment. This includes

discrimination based on gender. Females or males can be sexually discriminated on purely because of their gender in the workplace.

6. **Severe or Pervasive:** Sexual harassment can only be considered as such if it is severe or pervasive in sexual nature. For a singular incident to be regarded as sexual harassment, it must be severe. An example of this includes a single occurrence of attempted rape. In order to determine whether conduct is persistent is to establish the frequency of the incidents, as well as the length of time the instances have been occurring and how many people are affected by the sexual harassment.'[14]

Reasons of Sexual Harassment

'The causes of sexual harassment vary from person to person and from situation to situation. Social and political changes in recent years have changed power relationships. Some men feel threatened by the career advancement of women and people of colour, or are uncomfortable with women's newfound independence and assertiveness at home and / or at work. The prevalence of marital stress and divorce in our society means that some men and women come to work in a state of emotional distress that could make them vulnerable to sexual harassment.'[15]

'Sexual harassment occurs in the workplace or in a work-related environment because of the unwelcome, unwanted, uninvited, action or behaviour of a person that causes discomfort, humiliation, offence or distress to other. Majority of such cases are directed towards the opposite sex by men working high position in an organisation. Women are vulnerable to sexual harassment because they more often lack power and work in insecure positions. Due to the fear factor women often resign to their fate rather than raise voice against sexual harassment. Sometimes sexual harassment is also seen as a power game, where man insists on sexual favours in exchange for benefits he can dispense with due to his position.'[16]

Sexual Harassment: Global Perspectives

'Half of all women in the European Union have been sexually harassed and one-third has been the victim of sexual or physical violence at some point since they were 15 years old. These statistics come from a new report the European Agency for Fundamental Rights (FRA), which surveyed more than 42,000 women aged 18 to 74 living in EU states in 2012. The findings were presented at a conference in Brussels. "*This is no minor issue. We're talking about mothers, sisters, daughters across the EU who have been abused physically, sexually and psychologically,*" said Morten Kjaerum, FRA's director.'[17] 'Sexual harassment is common in both southern countries and northern countries. However, it seems that, save in France and Italy, much less importance is attached to the issue of sexual harassment in southern countries and the level of awareness is not very high. Almost all people suffering sexual harassment were reported negative consequences both private and regarding their job.

The highest incidence rates were found in the national surveys carried out in Austria, Germany and Luxembourg. The Austrian and Luxembourg surveys reported a rate of 80 per cent and the German research showed that 72 per cent of employees had been confronted with sexual harassment. The UK police research concluded that 90 per cent of the women had suffered sexual harassment of one kind or another. This could be one of the branches where sexual harassment occurs to a greater extent, opposed to other branches. Other high per centages of sexual harassment were found in a UK study amongst health service workers (89%) and in a Norwegian Women's Magazine study (90%).'[18]

'The Beijing Platform for Action, which was adopted at the United Nations Fourth World Conference on Women in Beijing in 1995, calls on governments, the international community and civil society to take strategic action in twelve critical areas of concern which include the area of violence against women. After the Beijing Conference, the European Council at its Madrid December 1995 meeting called on Member States to conduct an annual review of the implementation of the Platform for Action. In 1996 and 1997, this follow up process revealed the need for a more consistent and systematic observation and evaluation of Platform implementation in the European Union.'[19] 'European law tradition is said to have never really accepted the doctrinal theory according to which sexual harassment is a form of discrimination. It is said to rather focus on a different formula: 'the dignity of women' or even 'workers'.[20]

'In Bangladesh, large scale of women's entry into paid labour force has increased incidences of sexual harassment. Sexual harassment, work and mobility appear to be closely intertwined. In Nepal a research on Sexual Harassment at the Workplace revealed that the problem of sexual harassment is highly prevalent in workplaces, as 53.84 per cent of women employee/workers reported that they have faced the problem of sexual harassment in their workplaces, 57.14 per cent of male and 23.08 per cent women employee/workers were of the view that they were aware of sexual harassment at the workplace.'[21]

'According to the sexual harassment white paper by the National Human Rights Commission of South Korea (2012), 50.3 per cent of harassment cases occur in the workplace. Nearly 20 per cent takes place at dinner outings with coworkers and 4.2 per cent at education or training facilities. The report also indicated that power plays a significant role in sexual harassment, with 61.1 per cent of cases involving a boss and an employee. A survey conducted in 2012 by an employment website (www.career.co.kr) showed that four out of ten workers have experienced sexual harassment. Korea began to legally acknowledge sexual harassment in 1995, through the enactment of the framework act on women's development on December 30. It was triggered by the first-ever sexual harassment lawsuit in October 1993, when a teaching assistant at a university filed a complaint against a professor. The law now states that sexual harassment is when any member of a state organisation makes the other party feel sexual humiliation or aversion with verbal or physical behaviour of a sexual nature, or puts the other party at a disadvantage in employment for not complying with such action or demands.'[22]

'Sexual harassment is not a new phenomenon in South Africa but until recently nothing significant was done to address it. The problem is currently being addressed through legislation aimed at prevention and eradication. Sexual harassment in the employment environment is an area of great concern. With the advent of new legislation a positive duty has been placed on employers to take steps to combat the problem.'[23] 'The rate of sexual violence in South Africa is among the highest in the world. Sexual violence is the use of force or manipulation to get someone to engage in unwanted sexual activity without his or her consent. According to the report by the United Nations Office on Crimes and Drugs for the period 1998–2000, South Africa was ranked first for rapes per capita. While women's groups in South Africa estimate that a woman is raped every 26 seconds, the South African police estimate that a woman is raped every 36 seconds. The danger from rape and sexual assault is compounded because of the prevalence of HIV/AIDS in South African townships.'[24]

'In 2009 – 2010, 21 per cent of all complaints to the Australian Human Rights Commission were under the Sex Discrimination Act and 88 per cent of those complaints related to sex discrimination in the workplace. The wide use of new technologies such as mobile phones, e-mail and social networking websites creates new spaces where sexual harassment may occur. Sexual harassment at work is against the law. Sexual harassment can be committed by an employer, workmate or other people in a working relationship with the victim.'[25] 'All over the world girls and women face unwanted sexual harassment in school, at their jobs and also on the street. Respect for women's bodily autonomy should be a guaranteed human right and women throughout Latin America and the Caribbean are fighting to ensure they have the right to be safe when they walk down the street. In Bogota, Colombia, the Latin American Women and Habitat Network (LAWHN) launched a poster campaign on city buses that reads: "We don't need that kind of support." The Women Speak Project in Trinidad and Tobago provides an online platform for street harassment victims to share stories of discrimination and receive peer support.'[26]

'Sexual harassment is one of the most tolerated human rights violations against women in Latin American societies. Because it is often a hidden crime, Latin American governments have not specifically penalised sexual harassment in their domestic legislation. In Latin America, sexual harassment is a particular problem because certain groups of Latin American women are more vulnerable to sexual harassment due to their social and economic conditions. In Latin America, there are few specific laws or other legislation penalising sexual harassment. Most countries only prohibit sexual harassment in the workplace in the context of broader labour legislation. Uruguay, El Salvador and Mexico, however, regulate sexual harassment in their broader penal codes, while Costa Rica has a special law that protects against sexual harassment in the workplace and educational establishments. In 1993, Argentina enacted a narrowly tailored law prohibiting sexual harassment. Peru offers even less protection because sexual harassment is not considered an act of discrimination on the basis of sex. Costa Rica has fashioned a comprehensive law that extends beyond the workplace. The Mexican Penal Code has also criminalised sexual harassment, categorising it as a "Crime against Liberty and Normal Psychosexual Development.' Latin American countries have developed different approaches to sexual harassment. The most traditional approach is to include sexual harassment legislation within labour-based legislation."[27]

'Sexual harassment has long been recognised in Canada as a form of gender discrimination. For several years, gender discrimination (which includes discrimination based on breast feeding, sexual harassment, transgender and pregnancy) was the most commonly alleged ground of discrimination in both federal and provincial human rights commission complaints.'[28] 'Sexual harassment is not illegal in Canada; instead it is considered a human rights violation. Depending on where the harassment takes place, a complaint can be reported with the appropriate human rights organisation, such as the Canadian Human Rights Commission. Sexual harassment can happen anywhere: on the street, at school, at home, or in the workplace. It is a common occurrence. 87 per cent of women in Canada have reported being a victim of sexual harassment.'[29]

Sexual Harassment in India

'In India the concern of sexual harassment of women at work place is increasing. In the Sexual Harassment of Women at Workplace Act 2013 it is defined as "*unwelcome sexual gesture or behaviour whether directly or indirectly, sexually coloured remarks, physical contact and advances, showing pornography, a demand or request for sexual favours, any other physical, verbal/non verbal conduct being sexual in nature and passing offensive and unacceptable remarks.*" The issue of sexual harassment of women at workplace came into major lime light due to Bhavari Devi Case of 1992.'[30] 'Sexual harassment is defined as behaviour that is unwelcome and of a sexual nature.'[31]

'There are some women who may not have been harassed. But none have escaped the fear of harassment, of being misunderstood or of having been blamed for being provocative. *In India, every day a woman is harassed every 51 minutes and sexually molested every 26 minutes.* Most people will argue that sexual harassment either happens in isolated and dark roads or large organisations. The Gender Study Group of the University of Delhi, 1996 shows that 92 per cent of women in hostels and 88 per cent of women day scholars have faced sexual harassment on campus. A 1997 survey of colleges in Mumbai found that 39 per cent of women students have experienced harassment. Forms of sexual harassment that pertain to a campus environment include; demands for sexual favours accompanied by veiled or open promises of preferential treatment or threats concerning an individual's employment or student status, physical and verbal aggression arising from the above, communicating or displaying obscene letters, posters, cartoons, or photographs, disparaging remarks and gestures made with prejudicial intent in the work or study places, which specifically relate to the issue of gender, harassment through unwelcome telephone calls or e-mail, uninvited chasing or following/blackmailing in or outside the campus.'[32]

'The victims of sexual harassment are mostly girls/women. It indicates that it is not safe for girls to move out of their houses. They are harassed everywhere might be it an educational institute or workplace. Sexual harassment is illegal. If a girl is being harassed then she need not to be afraid but try to fight against it and get the harasser punished. If she is being sexually harassed then she should tell someone who could help her.'[33]

'Seventeen per cent of working women in India claim that they have experienced sexual harassment at workplace. This high incidence of sexual harassment, both in the organised and the unorganised sectors, was revealed in an opinion poll titled 'Sexual Harassment at Workplaces in India 2011-2012" released by Oxfam India. The survey for which women were interviewed in Delhi, Mumbai, Bangaluru, Chennai, Kolkata, Ahmedabad, Lucknow and Durgapur was jointly conducted by Oxfam India and Social and Rural Research Institute. Most women claimed to have faced incidents that were non-physical, according to the survey. "Sixty-six of the 400 respondents reported to have faced a cumulative of 121 incidents of sexual harassment, 102 of 121 incidents reported to be non-physical, whereas the remaining 19 incidents were physical in nature," indicated the survey. The report also noted that while 87 per cent of the general population and 93 per cent of working women respondents reported awareness of sexual harassment of women at work place, majority of the victims did not resort to any formal action against the perpetrator. The top three categories that have emerged unsafe for women are labourers (29 per cent), domestic help (23 per cent) and small scale manufacturing (16 per cent).'[34]

'The Indian Army has launched a court of inquiry against 12 officers and 39 soldiers allegedly involved in cases of sexual abuse while they were deployed as UN peacekeepers in strife-riven Congo. The inquiry is being held in Meerut in Uttar Pradesh, where the officers and soldiers are being questioned to conclude if they had sexually abused local women and also fathered children while on a UN peacekeeping mission in 2008. The sexual abuse allegations emerged after DNA tests commissioned by the UN on the children born to local women in Durla in the Congo showed they had distinctive Indian features. The UN wrote to Indian Army requesting further investigations, with the latest reminder coming in August 2010. Following the allegations, the regiment in which the officers and soldiers were serving was recalled from the Congo and attached to the Western Command headquarters. In March 2008, three officers were charged with sexual abuse of a local woman while on a holiday in South Africa. In 2007, there were allegations that some of the Indian peacekeepers had exchanged food and information with the locals for obtaining gold from rebels in North Kivu in the Congo. There were also allegations of Indian soldiers sexually exploiting minor girls in North Kivu.'[35]

Effects of Sexual Harassment

'Effects of sexual harassment can vary depending on the individuality of the recipient and the severity and duration of the harassment. Harassment may lead to temporary or prolonged stress and/or depression depending on the recipient's psychological abilities to cope and the type of harassment and the social support or lack thereof for the recipient.'[36] 'Psychologists and social workers report that severe/chronic sexual harassment can have the same psychological effects as rape or sexual assault.'[37] 'Sexual harassment can have a devastating impact on victims' lives. Victims of sexual harassment report greater instances of alcohol abuse and mental health problems. Harassment is a devious way to keep women out of the workplace or in traditional women's jobs with low pay and few benefits. Being sexually harassed can devastate psychological health, physical well-being and vocational development. Women who have been harassed often change their jobs, career goals, job assignments, educational programmes or academic majors. In addition, women have reported psychological and physical reaction to being harassed that is similar to reactions to other forms of stress.'[38]

'Harassment costs companies money by reducing productivity, morale and motivation. Companies may lose valuable staff. Many women resign rather than go through the unpleasantness of a confrontation. High absenteeism among women could also be a result (or a possible symptom) of harassment, as the stress caused by such an unresolved problem, or the fear of being harassed again can either cause illness, or encourage women to stay safely at home. Companies can incur legal costs if the problem is ignored. If a company has no clear policy on sexual harassment, it may also have problems if it needs to take disciplinary steps against a harasser.'[39] 'Women's participation in economic sector is crucial for their economic empowerment and their sustainability. However, problems such as sexual harassment in the workplace discourage women to continue working. Sexual harassment in the workplace though an age-old problem has emerged as a serious concern in Asia and the Pacific recently.'[40]

Preventing Sexual Harassment

'Sexual harassment in the workplace is a form of violence against women, a violation of their human rights and an offense that is incompatible with human dignity. Many countries recognise sexual harassment as a form of sex discrimination. In order to effectively prevent sexual harassment and appropriately address sexual harassment when it occurs, it is important to understand not just what sexual harassment is, but why it occurs and the effects it can have.'[41] 'Preventing sexual harassment must be an ongoing priority. Training that occurs over time, across settings and includes the entire faculty, staff and administrative personnel will be more effective than a one-time session of training for the teachers.'[42]

'Sexual harassment is a form of gender discrimination. Men may be subjected to sexual harassment but majority of the victims are women. In response to the growing awareness about the adverse impacts of sexual harassment, there have been increasing efforts around the world not only to break the silence on sexual harassment but also to take pro-active steps in addressing it.'[43]

'Various initiatives have slowly begun to address sexual harassment in Asia. Also, specific legislation exists, for example, in Belize, Costa Rica, France, Luxembourg and the Philippines. Awareness programmes have been conducted in South Asia. Also, business associations have started initiatives of providing awareness on the growing problem of sexual harassment in the workplaces. Both in Nepal and India, training programmes on Sexual Harassment in the Workplace have been provided in organisations. Such trainings have been developed in a way to promote understanding of the problem of sexual harassment as a violation of right to work in a safe environment and a problem that affects a woman's dignity and health.'[44]

Vishakha and others vs. State of Rajasthan

'Vishakha and others vs. State of Rajasthan was a 1997 Indian Supreme Court case where Vishakha and other women groups filed Public Interest Litigation against State of Rajasthan and Union of India to enforce the fundamental rights of working women under Articles 14, 19 and 21 of the Constitution of India. The petition was filed after Bhanwari Devi, a social worker in Rajasthan was brutally gang raped for stopping a child marriage. Articles 14, 15 19(1) (g) and 21 of the Constitution and the safeguards against sexual harassment are implicit therein. The petition resulted in what are popularly known as the Vicki Guidelines.

'In 1992 Bhanwari Devi a social worker in Rajasthan was brutally gang raped by a number of upper class men, because she had tried to stop a child marriage. Bhanwari Devi was determined to get justice and lodged a case against the offenders. During the 1990s, Rajasthan state government employee Bhanwari

Devi who tried to prevent child marriage as part of her duties as a worker of the Women Development Programme was raped by the landlords of the community. The feudal patriarchs who were enraged by her 'guts' decided to teach her a lesson and raped her repeatedly. The rape survivor did not get justice from Rajasthan High Court and the rapists were allowed to go free. This enraged a women's rights group called Vishaka that filed public interest litigation in the Supreme Court of India. In 1997, the Supreme Court passed a landmark judgment in the same Vishaka case laying down guidelines to be followed by establishments in dealing with complaints about sexual harassment. National Commission for Women has asked the government to ensure constitution of Internal Complaints Committee in accordance with Supreme Court guidelines in its departments, institutions and autonomous bodies to address such cases. It has also recommended conducting gender sensitisation workshops for top level management officials.'[45]

'The Supreme Court of India's judgment only proposed guidelines to alleviate the problem of sexual harassment in 1997. India finally enacted its law on prevention of sexual harassment against female employees at the workplace. The Sexual Harassment of Women at Workplace (Prevention, Prohibition and Redressal) Act, 2013 has been made effective on April 23, 2013 by way of publication in the Gazette of India.'[46]

Legal Mechanism

'The Sections 354, 509 and 376 of the Indian Penal Code which deal with sexual assault, namely, outraging the modesty of a woman, eve teasing and committing rape of a woman, all assume that men cannot be subjected to these crimes. The Vishakha guidelines which aim to prevent sexual harassment in work places are also just limited to women. The only form in which a wrong sexual advancement on a man is recognised as an offence is as sodomy under the Section 377 of the IPC. Apart from that there is no law to punish a person for molesting a man.'[47]

'The Sexual Harassment of Women at Workplace (Prevention, Prohibition and Redressal) Act, 2013 is a legislative act in India that seeks to protect women from sexual harassment at their place of work. It was passed by the Lok Sabha (the lower house of the Indian Parliament) on 3rd September 2012. It was passed by the Rajya Sabha (the upper house of the Indian Parliament) on 26th February 2013. The Bill got the assent of the President on 23rd April 2013. The Act came into force from 9th December 2013. According to the Press Information Bureau of the Government of India, The Act will ensure that women are protected against sexual harassment at all the work places, be it in public or private. This will contribute to realisation of their right to gender equality, life and liberty and equality in working conditions everywhere. The sense of security at the workplace will improve women's participation in work, resulting in their economic empowerment and inclusive growth.

The Act defines sexual harassment at the work place and creates a mechanism for redressal of complaints. It also provides safeguards against false or malicious charges. The definition of "aggrieved woman", who will get protection under the Act is extremely wide to cover all women, irrespective of her age or employment status, whether in the organised or unorganised sectors, public or private and covers clients, customers and domestic workers as well. The Committee is required to complete the inquiry within a time period of 90 days. On completion of the inquiry, the report will be sent to the employer or the District Officer, as the case may be, they are mandated to take action on the report within 60 days. Through the Criminal Law (Amendment) Act, 2013, Section 354 was added to the Indian Penal Code that stipulates what consists of a sexual harassment offence and what the penalties shall be for a man committing such an offence. Penalties range from one to three years imprisonment and/or a fine. Additionally, with sexual harassment being a crime, employers are obligated to report offences.'[48]

'The Act is enacted by the Indian Parliament to provide protection against sexual harassment of women at workplace and prevention and redressal of complaints of sexual harassment and for matters connected therewith or incidental thereto. Sexual harassment is termed as a violation of the fundamental rights of a woman to equality under Articles 14 and 15 of the Constitution of India and right to life and to live with dignity under Article 21 of the Constitution of India. The Act has adopted the definition of 'sexual harassment' from Vishaka Judgment and the term sexual harassment includes any unwelcome acts or behaviour (whether directly or by implication) such as physical contact and advances, demand or request for sexual favours, making sexually coloured remarks, showing pornography or any other unwelcome physical, verbal or non-verbal conduct of sexual nature. Section 3 of the Act provides that no woman shall be subjected to sexual harassment at any workplace. The Act makes it mandatory for every employer to constitute an internal complaints committee which entertains the complaints made by any aggrieved women'.[49]

'The Act in its Section 2n, defines sexual harassment. Sexual harassment includes any one or more of the following unwelcome acts or behaviour (whether directly or by implication), namely (a) Physical contact and advances, or (b) A demand or request for sexual favours, or (c) Making sexually coloured remarks, or (d) Showing pornography, or (e) Any other unwelcome physical, verbal, non-verbal conduct of sexual nature. Section 3 (2) of the Act further elaborates that if any of the following circumstances occurs or is present in relation to or connected with any act or behaviour of sexual harassment among other circumstances, it may amount to sexual harassment: (a) Implied or explicit promise of preferential treatment in her employment, or, (b) Implied or explicit threat of detrimental treatment in her employment, or, (c) Implied or explicit threat about her present or future employment status, or, (d) Interference with her work or creating an intimidating or offensive or hostile work environment for her, or, (e) Humiliating treatment likely to affect her health or safety.

According to the Act (Section 2a) aggrieved woman means: (a) In relation to a workplace, a woman of any age whether employed or not, who alleges to have been subjected to any act of sexual harassment by the respondent; (b) In relation to a dwelling place or house, a woman of any age who is employed in such a dwelling or house. Workplace includes: (a) Any department, organisation, undertaking, establishment, enterprise, institution, office, branch or unit which is established, owned, controlled or wholly or substantially financed by funds provided directly or indirectly by the appropriate government or the local authority or a government company or a corporation or a cooperative society; (b) Any private sector organisation or a private venture, undertaking, enterprise, institution, establishment, society, trust, non-governmental organisation, unit or service provider carrying on commercial, professional, vocational, educational, entertainmental, industrial, health services or financial activities including production, supply, sale, distribution or service; (c) Hospital or nursing homes; (d) Any sports institute, stadium, sports complex or competition or games venue, whether residential or not used for training, sports or other activities relating to it; (e) Any place visited by the employee arising out of or during the course of employment including transportation provided by the employer for undertaking such journey; (f) A dwelling or a house.

According to the Act (Section 2f), employee means a person employed at a workplace for any work on regular, temporary, adhoc or daily basis, either directly or through an agent, including a contractor, with or, without the knowledge of the principal employer, whether for remuneration or not, or working on a voluntary basis or otherwise, whether the terms of employment are express or implied and includes a co-worker, a contract worker, probationer, trainee, apprentice or called by any other such name. As per Section 19 of the Act, every employer shall: (a) Provide a safe working environment at the workplace which shall include safety from the persons coming into contact at the workplace; (b) Display at any conspicuous place in the workplace, the penal consequences of sexual harassments and the order constituting the Internal Complaint Committee; (c) Organise workshops and awareness programmes at regular intervals for sensitising the employees with the Act; (d) Organise orientation programmes for the members of the ICC; (e) Provide necessary facilities to the ICC or the LCC for dealing with the complaint and conducting an inquiry; (f) Assist in securing the attendance of respondent and witness before the ICC or the LCC; (g) Provide assistance to the woman if she chooses to file a complaint under IPC or any other law; (h) Treat sexual harassment as a misconduct under the service rules and initiate action for such misconduct.

Appropriate government means in relation to workplace which is established, owned, controlled or wholly or substantially financed by funds provided directly or indirectly by the Central

Government or the Union Territory administration it is the Central government, while those by the State Government, it is the State Government. The Act in Section 2(p) defines unorganised sector in relation to a workplace as an enterprise owned by individuals or self-employed workers and engaged in the production or sale of goods or providing service of any kind whatsoever and where the enterprise employs workers, the number of such workers is less than 10. According to the Act (Section 2e) domestic worker means a woman who is employed to do the household work in any household for remuneration whether in cash or kind, either directly or through any agency on a temporary, permanent, part time or full time basis, but does not include any member of the family of the employer. The Internal Complaint Committee should be located at all workplace. Where the offices or administrative units of the workplace are located at different places or divisional or sub-divisional level, the internal Committee shall be located at all administrative units or offices (Section 4(1) of the Act).'[50]

Conclusion

Sexual harassment defines violence against women and as discriminatory treatment, while national laws focus more closely on the illegal conduct. Unwelcome sexual advances, requests for sexual favours and other verbal or physical conduct of a sexual nature constitute sexual harassment when this conduct explicitly or implicitly affects an individual's employment, unreasonably interferes with an individual's work performance, or creates an intimidating, hostile, or offensive work environment. Sexual harassment can take a variety of forms. It includes both physical violence and more subtle forms of violence such as coercion or the creation of a hostile work environment.

Sexual harassment occurs in the workplace or in a work-related environment because of the unwelcome, unwanted, uninvited, action or behaviour of a person that causes discomfort, humiliation, offence or distress to other. Effects of sexual harassment can vary depending on the individuality of the recipient and the severity and duration of the harassment. Harassment may lead to temporary or prolonged stress and/or depression depending on the recipient's psychological abilities to cope and the type of harassment and the social support or lack thereof for the recipient.

References

1. Sexual harassment (2015), Retrieved from http://en.wikipedia.org/wiki/Sexual_harassment
2. Sexual harassment (2014), Retrieved from https://rainn.org/get-information/types-of-sexual-assault/sexual-harassment
3. Causes of Sexual Harassment, Retrieved from http://www1.umn.edu/humanrts/svaw/harassment/explore/3causes.htm
4. What is Harassment? Retrieved from https://www.westerncape.gov.za/general-publication/sexual-harassment- causes-consequences-and-cures?toc_page=1
5. Sexual harassment (2014), Retrieved from http://www.mywage.co.za/main/decent-work/fair-treatment/sexual-harassment
6. What is sexual harassment? Retrieved from http://www1.umn.edu/humanrts/svaw/harassment/explore/1whatis.htm
7. Sexual harassment (2014), Retrieved from http://www.nationalpartnership.org/issues/fairness/sexual-harassment.html
8. Facts about Sexual Harassment, Retrieved from http://www.eeoc.gov/eeoc/publications/fs-sex.cfm
9. Sexual harassment, Retrieved from http://www.eeoc.gov/laws/types/sexual_harassment.cfm
10. Ellie L. Young, NCSP, Melissa Allen, NCSP and Betty Y. Ashbaker, Sexual harassment, Retrieved from http://www.nasponline.org/educators/Sexual%20Harassment.pdf
11. What is Sexual Harassment, Retrieved from http://www.un.org/womenwatch/osagi/pdf/whatissh.pdf
12. https://www.humanrights.gov.au/our-work/sex-discrimination/guides/sexual-harassment
13. What is sexual harassment? Retrieved from http://www1.umn.edu/humanrts/svaw/harassment/explore/1whatis. htm
14. Steven V. Cates, The State of Sexual Harassment in America: What is the Status of Sexual Harassment in the US Workplace Today? Retrieved from http://www.jgbm.org/page/18%20Steven%20Cates.pdf
15. https://www.westerncape.gov.za/general-publication/sexual-harassment-causes-consequences-and-cures?toc_page=2

16. Sexual harassment in workplace: Causes and remedies - See more at: http://www.ummid.com/news/2013/December/12.12.2013/workplace-harassment.html#sthash.G3sbx7eg.dpuf
17. See http://www.pbs.org/newshour/rundown/half-eu-women-victims-sexual-harrasment-new-report-finds/
18. Sexual harassment in the workplace in the European Union (1998), Retrieved from http://www.un.org/womenwatch/osagi/pdf/shworkpl.pdf
19. Report on sexual harassment in the workplace in EU member states (2004), Retrieved from http://www.justice.ie/en/JELR/SexualHrrsmtRpt.pdf/Files/SexualHrrsmtRpt.pdf
20. Harassment related to Sex and Sexual Harassment Law in 33 European Countries, Retrieved from http://ec.europa.eu/justice/gender-equality/files/your_rights/final_harassement_en.pdf
21. Sapana Pradhan-Malla, Sexual harassment in workplace in Asia, Retrieved from http://www.un.org/womenwatch/daw/egm/vaw-gp-2005/docs/experts/pradhanmalla.sh.pdf
22. Sexual harassment haunts South Korea (2013), Retrieved from http://usa.chinadaily.com.cn/world/2013-06/10/content_16604393.htm
23. Sandra Govender, Sexual Harassment: The South African Perspective, Retrieved from http://jdi.sagepub.com/content/7/1-4/229.short
24. Sexual violence in South Africa (2014), Retrieved from http://en.wikipedia.org/wiki/Sexual_violence_in_South_Africa
25. See https://www.humanrights.gov.au/our-work/sex-discri mination /guides/sexual-harassment
26. http://rhrealitycheck.org/article/2012/03/20/whos-ending-street-harassment-in-latin-america-and-caribbean/
27. Gaby Oré-Aguilar (1997), Sexual Harassment and Human Rights in Latin America, Fordham Law Review, 66 (2), pp. 631-646.
28. See http://www.lawnow.org/sexual-harassment-is-a-continuing-issue-in-canada/
29. See http://www.consented.ca/basics/sexual-harassment/
30. Sexual harassment in workplace causes and remedies, Retrieved from http://www.civilserviceindia.com/subject/Essay/sexual-harassment-in-workplace-causes-and-remedies.html
31. Rebecca S. Merkin, Sexual Harassment Indicators: The Socio-Cultural and Cultural Impact of Marital Status, Age, Education, Race and Sex in Latin America, Intercultural Communication Studies XXI: 1 (2012), p. 155.

32. A Study on Sexual Harassment in Colleges in Mumbai: An Executive Summary, Retrieved from https://arajohannes.wordpress.com/writing/research/a-study-on-sexual-harassment-in-colleges-in-mumbai-an-excutive-summary/

33. Barkha Sethi (2011), Sexual Harassment of Women in India, Retrieved from http://www.youthkiawaaz.com/2011/11/sexual-harassment-of-women-in-india/

34. The Hindu (Nov 29, 2012), Sexual harassment at work place high, Retrieved from http://www.thehindu.com/todays-paper/tp-national/ sexual-harassment-at-work-place-high/article4144874.ece

35. NDTV (June 07, 2011), Indian Army probing sexual abuse charges against UN peacekeepers in Congo, Retrieved from http://www.ndtv.com/india-news/indian-army-probing-sexual-abuse-charges-against-un-peacekeepers-in-congo-457866

36. Sexual harassment (2014), Retrieved from http://www.nationalpartnership.org/issues/fairness/sexual-harassment.html

37. Sexual harassment (2014), Retrieved from http://en.wikipedia.org/wiki/Sexual_harassment

38. Sexual Harassment: The Facts, Retrieved from http://www.twu.edu/downloads/counseling/G-7_Sexual_ Harass ment_ The_Facts.pdf

39. https://www.westerncape.gov.za/general-publication/sexual-harassment-causes-consequences-and-cures?toc_page=5

40. Sapana Pradhan-Malla, Sexual harassment in workplace in Asia, Retrieved from http://www.un.org/womenwatch/daw/egm/vaw-gp-2005/docs/experts/pradhanmalla.sh.pdf

41. Causes, Theories and Effects of Sexual Harassment, Retrieved from http://www.stopvaw.org/uploads/causes_and_theories_sex_harassmt__2009.pdf

42. Ellie L. Young, NCSP, Melissa Allen, NCSP and Betty Y. Ashbaker, Sexual harassment, Retrieved from http://www.nasponline.org/educators/Sexual%20Harassment.pdf

43. Sapana Pradhan-Malla, Sexual harassment in workplace in Asia, Retrieved from http://www.un.org/womenwatch/daw/egm/vaw-gp-2005/docs/experts/pradhanmalla.sh.pdf

44. Sapana Pradhan-Malla, Sexual harassment in workplace in Asia, Retrieved from http://www.un.org/womenwatch/daw/egm/vaw-gp-2005/docs/experts/pradhanmalla.sh.pdf

45. Vishaka Guidelines (2014), Retrieved from http://en.wikipedia.org/wiki/Vishaka_Guidelines

46. Vishakha and others v State of Rajasthan (2014), Retrieved from http://en.wikipedia.org/wiki/Vishakha_and_ others_v_State_of_Rajasthan

47. The Indian Express (April 27, 2015), Sexual harassment of male a reality, but remains a taboo, Retrieved from http://indianexpress.com/article/india/sexual-harassment-of-male-a-reality-but-remains-a-taboo/

48. Sexual Harassment of Women at Workplace (Prevention, Prohibition and Redressal) Act, 2013, Retrieved from http://en.wikipedia.org/wiki/The_Sexual_Harassment_of_Women_at_Workplace_%28 Prevention,_Prohibition_and_Redressal%29_Act,_2013

49. Rajdutt S. Singh (2014), India: Overview of the Sexual Harassment of Women at Workplace, Retrieved from http://singhassociates.in/UploadImg/NewsImages/Vol%2520VII% 2520Issue% 2520IX.pdf?utm_sour ce=Mondaq&utm_ medium=syn dication&utm_campaign=View-Original

50. http://www.odisha.gov.in/schooleducation/Sexual_ Harassment_at_workplace_ACT_2013.pdf

15

Eve Teasing

"Clever and attractive women do not want to vote; they are willing to let men govern as long as they govern men."

—*George Bernard Shaw*

Introduction

'The meaning of the word "eve" is 'First woman in bible: in the Bible, the first woman created by God and Adam's companion in the Garden of Eden'. And the meaning of "tease" is 'to laugh at somebody and make jokes about them, either in a friendly way or in order to annoy or embarrass them. According to Encarta, the 'eve-teasing' is the harassment of young woman. Eve teasing stands for a kind of sexual harassment of a young woman.'[1] 'It is the sexual aggression in the form of sexually suggestive remarks, lewd comments to outright fondling. Sometimes, a wink or a low whistle may also follow. Many feminist writers have even termed it as 'little rapes'. It is the violation of woman's right to live in dignity. It was when more and more women started going out to colleges and work independently, the problem received both public and media attention. The concept emerged during the 60's and 70's. It grew to an alarming situation when women ventured on their own without the male escorts.'[2]

'Stalking creates uncertainty, instills fear and can completely disrupt lives. It can involve severe–even lethal–violence. Stalking involves a pattern of overtly criminal and/or apparently innocent behaviour that makes victims fear for themselves or other.'[3] 'Eve teasing, a colloquial word for gender harassment is popularly known and Tamil Nadu Prohibition of Eve-Teasing Act, 1998 on that was developed after the brutal killing of a girl named Sarika Shah in Chennai. Though, stalking is there in the past, it was not acknowledged with this terminology and it was always merged with Eve teasing.'[4] 'Violence against women is a common occurrence in India regardless of violence whether it is physical or mental. Women and girls are generally looked down upon, trapped within cultural framework and rigid perceptions of patriarchy. Any form of torture (physical or mental) can be considered as an offensive and inhuman act against women.'[5]

Meaning of the Concept

'Eve teasing is a ridiculous form of enjoyment for men and a physical as well as mental torment for women. This is one of the daily problems women in Indian society face. Of all the forms that violence against women can assume, eve teasing is the most ubiquitous and insidious because it is considered normal behaviour and not an assault to females.'[6] 'It is normally meant as teasing a girl or woman. It refers to public sexual harassment or street harassment to a girl by a boy, when it turns into a serious issue. Eve-teasing is a very common term in India, Bangladesh, Nepal and Pakistan. Eve teasing is not a new problem in Bangladesh. It is a concern since many years.'[7] 'Some feminist writers claim that this behaviour is a kind of little rape.'[8]

Eve teasing is a very different form of sexual assault. There are many forms the teaser behaves with the girls in a different manner. It ranges from whistle, catcalls, sexually evocative remarks, brushing in public places to outright groping and sometimes teasing by mobile phone and mobile tracking.'[9] 'It is mostly witnessed at public places, public transport, streets, coaching centre. Pertinently, coaching centres in Kashmir often feature in newspapers for wrong reason such as the growing menace of eve teasing.[10] It is generally indulged in by 'young Romeos on festival days e.g. Holi, in University/Colleges especially during opening sessions, submission of forms, cash counters, cinema houses, places of public entertainment, busy market centres and by miscreants including DTC staff in lone DTC buses etc.[11]

Reasons of Eve Teasing

'Eve teasers are any person on the street, in front of schools and colleges, in the bus, train, lift, shopping mall anywhere teases girls in any form of vocabulary, gesture, or directly physical assault. Among the eve teasers from rich to poor, being illiterate to educated, being young to middle age men are included. Eve teasing mainly occurs due to attitude towards girls, family culture and education and loss of morality. Sometimes too much restriction and religious fundamentalism not to intermix with the girls make the boys more curious towards the young girls.'[12]

'One of the great causes of eve teasing comes from the natural tendency of man and woman to attract each other when they openly see each other at the stage of puberty. When people are not religiously educated they will not understand respect of women by man and vice versa. Unfair dresses are great causes for eve teasing nowadays. Open sky culture, satellite communication, internet etc are to great stand responsible for eve teasing. Parents nowadays remain carefully careless about the movement of the son and daughter. Sometimes political parties do not take legal action against eve teaser for their political motives. Unemployed people are evil doers and engaged in eve teasing. Obscene cinema and drama sometimes encourage eve teasing. Absence of Law is a great factor of encouraging eve teasing.'[13]

'The portrayal of sex in Bollywood has long been euphemistic. The couple kisses behind a tree; intertwined feet indicate sexual intercourse; a rape is denoted by a flock of raucous birds disturbed from their peace and rising into the sky. Women are also shown as teasing. Young ladies – dressed in clothes far out of the social norm – thrusting breasts and hips at young men are commonly repeated dance scenes in Bollywood and Tollywood movies. Almost every movie has a song in which the young man pulls the *dupatta* (scarf) of a young girl and although she pretends to get angry, it is implied that secretly she loves the attention.'[14] 'The traditional mindset often blames the eve teasing incidents on women that they provoke male by wearing scanty clothes. That is actually a lame excuse. Even if females wear modern dresses it does not give men license to harass women.'[15]

Eve Teasing in India

'Eve teasing is a euphemism used in India for sexual harassment or molestation of women by men. The concept of eve-teasing vary among and within societies, depending on whether individuals are born and socialised as men or women in a specific socio-economic class in a society. It is probably the most common act of public violence against women which includes various forms of harassments like making vulgar comments, indecent proposals, unwelcome gestures with hands, legs, fingers or other organs, attempting to make physical contact etc. Any kind of verbal or non-verbal behaviour, physical conduct or display of objects or pictures and comments about a woman's looks or body can also be considered as eve-teasing. Eve teasing is a typical social crime.'[16]

'Though the problem received public and media attention in 1980s, it was in the following decades, when more and more women started going out to colleges and work independently, which means they are often no longer accompanied by a male escort as had been a norm in traditional society, that the problem grew to an alarming proportion. Eve-teasing has been a notoriously difficult crime to prove, as perpetrators devise ingenious ways to attack women, even though many feminist writers term it as little rapes and usually occur in public places, streets and public transport.'[17]

Effects of Eve Teasing

'The significant impact that education has on girls and their households is well documented. It has been shown that educated mothers are able to contribute more efficiently to enhance the quality of their children's education. Societies often impose physical restrictions on women's mobility. Eve teasing of school girls has many negative outcomes from increased school drop-out rate to many instances of suicide as the only way out. Drop-out rate of adolescent girls are strongly related to the increased prevalence of cultural and social norms that disempowered adolescents girls and make them vulnerable. Due to threat of eve teasing young girls are getting confined within the four walls, devoid of enjoying education, entertainment, outside work. Many girls become psychologically abnormal out of fear and social security.'[18]

'Eve teasing is a main cause of force marriage and child marriage. Eve teasing has become so alarming that many students and their guardian are compelled to stop education of their children. Most of the girls under prey of the eve teaser suffer from various types of mental disease and some go mad for all through their life. Some time eve teasing may bring new and unbelievable family trouble.'[19]

Constitutional and Legal Provision for Women

'The principle of gender equality is enshrined in the Indian Constitution in its Preamble, Fundamental Rights, Fundamental Duties and Directive Principles. The Constitution not only grants equality to women, but also empowers the State to adopt measures of positive discrimination in favour of women for neutralising the cumulative socio-economic, education and political disadvantages faced by them. Indian penal code 298 [a] and [b] prescribes three months prison and if repeated, five years prison with a fine of Rs 5000 while referring to the social crime as equable to observe, remarks or even songs, we still need to do a lot more. If the law would have been enough, then Delhi capital of India, would not have been referred to as 'one of the world's dangerous places for women.'[20]

'Section 294 punishes any obscene act or recital of any obscene songs or ballad or words in a public place with a punishment of three months or fine or both. Section 509 (Indian Penal Code) punishes anyone who, to intrude upon the privacy of a woman or with an intent to outrage her modesty utters any word, makes any sound or gesture or exhibits an object with an imprisonment for one year or fine or both. It is a cognizable as well as a bailable offence. A question can be raised as to what constitutes an obscene act. Another section is 354 (IPC) according to which anyone who uses forces or assaults a woman to outrage her modesty will be punished with two years of imprisonment or fine or both.'[21]

'Accordingly, the Tamil Nadu Prohibition of Eve-teasing Ordinance, 1998 (Tamil Nadu Ordinance No. 4 of 1998) was promulgated by the Governor and the same was published in the Tamil Nadu Government Gazette Extraordinary, dated the 30th July, 1998. The Bill seeks to replace the said Ordinance. Supreme Court dealing with a case of eve-teasing added about scenario, places and on legal aspect in the following words: *We may, in the facts and circumstances of this case, wish to add some aspects which are also of considerable public importance. We notice that there is no uniform law in this country to curb eve-teasing effectively in or within the precinct of educational institutions, places of worship, bus stands, metro-stations, railway stations, cinema theatres, parks, beaches, places of festival, public service vehicles or any other similar place.* SC observed that in the absence of effective legislation to contain eve-teasing, normally, complaints are registered under Section 294 or Section 509 IPC [Para 26].'[22]

'The Criminal Law (Amendment) Act, 2013 introduced changes to the Indian Penal Code, making sexual harassment an expressed offence under Section 354 A, which is punishable up to three years of imprisonment and or with fine. The Amendment also introduced new sections making acts like disrobing a woman without consent, stalking and sexual acts by person in authority an offence. The Indian Parliament has passed. The Sexual Harassment of Women at Workplace (Prevention, Prohibition and Redressal) Act, 2013, which add protections for female workers in most workplaces. The Act came into force from 9th December 2013.'[23]

Conclusion

Eve teasing is a ridiculous form of enjoyment for men and a physical as well as mental torment for women. This is one of the daily problems women in Indian society face. It is a ridiculous form of enjoyment for men and a physical as well as mental torment for women. This is one of the daily problems women in Indian society face. Eve teasers are any person on the street, in front of schools and colleges, in the bus, train, lift, shopping mall anywhere teases girls in any form of vocabulary, gesture, or directly physical assault. It is a euphemism used in India for sexual harassment or molestation of women by men.

References

1. Muhammad Aminul Hoque, Eve teasing in Bangladesh: causes and impact on society, a study from Islamic perspectives, Retrieved from http://www.tijoss.com/TIJOSS%2015th%20Volume/aminul%20hoque.pdf
2. Eve teasing in Delhi, Retrieved from http://www.ndtvmi.com/b5/B5_Dopesheets/Ritika_Dope.pdf
3. Karuppannan Jaishankar and Puthisigamani Kosalai, Victims of Stalking in India: A Study of Girl College Students in Tirunelveli City, TEMIDA, December 2007, pp. 13-21.
4. Karuppannan Jaishankar and Puthisigamani Kosalai, Victims of Stalking in India: A Study of Girl College Students in Tirunelveli City, TEMIDA, December 2007, pp. 13-21.
5. Mahmuda Khandker (2009), A Study Report on Situation of Violence Against Women (VAW) in Six Selected Districts under Dhaka Division, Retrieved from http://www.intrac.org/data/files/resources/619/PRIP-Violence-Against-Women-Study-Report-May-2009.pdf
6. Chesfeeda Akhtar, Eve teasing as a form of violence against women: A case study of District Srinagar, Kashmir, Academic journals, International Journal of Sociology and Anthropology, Vol. 5(5), pp. 168-178, August, 2013, p. 168.
7. Dr Zobaida Akhter, Eve Teasing, Tears of the Girls: Bangladesh Open University towards Women Empowerment, International Women Online Journal of Distance Education, October, 2013 Volume 2, Issue 4, Article 1, pp. 1-20.
8. Eve Teasing (2015), Retrieved from http://en.wikipedia.org/wiki/Eve_teasing
9. Dr Zobaida Akhter, Eve Teasing, Tears of the Girls: Bangladesh Open University towards Women Empowerment, International Women Online Journal of Distance Education, October, 2013 Volume 2, Issue 4, Article 1, pp. 1-20.
10. Reena Devi; Anu Jasrotia, Eve teasing in the Panjub university compass: A study of girls hostel students, Asian Journal of Multidimensional Research, Vol. 2, Issue 8, August 2013, pp. 80-87.
11. Check over eve-teasing, Retrieved from http://www.nipsa.in/uploads/country_resources_file/1166_5.pdf
12. Dr Zobaida Akhter, Eve Teasing, Tears of the Girls: Bangladesh Open University towards Women Empowerment, International Women Online Journal of Distance Education, October, 2013 Volume 2, Issue 4, Article 1, pp. 1-20.

13. Muhammad Aminul Hoque, Eve teasing in Bangladesh: causes and impact on society, a study from Islamic perspectives, Retrieved from http://www.tijoss.com/TIJOSS%2015th%20Volume/aminul%20hoque.pdf
14. Ranjani Iyer Mohanty (2013), The Term 'Eve-Teasing' Must Die, Retrieved from http://blogs.wsj.com/indiarealtime/2013/04/21/the-term-eve-teasing-must-die/
15. http://ken-foundation-awareness2.blogspot.in/p/eve-teasing-evils.html
16. Dr Moly Kuruvilla and Ms. Fathimath Suhara, Response Patterns of Girl Students to Eve-teasing: An Empirical Study in a University Setting, International Journal of Education and Psychological Research, Volume 3, Issue 3, September 2014, p. 60.
17. Reena Devi; Anu Jasrotia, Eve teasing in the Panjub university compass: A study of girls hostal students, Asian Journal of Multidimensional Research, Vol. 2, Issue 8, August 2013, pp. 80-87.
18. Dr Zobaida Akhter, Eve Teasing, Tears of the Girls: Bangladesh Open University towards Women Empowerment, International Women Online Journal of Distance Education, October, 2013 Volume 2, Issue 4, Articles 1, pp. 1-20.
19. Muhammad Aminul Hoque, Eve teasing in Bangladesh: causes and impact on society, a study from Islamic perspectives, Retrieved from http://www.tijoss.com/TIJOSS%2015th%20Volume/aminul%20hoque.pdf
20. Aadil Bashir and Shabana Khurshid, Eve Teasing and Molestation – A Case Study of District Srinagar, International Journal of Science and Research, Volume 2 Issue 12, December 2013, pp.196-201.
21. Reena Devi; Anu Jasrotia, Eve teasing in the Panjub university compass: A study of girls hostal students, Asian Journal of Multidimensional Research, Vol. 2, Issue 8, August 2013, pp. 80-87.
22. SC on Eve-Teasing: Human Rights of Woman in India, J Indian Acad Forensic Med. April-June 2013, Vol. 35, No. 2, Retrieved from http://medind.nic.in/jal/t13/i2/jalt13i2p98.pdf
23. Eve Teasing (2015), Retrieved from http://en.wikipedia.org/wiki/Eve_teasing

16

Honour Killing

"The connections between and among women are the most feared, the most problematic and the most potentially transforming force on the planet."

—*Adrienne Rich*

Introduction

'Honour is the most cherished value in the Indian sub-continental patriarchal families irrespective of the caste, regional and religious identities. Families gain and lose honour through money, power and improper behaviour of women.'[1] 'The so-called 'honour killings' are not peculiar to our country. It is an evil which haunts many other societies also. The belief that the victim has brought dishonour upon the family or the community is the root cause of such violent crimes. Such violent crimes are directed especially against women.'[2] 'Women are considered to be the pivotal point of their honour. Anything related to women is considered to be 'dishonour'. For women it's obligatory to follow a peculiar code of conduct in and outside home and refrain from certain behaviours, as its considered to bring 'Shame' and 'dishonour' for the family, which in most cases results in the death of the alleged woman.'[3]

'Under the wide scope of crimes of honour that happen, honour killing is perhaps the most heinous of them all. Under the crime of honour killing the victim is usually not a third person but rather the victim's own family member or social group member. Honour killing is originally the product of a particular social interaction amongst members of the society which believes in a strong patriarchal structure. The term Honour or Honor is derived from the Latin word 'honos' which is an abstract concept of a perceived quality of worthiness, respectability and moreover the perceived standing of an individual in large social bodies such as schools, neighbourhoods, cities or nations.'[4]

'Honour killing is an imprecise term for murder precipitated by the aggressor's loss of "honour" and can provisionally be defined as a ritualised form of violence usually with male perpetrators and often, but not always, female victims'.[5] 'Most honour killings occur in countries where the concept of women as a vessel of the family reputation predominates.'[6] 'In most domestic violence cases, women experience abuse by husbands or partners; though there are increases in women physically abusing men or elderly relatives. Domestic violence is commonly described as a form of emotional and/or psychological abuse often over many years.'[7]

Meaning of the Concept

'Honour killing is a form of violence that is almost without exception directed towards women. It is a murder which is an intentional, often especially malicious act with few causes that is, however, judged by family and society as a legitimate killing of a girl or a woman by a family member, when she is suspect of breaking the family honour code.'[8] 'Human Rights Watch defines "honour killings" as follows: *Honor killings are acts of vengeance, usually death, committed by male family members against female family members, who are held to have brought dishonour upon the family. A woman can be targeted by (individuals within) her family for a variety of reasons, including: refusing to enter into an arranged marriage, being the victim of a sexual assault, seeking a divorce—even from an abusive husband—or (allegedly) committing adultery. The mere perception that a woman has behaved in a way that "dishonours" her family is sufficient to trigger an attack on her life.*'[9]

'Honour killing, also known as honour murder is the killing of a member of a family or social group by other members, due to the belief of the perpetrators that the victim has brought dishonour upon the family or community. Honour killings are directed mostly against women and girls, but have been extended to men. In other words it is defined as a death that is granted to a woman of the family for marrying against the parent's desires, having extramarital and premarital relationships, marrying within the same *gotra* or outside one's caste or marrying a cousin from a different caste.'[10]

Reasons of Honour Killing

'Honour killings happen intentionally because as a rule the death of the girl or the woman is decided in a sort of family court, but the victim is not told the verdict. The act is most often done by a male relative, maybe even a brother, brother-in-law or father.'[11] 'It can be triggered by a woman or girl talking with an unrelated male, consenting to sexual relations outside marriage, being the victim of rape, or refusing to marry a man chosen by the family. Even a suspicion of the woman's committing any of these transgressions can be sufficient to trigger this action. The incidence of honour killings is presumed to increase in situations of economic crisis or conflict, or where traditional patriarchal values are under threat as, for example, when minority communities where honour killings are tolerated come into contact with mainstream societies which do not share the same views of appropriate gender roles.'[12]

'A woman can cause that stain on the family due to several reasons, including (a) refusing to enter an arranged marriage or choosing to marry by own choice (b) engaging in certain sexual acts; (c) marrying within same *gotra* (d) seeking divorce from an abusive husband etc. There main factors contribute against women in the name of honour, women's co-modification and conceptions of honour. Women are considered as the property of the males in their family, irrespective of their class, ethnic or religious groups. The sociologists are opined that the reason for increasing in honour killing is the fear of losing their caste status through which they gain many benefits which makes them commit this heinous crime.'[13]

Honour Killing: Global Perspectives

'Honour killings are a pre-Islamic practice that cannot be founded by Islamic theology. They are a characteristic of archaic, tribally organised societies, especially those found in the Middle East. Indeed in Islamic influenced societies, traditional views of what is honourable have a close relationship with socially accepted religious values as the Koran and the tradition hold numerous regulations for the demure behaviour of women.'[14] 'Honour killing is a global phenomenon and has been widely reported in countries such as Iran, Turkey, Afghanistan, Iraq, Saudi Arabia, Egypt, Palestine, Jordan, Bangladesh, Algeria, Brazil, Ecuador, Morocco, Israel, Ethiopia, Somalia, Uganda, the Balkans, Sweden, Holland, Germany, Italy, Yemen, India and many more countries. It is estimated by the United Nations Population Fund that as many as 5,000 women and girls are killed by the members of their families and/or relatives each year for the sake of honour around the world.'[15]

'Historically, honour-related violence has been practiced in North Africa, the Middle East, South Asia, Latin America and Southern Europe, with patterns of violence differing across the regions.'[16] 'While honour killings take place in many regions of the world, laws in some countries also reflect socio-cultural attitudes that underlie such killings. A number of countries have or recently had penal code provisions that applied to justify or excuse the killing of a wife, female ascendant, descendant or sister in order to restore the family honour.'[17] 'In many countries, the practice is so socially accepted that murderers are treated leniently, or not punished at all. In countries like Pakistan and Yemen, for example, the killings are often ignored by police and prosecutors. In Syria, the legal code states that if a man catches a female relative having illicit sex with another man and kills them (either just the woman or the partner as well), he is entitled to a reduced penalty of just two years in prison.

In the United Kingdom, one of the main news items at the moment is the trial of the parents of a teenage girl called Shafilea Ahmed. They have been charged with murdering their daughter after she refused to go through with an arranged marriage. As British Asians, they expected her to marry a partner of their choice, as well as to dress modestly and avoid contact with men outside her family. But Shafilea wanted to live a more westernised lifestyle, to wear fashionable clothes and become a lawyer. After a trip to Pakistan to meet her prospective husband, she attempted suicide by drinking bleach. A few weeks later, after an argument with her mother about wearing a sleeveless t-shirt, she disappeared. Her decomposed body was found in a river months afterwards. The prosecution's main witness is Shafilea's sister, who claims to have seen her parents suffocate her and dispose of the body. Whether Shafilea's parents are found guilty or not, this is a tragic reminder of how common the practice of honour killing is.'[18]

Honour Killing in India

'In India, honour-based violence and particularly the practice of honour killings is an olden phenomenon prevalent since centuries. There are reports of cases in almost all parts of India but the states of Punjab, Haryana, Rajasthan and Western Uttar Pradesh are the regions where these incidents occur more frequently.'[19] 'Though most of these killings and crimes are being reported from the States of Punjab and Haryana, Delhi, Western Uttar Pradesh and other parts of Northern and Western India, the problem is not confined to these areas alone and almost every part of the country has been witness to such incidents.'[20]

'Honor killings are rare in South India and the western Indian states of Maharashtra and Gujarat. In some other parts of India, notably West Bengal, honour killings completely ceased about a century ago. Haryana is notorious for incidents of honour killings, mainly in the upper caste of society, among Rajputs and Jaats. The Indian state of Punjab also has a large number of honour killings. According to data compiled by the Punjab Police, 34 honour killings were reported in the state between 2008 and 2010: 10 in 2008, 20 in 2009 and four in 2010. Bhagalpur in the eastern Indian state of Bihar has also been notorious for honour killings. Honor killings take place in Rajasthan, too. In 1990 the National Commission for Women set up a statutory body in order to address the issues of honour killings among some ethnic groups in North India. This body reviewed constitutional, legal and other provisions as well as challenges women face. In June 2010, scrutinising the increasing number of honour killings, the Supreme Court of India demanded responses about honour killing prevention from the federal government and the state governments of Punjab, Haryana, Bihar, Uttar Pradesh, Rajasthan, Jharkhand, Himachal Pradesh and Madhya Pradesh.'[21]

'This practice of honour killing is a form of murder without trial, which is contrary to Islam. Islam upholds the sanctity of human life, as the Holy Qur'an declares that killing one innocent human being is akin to killing the entire human race (Qur'an 5:32, 6:151, 17:33). Like all other faith traditions, Islam considers all forms of life as sacred. There is certainly no justification for such a practice of Honour Killing in Islamic Law (Shariah). The problem of honour killings is not a problem of morality or of ensuring that women maintain their own personal virtue; rather, it is a problem of domination, power and hatred of women who, in these instances, are viewed as nothing more than servants to the family, both physically and symbolically.'[22]

Effects of Honour Killing

'The psychological effects of the occurrence of honour killings are very detrimental. The presence of this violent practice induces a great deal of fear and many burdens on women, as they are most often the victims. It threatens the safety, physical and mental health of women, as honour killings not only works as a mode of social control, but a fear tactic, creating an environment of anxiety and risk. Children who have bore witness to or are aware of their mothers, sisters, or other relatives being victims of honour killings, are often incredibly traumatised and face an increased risk for behavioural issues, substance abuse and/or repeating the cycle of honour killings.'[23]

'Even victims of rape are vulnerable. In a widely reported case in March of 1999, a 16-year-old mentally retarded girl who was raped in the Northwest Frontier province of Pakistan was turned over to her tribe's judicial council. Even though the crime was reported to the police and the perpetrator was arrested, the Pathan tribesmen decided that she had brought shame to her tribe and she was killed in front of a tribal gathering'.[24]

Constitutional and Legislative Provisions in India

'Honour killings are violation of Articles 14, 15 (1) and (3), 17, 18, 19 and 21 of the Constitution of India. The Article 21 under the chapter of Fundamental Rights of the Indian Constitution guarantees the Right to Life and Liberty to all persons irrespective they are citizens or not. Article 14 of the

Indian Constitution guarantees to every person the right to equality before the law or the equal protection of the laws. Every person, whatever be his or her status or situation is subject to the jurisdiction of the ordinary courts. This right to equality is thus documented as one of the fundamental features of the Indian Constitution. Honour Killings are hideously against this very Constitutional Right provided for the protection of Indian citizens. Honour killings are mainly directed towards women and thus give rise to gender violence.'[25]

'Honour Killings are considered as brutal crimes of homicide under the IPC (Indian Penal Code). Sections 299 and 301 of the IPC, deals with culpable homicide not amounting to murder while Section 300, deals with murder. The perpetrators can be punished as per Section 302 of the IPC. The members of the family as well as community can be prosecuted under Section 302 of IPC for instigating suicide those who transgress the so called norms of the community.'[26] 'Honour killings involve the murder of a particular person especially a woman and thus come under the ambit of Section 299 and Section 300 of the Indian Penal Code. It is also violation of Article 19 and Article 21 of the Constitution. Such brutal murders, under the garb of saving the honour of the family, are clearly against the Constitutional provisions enshrined in Article 21.'[27]

'The Indian Majority Act, Section-3, 1857 states that every person domiciled in India shall attain the age of majority on completion of 18 years and not before. Unless a particular personal law specifies otherwise, every person domiciled in India is deemed to have attained majority upon completion of 18 years of age. However, in the case of a minor for whose person or property, or both, a guardian has been appointed or declared by any court of justice before the age of 18 years and in case of every minor the superintendence of whose property has been alleged by the Court of Wards, age of majority will be 21 years and not 18. The Protection of Women from Domestic Violence Act, 2005 provides for more effective protection of the rights of women guaranteed under the Constitution who are victims of violence of any kind occurring within the family and for matters connected therewith or incidental thereto. The Indian Evidence Act, 1872 makes provision to punish those who conceal facts, either before or at the time of, or after the alleged crime.'[28]

'In another landmark judgment (April 2011), a bench of Justices Markandey Katju and Gyan Sudha Mishra, while dismissing the appeal filed by one Bhagwan Dass challenging life imprisonment awarded to him by a Delhi Sessions Court for killing his daughter as she was allegedly in an incestuous relationship with her cousin despite being married, directed courts to view such cases as the rarest of the rare category for awarding death penalty to the convicts. It added that honour killing or inflicting atrocities on couples is wholly illegal and has to be ruthlessly stamped out. There is nothing honourable in such killings and in fact they are nothing but barbaric and shameful acts of murder committed by brutal, feudal minded persons who deserve harsh treatment. Only this way we can stamp out such acts of barbarism.

A bench of Supreme Court Justices H.S. Bedi and J.M. Panchel awarded (August 4, 2010) life sentence to three of accused who had caused the death of six persons of a family in a case of 'honour' killing in village Lakhanpur district Farrukhabad – Uttar Pradesh (10-11.8.1991). The Bench said, *"There is no manner of doubt that killing of six persons and wiping out almost the whole family on the flimsy ground of saving the honour of the family, would fall within the 'rarest of the rare' principle evolved by the Supreme Court and, therefore, the trial court was perfectly justified in imposing the capital punishment to the respondents. However, this court also noticed that the incident had taken place about 20 years ago. Further, the High Court had acquitted the respondents by a judgment dated April 12, 2002. Thereafter, nothing adverse against any of the respondents is reported to this court. To sentence the respondents to death after that acquittal in 2002 will not be justified on the facts and circumstances of this case."*[29]

International Human Rights Legislation

'Honour killing self-evidently violates the right to life of the individual victim, a right which is regarded as the most fundamental of all rights and which is enshrined in all major human rights instruments, not least in the Universal Declaration of Human Rights (1948). A major landmark in redressing the recognised gender bias in human rights legislation was the approval in 1979 of the Convention on the Elimination of All forms of Discrimination against Women (CEDAW) which is often called the international bill of rights for women. According to CEDAW States Parties must not only not commit any act of discrimination against women, but are also obligated to regulate actions of other public and private organisations and individuals. This provision makes the state responsible to regulate actions of in the private sphere such as various manifestations of Gender-based Violence or Violence against Women.

UN Declaration on the Elimination of Violence Against Women (1993) constitutes another important step, defining violence against women as "any act of gender-based violence that results in, or is likely to result in, physical, sexual or psychological harm or suffering to women, including threats of such acts, coercion or arbitrary deprivation of liberty whether occurring in public or in private life". The appointment in 1994 of the UN Special Rapporteur on Violence Against Women attached to the UN Office of the High Commissioner for Human Rights also represents a significant step. An important milestone at the European level is the European Convention for the Protection of Human Rights and Fundamental Freedoms (1950) which enshrines everyone's right to life, the prohibition of torture and slavery, the right to freedom and security and the prohibition of discrimination (Section 1, Articles 2, 3, 4, 5 and 14).'[30]

Conclusion

Honour killing is a form of violence that is almost without exception directed towards women. It is acts of vengeance, usually death, committed by male family members against female family members, who are held to have brought dishonour upon the family. It happen intentionally because as a rule the death of the girl or the woman is decided in a sort of family court, but the victim is not told the verdict. The act is most often done by a male relative, maybe even a brother, brother-in-law or father. In India, honour-based violence and particularly the practice of honour killings is an olden phenomenon prevalent since centuries. There are reports of cases in almost all parts of India but the states of Punjab, Haryana, Rajasthan and Western Uttar Pradesh are the regions where these incidents occur more frequently. The psychological effects of the occurrence of 'honour' killings are very detrimental. The presence of this violent practice induces a great deal of fear and many burdens on women, as they are most often the victims.

References

1. Jyothi Vishwanath and Srinivas C. Palakonda (2011), Patriarchal Ideology of Honour and Honour Crimes in India, International Journal of Criminal Justice Sciences (IJCJS) – Official Journal of the South Asian Society of Criminology and Victimology, January – December Vol. 6 (1 and 2): 386–395.
2. Prevention of Interference with the Freedom of Matrimonial Alliances (in the name of Honour and Tradition): A Suggested Legal Framework, Retrieved from http://lawcommissionofindia.nic.in/reports/report242.pdf
3. Noor Akbar Khalil (2010), Honor Killing in Pakistan: The Case of 5 Women Buried Alive (Political manipulation in human rights violation), Retrieved from http://www.humiliationstudies.org/documents/AkbarHonorKillinginPakistan.pdf
4. Navratan Singh Fateh (2012), Honour killing, Retrieved from https://tspace.library.utoronto.ca/bitstream/1807/33417/7/Fateh_Navratan_S_201211_LLM_thesis.pdf
5. Are Knudsen, Honour killings in Pakistan, Retrieved from http://www.cmi.no/publications/2004/wp/wp2004-1.pdf
6. Hillary Mayell (2002), Thousands of Women Killed for Family "Honour", Retrieved from http://www.unl.edu/rhames/courses/212/readings/%EE%80%80honor%EE%80%81-kil-ng.pdf
7. Ursula Smartt, Honour Killings, Retrieved from http://ursulasmartt.com/pdf/JustPeace%5B1%5D. Honour Killings. 9.1.06.pdf
8. Honour Killings, Retrieved from http://www.islaminstitut.de/uploads/media/Ehrenmorde.pdf
9. Navratan Singh Fateh (2012), Honour killing, Retrieved from https://tspace.library.utoronto.ca/bitstream/1807/33417/7/Fateh_Navratan_S_201211_LLM_thesis.pdf
10. Dr P. Neeraja, Honour Killing – An Insane to Human Kind, Retrieved from http://theglobaljournals.com/ijsr/file.php?val=November_2013_1383312704_3f4c2_163.pdf
11. Honour Killings, Retrieved from http://www.islaminstitut.de/uploads/media/Ehrenmorde.pdf
12. Dr Jane Hailé and Andrea Subhan (2007), Honour killing-Its causes and consequences: suggested strategies for the European parliament, Retrieved from http://www.europarl.europa.eu/

RegData/etudes/etudes/join/2007/385527/EXPO-JOIN_ET%282007% 29385527_ EN.pdf

13. Dr Pranab Kumar Rana and Bhabani Prasad Mishra, Honour Killings-A gross violation of Human rights and Its Challenges, International Journal of Humanities and Social Science Invention, Volume 2 Issue 6, June 2013, pp. 24-29.
14. Honour Killings, Retrieved from http://www.islaminstitut.de/uploads/media/Ehrenmorde.pdf
15. Satnam Singh Deol, Honour Killings in India: A Study of the Punjab State, International Research Journal of Social Sciences, Vol. 3(6), 7-16, June (2014), pp. 7-10.
16. Anna C. Korteweg, Understanding Honour Killing and Honour Related Violence in the Immigration Context: Implications for the Legal Profession and Beyond, Retrieved from http://www.learningtoendabuse.ca/sites/default/files/korteweg_cclr-understanding-honour-killing.pdf
17. Dr Amin A. Muhammad (2010), Preliminary Examination of so-called "Honour Killings" in Canada, Retrieved from http://www.justice.gc.ca/eng/rp-pr/cj-jp/fv-vf/hk-ch/hk_eng.pdf
18. Steve Taylor (2012), The Madness of Honor Killing, Retrieved from https://www.psychologytoday.com/blog/out-the-darkness/201205/the-madness-honor-killing
19. Satnam Singh Deol, Honour Killings in India: A Study of the Punjab State, International Research Journal of Social Sciences, Vol. 3(6), 7-16, June (2014), pp. 7-10.
20. The Prevention of Crimes in the Name of 'Honour' and Tradition Bill, 2010, Retrieved from http://ncw.nic.in/PDFFiles/Bill_against_honour_killing_crimes.pdf
21. Honor killing (2014), Retrieved from http://en.wikipedia.org/wiki/Honor_killing
22. Honour Killing: A Crime against Islam, Retrieved from http://www.islamawareness.net/HonourKilling/honour_killings.pdf
23. Factors that Lead to 'Honour' Killings and their Psychological Effects, Retrieved from http://whyhonorkillings.blogspot.in/
24. See http://news.nationalgeographic.com/news/2002/02/0212_020212_honorkilling_2.html
25. Puneet Kaur Grewal, Honour Killings and Law in India, IOSR Journal of Humanities and Social Science, Volume 5, Issue 6 (Nov. - Dec. 2012), pp. 28-31.

26. Satnam Singh Deol, Honour Killings in India: A Study of the Punjab State, International Research Journal of Social Sciences, Vol. 3(6), 7-16, June (2014), pp. 7-10.
27. Puneet Kaur Grewal, Honour Killings and Law in India, IOSR Journal of Humanities and Social Science, Volume 5, Issue 6 (Nov. - Dec. 2012), PP 28-31
28. *Ibid.*
29. Akshey Kumar, Public Policy Imperatives for Curbing Honour Killings in India, Journal of Politics and Governance, Vol. 1, No. 1, March 2012, Vol. 1, No. 1, pp. 33-37.
30. http://www.europarl.europa.eu/RegData/etudes/etudes/join/2007/385527/EXPO-JOIN_ET%282007%29385527_EN.pdf

17

Molestation

> "Women don't take enough risks. Men are just 'foot on the gas pedal.' We're not going to close the achievement gap until we close the ambition gap."
>
> —*Sheryl Sandberg*

Introduction

'Indian woman bearing the torch of cultured living through self-sacrifice, physical and mental endurance and compassion is waxing eloquence for retrogressive drudgery. It lends rationale for under-nutrition of girls, unequal healthcare, inequitable access to resources and denial of property rights all reserved for women born into a tradition that hails women's capacity for forbearance. Exploitation of women is various forms and different natures. It include crimes involving sexual exploitation for economic gains like prostitution and trafficking, adultery, abduction, rape, wrongful confinement and murder etc on the one hand and crimes related to women's property like dishonest misappropriation, criminal breach of trust, domestic violence, dowry extortion and outraging the modesty of women etc on the other.'[1]

'Although Women may be victims of any of the general crimes such as murder, robbery, cheating etc., only the crimes which are directed specifically against women are characterised as Crimes against Women. The United Nations defined Violence against Women in 1993 in Declaration on the Elimination of Violence against Women. It defines it as any act of gender-based violence that results in, or is likely to result in, physical, sexual or psychological harm or suffering to women, including threats of such acts, coercion or arbitrary deprivation of liberty, whether occurring in public or private life.'[2]

'Child sexual abuses are dark realities in Indian society like in any other nation. 53 per cent of our children are sexually abused, according to a statistic from a survey done by the Government of India. A 1985 study by the Tata Institute of Social Sciences reveals that one out of three girls and one out of 10 boys had been sexually abused as a child. Fifty per cent of child sexual abuse happens at home. In 19 per cent, Samvada, a Bangalore based NGO, conducted a study among 348 girls. Fifteen per cent were used for masturbation mostly by male relatives when they were less than 10 years old. Seventy Six per cent of the abusers were adult family members.'[3]

'Childhood sexual abuse (CSA) and its effect on symptomology and interpersonal relationships is a relatively new field historically. Legislation has been passed protecting children from rape and sodomy in many European countries. In the eighteenth and ninteenth centuries, books advised parents how to prevent child sexual abuse. But child sex abuse was not seen as a major problem in Europe and the United States until fairly recently. Only in the last two decades has childhood sexual abuse been seen in the field of mental health, psychiatry and social work as an important social problem with effects connected to this trauma.'[4]

Meaning of the Concept

'Molestation means forcing undesired sexual behaviour by one person upon another. When that force is immediate, of short duration, or infrequent, it is called sexual assault. The offender is referred to as a sexual abuser or molester. When the victim is younger than the age of consent, it is referred to as child sexual abuse. Sexual misconduct can occur where one person uses a position of authority to compel another person to engage in an otherwise unwanted sexual activity. Child sexual abuse is a form of child abuse in which a child is abused for the sexual gratification of an adult or older adolescent. Spousal sexual abuse is a form of domestic violence. When the abuse involves forced sex, it may constitute rape upon the other spouse, depending on the jurisdiction and may also constitute an assault.'[5]

'Child abuse can be defined as the willful and unjustifiable infliction of pain and suffering on children, sexual abuse is one type of abuse where the child is sexually violated by an assaulter. This type of abuse is devastating to the child in many ways; causing delays in physical growth, impaired language and cognitive abilities and problems in personality development, learning and behaviour.'[6] 'Child sexual abuse includes any activity that uses a child to create sexual gratification. Although the touching of children as a sign of affection and for hygiene is considered normal and necessary, there is a way to distinguish normal touching from child sexual abuse.'[7]

'Child sexual abuse is any interaction between a child and an adult (or another child) in which the child is used for the sexual stimulation of the perpetrator or an observer. Sexual abuse can include both touching and non-touching behaviours. Children of all ages, races, ethnicities and economic backgrounds are vulnerable to sexual abuse. It affects both girls and boys in all kinds of neighbourhoods and communities and in countries around the world.'[8] 'It exists in every community and at all levels of society, but allegations of molestation can sometimes be divisive for a community. Some people refuse to believe that the accused is capable of such a crime. It is not unheard of for parents, friends and coworkers to rally in support of the suspect, proclaim his innocence and even post his bond.'[9]

Reasons of Molestation

'The key is the intention by the perpetrator to be sexually aroused by the activity or the intention to create sexual arousal in others. The intent to use children in any way to create sexual arousal is illegal. This is criminal behaviour that is aggressively prosecuted and severely punished by our legal system.[10]

Child molestation can be caused by the following'[11]:

- Hormone imbalance
- Inadequate social skills
- Heightened arousal to children

- Early childhood experience
- Sexual anxiety
- Arrested development
- Socialisation to violence
- Sexual addiction
- Poor impulse control
- Alcohol and drugs
- Emotional immaturity
- Unresolved conflicts
- Child pornography and advertising
- Heredity
- Cultural tolerance
- Failure of incest taboo
- Situational stress
- Ignorance about sexuality

Source: Fuller, K. A. (1998). *Unacceptable risk: Child sexual abuse and AIDS*. Thomas College Press, 1501 Millpond Road, Thomasville, GA 31792.

Molestation Incidences in India

'The statistics can be read as either worrisome of hopeful; while there was a six per cent increase in reported crimes against women in India including rapes, kidnappings and dowry deaths. This can be indicative of more women willing to come forward to report these crimes. The number of women coming forward is increasing for sure, but it is still a very tiny amount. The murder and gang rape of a 23-year-old student on a moving bus in Delhi has galvanised women into action. Country-wide protests for better security have sparked national debate about gender inequalities in India. The number of rapes in the country rose by almost three per cent to 24,923, with Delhi reporting 706 rapes in 2012 making it the Indian city with the highest number of rapes and confirming its reputation as India's rape capital. Statistics showed that 244,270 crimes against women were reported to the Indian police in 2012 compared with 228,650 in 2011, according to the National Crimes Records Bureau.'[12]

(a) Moga Molestation Case

'The death of a 13-year-old Moga girl, after she was molested and thrown out of a moving bus on April 29, 2015 had shocked the nation especially since the bus was owned by Orbit Aviation, a company that belongs to Punjab deputy chief minister Sukhbir Badal. The girl was on late Sunday consigned to flames at her home in Moga village four days after her death. The Moga incident was the last one in recent cases in Punjab to shake the collective conscience of the country. Law and order in Punjab has deteriorated because the ruling Badal clan has hijacked all the businesses.'[13]

'Punjab and Haryana High Court directed the Punjab government to submit a report on the action taken against the bus staff in Moga molestation case and sought information about bus operators in the state including details of ownership. A bench of Justices Hemant Gupta and Lisa Gill issued notices to Punjab Chief Secretary, Director General of Police, owners of the transport company Orbit Aviation whose bus was involved in the incident and the state's Transport Commissioner, seeking their response by 15th May, 2015. The court directed the state to produce Action Taken Report against the driver, conductor and other staff of the bus, owned by Orbit Aviation belonging to Punjab Chief Minister Parkash Singh Badal's relatives. It also asked the counsel of Aam Aadmi Party RS Bains and another advocate HS Arora to withdraw their applications on the issue and appointed them as amicus curiae. The High Court asked the state to give information on the number of buses owned by Punjab Roadways, Pepsu RTC and private operators in Punjab along with details of ownership of each operator.

The High Court in Chandigarh had taken suo motu cognisance of a letter written to it regarding the Moga incident in which a teenaged girl had died after she and her mother were allegedly molested and thrown off a bus, belonging to Orbit Aviation which is owned by relatives of Chief Minister Parkash Singh Badal. However, a bench of the court had also recused from hearing the Moga bus molestation case. As the matter came up for hearing before the division bench of justices Satish Kumar Mittal and Harinder Singh Sidhu, it withdrew from the matter and referred it to the Chief Justice to be assigned to some other bench. No reason was given for recusing from the matter. The Moga molestation case had caused a huge uproar in the Parliament as both the houses were adjourned repeatedly as the Opposition protested, demanding a discussion on the case.'[14]

(b) Ruchika Girhotra Case[15]

The Ruchika Girhotra Case involves the molestation of 14-year-old Ruchika Girhotra in 1990 by the Inspector General of Police Mr Shambu in Haryana, India. After she made a complaint, the victim, her family and her friends were systematically harassed by the police leading to her eventual suicide. On 22nd December 2009, after 19 years, 40 adjournments and more than 400 hearings, the court finally pronounced Rathore guilty under Section 354 IPC (molestation) and sentenced him to six months imprisonment and a fine of Rs 1,000. Ruchika Girhotra was a student in Class X A (Batch of 1991) at Sacred Heart School for Girls in Chandigarh. Ruchika was a promising tennis player. On 11th August 1990, Rathore visited Ruchika's house and met her father S.C. Girhotra. As head of the Haryana Lawn Tennis Association, Rathore promised to get special training for Ruchika. On 12th August (Sunday), Ruchika, along with her friend Aradhana Prakash, went to play at the lawn tennis court and met Rathore in his office (in the garage of his house). On seeing both of them, Rathore asked Aradhana to call the tennis coach (Mr Thomas) to his room. Aradhana left and Rathore was alone with Ruchika. He immediately grabbed her hand and waist and pressed his body against hers. Ruchika tried to push him away, but he continued molesting her. On 20th September 1990, two weeks after the inquiry indicted Rathore, Ruchika was expelled from her school, Sacred Heart School for Girls, in Sector 26, Chandigarh. Ruchika had studied there from Class I. The school actively plotted against Ruchika. Ruchika's expulsion from school was later used by Rathore's lawyers to question her character.

Rathore deployed policemen in plainclothes in front of Ruchika's house to keep an eye on the family. False cases of theft, murder and civil defamation were filed against Ruchika's father and her 10-year-old brother Ashu. Aradhana, who is the sole witness in the molestation case, had ten civil cases filed against her by Rathore. On 23rd September 1993, Ruchika's then 13-year-old brother, Ashu, was picked up in the market place near his house by police in plain clothes. They drove him in a jeep to the Crime Investigation Agency (CIA) Staff Office in Mansa Devi. There, he was tortured by Sub-Inspector Prem Dutt and Assistant Sub-Inspectors Jai Narayan. After some time, Rathore also arrived there. Ashu was then tortured further. Ashu was picked up again on 11th November 1993. He was tortured again and was unable to walk due to the beatings. He was not given food or water for days at a stretch and was beaten mercilessly. On 28th December 1993, days after Ashu was paraded in handcuffs in his locality, Ruchika consumed poison. She died the next day. Rathore threw a party that night to celebrate. The government closed the case filed against Rathore less than a week after her death.

On 21st August 1998, the Punjab and Haryana High Court directed the CBI to conduct an inquiry. On 16th November 2000, the CBI filed a charge sheet against Rathore. The case was put to hearing in the CBI special court in Ambala from 17th November. The hearings in Ambala would continue till May 2006. On 5th November 2009, the case was transferred from the Ambala court to CBI Chandigarh. In December, the court closed all final arguments, gave its verdict and on 21st December, special judge J.S. Sidhu pronounced a six-month jail sentence and a fine of Rs 1000 to Rathore. The sentence was suspended until 20th January 2010.

(c) Guwahati Molestation Case[16]

On 9th July 2012, in Guwahati city, the capital city of Assam, an Indian state, a teenage girl was allegedly molested and manhandled by a crowd of approximately 30 men outside a bar, many of whom were subsequently arrested based on video footage of the even. On 9th July 2012, two women were exiting a bar and became involved in a physical struggle with a group of men standing outside. The case caused uproar in the national and local media right after the video was aired by News Live, going viral on YouTube and provoking debates about the safety of women and human rights in India, By 20th July 2012, 12 of the 22 accused were arrested. Eleven accused in this case including prime accused Amarjyoti Kalita, were convicted on December 7, 2012.

Effects of Molestation

'Effects of child sexual abuse include shame and self-blame, depression, anxiety, post-traumatic stress disorder, self-esteem issues, sexual dysfunction, chronic pelvic pain, addiction, self-injury, suicidal ideation, borderline personality disorder and propensity to re-victimisation in adulthood. Child sexual abuse is a risk factor for attempting suicide. Much of the harm caused to victims becomes apparent years after the abuse happens. Sexual abuse is a problem in some minority communities.'[17] 'Survivors of childhood sexual abuse experience an array of overwhelming and intense feelings. These may include feelings of fear, guilt and shame. Abusers have been known to tell children that it is the fault of the child that they are abused, shifting the blame away from the abuser, where it belongs and placing it on the child.'[18] 'Childhood sexual abuse infringes on the basic rights of human beings. Children should be able to have sexual experiences at the appropriate developmental time and within their control and choice. The nature and dynamics of sexual abuse and sexually abusive relationships are often traumatic. Survivors often experience guilt, shame and self-blame. It has been shown that survivors frequently take personal responsibility for the abuse. Stress and anxiety are often long-term effects of childhood sexual abuse. Body issues and eating disorders have also been cited as a long-term effect of childhood sexual abuse.'[19]

'The relationship between child sexual abuse and adult psychopathology tended initially to be conceptualised in terms of a chronic form of post-traumatic stress disorder. The post-traumatic stress model found its strongest support in the observations of clinicians dealing with individuals with histories of severe and repeated abuse'.[20]

Verma Committee Report

'A three-member Commission, headed by former Chief Justice of India, Justice J.S. Verma which was assigned to review laws for sexual crimes submitted its report to the government during January 2013. The Commission has recommended comprehensive changes in criminal laws to deal with crimes and atrocities against women. The panel has not recommended the death penalty for rapists. It suggests that the punishment for rape should be rigorous imprisonment of for seven years to life. It recommends that punishment for causing death or a persistent vegetative state should be RI for a term not be less than

20 years, but may be for life also, which shall mean the rest of the person's life. Gang-rape, it suggests should entail punishment of not less than 20 years, which may also extend to life and gang-rape followed by death, should be punished with life imprisonment.

Every complaint of rape must be registered by the police and civil society should perform its duty to report any case of rape coming to its knowledge. As a primary recommendation, all marriages in India should mandatorily be registered in the presence of a magistrate. The panel has observed that the "impunity of systematic sexual violence is being legitimised by the armed forces special powers act." It has said there is an imminent need to review the continuance of AFSPA (Armed Forces Special Power Act) in areas as soon as possible. It has also recommended posting special commissioners for women's safety in conflict areas. To inspire public confidence, the panel said, "police officers with reputations of outstanding ability and character must be placed at the higher levels of the police force." All existing appointments need to be reviewed to ensure that the police force has the requisite moral vision.'[21]

'By usual definition, sexual assault is defined as sexual actions or advances without the consent of one party. However, legal definitions tend to differ somewhat. Sections 375 and 376 of the Indian Penal Code refer to rape. This defines rape as penile penetration of the vagina only. The punishment for such a crime ranges from seven years upwards. Unfortunately, this law neglects sexual crimes that include digital, oral, or object penetration, as well as sexual crimes against men.'[22]

Conclusion

Child sexual abuses are dark realities in Indian society like in any other nation. It is forcing undesired sexual behaviour by one person upon another. Child sexual abuse is any interaction between a child and an adult (or another child) in which the child is used for the sexual stimulation of the perpetrator or an observer. Sexual abuse can include both touching and non-touching behaviours. The key is the intention by the perpetrator to be sexually aroused by the activity or the intention to create sexual arousal in others. The intent to use children in any way to create sexual arousal is illegal. This is criminal behaviour that is aggressively prosecuted and severely punished by our legal system. Survivors of childhood sexual abuse experience an array of overwhelming and intense feelings. These may include feelings of fear, guilt and shame.

References

1. Manikamma Nagindrappa and Radhika M.K, Women Exploitation in Indian modern society, International Journal of Scientific and Research Publications, Volume 3, Issue 2, February 2013, Retrieved from http://www.ijsrp.org/research-paper-0213/ijsrp-p14145.pdf
2. See http://www.catholic.org/news/international/asia/story.php?id=51381
3. Child Sexual Abuse in India, J Indian Acad Forensic Med. July-September 2011, Vol. 33, No. 3.
4. See https://ritualabuse.us/research/sexual-abuse/how-childhood-sexual-abuse-affects-interpersonal-relationships/
5. Sexual abuse (2014), Retrieved from http://en.wikipedia.org/wiki/Sexual_abuse
6. The Effects of Sexual Child Abuse on Female Victims, Retrieved from http://www.uoflife.com/wc/studentpapers/abuse.htm
7. Child Sexual Abuse and Pedophilia, Retrieved from http://www.emedicinehealth.com/child_abuse/page2_em.htm
8. Child Sexual Abuse Fact Sheet, Retrieved from http://nctsn.org/nctsn_assets/pdfs/caring/ChildSexualAbuseFactSheet.pdf
9. Tom O'Connor, Understanding the Psychology of Child Molesters: A Key to Getting Confessions, see http://www.policechief magazine.org/magazine/index.cfm? fuseaction= display_arch&article_id=770&issue_id=122005
10. Child Sexual Abuse and Pedophilia, Retrieved from http://www.emedicinehealth.com/child_abuse/page2_em.htm
11. Causes of Child molestation (2002), Retrieved from http://www.practicenotes.org/vol7_no2/causes.htm
12. See http://www.catholic.org/news/international/asia/story.php?id=51381
13. The Times of India (May 5, 2015), Moga molestation case: Amarinder to move adjournment motion today, Retrieved from http://timesofindia.indiatimes.com/india/Moga-molestation-case-Amarinder-to-move-adjournment-motion-today/articleshow/47155744.cms

14. Moga molestation case: Punjab and Haryana HC asks state govt to file report on action taken, Retrieved fromhttp://www.firstpost.com/india/moga-molestation-case-punjab-haryana-hc-asks-state-govt-file-report-action-taken-2232248.html
15. The Ruchika Girhotra Case (2015), Retrieved from http://en.wikipedia.org/wiki/Ruchika_Girhotra_case
16. 2012 Guwahati Molestation Case, Retrieved from http://en.wikipedia.org/wiki/2012_Guwahati_molestation_case
17. Sexual abuse (2014), Retrieved from http://en.wikipedia.org/wiki/Sexual_abuse
18. See https://www.rainn.org/get-info/effects-of-sexual-assault/adult-survivors-of-childhood-sexual-abuse
19. Melissa Hall and Joshua Hall, The Long-Term Effects of Childhood Sexual Abuse: Counseling Implications, Retrieved from http://counselingoutfitters.com/vistas/vistas11/Article_19.pdf
20. See http://www.aaets.org/article176.htm
21. Crime against women (2013), Retrieved from http://164.100.47.134/intranet/Crimeagainstwomen.pdf
22. Shannon (2001), Child Sexual Violence in India, Retrieved from http://www.pandys.org/csaindia.pdf

18
Rape

"Men are allowed to have passion and commitment for their work... a woman is allowed that feeling for a man, but not her work."

—*Barbra Streisand*

Introduction

'Violence against women is collectively, violent acts that are primarily or exclusively committed against women. The UN Declaration on the Elimination of Violence against Women states that:"violence against women is a manifestation of historically unequal power relations between men and women" and that violence against women is one of the crucial social mechanisms by which women are forced into a subordinate position compared with men. Kofi Annan, Secretary-General of the United Nations, declared in a 2006 report posted on the United Nations Development Fund for Women website that: Violence against women and girls is a problem of pandemic proportions. At least one out of every three women around the world has been beaten, coerced into sex, or otherwise abused in her lifetime with the abuser usually someone known to her. Although women may be victims of any of the general crimes such as murder, robbery, cheating, etc, only the crimes which are directed specifically against women are characterised as crimes against women.'[1]

'Some of the forms of violence perpetrated by individuals are rape; domestic violence; sexual harassment; coercive use of contraceptives; female infanticide; prenatal sex selection; obstetric violence and mob violence; as well as harmful customary or traditional practices such as honour killings, dowry violence, female genital mutilation, marriage by abduction and forced marriage.'[2]

Meaning of the Concept

'Rape is a type of sexual assault usually involving sexual intercourse or other forms of sexual penetration perpetrated against a person without that person's consent. The act may be carried out by physical force, coercion, abuse of authority or against a person who is incapable of valid consent, such as one who is unconscious, incapacitated, or below the legal age of consent. The term 'rape' originates in the Latin' rapere', to snatch, to grab, to carry off.'[3] 'Rape is a crime of violence; it is not sex. At common law, rape was defined as the unlawful carnal knowledge of a woman, without her consent. Carnal knowledge was defined as sexual intercourse. Sexual intercourse implied genital copulation.'[4]

Types of the Rape

Categories of rape look at the relationship of the perpetrator to the victim or the situation in which the rape occurs, such as date rape, gang rape, marital rape, incestual rape, child sexual abuse, prison rape, acquaintance rape, war rape and statutory rape.

(a) *Date Rape:* It is a form of acquaintance rape. The two phrases are often used interchangeably, but date rape specifically refers to a rape in which there has been some sort of romantic or potentially sexual relationship between the two parties. It occurs when a perpetrator uses physical or psychological intimidation to force a victim to have sex against his or her will, or when the perpetrator has sex with a victim who is incapable of giving consent because they have been incapacitated by drugs or alcohol. The concept of date rape is relatively new. Historically date rape has been taken less seriously than stranger rape. Researchers say date rape affects victims similarly to stranger rape, although the failure of others to acknowledge

and take the rape seriously can make it harder for victims to recover.[5]

(b) *Gang Rape:* It occurs when a group of people participate in the rape of a single victim. Rape involving at least two or more violators (typically at least three) is widely reported to occur in many parts of the world. It involved more alcohol and drug use, night attacks and severe sexual assault outcomes and less victim resistance and fewer weapons than individual rapes. Gang rape is sometimes referred to as "group rape", "party rape", or "multiple perpetrator rape" in scholarly literature. Gang rapes are more violent; the sexual and non-sexual injuries to the victim are often far more severe[6].

(c) *Marital Rape:* It is non-consensual sex in which the perpetrator is the victim's spouse. It is a form of partner rape, of domestic violence and of sexual abuse. The issues of sexual and domestic violence within marriage and the family unit and more generally, the issue of violence against women, have come to growing international attention from the second half of the twentieth century onward. Historically, many cultures have had a concept of spouses' conjugal rights to sexual intercourse with each other. This can be seen in Common law, in force in North America and the British Commonwealth, where the very concept of marital rape was treated as impossibility. Attributing the effects of marital rape in research is problematic as it is nearly impossible to find a large enough sample of spouses to study who have experienced sexual violence but have not also been physically assaulted by their spouse. It may occur as part of an abusive relationship. Trauma from the rape adds to the effect of other abusive acts or abusive and demeaning talk. Furthermore, marital rape is rarely a one-time event, but a repeated if not frequent occurrence.[7]

(d) *Incestual Rape:* Incest is sexual activity between family members or close relatives. This typically includes sexual activity between people in a consanguineous relationship and sometimes those related by affinity, such as individuals of the same household, step relatives, those related by adoption or marriage, or members of the same clan or lineage. Many studies found that stepfathers tend to be far more likely than biological fathers to engage in this form of incest. Adults who as children were incestuously victimised by adults often suffer from low self-esteem, difficulties in interpersonal relationships and sexual dysfunction and are at an extremely high risk of many mental disorders.[8]

(e) *Child Sexual Abuse:* Child sexual abuse is a form of child abuse in which an adult or older adolescent uses a child for sexual stimulation. It can occur in a variety of settings, including home, school, or work. Child marriage is one of the main forms of child sexual abuse. Child sexual abuse can result in both short-term and long-term harm, including psychopathology in later life. A well-documented, long-term negative effect is the repeated or additional victimisation in adolescence and adulthood. Child abuse, including sexual abuse, especially chronic abuse starting at early ages, has been found to be related to the development of high levels of dissociative symptoms, which includes amnesia for abuse memories.[9]

(f) *Prison Rape:* Prison rape is rape occurring in prison. It has come into common usage to refer to rape of inmates by other inmates and less commonly to the rape of inmates by staff and even less commonly rape of staff by inmates. Public awareness of the phenomenon of prison rape is a relatively recent development and estimates to its prevalence have varied widely for decades. The Prison Rape Elimination Act of 2003 was the first United States federal law passed specifically dealing with the sexual assault of prisoners. The bill was signed into law on September 4, 2003.[10]

(g) *Acquaintance Rape:* It is rape that is perpetrated by a person who is known to the victim. It includes a subcategory of incidents labeled date rape that involves people who are in romantic or sexual relationships with each other. From the legal perspective, the legal consequences of acquaintance rape are the same as for stranger rape. Acquaintance rape is a broad category that includes all rapes except those perpetrated by people previously unknown to the rape victim. Acquaintance rape by definition includes all date rape and marital and other intra-family rape, as well as rape between people such as classmates, co-workers, friends, neighbours and people in business, employment or caretaker relationships.[11]

(h) *War Rape:* It is rape or other forms of sexual violence committed by combatants during armed conflict or war or military occupation often as spoils of war; but sometimes, particularly in ethnic conflict, the phenomenon has broader sociological motives. Wartime sexual violence may include gang rape and rape with objects. During war and armed conflict, rape is frequently used as a means of psychological warfare in order to humiliate the enemy. Prosecution of rapists in war crime tribunals is a recent development. However, the lack of explicit recognition of war rape in international law or applicable humanitarian law may not be used as a defense by the perpetrator of war rape. Victims and survivors of war rape are at very high risk of psycho-social problems. In addition to the physical and psychological damages resulting from rape, sexual violence in the context of war often disrupt the linkages between the rape victims and their communities. Both during and even more in the aftermath of conflict, when abuses become known, victims of war rape risk finding themselves in situations of social isolation, often abandoned by their husbands and rejected by their communities.[12]

(i) *Statutory Rape:* It is sexual activity in which at least one person is below the age required to legally consent to the behaviour. The term statutory rape generally refers to sex between an adult and a sexually mature minor past the age of puberty. Sexual relations with a prepubescent child, generically called child sexual abuse or molestation, are typically treated as a more serious crime. Statutory rape laws are based on the premise that until a person reaches a certain age, that individual is legally incapable of consenting to sexual intercourse. Thus, the law assumes, even if he or she willingly engages in sexual intercourse, the sex is not consensual. The original purpose of statutory rape laws was to protect young, unwed females from males who might impregnate them and not take responsibility by providing support for the child.[13]

Effects of Rape

'Victims of rape can be severely traumatised by the assault and may have difficulty functioning as well as they had been used to prior to the assault, with disruption of concentration, sleeping patterns and eating habits. After being raped, it is common for the victim to experience acute stress disorder, including symptoms similar to those of post-traumatic stress disorder, such as intense, sometimes unpredictable emotions and they may find it hard to deal with their memories of the even. While sexual assault, including rape, can result in physical trauma, many people who experience sexual assault will not suffer any physical injury. Pregnancy can also result from rape. Rape may result in the transmission of HIV/AIDS. Rape acts both as a direct factor, as the virus can be transmitted through the forced sexual intercourse and as an indirect factor, as victims of rape are at higher risk of suffering psychological problems. In many cultures, those who are raped are at very high risk of suffering additional violence or threats of violence after the rape.'[14]

'Sexual violence can have psychological, emotional and physical effects on a survivor. These effects are not always easy to deal with, but with the right help and support they can be managed.'[15] 'Forced sexual assault frequently causes visible bruising or bleeding in and around the vaginal or anal area and bruises on other parts of the body from coercive violence. Victims experience both short and long-term psychological effects of rape. One of the most common psychological consequences of rape is self-blame. Victims use self-blame as an avoidance-based coping tool. Self-blame slows or, in many cases, stops the healing process. The aftermath of rape involves a cluster of acute and chronic physical and psychological effects. It's important that victims receive comprehensive care that addresses both the short and long-term effects of rape as they become apparent.'[16]

'Psychological effects in the medium to long-term encompass heightened fear, anger, anxiety, guilt, self-blame, loss of trust, flashbacks and PTSD, depression, dissociation, phobias, panic disorder and obsessive compulsive disorder. Women who have experienced sexual violence compared with their non-victimised counterparts have poorer self-rated health and increased rates of risky health behaviours including drinking, smoking and substance misuse as well as self-harming behaviours such as suicidal thoughts and actions.'[17] 'Rape impacts society by attacking the cohesion and mutual protection that makes a society. Rape is a hate crime, expressed in the violent exercise of physical violation as a means to an end.'[18]

Rape Cases in India

'Rape is one of the most common crimes against women in India. Criminal Law (Amendment) Act, 2013 defines rape as penile and non-penile penetration in bodily orifices of a woman by a man, without the consent of the woman. In India, a woman is raped every 29 minutes. Incidents of reported rape have increased three per cent from 2011 to 2012. Incidents of reported incest rape have increased 46.8 per cent from 268 cases in 2011 to 392 cases in 2012. Increased attention in the media and awareness among both Indians and the outside world is both bringing attention to the issue of rape in India and helping empower women to report the crime. After international news reported the gang rape of a 23-year old student on a moving bus that occurred in Delhi, in December 2012, Delhi experienced a significant increase in reported rapes. The number of reported rapes nearly doubled from 143 reported in January–March 2012 to 359 during the three months after the rape. After the Delhi rape case, Indian media has committed to report each and every rape case.'[19]

'Incest rape cases have increased by 36.7 per cent from 392 cases in 2012 to 536 cases in 2013 as compared to 35.2 per cent increase in overall rape cases. 20.1 per cent of such cases were registered in Maharashtra (108 out of 536 cases), wherein 117 victims of incest rape (rape by blood relatives) were reported. It is to be noted that 52.2 per cent of incest rape victims (286 out of 548 victims) were in age group of 10-18 years. There were 33,764 victims of rape out of 33,707 reported rape cases in the country during the year 2013. 13.1 per cent (4,427 out of 33,764) of the total victims of rape were girls under 14 years of age, while 26.3 per cent (8,877 victims out of 33,764) were teenaged girls (14-18 years). 46.1 per cent (15,556 victims) were women in the age-group 18-30 years.

Kidnapping and abduction cases have reported an increase of 35.6 per cent during 2013 as compared to 2012 (38,262 cases).

Uttar Pradesh with 9,737 cases has accounted for 18.8 per cent of the total cases at the national level. Delhi UT has reported the highest crime rate at 41.1 as compared to the national average of 8.8. The cases of 'Torture' committed on women in the country have increased by 11.6 per cent during 2013 over the previous year (1,06,527 cases). Most of these cases (40.8 per cent) were reported from West Bengal (18,116 cases) followed by Rajasthan 12.7 per cent (15,094 cases) and Andhra Pradesh 12.7 per cent (15,084). The highest crime rate of 56.4 was reported from Assam. Incidents of assault on women with intent to outrage her modesty in the country have increased by 56.0 per cent during 2013 over the previous year (45,351 cases). Madhya Pradesh has reported the highest incidence (8,252 cases) followed by Maharashtra (8,132 cases), amounting to 11.7 per cent and 11.5 per cent of total such incidences.'[20]

Criminal Law (Amendment) Act, 2013

'The Criminal Law (Amendment) Act, 2013 is an Indian legislation passed by the Lok Sabha on 19th March 2013 and by the Rajya Sabha on 21st March 2013, which provides for amendment of Indian Penal Code, Indian Evidence Act and Code of Criminal Procedure, 1973 on laws related to sexual offences. The Bill received Presidential assent on 2nd April 2013 and deemed to come into force from 3rd February 2013. It was originally an Ordinance promulgated by the President of India, Pranab Mukherjee, on 3rd February 2013, in light of the protests in the 2012 Delhi gang rape case. Six days after the incident, on 22th December 2012, the central government appointed a judicial committee headed by J. S. Verma, a former Chief Justice of India, to suggest amendments to criminal law to sternly deal with sexual assault cases. The committee, which also included retired judge Leila Seth and leading advocate Gopal Subramaniam, was given a month to submit its report.'[21]

'It amends sections 100, 228A, 354, 370, 370A, 375, 376, 376A, 376B, 376C, 376D and 509 of Indian Penal Code, 1860. It also inserts new sections 166A, 166B, 326A, 326B, 354A, 354B, 354C and 354D in Indian Penal Code, 1860. It also amends sections 26, 54A, 154, 160, 161, 164, 173, 197, 273, 309, 327 and First Schedule of Code of Criminal Procedure, 1973. It also inserts new sections 357B and 357C of Code of Criminal Procedure, 1973. It also amends sections 114, 119 and 146 of Indian Evidence

Act, 1872. It also inserts new Section 53A in Indian Evidence Act, 1872. It also amends Section 42 of Protection of Children from Sexual Offences Act, 2012.

Reforms in management of cases related to crime against women suggested by Justice Verma Committee: A Rape Crisis Cell should be set up. The Cell should be immediately notified when an FIR in relation to sexual assault is made. The Cell must provide legal assistance to the victim. All police stations should have CCTVs at the entrance and in the questioning room. A complainant should be able to file FIRs online. Police officers should be duty bound to assist victims of sexual offences irrespective of the crime's jurisdiction. Members of the public who help the victims should not be treated as wrong doers. The police should be trained to deal with sexual offences appropriately. Number of police personnel should be increased. Community policing should be developed by providing training to volunteers.'[22]

Conclusion

Rape is a type of sexual assault usually involving sexual intercourse or other forms of sexual penetration perpetrated against a person without that person's consent. Victims of rape can be severely traumatised by the assault and may have difficulty functioning as well as they had been used to prior to the assault, with disruption of concentration, sleeping patterns and eating habits. Psychological effects in the medium to long-term encompass heightened fear, anger, anxiety, guilt, self-blame, loss of trust, flashbacks and PTSD, depression, dissociation, phobias, panic disorder and obsessive compulsive disorder. The Criminal Law (Amendment) Act, 2013 is an Indian legislation passed by the Lok Sabha on 19th March 2013 and by the Rajya Sabha on 21st March 2013, which provides for amendment of Indian Penal Code, Indian Evidence Act and Code of Criminal Procedure, 1973 on laws related to sexual offences.

References

1. Crime against Women, Retrieved from http://ncrb.gov.in/CD-CII2013/Chapters/5-Crime%20against%20Women.pdf
2. Violence against women (2014), Retrieved from http://en.wikipedia.org/wiki/Violence_against_women

3. Rape (2015), Retrieved from http://en.wikipedia.org/wiki/Rape
4. See http://www.legalserviceindia.com/articles/rape_1.htm
5. Date rape (2014), Retrieved from http://en.wikipedia.org/wiki/Date_rape
6. Gang rape (2014), Retrieved from http://en.wikipedia.org/wiki/Gang_rape
7. Marital rape (2014), Retrieved from http://en.wikipedia.org/wiki/Marital_rape
8. Incest (2014), Retrieved from http://en.wikipedia.org/wiki/Incest
9. Child sexual abuse (2014), Retrieved from http://en.wikipedia.org/wiki/Child_sexual_abuse
10. Prison rape (2014), Retrieved from http://en.wikipedia.org/wiki/Prison_rape
11. Acquaintance rape (2014), Retrieved from http://en.wikipedia.org/wiki/Acquaintance_rape
12. Wartime sexual violence (2014), Retrieved from http://en.wikipedia.org/wiki/Wartime_sexual_violence
13. Statutory rape (2014), Retrieved from http://en.wikipedia.org/wiki/Statutory_rape
14. Rape (2015), Retrieved from http://en.wikipedia.org/wiki/Rape
15. Effects of Sexual Assault (2014), Retrieved from https://www.rainn.org/get-information/effects-of-sexual-assault
16. Effects of Rape: Psychological and Physical Effects of Rape, Retrieved from http://www.healthyplace.com/abuse/rape/effects-of-rape-psychological-and-physical-effects-of-rape/
17. Rape: How women, the community and the health sector respond, Retrieved from http://www.svri.org/svrisummary.pdf
18. See http://www.quora.com/How-would-you-say-rape-impacts-society
19. Violence against women in India (2014), Retrieved from http://en.wikipedia.org/wiki/Violence_against_women_in_India
20. Crime against Women, Retrieved from http://ncrb.gov.in/CD-CII2013/Chapters/5-Crime%20against%20Women.pdf
21. The Criminal Law (Amendment) Act, 2013, Retrieved from http://en.wikipedia.org/wiki/Criminal_Law_ %28Amendment %29_Act,_2013
22. Prof K.S. Suresh and Jagadish. A.T., An Overview of Criminal Law Amendment Act, 2013, Retrieved from http://www.atimysore. gov.in/workshops/wppts/gender_issues/crim_law_amnd_ 2013_drjagadeesh_jsslaw_college.pdf

19

Female Genital Mutilation

"Men are by nature merely indifferent to one another; but women are by nature enemies."

—*Arthur Schopenhauer*

Introduction

'The mutilation occurred not in Africa, where the practice is most prevalent, but in India where a small Muslim sub-sect known as the Dawoodi Bohra continues to believe that the removal of the clitoris is the will of God.'[1] 'Female genital cutting has for years been viewed as a barbaric traditional act that is used by men to subjugate women in the cultures of developing countries. Over the years the language of its description has moved from circumcision to mutilation and finally to cutting reflecting the different existing sentiments at each stage of the language development. The issue of female genital cutting is complex, not only because it cuts across human rights, culture and reproductive health, but also because of its perceived relationship with infant mortality and infertility in some of the communities in which it is practiced.'[2]

'Female genital mutilation includes procedures that intentionally alter or cause injury to the female genital organs for non-medical reasons. This harmful traditional practice is most common in the western, eastern and north-eastern regions of Africa; in some countries in Asia and the Middle East; and among migrant and refugee communities from these areas in Europe, Australia, New Zealand, Canada and the United States of America. FGM is recognised internationally as a violation of the human rights of girls and women'[3] 'The male genital alterations often take place in adolescence and they can involve major modifications. Considering the prevalence, timing and intensity of the relevant initiation rites and viewing genital alteration on a world wide scale, one is hard pressed to argue that it is an obvious instance of a gender inequity disfavouring girls.'[4]

'The practice of female circumcision in African countries did not attract the attention of many trained scholars until the 1980s. To be sure, European colonialists sought to eradicate the practice in parts of Kenya and Sudan in the 1920s and 1930s, as well as later, but these efforts proved isolated and ineffective. In the late 1920s, Protestant missionaries in Kenya sought to ban FGC for medical reasons. British authorities banned infibulation (narrowing or nearly closing the vaginal opening) but not clitoridectomy in Sudan in 1946, but very few arrests were made.'[5] 'Western feminism has represented African genital cutting as primitive, irrational, harmful and deserving of condemnation. The Western medical community has represented its genital cutting as modern, scientific, healing and above reproach.'[6]

Meaning of the Concept

'It is the ritual removal of some or all of the external female genitalia. The age at which it is conducted varies from days after birth to puberty; in half the countries for which national figures are available, most girls are cut before the age of five. The procedures differ according to the ethnic group. They include removal of the clitoral hood and clitoral glans, removal of the inner labia and, in the most severe form, removal of the inner and outer labia and closure of the vulva.'[7] 'Prior to the adoption of female genital mutilation, the practices were referred to as female circumcision, a term still in common use and preferred by the majority of people in communities where it is practiced.'[8]

'Female genital mutilation/cutting includes a range of practices involving the complete or partial removal or alteration of the external genitalia for nonmedical reasons. This procedure may involve the use of unsterilised, makeshift or rudimentary tools. The expression female genital mutilation gained growing support in the late 1970s.'[9] 'The practice of FGM can be viewed as an innovation that has gained wide acceptance and adoption in society and the move to medicalisation can be viewed as a form of reinvention of this practice.'[10] 'FGM/C is generally performed on girls between ages 4 and 12, although it is practiced in some cultures as early as a few days after birth or as late as just prior to marriage. Typically, traditional excisors have carried out the procedure, but recently a discouraging trend has emerged in some countries where medical professionals are increasingly performing the procedure.'[11]

Types of Female Genital Mutilation

'The World Health Organisation has classified these operations into four types. Type I involves the partial or total removal of the clitoris. Type II refers to partial or total removal of the clitoris together with partial or total excision of the labia minora. Type III is partial or total removal of the external genitalia and stitching or narrowing of the vaginal opening. Type IV is relatively rare and refers to other traditional genital surgeries such as pricking or stretching the clitoris and/or surrounding tissues.'[12]

1. *Clitoridectomy (Type I):* Partial or total removal of the clitoris (a small, sensitive and erectile part of the female genitals) and, in very rare cases, only the prepuce (the fold of skin surrounding the clitoris).
2. *Excision (Type II):* Partial or total removal of the clitoris and the labia minora, with or without excision of the labia majora (the labia are "the lips" that surround the vagina).
3. *Infibulation (Type III):* Narrowing of the vaginal opening through the creation of a covering seal. The seal is formed by cutting and repositioning the inner, or outer, labia, with or without removal of the clitoris.
4. *Other (Type IV):* All other harmful procedures to the female genitalia for non-medical purposes, e.g. pricking, piercing, incising, scraping and cauterising the genital area.[13]

Reasons of Female Genital Mutilation

'The practice is rooted in gender inequality, attempts to control women's sexuality and ideas about purity, modesty and aesthetics. It is usually initiated and carried out by women, who see it as a source of honour and who fear that failing to have their daughters and granddaughters cut will expose the girls to social exclusion.'[14] 'There are many reasons FGC is practiced, including social, economic and political reasons. Those who support FGC believe that it will empower their daughters, ensure the girls get married and protect the family's good name. In some groups, FGC is performed to show a girl's growth into womanhood and, as in the Masai community, marks the start of a girl's sexual debut. It also is performed to keep a woman's virginity by limiting her sexual behaviour. FGC is believed to stop a woman's sexual desire.'[15]

'Usually it is a girl's parents or her extended family that are responsible for arranging FGM. Some of the reasons given for the continued practice of FGM include; protecting family honour, preserving tradition, ensuring a woman's chastity, cleanliness and as a preparation for marriage.'[16]

1. *Psychosexual:* To attenuate sexual desire in the female, maintain chastity and virginity before marriage and fidelity during marriage and increase male sexual pleasure.
2. *Sociological:* For identification with the cultural heritage, initiation of girls into womanhood, social integration and maintenance of social cohesion and social acceptance.
3. *Hygiene and aesthetics:* Among some societies, the external female genitals are considered unclean and unsightly and so are removed to promote hygiene and provide aesthetic appeal.
4. *Religious*: Female genital mutilation is practiced in a number of communities, under the mistaken belief that it is demanded by certain religions.
5. *Others:* To enhance fertility and promote child survival, better marriage prospects and helps delivery of babies.[17]

Effects of Female Genital Mutilation

'The rates of infant resuscitation and perinatal death were higher among infants born to women who had undergone genital mutilation than among those born to mothers who had not and the severity of the adverse outcomes increased with the severity of female genital mutilation.'[18] 'FGM can have serious consequences for a woman's health and in some instances can lead to death. Infections, severe pain, bleeding and tetanus are just some of the short-term consequences. In the long-term women can suffer pain and discomfort during sex, chronic pain, infection, cysts, abscesses, difficulties with periods and fertility problems. Women also often suffer severe psychological trauma, including flashbacks and depression.'[19]

'Many health risks are associated with FGM, most notably among women who underwent infibulations. Short terms complications include pain, urinary infections and hemorrhage. In the long-term, women who had FGM complain of urinary incontinence, pelvic inflammatory diseases and infertility.'[20] 'Depending on the degree of mutilation FGM can cause severe pain and shock, uterus, vaginal and pelvic infections, complications in pregnancy and childbirth, sexual dysfunction, difficulties in menstruation and psychological damages among many consequences. In addition to these there are considerable psycho-sexual, psychological and social consequences of FGM.'[21]

Female Genital Mutilation: Global Perspectives

'FGM is concentrated in 27 African countries, Yemen and Iraqi Kurdistan and found elsewhere in Asia, the Middle East and among diaspora communities around the world. Over 130 million women and girls have experienced FGM in the 29 countries in which it is concentrated. The United Nations Population Fund estimates that 20 per cent of affected women have been infibulated, a practice found largely in northeast Africa, particularly Djibouti, Eritrea, Somalia and northern Sudan. UNICEF reported in November 2014 that prevalence rates for sub-Saharan Africa were 39 per cent for women and 17 per cent for girls aged 0–14; for Eastern and Southern Africa 44 and 14 per cent and for West and Central Africa 31 and 17 per cent. As of 2013, Egypt, Ethiopia and Nigeria had the highest number of women and girls living with FGM: 27.2 million, 23.8 million and 19.9 million respectively.

It is also practised in Jordan, Saudi Arabia, Indonesia and Malaysia and within immigrant communities around the world, including Australia, New Zealand, Europe, Scandinavia, the United States and Canada. The practice is sometimes an ethnic marker, but may differ along national lines. In the northeastern regions of Ethiopia and Kenya, which share a border with Somalia, the Somali people practise FGM at around the same rate as they do in Somali. In Iraq, for example, FGM is found mostly among the Kurds in Erbil, Sulaymaniyah and Kirkuk, giving the country a national prevalence of eight per cent.'[22]

'It is estimated that about 100–140 million girls and women worldwide have undergone FGM and each year a further two million girls and women are at risk of this practice. It is performed on girls aged 4–12 years and in some cultures as early as a few days after birth or as late as just before marriage. Most of the girls and women affected live in 28 African countries, but also in the Middle East and Asia. They are increasingly found in Europe, Australia, New Zealand, Canada and US, mostly among immigrants from cultures where FGM is a tradition.'[23] 'In industrialised countries, genital mutilation occurs predominantly among immigrants from countries where mutilation is practised. It has been reported in Australia, Canada, Denmark, France, Italy, the Netherlands, Sweden, the United Kingdom and the United States. Girls or female infants living in industrialised countries are sometimes operated on illegally by doctors from their own communities who reside there.'[24]

'Surveys have shown a widespread belief, particularly in Mali, Mauritania, Guinea and Egypt, that FGM is a religious requirement. Although FGM's origins in northeastern Africa are pre-Islamic, the practice became associated with Islam because of that religion's focus on female chastity and seclusion. FGM is also practised by animist groups, particularly in Guinea and Mali and by Christians. Because of poor access to information and because circumcisers downplay the causal connection, women may not associate the health consequences with the procedure.'[25]

'Most girls who are subjected to genital mutilation live in Africa, in almost 30 different countries. These countries lie within a geographical triangle that stretches from Egypt in the northeast to Tanzania in the south and Senegal in the west. Such mutilation is also practised in certain community's elsewhere in Africa and among certain ethnic groups outside Africa. The number of girls and women in the world who have undergone genital mutilation is estimated at between 100 million and 130 million, but these figures are uncertain. We know too little about women's reproductive health in the countries concerned. It is estimated that around two million girls are subjected to genital mutilation each year. The procedure is usually carried out by a traditional birth attendant, most often a woman.'[26]

Female Genital Mutilation in India

'In India, the Bohra community is a very small one compared to the entire population; added to that, the girls are generally circumcised just after/before they attain their puberty.'[27] 'The Bohris practice Type 1, whereby they cut the clitoris hood of a young girl, usually without any anaesthesia. Ninety per cent of the Bohri community still practices this ritual religiously. Only a small per centage of the progressive Dawood Bohri community has stopped this practice. Even the expats and NRIs who send their daughters to posh schools get FGM done. This is essentially done to prevent homosexuality, masturbation and to subdue a girl's desires so that she doesn't marry out of the community or have extra-marital relationships. The Bohras of India belong to the Shia Ismaili faith. Besides Bohras, there are similar two other Muslim sects - the Khojas and the Memons. All the three sects are petty business communities from Gujarat, are well structured and have similar and contemporaneous origin. Though these three Muslim sects hold similarities, but the Khojas and the Memos do not undertake the practice of female circumcision.'[28]

Human Rights Dimension

'Most contemporary human rights are based on international treaties signed by governments in the post-World War II era. In general, these treaties sought to establish universal standards by recognising fundamental rights and requiring governments to take action to ensure that such rights are respected. The standards set by governments around the world in their own countries are key to the development of human rights norms.'[29] 'Female genital mutilation of any type has been recognised as a harmful practice and a violation of the human rights of girls and women. Many of the United Nations human rights treaty monitoring bodies have addressed female genital mutilation in their concluding observations on how States are meeting their treaty obligations. The Committee on the Elimination of All Forms of Discrimination against Women, the Committee on the Rights of the Child and the Human Rights Committee have been active in condemning the practice and recommending measures to combat it, including the criminalisation of the practice. Female genital mutilation has been recognised as discrimination based on sex because it is rooted in gender inequalities and power imbalances between men and women and inhibits women's full and equal enjoyment of their human rights.'[30]

'The United Nations General Assembly adoption of the resolution intensifying global efforts for the elimination of female genital mutilations, on 20th December 2012, marked a milestone in global efforts to end the practice. The resolution demonstrated the political will of the international community to eliminate FGM/C. The term 'female genital mutilation' was adopted in 1990 by the Inter-African Committee on Traditional Practices Affecting the Health of Women and Children and in 1991 the World Health Organisation (WHO) recommended that the United Nations adopt it as well. UNICEF and the United Nations Population Fund (UNFPA) currently use a hybrid term, 'female genital mutilation/cutting' or FGM/C. This is meant to capture the significance of the term 'mutilation' at the policy level and highlight that the practice is a violation of the rights of girls and women.'[31]

'According to female genital mutilation was first recognised in the agenda of the United Nations in 1948 within the context of the universal declaration of human rights (UDHR). It was seen as a harmful tradition practice in the 70s and 80s, during the United Nation's year for women 1975-1989. Some of the international agencies, WHO consider FGM as a violation of human rights include; World Health Organisation (WHO), United Nation Children Education Fund (UNICEF), World Medical Association and the United Nations Population Fund.'[32]

'Moreover, Article 24 (3) of the United Nations Convention on the Rights of the Child (CRC) requires that State Parties "shall take all effective and appropriate measures with a view to abolishing traditional practices prejudicial to the health of the child'. The 1994 Fourth United Nations World Conference on Women held in Beijing, classified FGM as a form of violence against women, equated with battering, rape, sexual abuse and forced prostitution. Within the regional context, the African Charter on the Rights and Welfare of the Child (ACRWC) to which The Gambia acceded in 2002 stresses that positive traditional values and cultures be preserved and strengthened, while Article 21 requests Parties to take appropriate measures to eradicate traditional practices and customs, which are prejudicial to the child.'[33]

'The Protocol on the Rights of Women in Africa defines harmful practices as *"all behaviour, attitudes and/or practices which negatively affect the fundamental rights of women and girls, such as their right to life, health, dignity, education and physical integrity...."* Most societies have customs and traditions that can jeopardise the health, well-being, or dignity of women and young girls. Globally, the practices that are consistently recognised as harmful to women include, among others, female genital mutilation, child marriage, dowry-related deaths, honour killings and manifestations of son preference.'[34]

'The right to security of person, which protects women's right to physical integrity, ensures freedom from violence. Compulsory FGM robs women of the right to make independent decisions in matters affecting their bodies, rejects the state of the female body and its naturally occurring sexual functions and invades women's privacy regarding their sexuality. The right to freedom from FGM falls within the right to freedom from discrimination, because the practice of FGM distinguishes on the basis of sex and hinders the equal enjoyment by women of the fundamental rights. FGM obstructs women's right to health, both because the practice can lead to harmful physical and psychological complications and because subjecting someone to an invasive, medically unnecessary removal of healthy tissue violates the broadly understood right to the highest attainable standard of health. In those worst cases where girls bleed to death or suffer other grave complications, FGM deprives girls of their right to life.'[35]

'FGM is almost always carried out on minors who do not have sufficient knowledge to understand its implications. It is a human rights violation in the absence of any perceived medical necessity. While the right to participate in cultural life and freedom of religion are protected by international law, the latter also stipulates that freedom to manifest one's religion or beliefs might be subject to limitations necessary to protect the fundamental rights and freedoms of other. Social and cultural claims cannot be evoked to justify Female Genital Mutilation.'[36] 'It violates their right to health, security and physical integrity; the right to be free from torture and cruel, inhuman or degrading treatment; and the right to life when the procedure results in death.'[37]

Legal Mechanism

'Combating Female Genital Mutilation has emerged as an important policy goal among social activists and feminists in the present times. FGM is the cutting of the clitoris of girls in order to curb their sexual desire and preserve their sexual honour before marriage. Many girls who undergo FGM sometimes bleed to death or die of infection. Most are traumatised. Those who survive can suffer adverse health effects during marriage and pregnancy.'[38]

'The practice of female genital mutilation has received a great deal of attention in recent years at both the national and international levels. One of the most highly debated issues is the role that law should play in addressing a social practice that is strongly anchored in cultural beliefs and norms.[39] Because FGM is strongly linked to culture; it becomes an integration issue, in addition to being a health and human rights issue. In situations where integration is difficult, it often results in a withdrawal into the community and sometimes stricter application or toughening of cultural practices.'[40] 'Since the early 1990s, FGM/C has gained recognition as a health and human rights issue among African governments, the international community, women's organisations and professional associations. Global and national efforts to end FGM/C have supported legislation targeting excisors, medical professionals and families who perpetuate the practice, but political will and implementation remain an issue.'[41]

Conclusion

Female genital mutilation includes procedures that intentionally alter or cause injury to the female genital organs for non-medical reasons. This harmful traditional practice is most common in the western, eastern and north-eastern regions of Africa; in some countries in Asia and the Middle East; and among migrant and refugee communities from these areas in Europe, Australia, New Zealand, Canada and the United States of America. FGM is recognised internationally as a violation of the human rights of girls and women. The practice is rooted in gender inequality, attempts to control women's sexuality and ideas about purity, modesty and aesthetics. It is usually initiated and carried out by women, who see it as a source of honour and who fear that failing to have their daughters and granddaughters cut will expose the girls to social exclusion. FGM can have serious consequences for a woman's health and in some instances can lead to death. Infections, severe pain, bleeding and tetanus are just some of the short term consequences. In the long-term women can suffer pain and discomfort during sex, chronic pain, infection, cysts, abscesses, difficulties with periods and fertility problems.

References

1. Female circumcision anger aired in India (2012), Retrieved from http://www.dawn.com/news/712748/female-circumcision-anger-aired-in-india-fm
2. Edem Patricia Effiong (2006), Addressing Female Genital Cutting: A Public Health Perspective, Retrieved from http://cgi.unc.edu/uploads/media_items/addressing-female-genital-cutting-a-public-health-perspective.original.pdf
3. Female genital mutilation and asylum in the European union: A Statistical Overview (2013), http://www.unhcr.org/531880249.pdf
4. Richard A. Shweder, What about "Female Genital Mutilation"? And Why Understanding Culture Matters in the First Place, Daedalus, Vol. 129, No. 4, 2011, p. 221.
5. P. Stanley Yoder and Shanxiao Wang (2013), Female Genital Cutting: The Interpretation of Recent DHS Data, p.5, Retrieved from https://www.dhsprogram.com/pubs/pdf/CR33/CR33.pdf
6. Nancy Ehrenreich and Mark Barr, Intersex Surgery, Female Genital Cutting and the Selective Condemnation of "Cultural Practices", Retrieved from http://www.law.harvard.edu/students/orgs/crcl/vol40_1/ehrenreich.pdf
7. Female genital mutilation (2014), Retrieved from http://en.wikipedia.org/wiki/Female_genital_mutilation

8. Female Genital Mutilation: Integrating the Prevention and the Management of the Health Complications into the curricula of nursing and midwifery, Retrieved from http://www.who.int/gender/other_health/Studentsmanual.pdf
9. Changing a harmful social convention: Female Genital Mutilation/cutting, Retrieved from http://www.unicef-irc.org/publications/pdf/fgm_eng.pdf
10. Karim Naguib, The Effects of Social Interactions on Female Genital Mutilation: Evidence from Egypt, Retrieved from http://www.bu.edu/econ/files/2010/05/se_fgm_egypt.pdf
11. Female Genital Mutilation/ Cutting: Data and Trends (2010), Retrieved from http://www.prb.org/pdf10/fgm-wallchart2010.pdf
12. Linda Morison, Caroline Scherf, Gloria Ekpo, Katie Paine, Beryl West, Rosalind Coleman and Gijs Walraven, The long-term reproductive health consequences of female genital cutting in rural Gambia: a community-based survey, Tropical Medicine and International Health, Volume 6, No. 8, pp 643±653, August 2001.
13. Helen Baillot, Nina Murray, Elaine Connelly and Dr Natasha Howard (2004), Tackling Female Genital Mutilation in Scotland: A Scottish model of intervention, p.6, Retrieved from http://www.fgmnationalgroup.org/documents/2015_fgm_scotland.pdf
14. Female genital mutilation (2014), Retrieved from http://en.wikipedia.org/wiki/Female_genital_mutilation
15. Female Genital Cutting, Retrieved from http://www.womenshealth.gov/publications/our-publications/fact-sheet/female-genital-cutting.pdf
16. Female genital mutilation; the fact, Retrieved from https://www.gov.uk/government/uploads/system/uploads/attachment_data/file/300167/FGM_leaflet_v4.pdf
17. Nigeria: Female genital Mutilation, Retrieved from http://www.unicef.org/nigeria/FGM_.pdf
18. Effects of female genital mutilation on childbirth in Africa, Retrieved from http://www.who.int/reproductivehealth/publications/fgm/effect_of_fgm_on_childbirth_africa.pdf
19. Female genital mutilation: The fact, Retrieved from https://www.gov.uk/government/uploads/system/uploads/attachment_data/file/300167/FGM_leaflet_v4.pdf
20. Joseph Inungu and Yacouba Tou, Factors associated with female genital mutilation in Burkina Faso, Journal of Public Health and Epidemiology Vol. 5(1), pp. 20-28, January 2013.

21. Pinak Pani Datta (2012), Female Genital Mutilation: An Open Secret in India, Youth Ki Awaaz, Retrieved from http://www.youthkiawaaz.com/2012/04/female-genital-mutilation-an-open-secret-in-india/

22. Female genital mutilation (2014), Retrieved from http://en.wikipedia.org/wiki/Female_genital_mutilation

23. Wondimu Shanko Yirga1, Nega Assefa Kassa Mengistu Welday Gebremichael Arja R. Aro, Female genital mutilation: prevalence, perceptions and effect on women's health in Kersa district of Ethiopia, International Journal of Women's Health, 2012:4, p. 46.

24. Mohamed Moukhyer, Female genital mutilation (FGM): Against womens health and human rights, Retrieved from http://www.the-networktufh.org/sites/default/files/attachments/basic_pages/WHLP%20Female%20Genital%20Mutilation.pdf

25. Female Genital Mutilation (2014), Retrieved from http://en.wikipedia.org/wiki/Female_genital_mutilation

26. The Norwegian Government's International Action Plan for Combating Female Genital Mutilation (2003), Retrieved from https://www.regjeringen.no/globalassets/upload/ud/vedlegg/lemlestelse_e.pdf

27. Pinak Pani Datta (2012), Female Genital Mutilation: An Open Secret in India, Youth Ki Awaaz, Retrieved from http://www.youthkiawaaz.com/2012/04/female-genital-mutilation-an-open-secret-in-india/

28. Uproar over Female Genital Mutilation: Bohra Muslim woman activist launches campaign on Facebook to ban practice, Retrieved from https://www.facebook.com/notes/sijo-k-jose/uproar-over-female-genital-mutilation-bohra-muslim-woman-activist-launches-campa/329191643829952

29. Female Genital Mutilation: A Matter of Human Rights, Retrieved from http://www.reproductiverights.org/sites/default/files/documents/FGM_final.pdf

30. Eliminating Female genital mutilation: An interagency statement, Retrieved from http://www.un.org/womenwatch/daw/csw/csw52/statements_missions/Interagency_Statement_on_Eliminating_FGM.pdf

31. Female Genital Mutilation/Cutting: A statistical overview and exploration of the dynamics of change, Retrieved from http://www.childinfo.org/files/FGCM_Lo_res.pdf

32. Female Genital Mutilation- effects on women and young children, Retrieved from https://publications.theseus.fi/bitstream/handle/10024/22952/Karhu_Rose.pdf?sequence=1

33. Female Genital Mutilation in the Gambia: A Desk Review, Retrieved from http://www.unicef.org/wcaro/wcaro_gambia_FGM_Desk_Review.pdf

34. Harmful Practices—the Case of Female Genital Mutilation, Retrieved from https://www.k4health.org/sites/default/files/pub_bo_GG_FGM.pdf

35. Harmful Practices—the Case of Female Genital Mutilation, Retrieved from https://www.k4health.org/sites/default/files/pub_bo_GG_FGM.pdf

36. Protecting girls from undergoing Female Genital Mutilation: The experience of working with the Maasai communities in Kenya and Tanzania, Retrieved from http://www.equalitynow.org/sites/default/files/Protecting%20Girls_ FGM_ Kenya_Tanzania.pdf

37. The dynamics of social change towards the abandonment of Female Genital Mutilation in five African countries, Retrieved from http://www.unicef-irc.org/publications/pdf/fgm_insight_eng.pdf

38. Uproar over Female Genital Mutilation: Bohra Muslim woman activist launches campaign on Facebook to ban practice, Retrieved from https://www.facebook.com/notes/sijo-k-jose/uproar-over-female-genital-mutilation-bohra-muslim-woman-activist-launches-campa/329191643829952

39. Female Genital Mutilation: A Matter of Human Rights, Retrieved from http://www.reproductiverights.org/sites/default/files/documents/FGM_final.pdf

40. Supporting the Abandonment of Female Genital Mutilation in the Context of Migration, Retrieved from https://www.iom.int/jahia/webdav/shared/shared/mainsite/projects/documents/fgm_infosheet.pdf

41. Female Genital Mutilation/Cutting: Data and Trends, Retrieved from http://www.prb.org/pdf08/fgm-wallchart.pdf

20

Child Marriage

"Women have simple tastes. They get pleasure out of the conversation of children in arms and men in love."

—H.L. Mencken

Introduction

'A child is a human between the stages of birth and puberty. The United Nations Convention on the Rights of the Child defines child as a human being below the age of 18 years unless under the law applicable to the child, majority is attained earlier. Every child goes through many stages of social development. Social attitudes toward children differ around the world in various cultures. These attitudes have changed over time. Protection of children from abuse is considered an important contemporary goal. This includes protecting children from exploitation such as child labour, child trafficking and selling, child sexual abuse, including child prostitution and child pornography, military use of children and child laundering in illegal adoptions.'[1]

'Investing financial resources to help children survive and develop to their full potential is, first and foremost, a moral imperative. The world can afford to address the most disturbing aspects of poverty through child-related interventions. Seven out of the top ten most productive investments in the updated

Copenhagen Consensus initiative list directly relate to children. These investment initiatives include expanding micronutrients for children, increasing immunisation coverage, lowering the price of schooling and removing education barriers for girls.'[2]

Meaning of the Concept

'Child marriage is a formal marriage or informal union entered into by an individual before reaching the age of 18. UNICEF defines child marriage as a formal marriage or informal union before 18 years of age. UN Women has proposed that child marriage be defined as a forced marriage because they believe children under age 18 are incapable of giving a legally valid consent.

Child Marriage denies a child the basic right to good health, nutrition and education. Evidence shows that early marriage makes girls more vulnerable violence, abuse and exploitation. For both girls and boys, marriage has a strong physical, intellectual, psychological and emotional impact, cutting off educational opportunities and chances of personal growth. While boys are affected by child marriage, this is an issue that impacts upon girls in far larger numbers and with more intensity.'[3]

Reasons of Child Marriage

'Poverty is one of the major factors underpinning early marriage. Early marriage is one way to ensure that a wife is protected, or placed firmly under male control; that she is submissive to her husband and works hard for her in-laws household; that the children she bears are legitimate; and that bonds of affection between couples do not undermine the family unit. Parents may genuinely feel that their daughter will be better off and safer with a regular male guardian.'[4]

Child Marriage: Global Perspectives[5]

'Historically, child marriage was common around the world. The practice began to be questioned in the twentieth century, with the age of individuals' first marriage increasing in many countries and most countries increasing the minimum marriage age. In Greece, early marriage and motherhood for girls was encouraged. Child marriages were common throughout history for a variety of reasons, including poverty, insecurity, as well as for political and financial reasons. Today, one in six adolescent girls between the ages of 15 and 19 are formally married or in a union. On a global scale, rates of child marriage are highest in South Asia followed by West and Central Africa and Sub-Saharan Africa.

Niger has one of the highest rates of early marriage in sub-Saharan Africa. African countries have enacted marriageable age laws to limit marriage to a minimum age of 16 to 18, depending on jurisdiction. In Ethiopia, Chad and Niger, the legal marriage age is 15, but local customs and religious courts have the power to allow marriages below 12 years of age. In Morocco, child marriage is a common practice. Over 41,000 marriages every year involve child brides. More than half of all child marriages occur in the South Asian countries of India, Pakistan, Bangladesh and Nepal. According to two 2013 reports, over 50 per cent of all marriages in Pakistan involve girls less than 18 years old. Child marriage rates in Bangladesh are amongst the highest in the world. Every two out of three marriages involve child marriages. According to statistics from 2005, 49 per cent of women then between 25 and 29 were married by the age of 15.

A 2013 report claims 53 per cent of all married women in Afghanistan were married before age 18 and 21 per cent of all were married before age 15. Afghanistan's official minimum age of marriage for girls is 15 with her father's permission. Child marriage is common in Latin America and the Caribbean island nations. About 29 per cent of girls are married before age one (from Wikipedia). There are International Human Rights instruments that have been put in place in relation to the problem of early marriage. The key ones are Universal Declaration of Human Rights; Supplementary Convention on the Abolition of Slavery, the Slave Trade and Institutions and Practices Similar to Slavery; Convention on Consent to Marriage, Minimum Age for Marriage and Registration of Marriages; International Covenant on Economic, Social and Cultural Rights; Convention on the Elimination of All Forms of Discrimination against Women) and Convention on the Rights of the Child.'[6]

Child Marriage in India

Child marriages are prevalent in India. Since 2001, child marriage rates in India have fallen another 46 per cent, reaching an overall nationwide average seven per cent child marriage rates by 2009.'[7] 'Child marriage in India are continues to thrive by and large in the rural areas more than elsewhere in the country. The factors that encourage its subsistence are usually a combination of poverty, the lack of education, continued perpetration of patriarchal relations that encourage and facilitate gender inequalities and cultural perspectives that encourage the phenomenon to thrive. Child marriage in India is not a new phenomenon. The practice as it prevails now, though, continues to thrive in economically disadvantaged communities, especially those that are coloured by customary and cultural practices and perspectives that encourage the early marriage of a girl child.'[8]

'Legislation prohibiting early marriage in India was put in place way back in 1929, however, even in the modern times, in spite of the new law (Prohibition of Child Marriage Act, 2006); the problem continues to haunt states like Jharkhand, Bihar, Chhattisgarh, West Bengal, Rajasthan, Andhra Pradesh, Madhya Pradesh, Uttar Pradesh and Jammu and Kashmir. The problem is worse in rural areas in comparison to urban areas. These marriages are low profile, solemnised in complete secrecy and are underreported.'[9] 'Despite legislation forbidding child marriage in existence in India since 1929 (Child Marriage Restraint Act), the adoption of the much more progressive Prohibition of Child Marriage Act in 2006 and the presence of many initiatives, by both government and non-government organisations to prevent child marriage, there is wide acceptance amongst sections of society for early marriage of girls and boys.'[10]

Effects of Child Marriage

'Child marriage has lasting consequences on girls, which last well beyond adolescence. Women married in their teens or earlier, struggle with the health effects of getting pregnant at a young age and often with little spacing between children. Early marriages followed by teen pregnancy significantly increase birth complications and social isolation. Girls in child marriages are more likely to suffer from domestic violence, child sexual abuse and marital rape. Child marriage often ends a girl's education, particularly in impoverished countries where child marriages are common. Without education, girls and adult women have fewer opportunities to earn an income, financially provide for herself and her children. Early marriage places young girls in a vulnerable situation of being completely dependent on her husband.'[11]

The Child Marriage Restraint Act of 1929[12]

It extends to the whole of India except the State of Jammu and Kashmir and it applies also to all citizens of India without and beyond India. It shall come into force on the 1st day of April, 1930. Whoever, being a male above eighteen years of age and below twenty-one, contracts a child marriage shall be punishable with simple imprisonment which may extend to fifteen days, or with fine which may extend to one thousand rupees, or with both. Whoever, being a male above twenty-one years of age, contracts a child marriage shall be punishable with simple imprisonment which may extend to three months and shall also be liable to fine. Whoever performs conducts or directs any child marriage shall be punishable with simple imprisonment which may extend to three months and shall also be liable to fine, unless he proves that he had reason to believe that the marriage was not a child marriage.

Where a minor contracts a child marriage, any person having charge of the minor, whether as parent or guardian or in any other capacity, lawful or unlawful, who does any act to promote the marriage or permits it to be solemnised, or negligently fails to prevent it from being solemnised, shall be punishable with simple imprisonment which may extend to three months and shall also be liable to fine, provided that no woman shall be punishable with imprisonment. For the purposes of this section, it shall be presumed, unless and until the contrary is proved, that where a minor has contracted a child marriage, the person having charge of such minor has negligently failed to prevent the marriage from being solemnised.

No Court shall take cognisance of any offence under this Act after the expiry of one year from the date on which the offence is alleged to have been committed. Notwithstanding anything to the contrary contained in this Act, the Court may, if satisfied from information laid before it through a complaint or otherwise that a child marriage in contravention of this Act has been arranged or is about to be solemnised, issue an injunction against any of the persons mentioned in Sections 3, 4, 5 and 6 of this Act prohibiting such marriage.

The State Government may, by notification in the official Gazette, invested the Child Marriage Prevention Officer* with such powers of a Police Officer as may be specified in the notification and the Child Marriage Prevention Officer shall exercise his powers subject to such limitations and conditions as may be specified in the notification. The State Government may associate with each Child Marriage Prevention Officer a non-official advisory body consisting of not more than five social welfare workers, of whom at least two shall be women workers known in the area within the jurisdiction of the officer for the purposes of advising and assisting him in the performance of his functions under this Act.

The Prohibition of Child Marriage Act, 2006

'The act includes punitive measures against those who perform, permit and promote child marriage. It also provides for annulment of a child marriage and gives a separated female the right to maintenance and residence from her husband if he is above 18 or in-laws if he is a minor until she is remarried. This Act came into effect in January 2007. Unless and until the rural people are enlightened about the horrible impacts of early marriage, no laws will be able to change the present appalling situation that the nation is facing. Also, stress needs to be put on education, gender equality and changing the patriarchal mindset.'[13]

Conclusion

Child marriage is a formal marriage or informal union entered into by an individual before reaching the age of 18, is one way to ensure that a wife is 'protected', or placed firmly under male control; that she is submissive to her husband and works hard for her in-laws' household; that the children she bears are 'legitimate'; and that bonds of affection between couples do not undermine the family unit. Child marriages are prevalent in India. Legislation prohibiting early marriage in India was put in place way back in 1929, however, even in the modern times, in spite of the new law (Prohibition of Child Marriage Act, 2006); the problem continues to haunt states like Jharkhand, Bihar, Chhattisgarh, West Bengal, Rajasthan, Andhra Pradesh, Madhya Pradesh, Uttar Pradesh and Jammu and Kashmir. The problem is worse in rural areas in comparison to urban areas.

Child marriage has lasting consequences on girls, which last well beyond adolescence. Women married in their teens or earlier, struggle with the health effects of getting pregnant at a young age and often with little spacing between children.

References

1. Child (2015), Retrieved from http://en.wikipedia.org/wiki/Child
2. Importance of investing in children, Retrieved from http://www.unicef.org/socialpolicy/index_53294.html
3. National Strategy Document on Prevention of Child Marriage (2013), Retrieved from http://wcd.nic.in/childwelfare/Strategychildmarrige.pdf
4. Early marriage: Child spouses, Innocenti digest (No. 7 - March 2001), Retrieved from http://www.unicef-irc.org/publications/pdf/digest7e.pdf
5. Child marriage (2014), Retrieved from http://en.wikipedia.org/wiki/Child_marriage
6. See http://www.breakthrough.tv/earlymarriage/2013/08/impact-early-marriage-domestic-violence-sexuality/
7. Child marriage in India (2014), Retrieved from http://en.wikipedia.org/wiki/Child_marriage_in_India
8. Child Marriages in India: An insight into Law and Policy (2013), Retrieved from http://www.ohchr.org/Documents/Issues/Women/WRGS/ForcedMarriage/NGO/TheRedElephantFoundation.pdf
9. See http://www.breakthrough.tv/earlymarriage/2013/08/impact-early-marriage-domestic-violence-sexuality/
10. National Strategy Document on Prevention of Child Marriage (2013), Retrieved from http://wcd.nic.in/childwelfare/Strategychildmarrige.pdf
11. Child marriage (2014), Retrieved from http://en.wikipedia.org/wiki/Child_marriage
12. The Child Marriage Restraint Act of 1929, Retrieved from http://highcourtchd.gov.in/hclscc/subpages/pdf_files/5.pdf
13. See http://www.breakthrough.tv/earlymarriage/2013/08/impact-early-marriage-domestic-violence-sexuality/

Bibliography

Books

1. A. Kumar (2006). *Women and Crime: Dimensions and Remedial Measures,* Anmol Publications Pvt. Limited.
2. A.S. Garg (1990). *Bride burning: crime against women,* Sandeep Publication.
3. A. S. Srinivasar Aiyar (1930). *The Child Marriage Restraint Act, 1929,* Universal Law Publishing.
4. Abdul Matin (1992). *The Law on Dowry Prohibition and Child Marriage Restraint,* Palak Publishers.
5. Adam Hibbert (2004). *Children's Rights,* Sea-To-Sea Publisher.
6. Ahmed, S.M. (2009). Capability Development among the Ultra Poor in Bangladesh: A Case Study. Journal of Health, Population and Nutrition, 4:528-535.
7. Alessandro Cigno and Furio Camillo Rosati (2005). *The Economics of Child Labour,* Oxford University Press.
8. Alexandra Stiglmayer (1994). *Mass Rape: The War Against Women in Bosnia-Herzegovina,* U of Nebraska Press.
9. Al-Mamun, A. Malarvizhi, C.A. Wahab, S.A. and Mazumder, M.N.H. (2011) Investigating The Effect of Microcredit on Microenterprise Income in Peninsular Malaysia. European Journal of Economic, Finance and Administrative Sciences, 29, 122-133.
10. Anaclaudia Gastal Fassa, David L. Parker and Thomas J. Scanlon (2010). *Child Labour: A Public Health Perspective,* Oxford University Press.

11. Andrea Dworkin (1981). *Pornography: Men Possessing Women*, Women's Press.
12. Andrea Dworkin (1989). *Pornography: men possessing women*, Dutton.
13. Andrea Warren (1998). *Orphan Train Rider: One Boy's True Story*, Houghton Mifflin Harcourt.
14. Andrea Warren (2004), *We Rode the Orphan Trains*, Houghton Mifflin Harcourt.
15. Andrea Warren (2011). *Charles Dickens and the Street Children of London*, Houghton Mifflin Harcourt.
16. Arjun Prakash Aggarwal (1992). *Sexual Harassment in the Workplace*, Edition 2, Butterworth Pub Limited.
17. Arvind Ganesan and Patricia Gossman (1996). *Police Abuse and Killings of Street Children in India*, Human Rights Watch Children's Rights Project.
18. Asha Bajpai (2003). *Child Rights in India: Law, Policy and Practice*, Oxford University Press.
19. Assefa Bekele and Jo Boyden (1988). *Combating Child Labour*. International Labour Organisation.
20. Assefa Bekele and William E. Myers (1995). *First Things First in Child Labour: Eliminating Work Detrimental to Children*, International Labour Organisation.
21. B. S. Nagi (1993). *Child Marriage in India: A Study of Its Differential Patterns in Rajasthan*, Mittal Publications.
22. Bella Chagall (1988). *Burning Lights: A Unique Double Portrait of Russia*, Knopf Doubleday Publishing Group.
23. Bernie Anderson (2007). *Breaking the Silence: A Pastor Goes Public about His Battle with Pornography*, Autumn House Publishing.
24. Beryl Rawson (1996). *Marriage, Divorce and Children in Ancient Rome*, Humanities Research Centre.
25. Bi, Z. and Pandey, S.L.D. (2011). Comparison of Performance of Microfinance Institutions with Commercial Banks in India. Australian Journal of Business and Management Research, 1(6), 110-120.
26. C. P. Rai (2002). *Child labour: A reality*, Volume 2, Laxmi Shikshan Sansthan.
27. Carol J. Adams (2004). *The Pornography of Meat*, Continuum.
28. Carol Neel (2004). *Medieval Families: Perspectives on Marriage, Household and Children*, University of Toronto Press.

29. Catharine A. MacKinnon (1979). *Sexual Harassment of Working Women: A Case of Sex Discrimination,* Yale University Press.
30. Catharine A. MacKinnon and Andrea Dworkin (1997). *In Harm's Way: The Pornography Civil Rights Hearings,* Harvard University Press.
31. Catharine A. MacKinnon and Reva B. Siegel (2004). *Directions in Sexual Harassment Law,* Yale University Press.
32. Cathryne L. Schmitz, Elizabeth KimJin Traver and Desi Larson (2004). *Child Labor: A Global View,* Greenwood Publishing Group.
33. Chitra Banerjee Divakaruni (2000). *Black Candle: Poems about Women from India, Pakistan and Bangaladesh,* CALYX Books.
34. Chowdhury, A. (2009) Microfinance as a Poverty Reduction Tool-A Critical Assessment. DESA Working Paper, 9:1-11.
35. Claire M. Renzetti, Jeffery L. Edleson and Raquel Kennedy Bergen (2001). *Sourcebook on Violence Against Women,* SAGE.
36. Clive Gifford (2009). *Child Labour,* Evans Brothers.
37. Colin Wringe (1981). *Children's rights: a philosophical study,* Routledge and Kegan Paul.
38. Courtney Farrell (2010). *Children's Rights,* ABDO.
39. D.C. Nanjunda (2008). *Child Labour and Human Rights: A Prospective,* New Delhi: Gyan Publishing House.
40. David Archard (2004). *Children: Rights and Childhood,* Routledge.
41. David Finkelhor, Kersti Yllö (1987). *License to Rape: Sexual Abuse of Wives,* Free Press.
42. Debarati Halder and K. Jaishankar (2011). *Cyber Crime and the Victimisation of Women: Laws, Rights and Regulations,* Idea Group Inc (IGI).
43. Deborah M. Merrill (2011). *When Your Children Marry: How Marriage Changes Relationships with Sons and Daughters,* Rowman and Littlefield Publishers.
44. Dennis Frederick (2007). *Conquering Pornography: Overcoming the Addiction: A Practical,* WinePress Publishing.
45. Diana E. H. Russell (1990). *Rape in Marriage,* Indiana University Press.
46. Eleanor Flexner and Ellen Frances Fitzpatrick (1996). *Century of Struggle: The Woman's Rights Movement in the United States,* Harvard University Press.
47. Elizabeth Podnieks, Jordan I. Kosberg and Ariela Lowenstein (2005). *Elder Abuse: Selected Papers from the Prague World Congress on Family Violence,* Haworth Maltreatment and Trauma Press.

48. Elizabeth Russell Connelly (2000). *Child Abuse and Neglect: Examining the Psychological Components,* Chelsea House.

49. Ellen Carol DuBois (1998). *Woman Suffrage and Women's Rights,* NYU Press.

50. Ellen Lynn Hall and Jennifer Kofkin Rudkin (2011). *Seen and Heard: Children's Rights in Early Childhood Education,* Teachers College Press.

51. Elumilade, D.O, Asaolu, T.O. and Adereti, S.A. (2006) Appraising the Institutional Framework for Poverty Alleviation Programmes in Nigeria. International Research Journal of Finance and Economics, 3:67-79.

52. Emma Guest (2003). *Children of AIDS: Africa's orphan crisis,* Pluto Press.

53. Eugeen Verhellen (1996). *Monitoring Children's Rights,* Martinus Nijhoff Publishers.

54. F.M. Christensen (1990). *Pornography: The Other Side,* Greenwood Publishing Group.

55. Facts on File and Incorporated (2002). *Crimes Against Women,* Infobase Publishing.

56. Francis Achampong (1999). *Workplace Sexual Harassment Law: Principles, Landmark Developments and Framework for Effective Risk Management,* Greenwood Publishing Group.

57. Gail Dines, Robert Jensen and Ann Russo (1998). *Pornography: The Production and Consumption of Inequality,* Psychology Press.

58. Gamini Herath and Kishor Sharma (2007). *Child Labour in South Asia,* Ashgate Publishing Ltd.

59. Geoffrey Steven Kyeyune (1996). *Street children: why are they out?,* Fountain Publishers.

60. Georges Kristoffel Lieten (2005). *Child Labour: Burning Questions : Inaugural Lecture,* Amsterdam University Press.

61. Geraldine Terry (2007). *Women's Rights,* Copenhagen: Oxfam GB and Pluto Press.

62. Geraldine Terry (2008). *Sex Trafficking: Inside the Business of Modern Slavery.* Columbia University Press.

63. Geraldine Van Bueren (1998). *The International Law on the Rights of the Child,* Martinus Nijhoff Publishers.

64. Geraldine Van Bueren (2007). *Child Rights in Europe: Convergence and Divergence in Judicial Protection,* Council of Europe.

65. Gopal Bhargava (2003). *Child Labour,* Volume 2, New Delhi: Gyan Publishing House.

66. Haque, M.S and Yamao, M. (2008). Can micro-credit alleviate rural poverty? A Case Study of Bangladesh. Proceedings of World Academy of Science, Engineering and Technology, 36:1-12.

67. Herma Silverstein (1994). *Date Abuse*, Enslow Pub Incorporated.

68. Holly Johnson, Natalia Ollus and Sami Nevala (2007). *Violence Against Women: An International Perspective*, Springer.

69. Holly Littlefield (2001). *Children of the Orphan Trains*, Lerner Publications.

70. Hossain, M.K (2012) Measuring The Impact of BRAC Microfinance Operations; A Case Study of a Village. International Business Research, 5(4):112-124.

71. Hugh D. Hindman (2002). *Child Labor: An American History*, M.E. Sharpe.

72. Hugh D. Hindman (2011). *The World of Child Labor: An Historical and Regional Survey*, M.E. Sharpe.

73. Human Rights Watch (Organisation), Women's Rights Project (Human Rights Watch) (1991). *Criminal Injustice: Violence against Women in Brazil*, Human Rights Watch.

74. Ibru, C. (2007). Providing Operational Financing for Small Businesses-Challenges and Opportunities. A paper presented at the Cultural Centre (Main Auditorium), Calabar. 8th November. Retrieved from www.oceanicbanknigeria.comon 13th August, 2012.

75. Irobi, N.C. (2008). Microfinance and Poverty Alle-viation: A Case Study of Obazu Progressive Women Association, Mbieri, Imo State, Nigeria. Master Thesis. Sweden: Uppsala, SverigesLantbruksUniversitet.

76. Jane Fortin (1998). *Children's Rights and the Developing Law*, Butterworth, (Publishers) Limited.

77. Jane Fortin (2003). *Children's Rights and the Developing Law*, Cambridge University Press.

78. Jane Gallop (1997). *Feminist Accused of Sexual Harassment*, Duke University Press.

79. Jane Humphries (2010). *Childhood and Child Labour in the British Industrial Revolution*, Cambridge University Press.

80. Jaya Sagade (2005). *Child Marriage in India: Socio-legal and Human Rights Dimensions*, Oxford University Press

81. Jessica Spector (2006). *Prostitution and Pornography: Philosophical Debate about the Sex Industry*, Stanford University Press.

82. Joan Nordquist (1986). *Domestic violence: spouse abuse/marital rape,* Reference and Research Services.

83. Joanne Belknap (2007). *The invisible woman: gender, crime and justice,* Thomson/Wadsworth.

84. Joanne Mariner (2001). *No Escape: Male Rape in U.S. Prisons,* Human Rights Watch.

85. Joe Lugalla and Colleta G. Kibassa (2002). *Poverty, AIDS and street children in East Africa,* Edwin Mellen Press.

86. John Kabutha Mugo (2004). *Rehabilitation of Street Children in Kenya: Approaches, Quality and Challenges, IKO,* Verlag für Kulturelle Kommunikation.

87. John T. Pardeck (2006). *Children's Rights: Policy and Practice,* Psychology Press.

88. Joseph W. Slade (2001). *Pornography and Sexual Representation: A Reference Guide,* Volume 2, Greenwood Publishing Group.

89. Joyce Hart (2009). *Human Trafficking,* The Rosen Publishing Group.

90. Judy Westwater and Wanda Carter (2006). *Street Kid: One Child's Desperate Fight for Survival,* Harper Element.

91. Julia Sloth-Nielsen (2008). *Children's Rights in Africa: A Legal Perspective,* Ashgate Publishing Ltd.

92. Julie K. Ehrhart and Bernice Resnick Sandler (1985). *Campus gang rape: party games? Project on the Status and Education of Women,* Association of American Colleges.

93. Julie Peters and Andrea Wolper (1995). *Women's Rights, Human Rights: International Feminist Perspectives,* Psychology Press.

94. Karla Fitzhugh (2005). *Prescription Drug Abuse,* Crabtree Publishing Company.

95. Kate Walker (2009). *Cordero's Forced Bride,* Harlequin.

96. Kathleen Barry (1984). *Female Sexual Slavery,* NYU Press.

97. Kathryn Farr (2004). *Sex Trafficking: The Global Market in Women and Children,* Worth Publishers.

98. Kaye Stearman (2004). *Child Labor,* Raintree.

99. Keith Burgess-Jackson (1999). *A Most Detestable Crime: New Philosophical Essays on Rape,* Oxford University Press.

100. Kelly Dawn Askin (1997). *War Crimes Against Women: Prosecution in International War Crimes Tribunals,* Martinus Nijhoff Publishers.

101. Kevin Bales and Ron Soodalter (2010). *The Slave Next Door: Human Trafficking and Slavery in America Today, New Preface edition,* University of California Press.

102. Kristoffel Lieten and Benjamin White (2001). *Child labour: policy options*, Aksant Academic Publishers.

103. Laxmi Devi (1998). *Crime Atrocities and Violence against Women and Related Laws and Justice*, Anmol Publications Pvt. Limited.

104. Library Binding (2000). *Child Slavery in Modern Times*, Scholastic Library Publishing.

105. Lisa M. Cuklanz (1996). *Rape on Trial: How the Mass Media Construct Legal Reform and Social Change*, University of Pennsylvania Press.

106. Louise Shelley (2010). *Human Trafficking: A Global Perspective*, Cambridge University Press.

107. Lynn Hunt (1996). *The Invention of pornography: obscenity and the origins of modernity, 1500-1800*, Zone Books.

108. Lynn Walter (2001). *Women's Rights: A Global View*. Greenwood Publishing Group.

109. Lynne Eisaguirre (1997). *Sexual harassment: a reference handbook*, ABC-CLIO.

110. Mamta Rajawat (2004). *Child Labour: The Indian Perspective*, Kilaso Books.

111. Margaret Moberly (1999). *Fire Bride*, Charisma Media.

112. Marian Meyers (1997). *News Coverage of Violence Against Women: Engendering Blame*, SAGE.

113. Mark S. Fleisher and Jessie L. Krienert (2009). *The Myth of Prison Rape: Sexual Culture in American Prisons*, Rowman and Littlefield Publishers.

114. Marlene Webber (1991). *Street Kids: The Tragedy of Canada's Runaways*, University of Toronto Press.

115. Martin Guggenheim (2005). *What's Wrong with Children's Rights?*, Harvard University Press.

116. Mary Ellen Richmond and Fred Smith Hall (2007). *Child Marriages*, Russell Sage Foundation.

117. Mary L. Boland (2005). *Sexual Harassment in the Workplace*, Sphinx Legal.

118. Matt Bernstein Sycamore (2000). *Tricks and Treats: Sex Workers Write about Their Clients*, Harrington Park Press.

119. Maxwell Taylor and Ethel Quayle (2003). *Child Pornography: An Internet Crime*, Psychology Press.

120. Mejeha, R.O. and Nwachukwu, I.N., (2008). Micro-finance Institutions in Nigeria. MPRA Paper, 13711.Retrieved from http://mpra.ub.uni.muenchen.de/13711 on 23rd August 2011.

121. Michael D.A. Freeman and Michael Freeman (2011). *Children's Rights: Progress and Perspectives: Essays from the International Journal of Children's Rights,* Martinus Nijhoff Publishers.

122. Michael D.A. Freeman and Philip E. Veerman (1992). *The Ideologies of Children's Rights,* Brill Academic Pub.

123. Michael Freeman and Michael David Alan Freeman (2006). *Children's Health and Children's Rights,* Martinus Nijhoff Publishers.

124. Michele Antoinette Paludi, Richard B. Barickman and Richard Barickman (1991). *Academic and Workplace Sexual Harassment: A Resource Manual,* SUNY Press.

125. Mohd Umar (2005). *Bride Burning in India: A Socio Legal Study,* APH Publishing.

126. Nab Kishore Behura, Ramesh P. Mohanty (2005). *Urbanisation, Street Children and Their Problems,* New Delhi: Discovery Publishing House.

127. Nazir Ahmad Shah (1992). *Child Labour in India,* New Delhi: Anmol Publications Pvt. Limited.

128. Neera Burra (1997). *Born to work: child labour in India,* Oxford University Press.

129. Neera Burra (1994). *Child labour: impact assessment,* Cornell University.

130. Nelien Haspels and Michele Jankanish (2000). *Action Against Child Labour,* International Labour Organisation.

131. Obamuyi, T.M. (2011). Comparative Loan Performance in Banks and Micro-Credit Institution. Global Journal of Management and Business Research, March, 11(4):60-69.

132. Oriahi, C.I. and Aitufe, A.O. (2010) Education for the Eradication of Poverty. Current Research Journal of Social Sciences, 2(6):306-310.

133. Orient Blackswan (2005). *Trafficking in Women and Children in India,* Orient Blackswan.

134. Pamela Paul (2007). Pornified: *How Pornography Is Transforming Our Lives, Our Relationships and Our Families,* Macmillan.

135. Paras Diwan and Peeyushi Diwan (1997). *Law relating to dowry, dowry deaths, bride burning, rape and related offences,* Universal Law Pub. Co.

136. Parveen Nangia (1987). *Child labour: cause-effect syndrome,* Janak Publishers.

137. Patricia Nieuwenhuizen (2006). *Street Children in Bangalore (India): Their Dreams and Their Future,* Het Spinhuis.

138. Peggy Reeves Sanday (1992). Fraternity Gang Rape: Sex, Brotherhood and Privilege on Campus, NYU Press.

139. Phil Jones, Sue Welch and Susan Welch (2010). *Rethinking Children's Rights: Attitudes in Contemporary Society,* Continuum.

140. Philip Alston and Stephen Parker (1992). *Children, Rights and the Law,* Oxford University Press.

141. Philip Jenkins (2003). *Beyond Tolerance: Child Pornography on the Internet,* NYU Press.

142. Philip Leroy Kilbride, Collette A. Suda and Enos Hudson Nthia Njeru (2000). *Street Children in Kenya: Voices of Children in Search of a Childhood,* Greenwood Publishing Group.

143. Prabhat Chandra Tripathy (1998). *Crime against working women,* New Delhi: APH Publication.

144. Prachi Jaiswal (2000). *Child labour: a sociological study,* New Delhi: Shipra Publications.

145. Pramila H. Bhargava (2003). *The Elimination of Child Labour: Whose Responsibility?,* New Delhi: SAGE Publisher.

146. Premacanda and David Rubin (1998). Widows, wives and other heroines: twelve short stories, Oxford University Press.

147. Priscilla Alderson (2000). *Young Children's Rights: Exploring Beliefs, Principles and Practice,* Jessica Kingsley Publishers.

148. Raghbirlal Bhagatram Sethi (2007). *The Child marriage restraint act, as amended up to date,* Edition: 2, Law Book Co.

149. Ram Ahuja (1987). *Crime against Women,* Rawat Publications.

150. Ranjana Kumari (1989). *Brides Are Not for Burning: Dowry Victims in India,* Radiant Publisher.

151. Rashmi Agrawal (1999). *Street children: a socio-psychological study,* Shipra Publications.

152. Raymond Chandler (2002). *The High Window: A Novel,* Knopf Doubleday Publishing Group.

153. Rebecca J. Cook (1994). *Human Rights of Women: National and International Perspectives,* University of Pennsylvania Press.

154. Richard Procida and Rita James Simon (2007). *Global Perspectives on Social Issues: Pornography,* Lexington Books.

155. Richard Wortley and Stephen Smallbone (2012). *Internet Child Pornography: Causes, Investigation and Prevention,* ABC-CLIO.

156. Robin Warshaw (1994). *I Never Called It Rape,* Harper Collins.

157. Rory C. Reid and Dan Gray (2006). *Confronting Your Spouse's Pornography Problem,* Silverleaf Press.

158. Sambodh Goswami (2007). *Female Infanticide and Child Marriage,* Rawat Publications.

159. Samya Burney (1999). *Crime Or Custom?: Violence Against Women in Pakistan,* Human Rights Watch.

160. Sandy Hobbs, Jim McKechnie and Michael Lavalette (1999). *Child Labor: A World History Companion,* ABC-CLIO.

161. Selda Altun, Tom Burke and Jabran Ali (2001). *Stand Up Speak Out: A Book about Children's Rights,* Cooper Square Pub.

162. Shane Mountjoy and Tim McNeese (2009). *The Women's Rights Movement: Moving Toward Equality,* Infobase Publishing.

163. Shasta Gaughen (2003). *Women Rights,* Pennsylvania State University: Greenhaven Press.

164. Shastri, R.K. (2009). Micro Finance and Poverty Reduction in India (A Comparative Study with Asian Countries). African Journal of Business Management, 3(4):136-140.

165. Shobha Saxena (1995). *Crimes against Women and Protective Laws,* Deep and Deep Publications.

166. Shobhan Bantwal (2007). *The Dowry Bride,* Kensington Books.

167. Siddharth Kara (2010). *Sex Trafficking: Inside the Business of Modern Slavery,* Columbia University Press.

168. Simon Watney (1987). *Policing Desire: Pornography, AIDS, And the Media,* University of Minnesota Press.

169. Simon Watney (1996). *Policing Desire: Pornography, AIDS and the Media,* U of Minnesota Press.

170. Stanley G. French, Wanda Teays, Laura Martha Purdy (1998). *Violence against women: philosophical perspectives,* Cornell University Press.

171. Stuart N. Hart (2001). *Children's Rights in Education,* Jessica Kingsley Publishers.

172. Susan Griffin (1981). *Pornography and silence: culture's revenge against nature,* Harper and Row.

173. Susanna Paasonen (2011). *Carnal Resonance: Affect and Online Pornography,* MIT Press.

174. Sydney Newton and Julie Gerrits (2010). *Child Abuse,* Crabtree Publishing Company.

175. Thoko Kaime (2011). *The Convention on the Rights of the Child: A Cultural Legitimacy Critique,* Sussex Academic Press.

176. Tobias Hecht (1998). *At Home in the Street: Street Children of Northeast Brazil,* Cambridge University Press.

177. Ugoh, S.C. and Ukpere, W.I. (2009) Appraising the Trend of Policy on Poverty Alleviation Programmes in Nigeria with Emphasis on A National Poverty Eradication Programme (NAPEP). *African Journal of Business Management*, 3(12), 847-854.

178. United Nations Children's Fund (UNICEF) (2005). *Early Marriage: A Harmful Traditional Practice, a Statistical Exploration*, UNICEF.

179. Usha Sharma (2006). *Child Labour in India*, New Delhi: Mittal Publications.

180. Veena Talwar Oldenburg (2002). *Dowry Murder: The Imperial Origins of a Cultural Crime*, Oxford University Press.

181. Walter M. Kendrick (1987). *The Secret Museum: Pornography in Modern Culture*, University of California Press.

182. Werner Menski (1998). *South Asians and the Dowry Problem*, Trentham Books.

183. William M. Struthers (2009). *Wired for Intimacy: How Pornography Hijacks the Male Brain*, Inter Varsity Press.

184. William Petrocelli and Barbara Kate Repa (1998). *Sexual harassment on the job: what it is and how to stop it*, Nolo Press.

185. William Pinar (2001). *The Gender of Racial Politics and Violence in America: Lynching, Prison Rape and the Crisis of Masculinity*, Lang.

Reports/Articles

1. *2012 Trafficking in Persons Report: El Salvador*, Retrieved from http://sansalvador.usembassy.gov/reports/2012/tip.html

2. *2014 Trafficking in Persons Report: Uzbekistan*, Retrieved from http://uzbekistan.usembassy.gov/tip2014.html

3. *A brief history of the battle against sexual harassment at the workplace*, Retrieved from http://infochangeindia.org/women/analysis/a-brief-history-of-the-battle-against-sexual-harassment-at-the-workplace.html

4. A Statistical Study to Estimate the Prevalence of Female Genital Mutilation in England and Wales: Summary Report.

5. *Afghanistan: A Human Rights Report on Trafficking in Persons, Especially Women and Children*, Retrieved from http://www.protectionproject.org/wp-content/uploads/2010/09/Afghanistan.pdf

6. *Afghanistan: Lack of institutional mechanisms to tackle human*, Retrieved from http://www.irinnews.org/report/73300/afghanistan-lack-of-institutional-mechanisms-to-tackle-human-trafficking

7. *Afghanistan: Urgent need to tackle human trafficking,* Retrieved from http://www.irinnews.org/report/93318/afghanistan-urgent-need-to-tackle-human-trafficking

8. *Africa (2014),* Retrieved from http://en.wikipedia.org/wiki/Africa

9. *An Introduction to Human Trafficking: Vulnerability, Impact and Action,* Retrieved from http://www.unodc.org/documents/human-trafficking/An_Introduction_to_Human_Trafficking_-_Background_ Paper.pdf

10. *Analysis: Southeast Asia's human trafficking conundrum,* Retrieved from http://www.irinnews.org/report/97979/southeast-asia-s-human-trafficking-conundrum

11. Anam Rizvi (2014), *A Pinch of Skin: A documentary that attempts to lift the silence on female genital mutilation,* Retrieved from http://www.dnaindia.com/lifestyle/report-a-pinch-of-skin-a-documentary-that-attempts-to-lift-the-silence-on-female-genital-mutilation-1986973

12. *Appropriate Legal Responses to Combating Trafficking in Persons in Afghanistan (2008),* Retrieved from http://www.unodc.org/documents/human-trafficking/Legal_Responses_to_Trafficking_in_ Persons_Manual_ for_Parliamentarians_of_Afghanistan.pdf

13. *Argentina: A Human Rights Report on Trafficking in Persons, Especially Women and Children,* Retrieved from http://www.protectionproject.org/wp-content/uploads/2010/09/Argentina.pdf

14. *Bangladesh: A Human Rights Report on Trafficking in Persons, Especially Women and Children,* Retrieved from http://www.protectionproject.org/wp-content/uploads/2010/09/Bangladesh2.pdf

15. Bethany Bell (2014), *Violence against women: One-third of EU women affected – survey.*

16. *Bhutan: Working against human trafficking - focusing on rights, not on numbers,* Retrieved from http://www.unodc.org/southasia//frontpage/2013/April/bhutan-working-against-human-trafficking-focussing-on-rights-not-on-numbers.html

17. *Bolivia: A Human Rights Report on Trafficking in Persons, Especially Women and Children,* Retrieved from http://www.protectionproject.org/wp-content/uploads/2010/09/Bolivia-FINAL.pdf

18. *Brazil and Argentina among biggest contributors to UNODC human trafficking database,* Retrieved from http://www.unodc.org/lpo-brazil/en/frontpage/2014/05/06-brasil-e-argentina-estao-entre-maiores-contribuidores-de-base-de-dados-sobre-trafico-de-pessoas-do-unodc.html

19. *Causes of Sexual Harassment,* Retrieved from http://www1.umn.edu/humanrts/svaw/harassment/explore/3causes.htm

20. *Causes, Theories and Effects of Sexual Harassment,* Retrieved from http://www.stopvaw.org/uploads/causes_and_theories_sex_harassmt__2009.pdf

21. *CBC News (Oct 30, 2013),* Quebec women's council unveils 7 steps to stop 'honour crimes', Retrieved from http://www.cbc.ca/news/canada/montreal/quebec-women-s-council-unveils-7-steps-to-stop-honour-crimes-1.2288389

22. *Central African Republic (2014),* Retrieved from http://www.protectionproject.org/wp-content/uploads/2010/09/Central-African-Republic.pdf

23. *Central Asia: Special report on human trafficking (2014),* Retrieved from http://www.irinnews.org/report/20782/central-asia-special-report-on-human-trafficking

24. *Chad: 2013 Findings on the Worst Forms of Child Labor,* Retrieved from http://www.dol.gov/ilab/reports/child-labor/chad.htm

25. *Changing a harmful social convention: Female Genital Mutilation/Cutting (2005),* Retrieved from http://www.unicef-irc.org/publications/pdf/fgm_eng.pdf

26. *Child Sexual Abuse, Exploitation and Trafficking in Bangladesh,* Retrieved from http://www.unicef.org/bangladesh/Child_Abuse_ Exploitation_and_Trafficking.pdf

27. *Child trafficking in Guinea-Bissau: An explorative study,* Retrieved from https://www.unicef.is/efni/annad_utgefid_efni/Mansal_islskyrsla.pdf

28. *Child trafficking in India (2014),* Retrieved from http://en.wikipedia.org/wiki/Child_trafficking_in_India

29. *Chile Human Trafficking 'Invisible Problem' For Lack of Investigation,* Retrieved from http://www.insightcrime.org/news-briefs/lack-of-investigation-makes-chile-human-trafficking-invisible-problem

30. *Chile ranked in the highest tier in combatting human trafficking (2014),* Retrieved from http://dialogo-americas.com/en_GB/articles/rmisa/features/regional_news/2014/07/16/chile-human-trafficking

31. Clare Ribando Seelke (2013), *Trafficking in Persons in Latin America and the Caribbean,* Retrieved from http://www.fas.org/sgp/crs/row/RL33200.pdf

32. *CNN Report (December 5, 2008),* 13 yearold girl Gang raped by five indian soldiers in Kashmir.

33. *Combating human trafficking in Zambia (2014),* Retrieved from http://www.comboniane.org/progetti/images/upload/combatting_ human_trafficking-in_zambia.pdf

34. *Combating Trafficking in South-East Asia: A Review of Policy and Programme Responses (2000),* Retrieved from http://www.unesco.org /most/migration/ctsea.pdf

35. Desai, Mihir. March 2005. Mumbai: India Together. Accessed on 12 May 2004 at http://www.indiatogether.org/combatlaw/vol3/issue5/visakha.htm.The excerpts on Bhanwari devi's case has been taken from the book- The Politics of Silence, published by Sanhita, Kolkata, Aug- 2001)

36. *Dowry death (2014),* Retrieved from http://en.wikipedia.org/wiki/Dowry_death

37. Dr Jyoti Sanghera and Ms. Ratna Kapur, *An Assessment of Laws and Policies for the Prevention and Control of Trafficking in Nepal,* Retrieved from http://asiafoundation.org/resources/pdfs/nepaltrafficking assesment.pdf

38. Dr P.M. Nair (2007), *Trafficking Women and Children for Sexual Exploitation,* Retrieved from http://www.unodc.org/documents/human-trafficking/India_Training_material/Handbook_for_Law_Enforcement_Agencies_in_India.pdf

39. Dr P. M. Nair, *Trafficking Women and Children for Sexual Exploitation,* Retrieved from http://www.unodc.org/documents/human-trafficking/India_Training_material/Handbook_for_Law_Enforcement_Agencies_in_India.pdf

40. *East Africa (2014),* Retrieved from http://en.wikipedia.org/wiki/East_Africa

41. *Ecuador: A Human Rights Report on Trafficking in Persons, Especially Women and Children,* Retrieved from http://www.protectionproject.org/wp-content/uploads/2010/09/Ecuador1.pdf

42. Education, Race and Sex in Latin America, Intercultural Communication Studies XXI: 1 (2012). Retrieved from http://www.uri.edu/iaics/content/2012v21n1/15RebeccaSMerkin.pdf

43. *Effects and consequences of trafficking in women,* Retrieved from http://www1.umn.edu/humanrts/svaw/trafficking/explore/4effects.htm

44. *Effects of FGM,* Retrieved from http://www.endfgm.eu/en/female-genital-mutilation/what-is-fgm/effects-of-fgm/

45. Eileen Mariano, *Health and Sex Trafficking in Nepal,* Retrieved from http://med.stanford.edu/schoolhealtheval/files/Eileen Mariano_SocialProg_final.pdf

46. Eira Mishra, Combating Human Trafficking: A Legal Perspective with Special Reference to India, *Sociology and Anthropology* 1(4): 172-179, 2013.

47. *Eradication of female genital mutilation in Somalia,* Retrieved from http://www.unicef.org/somalia/SOM_FGM_ Advocacy_ Paper.pdf

48. *Essay on the Role of Women in India,* Retrieved from http://www.preservearticles.com/201104105204/the-role-of-women-in-india.html

49. *EU saves thousands of girls from female genital mutilation/cutting and child marriage,* Retrieved from http://www.enpi-info.eu/files/publications/female%20genital%20mutilation.pdf

50. *Factsheet: Understanding human trafficking,* Retrieved from http://africacheck.org/factsheets/factsheet-understanding-human-trafficking/

51. *Female circumcision anger aired in India,* Retrieved from http://www.dawn.com/news/712748/female-circumcision-anger-aired-in-india-fm

52. *Female Genital Mutilation – The Facts,* Retrieved from http://www.path.org/files/FGM-The-Facts.htm

53. *Female genital mutilation (2014),* Retrieved from http://www.forwarduk.org.uk/key-issues/fgm

54. *Female genital mutilation (2014),* Retrieved from http://www.nhs.uk/Conditions/female-genital-mutilation/Pages/Introduction.aspx

55. *Female genital mutilation (2014),* Retrieved from http://www.who.int/mediacentre/factsheets/fs241/en/

56. *Female Genital Mutilation A Matter of Human Rights: An Advocate's Guide to Action,* Retrieved from http://reproductiverights.org/sites/default/files/documents/FGM_final.pdf

57. *Female genital mutilation (2014),* Retrieved from http://www.forwarduk.org.uk/key-issues/fgm

58. *Female genital mutilation,* Retrieved from http://www.nhs.uk/Conditions/female-genital-mutilation/Pages/Introduction.aspx

59. *Female Genital Mutilation/Cutting: Data and Trends,* Retrieved from http://www.prb.org/pdf08/fgm-wallchart.pdf

60. *Female genital mutilation: An RCN educational resource for nursing and midwifery staff,* Retrieved from https://www.rcn.org.uk/__data/assets/pdf_file/0012/78699/003037.pdf

61. *Female genital mutilation: issues and impact,* Retrieved from http://www.unicef.org/egypt/protection_148.html

62. Gaby Oré-Aguilar (1997), *Sexual Harassment and Human Rights in Latin America,* Retrieved from http://ir.lawnet.fordham.edu/cgi/viewcontent.cgi?article=3401&context=flr&sei-redir=1

63. *Global Consultation on Female Genital Mutilation/Cutting,* Retrieved from http://www.unfpa.org/sites/default/files/pub-pdf/fgm_2008.pdf

64. *Global Report on Trafficking in Persons 2012,* Retrieved from http://www.unodc.org/documents/data-and-analysis/glotip/Trafficking_in_Persons_2012_web.pdf

65. *Global Report on Trafficking in Persons 2012,* Retrieved from http://www.unodc.org/documents/data-and-analysis/glotip/Trafficking_in_Persons_2012_web.pdf

66. *Hindustan Times (July 05, 2014),* New low for Delhi: Capital sees 125 dowry deaths in 2013, highest among cities, Retrieved from http://www.hindustantimes.com/india-news/new-low-for-delhi-125-dowry-deaths-in-2013-highest-among-cities/article1-1236937.aspx

67. *Honor killing in India,* Retrieved from http://www.civilserviceindia.com/subject/Essay/honor-killing-in-india2.html

68. *Honour Killing (2014),* Retrieved from http://en.wikipedia.org/wiki/Honor_killing

69. *Honour killing by reasons,* Retrieved from http://hbv-awareness.com/regions/

70. *Honour Killing, its Causes and Consequences: suggested strategies for the European Parliament,* Retrieved from http://edz.bib.uni-mannheim.de/daten/edz-ma/ep/07/EST18859.pdf

71. *Honour Killing, its Causes and Consequences: suggested strategies,* Retrieved from http://edz.bib.uni-mannheim.de/daten/edz-ma/ep/07/EST18859.pdf

72. *Honour Killings,* Retrieved from http://www.islaminstitut.de/uploads/media/Ehrenmorde.pdf

73. *How to put an end to the practice of female genital mutilation (FGM)?* See http://www.ipu.org/PDF/publications/fgm08-e.pdf

74. *Human rights abuses in Kashmir,* Retrieved from http://en.wikipedia.org/wiki/Human_rights_abuses_in_Kashmir

75. *Human Trafficking - Medical effects on victims*, Retrieved from https://ec.europa.eu/anti-trafficking/sites/antitrafficking/files/forum_magazine_on_medical_effects_1.pdf
76. *Human Trafficking - Medical effects on victims*, Retrieved from https://ec.europa.eu/anti-trafficking/sites/antitrafficking/files/forum_magazine_on_medical_effects_1.pdf
77. *Human Trafficking and Modern-day Slavery*, Retrieved from http://gvnet.com/humantrafficking/SriLanka.htm
78. *Human Trafficking and Modern-day Slavery*, Retrieved from http://gvnet.com/humantrafficking/KyrgyzRepublic.htm
79. *Human Trafficking and Modern-day Slavery*, Retrieved from http://gvnet.com/humantrafficking/Turkmenistan.htm
80. *Human Trafficking and Modern-day Slavery*, Retrieved from http://gvnet.com/humantrafficking/Togo.htm
81. *Human Trafficking and Modern-day Slavery*, Retrieved from http://gvnet.com/humantrafficking/Ethiopia.htm
82. *Human Trafficking and Modern-day Slavery*, Retrieved from http://gvnet.com/humantrafficking/Colombia.htm
83. *Human Trafficking and Modern-day Slavery*, See http://gvnet.com/humantrafficking/Ghana.htm
84. *Human trafficking (2014)*, Retrieved from http://en.wikipedia.org/wiki/Human_trafficking
85. *Human trafficking (2014)*, Retrieved from http://en.wikipedia.org/wiki/Human_trafficking_in_Uruguay
86. *Human trafficking assessment tool report for Nepal*, Retrieved from http://www.americanbar.org/content/dam/aba/directories/roli/nepal/nepal_human_trafficking_ assessment_report_2011.authcheckdam.pdf
87. *Human trafficking has wide-reaching social impact (2014)*, Retrieved from http://www.montgomerynews.com/articles/2014/01/21/souderton_independent/news/doc52d735fdbe3eb165162138.txt
88. *Human Trafficking in Canada (2014)*, Retrieved from http://www.publiclegaled.bc.ca/wp-content/uploads/2013/07/English_Human-Trafficking-In-Canada_2010.pdf
89. *Human trafficking in Canada, Frequent asked questions*, Retrieved from http://salvationist.ca/wp-content/uploads/2011/08/Human-Trafficking-in-Canada-FAQs.pdf
90. *Human trafficking in Columbia: A Modern Slavery*, Retrieved from http://www.africanafrican.com/folder14/alot%20more%20of%20african%20&%20african%20american%20history11/slavery/Human%20Trafficking%20In%20Colombia.pdf

91. *Human Trafficking in Mozambique: Root Causes and Recommendations,* Retrieved from http://unesdoc.unesco.org/images/0014/001478/147846e.pdf

92. *Human Trafficking in South Africa: Root Causes and Recommendations,* Retrieved from http://unesdoc.unesco.org/images/0015/001528/152823e.pdf

93. *Human Trafficking in South-East Asia | Overview,* Retrieved from http://www.afppd.org/files/1113/8206/9530/Policy_Brief.pdf

94. *Human Trafficking in sub-Saharan Africa, the Caribbean and the Pacific (2011),* Retrieved from http://www.acpmigration-obs.org/sites/default/files/EN-BN01-trafficking.pdf

95. *Human Trafficking Still a Major Concern in Asia,* Retrieved from http://dailysignal.com/2013/06/26/human-trafficking-still-a-major-concern-in-asia/

96. *Human trafficking,* Retrieved from http://www.stopthetraffik.org/the-scale-of-human-traffiking

97. *Human trafficking,* Retrieved from https://www.unodc.org/unodc/en/human-trafficking/what-is-human-trafficking.html#What_ is_Human_Trafficking

98. *Human trafficking, Understanding and addressing violence against women,* Retrieved from http://apps.who.int/iris/bitstream/10665/77394/1/WHO_RHR_12.42_eng.pdf

99. *Human Trafficking: An Overview,* Retrieved from http://www.ungift.org/doc/knowledgehub/resource-centre/GIFT_Human_Trafficking_An_Overview_2008.pdf

100. *Human Trafficking: An Overview,* Retrieved from http://www.ungift.org/doc/knowledgehub/resource-centre/GIFT_Human_Trafficking_An_Overview_2008.pdf

101. *Human Trafficking: The Sinai Phenomenon (2014),* Retrieved from http://www.worldpolicy.org/blog/2014/09/23/human-trafficking-sinai-phenomenon

102. *Impact of Human Trafficking on Victims,* Retrieved from http://www.justice.gov/usao/ian/htrt/htrt_impact.html

103. *Indian Defense Review (June 26, 2007),* Women in the arm force.

104. *Inside the brutal and hopeless world of Mumbai's trafficked teenage sex slaves (2013),* Retrieved from http://www.theguardian.com/world/2013/sep/28/trafficked-india-red-light-districts

105. International Business Times (Oct 5, 2013), Kunan-Poshpora: Can Kashmiri Rape Victims Get Justice.

106. *Israel: Still a destination for human trafficking*, Retrieved from http://www.irinnews.org/report/84897/israel-still-a-destination-for-human-trafficking

107. Jacqueline Joudo Larsen, *Migration and people trafficking in Southeast Asia*, Retrieved from http://www.aic.gov.au/media_library/publications/tandi_pdf/tandi401.pdf

108. Judy Hemming and Nicola Piper, *Trafficking and Human Security in Southeast Asia: A Sociological Perspective*, Retrieved from http://www.rsis-ntsasia.org/resources/publications/research-papers/transnational-crime/Judy_Nicola.pdf

109. June JH Lee, *Human Trafficking in East Asia: Current Trends, Data Collection and Knowledge Gaps*, Retrieved from http://www.hks.harvard.edu/cchrp/isht/study_group/2010/pdf/Human%20Trafficking%20in%20East%20Asia.pdf

110. Kate Zdrojewski, *The Development of Sex Trafficking in Central America*, Retrieved from https://www.du.edu/korbel/hrhw/researchdigest/trafficking/CentralAmerica.pdf

111. Kieran Guilbert (2014), *Human Trafficking Victims in India Need Greater Legal Support*, Retrieved from http://www.newindianexpress.com/nation/Human-Trafficking-Victims-in-India-Need-Greater-Legal-Support/2014/11/19/article2531294.ece

112. *Legal education to counteract human trafficking in Kazakhstan*, Retrieved from http://ec.europa.eu/europeaid/documents/case-studies/kazakhstan_human-trafficking_legal-edu_en.pdf

113. Legislation and other national provisions: India, Indonesia, Ireland, Israel, Italy, Japan, Kenya, Lesotho, Liberia, Libyan Arab Jamahiriya, Luxembourg.

114. *Los Angeles Times (Sep 05, 2013)*, India 'dowry deaths' still rising despite modernisation, Retrieved from http://articles.latimes.com/2013/sep/05/world/la-fg-wn-india-dowry-deaths-20130904

115. *Love marriage (2014)*, Retrieved from http://en.wikipedia.org/wiki/Love_marriage

116. M. Bashir Uddin, Human Trafficking in South Asia: Issues of Corruption and Human Security, *International Journal of Social Work and Human Services Practice*, Vol. 2. No. 1 Feb., 2014, pp. 18-27.

117. Majeed A. Rahman, *Human Trafficking in the era of Globalisation: The case of Trafficking in the Global Market Economy*, Transcience Journal Vol. 2, No. 1 (2011), Retrieved from http://www2.hu-berlin.de/transcience/Vol2_Issue1_2011_54_71_Glossary.pdf

118. *Manoj-Babli honour killing case,* Retrieved from http://en.wikipedia.org/wiki/Manoj-Babli_honour_killing_case

119. Marianela Jarroud (2014), *Modern Slavery Rears its Ugly Head in Chile,* Retrieved from http://www.ipsnews.net/2013/02/modern-slavery-rears-its-ugly-head-in-chile/

120. Marja Exterkate (2013), *Female Genital Mutilation in the Netherlands: Prevalence, incidence and determinants,* Retrieved from http://www.awepa.org/wp-content/uploads/2013/05/Female-Genital-Mutilation-in-the-Netherlands.pdf

121. *Marriage (2014),* Retrieved from http://en.wikipedia.org/wiki/Marriage

122. Maryam Sheikh Abdi and Ian Askew (2009), *A Religious Oriented Approach to Addressing Female Genital Mutilation/ Cutting among the Somali Community of Wajir, Kenya,* Retrieved from http://www.popcouncil.org/uploads/pdfs/frontiers/reports/Kenya_Somali_FGC.pdf

123. *Measures to Combat Trafficking in Human Beings in Benin, Nigeria and Togo,* Retrieved from http://www.unodc.org/documents/human-trafficking/ht_research_report_nigeria.pdf

124. Mohammad Barad Hossain Chowdhury, *Trafficking in persons in Bangladesh,* Retrieved from http://www.unafei.or.jp/english/pdf/RS_No89/No89_PA_Chowdhury.pdf

125. Ms. Mahek Singh, Dowry as a factor of violence in Marriage: A study of Women seeking help in Family Counseling Centers in Chandigarh, *International Journal of Advancements in Research and Technology,* Volume 2, Issue 6, June-2013, Retrieved from http://www.ijoart.org/docs/Dowry-as-a-factor-of-violence-in-Marriage-A-study-of-Women-seeking-help-in-Family-Counseling-Centers-in-Chandigarh.pdf

126. *National Action Plan to Combat Human Trafficking (2014),* Retrieved from http://www.publicsafety.gc.ca/cnt/rsrcs/pblctns/ntnl-ctn-pln-cmbt/index-eng.aspx

127. *Nepal: the problems of trafficking in women and children,* Retrieved from http://www.asiapacificforum.net/about/annual-meetings/7th-india-2002/downloads/thematic-issues/nepal_trafficking.pdf

128. *News Africa (June 14, 2011),* Libya rape victims 'face honour killings', Retrieved from

129. *Odisha frames new policy to check human trafficking,* Retrieved from http://zeenews.india.com/news/nation/orissa-frames-new-policy-to-check-human-trafficking_587388.html

130. *Pakistan Defense (June 8, 2010)*, Sexual harassment in Indian Army, Retrieved from http://defence.pk/threads/sexual-harassment-in-indian-army.60978/

131. *Pakistan: Sharp rise in human trafficking in Sindh Province*, Retrieved from http://www.irinnews.org/report/95117/pakistan-sharp-rise-in-human-trafficking-in-sindh-province

132. *Panama: A Human Rights Report on Trafficking in Persons, Especially Women and Children*, Retrieved from http://www.protection project. org/wp-content/uploads/2010/09/Panama.pdf

133. *Peru: A Human Rights Report on Trafficking in Persons, Especially Women and Children*, Retrieved from http://www.protection project. org/wp-content/uploads/2010/09/Peru1.pdf

134. Peter Clarke, *Types of sexual harassment*, Retrieved from http://www.legalmatch.com/law-library/article/types-of-sexual-harassment.html

135. Petra Follmar-Otto and Heike Rabe (2009), *Human Trafficking in Germany*, Retrieved from http://www.stiftung-evz.de/fileadmin/user_upload/EVZ_Uploads/Publikationen/Englisch/study_human_trafficking_in_germany.pdf

136. Phyllis Chesler (2010), *Worldwide Trends in Honor Killings*, Retrieved from http://www.meforum.org/2646/worldwide-trends-in-honor-killings

137. Pinak Pani Datta (2012), *Female Genital Mutilation: An Open Secret in India*, Retrieved from

138. Praggnaparamita Biswas, Politics of Dowry Deaths in India: A Study of Dina Mehta's Brides Are Not for Burning, *The Criterion: An International Journal in English*, See http://www.the-criterion.com/V4/n2/Biswas.pdf

139. Praggnaparamita Biswas, Politics of Dowry Deaths in India: A Study of Dina Mehta's Brides Are Not for Burning, *The Criterion: An International Journal in English*, See http://www.the-criterion.com/V4/n2/Biswas.pdf

140. *Preventing and Combating the Trafficking of Girls in India Using Legal Empowerment Strategies (2011)*, Retrieved from http://www.idlo.org/Publications/FinalReportGirlsProject.pdf

141. Priya Prakashan (2014), *Female genital mutilation: What is FGM? Know more about the brutal practice*, Retrieved from http://www.india.com/whatever/female-genital-mutilation-what-is-fgm-know-more-about-the-brutal-practice-102516/

142. *Prostitution in Kolkata (2014)*, Retrieved from http://en.wikipedia.org/wiki/Prostitution_in_Kolkata

143. *Protecting girls from undergoing Female Genital Mutilation: The experience of working with the Maasai communities in Kenya and Tanzania,* Retrieved from http://www.equalitynow.org/sites/default/files/Protecting%20Girls_FGM_Kenya_Tanzania.pdf

144. *Protecting girls from undergoing Female Genital Mutilation: The experience of working with the Maasai communities in Kenya and Tanzania,* Retrieved from http://www.equalitynow.org/sites/default/files/Protecting%20Girls_FGM_Kenya_Tanzania.pdf

145. Puneet Kaur Grewal, Honour Killings and Law in India, *IOSR Journal of Humanities and Social Science,* Volume 5, Issue 6 (Nov. - Dec. 2012), pp. 28-31.

146. R.H.Waghamode , J. L. Kalyan and S. S. Angadi, Human trafficking in India, Retrieved from http://researchdirection.org/UploadArticle/153.pdf

147. Radhika, R.H and Ananda.K, An Autopsy Study of Socio-Etiological Aspects in Dowry Death Cases, J Indian Acad Forensic Med. July-September 2011, Vol. 33, No. 3, Retrieved from http://medind.nic.in/ jal/t11/i3/jalt11i3p224.pdf

148. Read more at

149. Rebecca S. Merkin, Sexual Harassment Indicators: The Socio-Cultural and Cultural Impact of Marital Status, Age.

150. Rebecca S. Merkin, *South American Perspectives on Sexual Harassment: The Standpoint in Argentina, Brazil and Chile,* Retrieved from http://www.ibam.com/pubs/jbam/articles/vol10/no3/Merkin_4.pdf

151. Renu Sharma, *Trafficking in Women and Children in India: A Situational Analysis in Maharashtra,* Retrieved from http://www.sascv.org/ijcjs/renusharma.html

152. *Report Female genital mutilation in Sudan and Somalia,* Retrieved from http://www.landinfo.no/asset/764/1/764_1.pdf

153. *Report Shows Dynamics of Human Trafficking In Argentina,* Retrieved from http://www.insightcrime.org/news-briefs/report-breaks-down-dynamics-of-human-trafficking-in-argentina

154. *Responding to Trafficking for Sexual Exploitation in South Asia (2007),* Retrieved from http://www.ungift.org/docs/ungift/pdf/world/INDIA.pdf

155. *Review of Laws against Human Trafficking in Bangladesh,* Retrieved from http://actbd.org/doc/Law%20Review% 20Study%20 Report% 20 Edited%20LH%20Revised% 20FINAL.pdf

156. Ruh Afza Ruhi, *Human trafficking in Bangladesh: An overview*, Retrieved from http://www.cdrb.org/journal/2003/4/3.pdf

157. Sankar Sen, *Final Report of Action Research on Trafficking in Women and Children*, Retrieved from http://nhrc.nic.in/Documents/ReportonTrafficking.pdf

158. Sapana Pradhan-Malla, *Sexual harassment in the workplace in Asia*, Retrieved from http://www.un.org/womenwatch/daw/egm/vaw-gp-2005/docs/experts/pradhanmalla.sh.pdf

159. Satnam Singh Deol, Honour Killings in India: A Study of the Punjab State, *International Research Journal of Social Science*, Vol. 3(6), 7-16, June (2014), pp. 7-11.

160. *Sex Ratio (2014)*, Retrieved from http://www.google.co.in/search?noj=1&biw=1024&bih=677&q=gender+ratio&oq=gender+ratio&gs_l=serp.3...3964.7328.0.7828.12.9.0.0.0.0.0.0 ..0.0.msedr...0...1c.1.60. serp.. 12.0.0.R0Ttg9ZbbSc

161. *Sexual assault (2014)*, Retrieved from http://en.wikipedia.org/wiki/Sexual_assault

162. *Sexual harassment (2014)*, Retrieved from http://www.eeoc.gov/laws/types/sexual_harassment.cfm

163. *Sexual harassment (2014)*, Retrieved from https://rainn.org/get-information/types-of-sexual-assault/sexual-harassment

164. *Sexual harassment in education, OHRC*, Retrieved from http://www.ohrc.on.ca/en/sexual-harassment-education-brochure

165. *Sexual harassment in education*, Retrieved from http://en.wikipedia.org/wiki/Sexual_harassment_in_education

166. *Sexual harassment in the workplace (2008)*, Retrieved from http://www.slsedmonton.com/userfiles/file/Sexual% 20 Harassment.pdf

167. *Sexual Harassment: The Facts*, Retrieved from http://www.twu.edu/downloads/counseling/G-7_Sexual_Harassment_The_Facts.pdf

168. *Sexual violence in South Africa (2014)*, Retrieved from http://en.wikipedia.org/wiki/Sexual_violence_in_South_Africa

169. *Significance of Women's Day*, Retrieved from http://www.indiaparenting.com/womens-issues/177_3931/significance-of-women's-day.html

170. *South Asia in Action: Preventing and responding to child trafficking*, Retrieved from http://www.unicef.org/media/files/IRC_CT_Asia_ Summary_FINAL4.pdf

171. *South Asia in action: Preventing and responding to child trafficking analysis of anti-trafficking initiatives in the region*, Retrieved from http://www.unicef-irc.org/publications/pdf/ii_ct_southasia_analysis.pdf

172. *Stop Trafficking : Learn More : Sex Trafficking FAQ*, Retrieved from http://www.soroptimist.org/trafficking/faq.html

173. *Stop violence against Sexual harassment (2014)*, Retrieved from http://www1.umn.edu/humanrts/svaw/harassment/explore/1whatis.htm

174. *Stopping sexual harassment at work: A trade union guide*, Retrieved from http://www.ituc-csi.org/IMG/pdf/Harcelement_ENG_12pgs_ BR.pdf

175. *Syria: First shelter for trafficked people opens in Damascus*, Retrieved from http://www.irinnews.org/report/82686/syria-first-shelter-for-trafficked-people-opens-in-damascus

176. *Tajikistan: National conference on human trafficking opens in Dushanbe*, Retrieved from http://www.irinnews.org/report/24225/tajikistan-national-conference-on-human-trafficking-opens-in-dushanbe

177. *The Guardian (June 23, 2014)*, Let's stop talking about 'honour killing'. There is no honour in murder, Retrieved from http://www.theguardian.com/commentisfree/2014/jun/23/stop-honour-killing-murder-women-oppresive-patriarchy

178. *The Hindu (August 7, 2013)*, Rising number of dowry deaths in India: NCRB, Retrieved from http://www.thehindu.com/news/national/rising-number-of-dowry-deaths-in-india-ncrb/article4995677.ece

179. *The Hindu (June 30, 2013)*, Special law will deter honour killings, says Sathasivam, Retrieved from http://www.thehindu.com/news/national/special-law-will-deter-honour-killings-says-sathasivam/article4864168.ece

180. *The Hindu* (Oct 18, 2013), High Court upholds conviction of man in dowry death case, Retrieved from http://www.thehindu.com/news/cities/Delhi/high-court-upholds-conviction-of-man-in-dowry-death-case/article5247196.ece

181. *The Horrendous Realities of Human Trafficking in India*, See http://indiaopines.com/human-trafficking-indiarising-problem/

182. *The Horrendous Realities of Human Trafficking in India*, See http://indiaopines.com/human-trafficking-indiarising-problem/

183. The importance of women in society, Retrieved from http://socialactionnow.wordpress.com/2014/02/04/the-importance-of-the-woman-in-the-society/

184. *The Indian Express (Oct 01, 2012),* Law panel for making honour killings non-bailable offence, Retrieved from http://archive.indianexpress.com/news/law-panel-for-making-honour-killings-nonbailable-offence/1010261/2

185. *The Occupied Palestinian Territory West Bank and Gaza Strip,* Retrieved from http://www.protectionproject.org/wp-content/uploads/2010/09/Palestine-FINAL-2012.pdf

186. *The social construction of 'dowry deaths',* Retrieved from http://www.sciencedirect.com/science/article/pii/S0277953614004730

187. *The Telegraph (Feb 27, 2012),* Indian dowry deaths on the rise, Retrieved from http://www.telegraph.co.uk/news/worldnews/asia/india/9108642/Indian-dowry-deaths-on-the-rise.html

188. *The Telegraph (Sep 2, 2013),* Woman killed over dowry 'every hour' in India, Retrieved from http://www.telegraph.co.uk/news/worldnews/asia/india/10280802/Woman-killed-over-dowry-every-hour-in-India.html

189. *The Times of India (Dec 27, 2013),* 25 more anti-human trafficking cells in Odisha, Retrieved from http://timesofindia.indiatimes.com/city /bhubaneswar/25-more-anti-human-trafficking-cells-in-Odisha/articleshow/27989655.cms

190. *The Times of India (Jan 27, 2012),* Dowry death: One bride burnt every hour, Retrieved from http://timesofindia.indiatimes.com/india/Dowry-death-One-bride-burnt-every-hour/articleshow/11644691.cms

191. *The Times of India (July 4, 2010),* More than 1000 honour killings in India every year: Experts, Retrieved from http://timesofindia.indiatimes.com/india/More-than-1000-honour-killings-in-India-every-year-Experts/articleshow/6127338.cms

192. *The Times of India (Mar 13, 2013),* NID student's film on female genital mutilation, Retrieved from http://timesofindia.indiatimes. com/entertainment/hindi/bollywood/news/NID-students-film-on-female-genital-mutilation/articleshow/19304011.cms

193. *The Times of India (Nov 15, 2013),* Separate law against honour killings sought, Retrieved from http://timesofindia.indiatimes.com/india/Separate-law-against-honour-killings-sought/articleshow/25785687.cms

194. *The Times of India (Nov 5, 2013),* In India, Karnataka stands third in human trafficking, Retrieved from http://timesofindia.indiatimes.com/india/In-India-Karnataka-stands-third-in-human-trafficking/articleshow/25234883.cms

195. *The Times of India (November 12, 2014),* HC orders CBI probe in honour killing case, Retrieved from http://timesofindia.indiatimes. com/city/chennai/HC-orders-CBI-probe-in-honour-killing-case/articleshow/45117542.cms

196. *The Times of India (November 16, 2014),* 21 states, UTs join Centre in fight against honour killings, Retrieved from http://timesofindia.indiatimes.com/india/21-states-UTs-join-Centre-in-fight-against-honour-killings/articleshow/45162780.cms

197. *The Times of India (November 19, 2014),* Pakistani family sentenced to death over 'honour killing', Retrieved from http://timesofindia.indiatimes.com/world/pakistan/Pakistani-family-sentenced-to-death-over-honour-killing/articleshow/45204166.cms

198. *The Times of India (November 20, 2014),* Parents held for 'honour' killing of 21-year-old Delhi University girl, Retrieved from http://timesofindia.indiatimes.com/city/delhi/Parents-held-for-honour-killing-of-21-year-old-Delhi-University-girl/articleshow/45210903.cms

199. *The Times of India (November 7, 2014),* Polytechnic student found hanging from tree in Muradnagar, Retrieved from http://timesofindia.indiatimes.com/city/noida/Polytechnic-student-found-hanging-from-tree-in-Muradnagar/articleshow/45063997.cms

200. *The Times of India (Oct 26, 2014),* Two get life sentence in case of honour killing, Retrieved from http://timesofindia.indiatimes.com/city/allahabad/Two-get-life-sentence-in-case-of-honour-killing/articleshow/44942038.cms

201. *Trafficking and Forced Prostitution of Palestinian Women and Girls (2008),* Retrieved from http://www.refworld.org/pdfid/4bcc13862.pdf

202. *Trafficking and human rights in Nepal,* Retrieved from http://www.popcouncil.org/uploads/pdfs/horizons/trafficking sum1.pdf

203. *Trafficking in persons especially on women and children in Nepal,* Retrieved from http://www.nhrcnepal.org/nhrc_new/doc/newsletter/National%20Report%20on%20Traffiking%20in%20Persons%20%20Es pecially%20%20on%20 women%20 and% 20Children%20in%20Nepal%20-%202012.pdf

204. *Trafficking in Persons in Afghanistan (2008)*, Retrieved from http://www.iom.int/jahia/webdav/shared/shared/mainsite/activities/countries/docs/afghanistan/iom_report_ trafficking_afghanistan.pdf

205. *Trafficking in Persons Report 2014 Turkmenistan*, Retrieved from Trafficking in Persons Report 2014 Turkmenistan

206. *Uproar over Female Genital Mutilation: Bohra Muslim woman activist launches campaign on Facebook to ban practice*, Retrieved from https://www.facebook.com/notes/sijo-k-jose/uproar-over-female-genital-mutilation-bohra-muslim-woman-activist-launches-campa/329191643829952

207. *Vishaka Guidelines (2014)*, see http://en.wikipedia.org/wiki/Vishaka_Guidelines

208. *Vishakha and others v State of Rajasthan*, http://en.wikipedia.org/wiki/Vishakha_and_ others_v_ State_of_ Rajasthan

209. *What is sexual harassment?* (2014), Retrieved http://news.bbc.co.uk/2/hi/africa/4791625.stm

210. *Why do dowry deaths occur?* (2014), Retrieved from http://www.pucl.org/from-archives/Gender/dowry-deaths.htm

211. *Women (2014)*, Retrieved from http://en.wikipedia.org/wiki/Woman

212. Zeynep Zileli Rabanea (2014), *Brazil's blind eye to sexual harassment*, Retrieved from http://www.aljazeera.com/indepth/opinion/2014/03/cloneofbrazil-blind-eye-sexual-h-20143118227832386

213. Zofeen Ebrahim (2014), *Pakistan-India: Women Expose Secret Genital Cutting Rite*, Retrieved from http://www.ipsnews.net/2012/01/pakistan-india-women-expose-secret-genital-cutting-rite/

214. Wikipedia of Human trafficking in *Afghanistan, Algeria, Angola, Antigua and Barbuda, Argentina, Austria, Bangladesh, Belarus, Benin, Bosnia and Herzegovina, Botswana, Brazil, Bulgaria, Burkina Faso, Burundi, Canada, Central African Republic, Chad, Costa Rica, Croatia, Czech Republic, Denmark, Dominican Republic, Ecuador, Egypt, Eritrea, Ethiopia, El Salvador, Europe, Finland, Germany, Greece, Guina, Guinea-Bissau, Guyana, Honduras, India, Iran, Israel, Jamaica, Kazakhstan, Kenya, Kosovo, Latvia, Lebanon, Lesotho, Liberia, Libya, Lithuania, Malawi, Maldives, Mali, Mauritania, Mexico, Morocco, Mozambique, Nepal, Nicaragua, Nigeria, Norway, Panama, Pakistan, Paraguay, Poland, Romania, Russia, Serbia, Sierra Leone, Slovenia, South Africa, South East Asia, Spain, Sri Lanka, Sudan, Surinam, Sweden, Switzerland, Syria, Tajikistan, Tanzania, Democratic Republic of the Congo, Republic of Congo, United States, Trinidad and Tobago,*

Tunisia, Turkmenistan, Ukraine, United Arab Emirates, United Kingdom, Uzbekistan, Venezuela, Zambia, Zimbabwe, Ivory Coast.

215. Women Empowerment in India – A Burnings Issue, Retrieved from http://www.womenempowermentinindia.com

216. Yahaya, K.A., Osemene, O.F. and Abdulraheem, A. (2011), Effectiveness of Microfinance Banks in Alleviating Poverty in Kwara State Nigeria. Global Journal of Management and Business Research, March, 11(4), 12-21.

Websites

1. http://www.brainyquote.com/quotes/authors/m/martin_luther_king_jr.html#JbW5OxFH4weA46H7.99
2. http://www.brainyquote.com/quotes/keywords/crime.html#pROPkYjtSIWqlKD9.99
3. http://www.brainyquote.com/quotes/keywords/violence.html#YXLgWjWUbruW77id.99
4. http://www.brainyquote.com/quotes/keywords/violence_2.html#iMg75slXimIEP0hY.99
5. http://allafrica.com/stories/201306121100.html
6. http://amandala.com.bz/news/belize-downgraded-human-trafficking-report/
7. http://dialogo-americas.com/en_GB/articles/saii/features/main/2013/05/09/feature-02
8. http://digital.library.upenn.edu/women/stopes/married/1918.html
9. http://en.wikipedia.org/wiki/Human_trafficking_in_Ghana
10. http://en.wikipedia.org/wiki/Sexual_harassment
11. http://forcechange.com/2870/stop-honor-killing-of-innocent-women-and-girls-around-the-world/
12. http://freethoughtblogs.com/taslima/2012/06/05/bride-burning/
13. http://godswordtowomen.org/kyrgyzstan.htm
14. http://guardianlv.com/2014/02/human-trafficking-and-sexual-abuse-rates-are-on-the-rise/
15. http://gulfnews.com/news/world/india/dowry-deaths-on-the-rise-across-india-1.1227758
16. http://jdi.sagepub.com/content/7/1-4/229.abstract
17. http://kazakhstan.usembassy.gov/tip2012.html
18. http://legal-dictionary.thefreedictionary.com/sexual+harassment

19. http://mahacid.com/AHTU.html
20. http://ncrb.nic.in/CD-CII2011/cii-2011/Chapter%205.pdf
21. http://news.bbc.co.uk/2/hi/south_asia/431607.stm
22. http://niamey.usembassy.gov/2011_traffickinginpersons.html
23. http://nicaragua.usembassy.gov/rpt_tip_2012.html
24. http://notforsalecampaign.org/our-strategy/romania/
25. http://notforsalecampaign.org/stories/2012/08/27/the-state-of-human-trafficking-in-syria/
26. http://panama.usembassy.gov/062711.html
27. http://panama.usembassy.gov/tip13pty.html
28. http://paraguay.usembassy.gov/tip.html
29. http://reliefweb.int/report/sudan/sudan-calls-support-combating-human-trafficking
30. http://rhrealitycheck.org/article/2012/03/20/whos-ending-street-harassment-in-latin-america-and-caribbean/
31. http://tunisia.usembassy.gov/rpt-trafficking-in-person-2011.html
32. http://womennewsnetwork.net/2014/04/28/crimes-children-honduras/
33. http://www.actnowsrilanka.org/en/vaw/trafficking
34. http://www.africa-eu-partnership.org/success-stories/zambia-develops-national-plan-action-against-trafficking-human-beings
35. http://www.aljazeera.com/indepth/opinion/2013/11/honour-killings-india-crying-shame-20131127105910392176.html
36. http://www.britannica.com/EBchecked/topic/556618/Southern-Africa
37. http://www.dnaindia.com/mumbai/report-mumbai-students-work-to-empower-victims-of-human-trafficking-1998652
38. http://www.dol.gov/ilab/reports/child-labor/el_salvador.htm
39. http://www.dol.gov/ilab/reports/child-labor/uruguay.htm
40. http://www.dw.de/growth-makes-brazil-a-hub-for-human-trafficking/a-16855897
41. http://www.dw.de/human-trafficking-prostitution-thrive-in-afghanistan/a-16327746
42. http://www.dw.de/human-trafficking-the-eus-dirty-secret/a-17412036
43. http://www.examiner.com/article/bride-burning-india-

pakistan-and-bangladesh-is-acceptable-murder

44. http://www.hhrjournal.org/wp-content/uploads/sites/13/2014/02/How-do-social-determinants-affect-human-trafficking-in-southeast-asia-and-what-can-we-do-about-it_-A-systematic-review2-27.pdf
45. http://www.hrw.org/news/2014/02/11/egyptsudan-traffickers-who-torture
46. http://www.indg.in/social-sector/socialwelfare-faqs/2.dowrydeath.pdf
 a. http://www.indiandefencereview.com/spotlights/women-in-the-armed-forces-part-2/
47. http://www.indiatribune.com/index.php?option=com_content&id=3557:uttar-pradesh-bihar-madhya-pradesh-report-most-dowry-deaths&Itemid=400
48. http://www.insightcrime.org/news-briefs/report-reveals-extent-of-human-trafficking-in-colombia
49. http://www.iom.int/cms/en/sites/iom/home/news-and-views/press-briefing-notes/pbn-2013/pbn-listing/maldives-passes-bill-to-criminal.html
50. http://www.iom.int/cms/en/sites/iom/home/where-we-work/africa-and-the-middle-east/east-africa/kenya.default.html?displayTab=latest-news
51. http://www.islamweb.net/emainpage/articles/148077/mozambique-fights-human-trafficking
52. http://www.justice.gc.ca/eng/rp-pr/cj-jp/fv-vf/hk-ch/p5.html
53. http://www.kidpower.org/library/article/sexual-harassment-schools/
54. http://www.lawyerscollective.org/blog/sexual-harassment-women-workplace-bill-2012-passed-lok-sabha.html
55. http://www.ndtv.com/article/india/indian-army-probing-sexual-abuse-charges-against-un-peacekeepers-in-congo-110764
56. http://www.oas.org/atip/belize/belize-%20petit.pdf
57. http://www.pbs.org/newshour/rundown/half-eu-women-victims-sexual-harrasment-new-report-finds/
58. http://www.sunday-guardian.com/investigation/sexual-harrasment-not-new-in-army
59. http://www.thebetterindia.com/9556/rescue-foundation-rescuing-victims-human-trafficking/
60. http://www.thedailybeast.com/articles/2014/06/23/how-

mexico-s-cartels-are-behind-the-border-kid-crisis.html

61. http://www.theguardian.com/lifeandstyle/2013/apr/20/love-not-all-need-marriage
62. http://www.ticotimes.net/2014/06/12/sex-tourism-a-driver-for-human-trafficking-in-costa-rica-says-foundation
63. http://www.ticotimes.net/2014/08/19/5-cases-of-human-trafficking-under-investigation-in-costa-rica-this-year-says-immigration-administration-director
64. http://www.un.org/womenwatch/osagi/pdf/whatissh.pdf
65. http://www.usccb.org/issues-and-action/marriage-and-family/marriage/love-and-life/upload/Love-and-Life-Abridged-Version.pdf
66. http://www.usip.org/sites/default/files/PW96-Illicit-Trafficking-and-Libyas-Transition.pdf
67. http://www.voanews.com/content/un-human-trafficking-increasing-in-pakistan/1836345.html
68. http://www.wbsjournal.co.za/articles/sexual-harassment-in-the-workplace-sorting-the-grey-areas-from-the-black-and-white-921.html
69. http://www.westerncape.gov.za/general-publication/sexual-harassment-causes-consequences-and-cures?toc_page=1
70. http://www.westerncape.gov.za/general-publication/sexual-harassment-causes-consequences-and-cures?toc_page=2
71. http://www.westerncape.gov.za/general-publication/sexual-harassment-causes-consequences-and-cures?toc_page=5
72. http://www.wikigender.org/index.php/Bride_Burning
73. http://www.wsws.org/en/articles/2001/07/ind-j04.html
74. https://www.humanrights.gov.au/sexual-harassment-education
75. http://indiatogether.org/combatlaw/vol2/issue3/harass.htm#sthash.03k5SOkH.dpuf
76. http://www.ummid.com/news/2013/December/12.12.2013/workplace-harassment.html#sthash.v3qu4iML.dpuf
77. http://www.ummid.com/news/2013/December/12.12.2013/workplace-harassment.html#sthash.v3qu4iML.dpuf
78. http://www.ummid.com/news/2013/December/12.12.2013/workplace-harassment.

Index

W